LAUREL and HARDY
The U.S. Tours

by

"A.J" Marriot

Marriot Publishing

LAUREL and HARDY – The U.S. Tours

First published November 2011
ISBN 978-0-9521308-2-6
This second revised edition published November 2019
ISBN 978-0-9521308-6-4
Marriot Publishing
Ciudad Quesada, Alicante, Spain
Text Copyright © by "A.J" Marriot 2011
Printed via "LULU"

Written, compiled, and designed by "A.J" Marriot. Layout by "A.J" Marriot
COVER DESIGN by "A.J" Marriot
Cover artwork by Paul Wood (TT Litho, Rochester, Kent. ME1 1NN. – www.ttlitho.co.uk)
Cover photo by courtesy of Tyler St. Mark
All rights reserved

A.J Marriot is hereby identified as author of this work in accordance with Section 77 of the Copyright, Designs and Patent Act 1988

o-o-0-o-o

This book is sold subject to the condition that it shall not, by way of trade or otherwise, be lent, resold, hired out or otherwise circulated without the publisher's prior consent in any form of binding cover other than that in which it is published and without a similar condition – this condition being imposed on the subsequent purchaser.

o-o-0-o-o

PREFACE

My original concept in documenting Laurel and Hardy's U.S. stage tours in the years 1940-42, was to insert just one extra chapter into a revised edition of my book "*LAUREL & HARDY – The British Tours.*" However, the more I dug, the more previously undiscovered material I found until, four years later, this book-size document emerged.

At the outset I had no intention of documenting Stan Laurel's marital history; as to do so is to walk into a literary minefield of legal terms. However, because Laurel's many strives with his many wives impacted on his film work and his public life, I felt it necessary to paint at least some background, so that the reader could see things in context.

I have omitted most of the background information on the production of the Laurel & Hardy films except, again, where happenings in the studio spilled over into Stan and Babe's private lives. In some instances I do include short accounts on film production, but only where new information has come to light.

As for the "Roach years" (1925-1940), all previous accounts paint a picture of the lives of Laurel and Hardy as being equivalent to that of circus animals; in that they supposedly went from their sleeping quarters to the performance area; did their act; then returned to their individual quarters. We have been brainwashed into believing that they never socialised off-screen; did not frequent nightclubs or Hollywood parties, and preferred their different hobbies. This book will totally blow apart those claims by revealing details of numerous visits to nightclubs the comedy couple made, and a number of Hollywood parties they attended. Readers will also discover previously unrecorded attendances at award ceremonies, benefit shows, film premieres, openings of theatres and hotels, sporting events, junkets, "Goodwill" visits, fund-raising tours, and troop shows.

As for hobbies, there are accounts of THREE different ones which Stan and Babe not only practised individually, but participated in – TOGETHER.

In the chapters detailing Laurel and Hardy's stage tours, every care has been taken to make the date-sheets as accurate as possible, but there may be instances of minor errors. In British Variety theatres, shows ran from Monday to Saturday – almost without exception; but in American theatres there was no standardisation. The bulk of shows Laurel and Hardy played were from Friday to Thursday; but, if there was a long distance between cities, it would mean a shorter stay, so as to give adequate travel time to make the next one. And theatres in smaller towns might take the show for only three or four nights as, by then, the theatregoing members of the population would have been accommodated. Sometimes, the stage show would run for only six days, so as to allow for the release of a major film on the one vacated. So please realise the enormity of the task in getting every date exact. Add to that the difficulty of being based in England, and researching cities located across the full expanse of the U.S.A.

Some readers may question why I quote so many newspaper articles in this book. The logic is similar to that of one prolific bank robber who, when asked why he always robbed banks, replied: "Because that's where the money is." I would be the first to acknowledge that newspapers do not always give the most accurate information, but at least that information is contemporary. Ask yourself this, "Which Chinese whisper would you consider the more reliable – the first one, or the last in a long network?"

Someone once said that it is the duty of a writer to tell people something they don't already know.

I trust I have done my duty.

"A.J" Marriot

Bouquets to the author at ajmarriot@aol.com (but not too many brickbats, please! I'm sensitive.) Suggested amendments will be better received, and additions gratefully so.

o-o-0-o-o

CONTENTS

Chapter 1	CONVERGING PATHS	1910-24	1
Chapter 2	ALL ROADS LEAD TO ROACH	1921-27	13
Chapter 3	THE FIRST STAGE	1918-29	21

Chapter 4	THE NEXT STAGE	1929-31	31
Chapter 5	HABLAS ESPAÑOL?	1932	43
Chapter 6	BEWARE! SAILORS	1933 pt1	51
Chapter 7	NO TIME FOR LEVITY	1933 pt2 - 1934 pt1	57
Chapter 8	SPLIT MILK	1934 pt2 – 1935 pt1	65
Chapter 9	GONE FISHIN'	1935 pt2	77
Chapter 10	TWO GOLFS AND THREE FISHES	1936 pt1	87

Chapter 11	THERE'S GOING TO BE A FIGHT	1936 pt2 – 1937 pt1	95
Chapter 12	FIFTY-SIX DAYS AT THE RACES	1937 pt2	101
Chapter 13	HELLO VERA	1938 pt1	109
Chapter 14	THREE'S A CROWD	1938 pt2	117
Chapter 15	INTO THE BREACH	1938 pt3	123
Chapter 16	WAR AT HOME	1939 pt1	129
Chapter 17	DROP THE LOT	1939 pt2 – 1940 pt1	137
Chapter 18	LIFE BEGINS AT 1940	1940 pt2	145
Chapter 19	BLEW IN – BLOWN OUT	1940 pt3	151
Chapter 20	THE OTHER MONKEY	1940 pt4	161
Chapter 21	COP OUT	1940 pt5	167

CONTENTS

Chapter 22	COAST TO COAST	1941 pt1	175
Chapter 23	HAVING THE TIME OF OUR LIVES	1941 pt2	185
Chapter 24	PILOTS OF THE CARIBBEAN	1941 pt3	199

Chapter 25	HEAT AND DRINK	1941 pt4	211
Chapter 26	LAUGH FOR MORALE	1941 pt5 – 1942 pt1	221
Chapter 27	TOUR DE FOX	1942 pt2	231
Chapter 28	ON THE RIGHT TRACK	1942 pt3	241

Chapter 29	TRAIN KEEPS A ROLLIN'	1942 pt4	253
Chapter 30	LAST TRAIN TO SAN FERN … CISCO	1942 pt5	261
Chapter 31	FORT AND LOST	1942 pt6 – 1945 pt1	269
Chapter 32	THE BOYS IN FOREIGN	1945 pt2 – 1948	279
Chapter 33	AT WHAT PRICE?	1949 – 1951 pt1	285
Chapter 34	PROMISES, PROMISES	1951 pt2 – 1953 pt1	295
Chapter 35	THE LAST STAGE	1953 pt2 – 1954	303
Chapter 36	A MAN OF LETTERS	1955 onwards	311

THE END

ACKNOWLEDGEMENTS and BIBLIOGRAPHY	321
U.S. FILM FOOTAGE and TV BROADCASTS	323
Other Books by the Author	327

o-o-0-o-o

KEY

Laurel **&** Hardy = on-screen – Laurel **and** Hardy = off-screen

(*ibid.*) = previously mentioned

(*circa*) = around this time

(*sic*) = copied correctly from original

[Square brackets] = author's comments.

[FILM] = refer to U.S. Film Footage and TV Broadcasts. (P323-326)

American variant spellings of such words as "defense" (UK = "defence"), "license" (UK = licence), color (colour), and honor (honour), have been left unchanged, where the original text is in U.S. English.

"Theatre" and "Theatre" are seemingly used equally in U.S. English.

All grammatical errors and mis-spellings in the "Laurel Letters" have been left in.

Any other mistakes are attributable to the author.

-----0-----

CHAPTER 1

CONVERGING PATHS

STAN JEFFERSON (1910)

Publicity photo from c1910, but also used in subsequent years.

It was September 1910. For the last four of his twenty years Englishman Arthur Stanley Jefferson had been learning his stagecraft as a member of small touring companies playing in pantomimes and plays, in variety halls and theatres around Britain. His ambition to become a comedian had taken a decided upturn when, in December 1909, he became a member of the best stable of comedians the variety stage has ever hosted – the Fred Karno Company.

Karno managed several comedy troupes from his London-based premises, and booked them in theatres throughout the U.K. – performing various comedy sketches. Young Stanley joined the troupe playing the most famous of all Karno music-hall sketches, *"Mumming Birds,"* a sketch which parodied the acts on a typical music-hall bill.

At the start of Jefferson's sixth week with the Karno Company, another young comedy acrobat joined the cast. This was to be the troupe's last week of performing *"Mumming Birds."* For the next twelve, they would be playing in a new sketch, *"Skating,"* with the new boy as principal comic. His name – CHARLIE CHAPLIN.

"Skating" went on a tour around Lancashire and Yorkshire, before ending its twelve-week run in London. There, the troupe went into rehearsals for a brand-new Karno sketch, *"Jimmy the Fearless,"* which subsequently ran for twenty weeks. Next, Stan and Charlie played just two weeks in *"The Wow-Wows,"* after which they had rather a fair few miles to travel to do their next run of shows – North America.

Some of the Karno Comedians from SKATING, doubling up as a competitive hockey team, playing at a local rink.
Laurel – back row, left. Chaplin front row, 2nd from left.

OLIVER NORVELL HARDY (1910)

Meanwhile, over in the small southern American town of Milledgeville, Georgia, eighteen-year-old Oliver Norvell Hardy was working at the Electric Theater, of which he later told a reporter:

In 1910, I started work at Milledgeville's first movie theatre, checking tickets and helping to clean the projector, and of course, singing in the evenings.

In 1913, after wasting three years of his life doing a job in which the public never saw him, Hardy moved to Atlanta, Georgia, where he found work doing something he really enjoyed – singing on stage.

BABE HARDY – 1913
Looking at those chubby, cherubic cheeks it is not hard to see how the nickname "Babe" story came about.

One of his regular bookings was at the Montgomery Theatre, where he got to know the resident pianist, Madelyn Saloshin. But Hardy's performing skills had still not reached their potential; and so, having viewed countless film comedies over the last four years, and convinced he could do as well as any of the actors in them, Norvell set out for their place of origin – Jacksonville, Florida.

On 7 November 1913, just before the move, Norvell and Madelyn married, which meant they could now legally live as man and wife in Jacksonville – a status which had probably prompted the marriage. Madelyn secured the job of resident pianist in the pit orchestra at the Orpheum Theatre, whilst Norvell undertook two jobs. During the day he worked as a labourer at the Lubin film studios, and in the evenings as a singer in cabaret and in vaudeville.

Within one month of his arrival in Jacksonville, Hardy was promoted to playing bit parts in films. Come January 1914 he knew he had truly arrived when he got his first credited role, in the film "*Outwitting Dad.*" The credits listed him as "O.N. Hardy" – a contraction of Oliver Norvell Hardy, and the name he was to so proudly announce himself as in later films.

In his next film, "*Casey's Birthday,*" O.N. Hardy's screen name had become "Babe" Hardy. The story goes that the Italian barber, across from the Lubin studios, would pat Hardy's cherubic cheeks with talcum powder after shaving him, whilst uttering: "Nice-a-babee, nice-a-babee." After a period of playful taunting by the other actors, the nickname "Babe" eventually stuck, and was to stay with him the rest of his life, both on screen and off.

JACKSONVILLE
This sad-looking outsider-figure, would soon emerge as the most popular and talented boy on set.

After Hardy had made just twenty films, Lubin took out a huge advert in the trade papers proclaiming Babe Hardy to be "The funniest fat Comedian in the world." The "funniest" part was extremely complimentary, but the "fat" bit was an epithet which would never sit easy with Hardy, but one he always had to bear in the course of making a living. In *"The Honor of Force,"* just a few films later, the name was even more firmly embedded when Hardy's character part was listed as "Fattie."

BABE at LUBIN – 1914
You wouldn't call him 'Fattie' if he was charging at you during a football game, would you!

During the first fourteen months with Lubin, Hardy appeared in the staggering number of fifty-eight films – that's one per week, *every* week.

In many of the films he was just a bit-part actor; but, as time went on, he got to play featured roles and bigger parts. [No pun intended]

-----0-----

Babe holding the screen in the 1915 release of the Lubin film:
AN EXPENSIVE VISIT

But it all came to a dead stop when, in February 1915, Lubin closed their Jacksonville studios. The Southern homeboy was going to have to move north if he wished to continue in films.

o-o-0-o-o

STAN JEFFERSON (1910 – 1915)

Stanley Jefferson, Charlie Chaplin, and the other thirteen members of the Karno company who had come "to conquer" America, opened on 3 October 1910 at the Colonial Theatre, New York. Reviews for their sketch, *"The Wow-Wows"* (re-titled for American audiences, *"A Night in a London Secret Society"*), were scathing. One newspaper reviewer described the company as "a lot of blithering, blathering Englishmen," and advised people to stay away. They took the advice.

Dropping this sketch in favour of the acclaimed *"Mumming Birds"* (*"A Night in an English Music Hall"*), the players fared much better, and the initial six-week run had a succession of extensions, which took them right through to August 1911, and as far as the West Coast.

THE KARNO COMPANY – Sacramento, June 1911.
Stan is back row, second from left, and Chaplin third from right.

The experience young Jefferson was gaining with the Karno Company was to prove invaluable to him in years to come but, at the time, the lack of a decent wage seemed too high a price to pay. So in August 1911, along with fellow comedian Arthur Dandoe, he quit; and the two home-sick Brits took a train to New York and sailed home on the *Lusitania*.

Once back in London, Stan and Dandoe formed as The Barto Brothers, playing a sketch written by Stan titled, *"The Rum 'Uns from Rome,"* but found bookings difficult to come by.

They thought they had been rescued from Poverty Corner when invited to join 'The Eight Comics' (Comiques) and, in May 1912, set off for a tour of the Continent, with the sketch *"Fun on the Tyrol."* Of all the tours Stanley had been on, this was to prove the most ill-fated of them all. Their engagement at the Circus Variété, in Rotterdam, was cancelled without a single performance having been played.

Moving on to the Palace in Liège, Belgium, the depleted company were plagued by more bad luck, which left them stranded – with no work, and no money.

'The Two Arthurs' – who left the U.S. to find their fame and fortune in London – but found only London.

Converging Paths

The Barto Bros' – Dando and Jefferson – who were also two of the 8 Komiks

Upon scraping their way back to London, Stan called in on his older brother Gordon, who was acting manager at the newly built Princes Theatre. Accepting some fraternal charity, he played a small role in the play "*Ben My Chree,*" which ran from July to September 1912. Then, by a stroke of luck, Stan bumped into Alf Reeves, manager of the Karno Company he had been to the U.S. with – who were now back in England. Reeves offered him a pay-rise and, one week later, on 2 October, Stan Jefferson set sail for America once again.

FRED KARNO COMPANY
SS Cairnrona - 20th September 1910
Back L-R: Albert Austin, Fred Palmer, Bert Williams, George Seaman, Frank Melroyd
Stan Jefferson, Fred Westcott, Charlie Chaplin, Arthur Dandoe
Muriel Palmer, Mike Asher, Amy Minister, Capt. C.J. Slooke

Chaplin was again the lead comic and, as the months went by, he continued to attract rave reviews. Come November 1913, Charlie was finally lured away from vaudeville by Mack Sennett, and put into films. With their star player gone the troupe struggled on for a further six months, before finally calling it a day.

So what was Stan to do now? He was stranded in America with no act, no money, and no prospects.

o-o-0-o-o

OLIVER NORVELL HARDY (1915 – 1917)

With no suitable film companies operating in the South, Hardy went on a job-finding mission to New York, but soon returned to Florida, where he made out by singing in cinemas, to accompany news-reel footage. Raymond McKee, a friend and fellow-actor from the former Lubin company, then sent word to Hardy that he could guarantee him work if he returned to New York.

Hardy took up the offer and joined McKee in the Edison Company, located in the Bronx. Having lost the status he had built up at Lubin, Hardy now had to start off again in minor roles, which is the probable reason he left the Edison Company after making just five films. Within a week he was working in Ithaca, an area of New York rich with filmmakers, his chosen one being Wharton Brothers, of whom he later related the account:

> I then worked for a film company who were producing a twelve-reel series of 'Get-Rich-Quick-Wallingford' stories, for which I was used as 'comic relief'. This consisted mainly of my being the target of custard pies, and having my false beard painfully tugged. I did however learn the art of taking a tumble, which stood me in good stead for what was to come later.

HOLD THAT TRAIN
One of the four
"Get-Rich-Quick-Wallingford" films which Babe Hardy made circa July-August 1915.

Just four Wallingford films later, Babe had had enough of custard pies, for now anyway, and moved on to Bayonne, New Jersey, to work for Vim Comedies. Here he actually got to appear in as many as eight films, at which point the Vim studios decided to up sticks, and move out. However, this didn't signal the end of a Babe's working relationship with Vim – far from it.

First good news was that the Vim company was relocating to the former Lubin Studios in Jacksonville. Second piece of good news was that pretty well the whole of the then current employees were going there too, including Babe Hardy. He had never been at ease with New York living. What suited others hadn't suited Hardy. Soon he would be back in his comfort zone.

In New York, Babe had been playing support parts in a series of Vim comedies featuring the characters 'Pokes and Jabs.' Once the cameras began rolling in Jacksonville, in November 1915, Hardy did a couple more of these, but then went into a new series of films known as the 'Plump and Runt' comedies, with Billy Ruge playing the name role of 'Runt' and Hardy that of 'Plump.'

For some reason, Hardy had used the name 'O.N. Hardy' for all his film credits in New York, but now reverted to 'Babe Hardy.'

Before the Plump and Runt comedies could get up a head of steam they had to give way to a series of films with the lead character called 'Bungles,' in which Hardy was back to minor roles. When these seemed to be heading nowhere, the 'Plump and Runt' series was given a prolonged run and, from January to September 1916, were made at the rate of one a week.

Despite all the experimental on-screen time that was allowed them, the two 'Plump and Runt' characters never became truly defined. Nor was there any consistency in the way they played together. It was a process that would develop almost instantly once Hardy was teamed with the right foil. But that was yet a decade, and a different partner, away.

The 'Plump and Runt' comedies were therefore terminated, and well-known film comedienne of her day, Kate Price, was brought in to play opposite Hardy. The pairing stayed together for eleven films, but then irregularities in the finances of Vim led to the company dissolving. It was a sad ending to a happy time for Babe.

THE CANDY TRAIL (1916)
Babe Hardy with Billy Ruge, and Florence McLoughlin, in one of the "Plump & Runt" films.

Within a few months, the newly-formed King Bee took over the Vim Studios, and recalled many of the Vim players, including Hardy. The main difference now was that they were there to service star player Billy West – a Chaplin impersonator, mimicking the plots and characters from the Chaplin films. But work was work, and Hardy even stayed with King Bee when, after making just five films in Jacksonville, they moved lock, stock and barrel to New York. Although Hardy had not enjoyed the time he had spent there previously, his return was under different circumstances – he was now an established actor, working with people who knew him and respected his work and worth.

Gone is the lonely outsider figure from his early days, and in his place, a prominent place, sits a very confident and at-ease Babe Hardy.
King Bee studios Jacksonville. (c. April 1917)

After just four weeks in New York, during which Hardy made two more Billy West comedies, the King Bee company moved into newly refurbished premises in Bayonne, New Jersey, where they made just seven films and stayed only thirteen weeks.

Babe in Jacksonville – 1916
Up till now, the whole of Hardy's cherubic baby features had been on view to cinemagoers. But now, as the antagonist to Billy West's Chaplinesque character, he was having to cover up with a scrubbing-brush moustache, and/or a raggedy beard, so as to resemble Chaplin's nemesis – Eric Campbell.

"THE ROGUE" (1917) King Bee Films Corporation, Hollywood
It looks like Babe Hardy has just discovered that this isn't the real Charlie Chaplin, and is letting Billy West know what he thinks of the deception.

This was one hell of a peripatetic profession, and the next move (October 1917) was going to prove the farthest of them all, when the company were offered to go to King Bee's new studios. This would take them from New Jersey on the East Coast, all the way to the West Coast, to a small, little-known film community in Los Angeles known as – Hollywoodland.

It was a big decision for homeboy Hardy. Would he take it? Let us hope so, or this story will have one heck of a tame ending!

o-o-0-o-o

STAN LAUREL (1915 – 17)

Seeing no advantage in returning to England, Stan decided to stay on and make a go of it. Enlisting Edgar Hurley and his wife Ethel, from the disbanded Karno Company, Stan formed The Three Comiques, for whom he wrote "*The Nutty Burglars*," a sketch about two burglars breaking into a lady's apartment. The problem was they couldn't break into the vaudeville circuit, and were out of work for more weeks than they were in it.

It was February 1915 before they finally obtained bookings on one of the better circuits. Cleverly, they had won over the agent with a revamped stage sketch which mimicked the screen characters of Chaplin, Chester Conklin, and Mabel Normand – who by this time were popular with cinema-goers; thus beating all others to the idea. The new act also had a new name: The Keystone Trio – which reinforced the association with the Chaplin films.

The Keystone Trio – Jefferson, Hurley and Wren (Ethel)

After an internal disagreement led to The Keystone Trio separating, Stan formed The Stan Jefferson Trio (September 1915), with man and wife team Baldwin and Alice Cooke, playing "*The Crazy Cracksman*" – a hybrid of Stan's two previous sketches.

Early in 1917, Stan appeared on the bill with an Australian duo called The Hayden Sisters. One of them was Mae Charlotte Dahlberg, whom Stan immediately fell for. Knowing he might never see her again if she continued touring with The Hayden Sisters, Stan persuaded her to leave and come on tour with him. But this meant dropping the Cookes – so he had effectively broken up two partnerships to get the one which suited HIM. It was a trait that would reveal itself on other occasions.

Mae was already married, so Stan had to make out that she was actually his wife during the eight years they were to spend together. The change of partner also brought about a change of stage name and, from now on in, Stan Jefferson would be known professionally (but not legally) as "Stan Laurel." He was also working on his new character, having discarded the Chaplin impersonation, as so many others were now doing it.

So, in March 1917, with yet another burglar sketch, "*Raffles – The Dentist*" (in which Stan played not 'Raffles' but 'Waffles' – a burglar mistaken for a dentist), the act of Stan & Mae Laurel hit the vaudeville circuit.

STAN LAUREL
This is how Stan looked,
when not impersonating Chaplin.

MAE 'LAUREL'
And this is how Mae looked,
when not throwing a tantrum.

In May 1917, whilst appearing at the Hippodrome in Los Angeles, Stan was approached backstage by a representative from Bernstein Productions who asked if he would be interested in making a series of pictures. He didn't have to deliberate long before saying, "Yes." The first film of the 'Stanley Comedies' – "*Nuts in May*" – was shot in June 1917, but a backer couldn't be found to make the others, and so Stan, and Mae, who had also appeared in the film, were released. After the preview of "*Nuts in May*," shown late-August, Laurel was picked up by Universal Pictures, for whom he made four films with L-KO and Nestor, on the Universal lot in Los Angeles, but was then let go.

STAN & MAE LAUREL – 1918

Chaplin had now been making films for four years, and was one of the screen's highest paid stars. Stan Laurel, meanwhile, would have to carry on scraping his way around the vaudeville circuit for some time yet.

o-o-0-o-o

OLIVER NORVELL HARDY (1917 – 1924)

"BRIGHT and EARLY"
(filmed 1917)
King Bee Films
Corporation, Hollywood

It was October 1917, and Oliver and Madelyn Hardy were now in Hollywoodland. But this wasn't the Hollywood we know of today – it was still an area of wide open spaces and orange groves. The main influx of immigrants was from the film communities, who were looking to gain from the extended hours of sunshine they expected in these here parts. Hardy continued playing supporting roles for Billy West with King Bee, for whom, up till mid-June 1918, he made twelve films, after which he then left their employ.

Within a few weeks Babe had been taken on by L-KO, with whom he made just nine films, before switching to Vitagraph in January 1919. This was to prove a long-lasting working relationship, as Babe was to spend the best part of the next five years on the Vitagraph lot.

Twenty-six of the first twenty-nine films he made for Vitagraph were with an English comedian from Lancashire, who had first come to the U.S. playing in vaudeville with the Fred Karno Company. His name was Jimmy Aubrey. If you thought I was going to say "Stan Laurel," you are racing too far ahead.

The end of Hardy's working relationship with Jimmy Aubrey coincided with the end of his marriage to Madelyn. Babe had been having an affair with actress Myrtle Lee Reeves and, just days after the divorce, they married. The two had met during film work: "*I was in drama, and he was in comedy, and so we met and were married*," Myrtle was later quoted as saying.

"THE FLY COP
(filmed 1917)
King Bee Films
Hardy again beetle-browed and moustachieod, and threatening to inflict severe and painful retribution.

The meeting she speaks of could have been as far back as May-July 1915, when Babe made a handful of films with the Edison Company, in Brooklyn, where Myrtle was both residing and working in films at that time. Or it may have been later, when both were working in California. Myrtle is confirmed as residing in Los Angeles in 1916, where she already had a number of films to her credit, made by Balboa Feature Films. This would fix her arrival in the Golden State at least one and a half years, and possibly up to two and a half years, before Hardy's. I was quite willing to accept, therefore, that Ms. Reeves and Mr. Hardy's second meeting, in California, was more by coincidence, and less by collusion. That is, until I spotted an entry in Simon Louvish's book: "*STAN & OLLIE – The Roots of Comedy*," which ran:

> In the summer of 1916 they [Babe and Madelyn] had a blow-up about a young unnamed actress in New York. This kind of behaviour continued after their move to Los Angeles.

Although the blow-up occurred when Myrtle was known to have already left New York, it is not to say that the incident which Madelyn was raking up had not happened some time before then. It would seem, therefore, there is a chain of evidence to suggest that Hardy had had an affair with Myrtle in New York, which was rekindled when both met up again in California.

Madelyn had further cause to vent her wrath when Hardy moved in with Myrtle before the divorce was finalised (petition submitted 1 March 1920 – interlocutory judgement 17 Nov 1920 – Interlocutory Divorce 17 November 1921). Myrtle was sharing a residence, at 4401 Clayton Avenue, Hollywood, with her sister Mary, also an actress; and so Hardy was admitted under the guise of "a boarder." After the wedding, on 24 November 1921, at the Church of Christ, 600 North Rossmore Avenue, Hollywood, Hardy and his new bride, Myrtle, moved into their own home at 2425 Russell Avenue, Hollywood.

Myrtle's hometown (born 15 January 1897) was Dublin, Georgia – less than fifty miles from Milledgeville – which would make for a common bond with Hardy. Among the films she had made up till becoming Mrs. Hardy were: "*The Red Circle*" (1915), "*The Millionaire's Son*" (1916), "*The Dawn of Wisdom*" (1917), "*Her Primitive Man*" (1917), "*Playthings*" (1918), "*A Bachelor's Wife*" (1919), and "*Beautifully Trimmed*" (1921) – after which she appears to have ceased making films to become a full-time wife.

As for Babe, the other three of the twenty-nine films he had so far made at Vitagraph were with Larry Semon. Now he was to stay exclusively with Semon, right through from March 1921 to December 1924 – even through a change of film studios, and a change of home address to 1719 Talmadge Street, Hollywood.

Hardy's last ever film with Semon was "*The Wizard of Oz*," which is totally unfaithful to the L. Frank Baum book, and bears no comparison whatsoever to the 1939 Judy Garland classic.

When Semon brought about his own demise, by making films at four times the cost, and taking four times longer than what was considered reasonable, Babe Hardy followed the 'Yellow Brick Road' to the Hal Roach Studios. It wouldn't be long now!

THE BELLHOP (1921)
Babe Hardy giving instructions to the bellhop, Larry Semon – looking identical to the role he had played in *The Fly Cop*, some four years earlier.

o-o-0-o-o

CHAPTER 2

ALL ROADS LEAD TO ROACH
STAN LAUREL (1918-25)

STAN & MAE LAUREL
"No Mother to Guide Her"
Des Moines – 23 February 1919

Upon returning to Los Angeles for a vaudeville engagement, in May 1918, Stan was hired to make a series of films at the Rolin Studios. "Rolin" was an acronym formed from the initial letters of the surnames of Hal ROach and his financial partner Dan LINthicum. The former was soon to transform Laurel's life but, at that moment in time, he let him go after the completion of just five pictures.

Stan didn't have to wait long for his next spell in front of the cameras. He bounced straight into the Vitagraph Studios, where he made three films as support to comedy star Larry Semon; then, due to a slice of bad luck, bounced straight out again. Just as Stan had been about to make his mark in the Semon films, Los Angeles was stricken by a flu epidemic, and the studio had to close its doors until the epidemic could be controlled. Would Stan ever get past spending five weeks in one place?

When the Vitagraph Studios re-opened, after a month of enforced inactivity, Stan was already back in vaudeville. Larry Semon did not seek to recall Laurel, as the latter had been getting too many laughs for Semon's liking. The lay-off did however do Stan a bit of good, as it gave him time to write and rehearse a new sketch, "*No Mother to Guide Her*," to replace the previous vaudeville sketch, "*Raffles the Dentist*."

It was some fifteen months later before Stan and Mae returned to L.A. (November 1919), but this time there were no film offers, and they continued on their vaudeville tour without so much as a hiccough. In March 1920 they hit the East Coast, where they stayed until October, before heading west again. Upon landing back in Los Angeles, in January 1921, Stan was picked up by G.M. "Broncho Billy" Anderson, a former screen cowboy, who then made a pilot film to showcase Laurel's talents – "*The Lucky Dog*." The film was in the can by February 1921 but, when no backers could be found to finance a series starring Laurel, he and Mae returned yet again to vaudeville.

This is pretty well a metaphor, as Semon seems to be frustrated that Laurel is in the foreground, and he is in his shadow.

The "heavy" in "*The Lucky Dog*" had been none other than Babe Hardy; but, such was the briefness of their meeting, that the chemistry between the two of them had no time to work its magic; and so both went on their separate ways without any inkling of what the future held.

THE LUCKY DOG
The luckiest thing here, is that Laurel and Hardy were to team up at a later date.

Roll forward to January 1922, and we find Stan and Mae back in Los Angeles. On the strength of his, by then, having sold "*The Lucky Dog*," G.M. Anderson pulled Laurel out of vaudeville, and took a gamble by beginning to shoot a series of films with Stan as the star. By December he had seven films in the can: "*The Weak-End Party*," "*The Handy Man*," "*The Egg*," "*The Pest*," "*Mixed Nuts*," "*Mud and Sand*," and "*When Knights Were Cold*" – six of which were released by Metro Pictures on a monthly basis, up till March 1923. For reasons not totally clear, Metro did not ask for more "Stan Laurel Comedies," and so Anderson and Laurel parted company.

MIXED NUTS – 1922 G.M Anderson film
The guy on the left is Stan's younger brother Teddy Jefferson.

Hal Roach, having seen one or more of the films in the Stan Laurel series, was impressed enough to recall him to his studio, for a trial period. Roach, it may be remembered, had been half of the Rolin Film Company, with whom Stan had made five films back in the summer of 1918. Roach was now sole owner of the newly built Hal Roach Studios, located at 8822 Washington Boulevard, in Culver City, California. The contract, signed late January 1923, was for twelve weeks, with a one- or two-year extension.

Filming began a week later, with one-reelers being made at the rate of roughly one every ten days. Happy with the nine films they had in the can during the provisional twelve week try-out, the two parties agreed to the one year extension, during which an additional fifteen films were shot – ending with "*Short Kilts*," in January 1924.

It is believed that Roach didn't take up the second year option on Laurel's contract because of Mae Laurel. He wasn't enamoured with her looks; didn't like her acting; and was totally infuriated by her private life and the way it affected Stan and his film work. As Stan would not agree to Mae being left out of the films, Roach felt he had no option but to keep Stan out of the frame as well – literally.

Luckily for Laurel, a friend of his persuaded independent film producer Joe Rock to take him on. Rock, however, had heard of the trouble Mae could make, and made it clear from the outset that her face was not about to be seen on film, nor even on set. However, things came to a head when Mae was allowed to accompany Stan on location during filming of the "*Snow Hawk*" (*circa* December 1924). A few days in she caused a major incident, by telling Stan that Joe Rock had made a pass at her. After proving to Laurel that he had been nowhere near Mae, Rock finally persuaded Laurel to send her packing, and even paid for her boat fare back to Australia.

Laurel waits patiently while Scott Pembroke (kneeling) discusses the next scene with JOE ROCK, in this 1924 Stan Laurel Comedy – "*Mandarin Mix-Up*"

The shrewd Mr. Rock then introduced Stan to Lois Neilson, another actress he employed, whom Laurel immediately fell for. But this was to be no short-time infatuation. Lois would turn out to be the biggest love in Laurel's life.

Lois Neilson was born Lois Nelson, in Tulare, California on 7 September 1895, of an American mother, Ella, and a Danish father, Albert. She had two older sisters, Ella and Lena. When the family moved to Santa Cruz, California, Lois attended Santa Cruz High School. There, one of her school-friends encouraged her to go into acting – her name, ZaSu Pitts. It was when Lois became an actress that she inserted the "i" into her surname, although she was to be billed by both names in the many films she made.

In 1919 Lois, who was then living in Los Angeles, had already appeared in the films: *"Farms and Fumbles," "Boarders and Bums," "Life Savers and Love Cravers," "Chumps and Cops,"* and *"Subs and Dubs."* In June 1918 she had made *"Do You Love Your Wife?"* (released January 1919) at Rolin Studios, a film in which Stan Laurel also appeared. During the five and a half years since then Lois had remained in Los Angeles, and made films with L-KO; United States Moving Picture Corporation; Century Films; and Universal; before ending up at the Joe Rock Studios.

In 1925, a few months after meeting Lois, Stan moved out of the Somerset Apartments, at 6075 Franklin Avenue, Hollywood; and moved in with her at Florence Avenue, Hollywood. He wasn't going to drift away a second time.

The twelve films which Laurel made with Rock, between February 1924 and February 1925, were pretty good quality, even though Rock had made them in an average of ten days per picture. But there was a problem. Rock was making out that the films were taking a whole month to shoot, and was charging the distributors accordingly. Consequently, when the films came in five months ahead of schedule, Rock had to keep up the pretence that the full series had not yet been shot. This meant he wasn't able to start shooting any further films with Laurel until that time was up. The problem now was that, during the wait, Laurel would have no income and could not appear on film for other companies for fear of blowing Rock's ruse.

Joe Rock Comedy – 1925
"Dr. Pyckle & Mr. Pride"
with Stan Laurel looking somewhat different to his publicity portrait, above.

Then, one of those twists of fate happened, which one can never explain, but which have life-changing outcomes. In April 1925 Laurel was invited back to the Hal Roach studios – not as an actor, but as a gag-writer.

Stan was now in the right mixing-bowl, working with all the best ingredients. Right in there with him was one ingredient which, when combined, would make the two of them so very, very special. All that was needed now was for someone to spot the potential!

o-o-0-o-o

THE TEAMING (1925-27)

OLIVER NORVELL HARDY had commenced work at the Hal Roach studios in January 1925, three months before Laurel. However, Hardy was not yet under contract, and so was allowed to do freelance work with other studios when not filming for Roach. His old pal Billy West put him into seven of the films he was producing for Cumberland Productions. In three of these Billy himself is the star but, in the other four, West paired Babe with comedian Bobby Ray.

Babe has now escaped the role of the heavy, and discarded most of the wild hair from his face. In fact, in some of the Billy West films, and even in his early films with Roach, his top lip is hairless. This then was a much gentler Hardy, whose facial expressions could be valued to the full and who, with Bobby Ray, was able to practise that "dumb and dumber" partnership which was so soon to become his stock-in-trade.

In the John McCabe book "*Mr Laurel & Mr Hardy*," Hardy speaks of the film "*The Paperhanger's Helper*," which he made with Bobby Ray, as having an influence on his later partnership with Stan Laurel:

> Bobby Ray was a slight man, on the short side. Didn't look like Stan, but he was an opposite to me. We were paperhangers. I was the boss, Bobby was my helper. I was always giving him orders, and he was always getting the wrong end of the stick. Bobby always played the fall guy; I was the wise guy, just as I am in Laurel and Hardy (only in Laurel and Hardy I am always the fall guy). I think of that picture once in a while as being the start of the Laurel and Hardy idea as far as I was concerned.

What was needed now was for Hardy to meet that man – under the right conditions. He was very close by, but not in the right environment. Hardy had been brought in to play supporting roles to other comedians on the Roach Lot, including: Charley Chase, Frank Butler, Clyde Cook, Max Davidson, James Finlayson, Glenn Tryon, Mabel Normand, Theda Bara, and the 'Our Gang' kids. Laurel, meanwhile, wasn't even in front of the camera.

Stan was happy with his position as writer and gag-man at the Roach Studios, as he had never rated himself as a film comedian in any case. But he didn't just limit himself to writing. After showing interest in everything about filmmaking, he was rewarded by being trained as a director. One year on and Laurel had co-directed a handful of films, including three with Oliver Hardy – who was by then under contract with Roach.

One day in June 1926 Hardy was unable to turn up for filming, having badly scalded his arm at home, while basting a leg of lamb he was roasting. Unable to find an immediate stand-in, Hal Roach pitched Laurel into the role. Liking Stan's contribution to the finished film, "*Get 'Em Young*," Roach gave him the go-ahead to write himself a part in the next picture. Hardy had by then recovered sufficiently to return, whereupon the two of them inadvertently appeared in the same film. For Stan Laurel and Oliver Hardy, the wheels had been set in motion. It was now only a matter of time!

Further films ensued in which the two of them appeared, until – by a process of almost "natural selection" – the potential of playing them against one another was spotted, and exploited. Here is how the metamorphosis happened – starting in August 1926:

45 MINUTES FROM HOLLYWOOD – Stan plays a hotel guest, and Hardy plays a policeman called to the hotel. They don't appear together in the same scene – so no pairing there!

DUCK SOUP – Laurel and Hardy are vagrants, on the run from a posse of Forest Rangers who want to recruit them for a work-party to fight a forest fire. If we were to shave Hardy's face, and fit out both men with better clothes, we would pretty well have the characters we are looking for, as everything else is in there – right down to Laurel's cry. In fact, the characters were so close to the finished article that, when sound came in, "*Duck Soup*" was remade as the Laurel & Hardy talkie "*Another Fine Mess*" – with the prescribed make-over implemented.

The chemistry between Hardy and Laurel during filming of "*Duck Soup*" had been noticed and noted, but in the next few films they were just allocated roles at random, and it would be a further fourteen weeks before they were so much as to appear in the same shot together.

SLIPPING WIVES – Having come so close to nailing the characters of "The Boys" in their first ever film together, Laurel and Hardy are split up here – one to play a delivery man, the other to play a butler. This film too was remade as a talkie – "*The Fixer-Uppers*." The second version has them as partners in deceit, which works perfectly. However, this earlier version misses by a mile.

LOVE 'EM AND WEEP – Laurel has some recognisable traits in his character, but Hardy is sporting a Kitchener moustache, and has little screen time. This is now the third of their first four films which would be remade as a talkie, and again the remake will fix the problems.

WHY GIRLS LOVE SAILORS – is a Stan Laurel comedy, and sees him for the second time, but certainly not the last, pretending to be a woman. Hardy appears as the Captain's mate, who tries to become Stan's mate (the "female" Stan, that is!).

WITH LOVE AND HISSES – has what is now a very over-used scenario of the raw recruit joining the army, and having his life being made a misery by a bullying sergeant. In later films in which Laurel & Hardy appear as soldiers, Ollie is there to

protect Stan, whereas, in this film, Hardy is the sergeant who adds to the discipline dished out by the Captain (James Finlayson). So, again, it's no "buddy picture."

NOW, I'LL TELL ONE – both Laurel AND Hardy appear in this; but, as it is actually a Charley Chase comedy, it doesn't really advance the cause.

SAILORS, BEWARE! – Similar in size of roles, and Stan and Babe's respective on-screen time, to "*Why Girls Love Sailors*." And again, when they do meet, it's for a confrontation. We do however get to see the first try-out of Hardy's look to camera, accompanied by a "tie-twiddle" to cover his embarrassment.

DO DETECTIVES THINK? – Now we're getting somewhere! Here we see the template being laid down for what would become consistent and recognisable in Laurel & Hardy films. Firstly, the two characters are working partners. Secondly, their faces have been stripped of all the adornments which masked them in earlier pictures. Thirdly, they are wearing what was to become their regular attire: Laurel's tatty ill-fitting suit, spotted bow-tie, wing-collar shirt, and flat-heeled shoes; and Hardy's dark trousers, non-matching jacket, and what would become the trademark tie. And they have taken to wearing their most famous of trademarks – the Derby hats. If we can reinforce these elements in the next few pictures, we'll be there in a jiffy.

FLYING ELEPHANTS – No-ohhh! Where are those two men we saw in the last film? Here we have Stan playing a caveman who loves women, but whose mannerisms would suggest otherwise, and Hardy playing his rival. My advice: Stick this film in a cave, and dig it up later when it may be viewed more as a novelty find. (Which they did. Well! – not literally.)

SUGAR DADDIES – Again, no partnership here. Stan and Ollie are basically there to support one of the other stars in the "Roach All-Star" series – Jimmy Finlayson.

THE SECOND HUNDRED YEARS – Here we are very close to a confirmed partnership. Disguised under their prison outfits are the two guys we are looking for. The press releases bill this as another in the "Roach All-Star" series, but the main star, Jimmy Finlayson, has been deposed; and in his place on the posters we see "Oliver Hardy and Stan Laurel" – accompanied by phrases such as: "new starring team," and "in first picture as comedy duo."

This appears to be the exact moment when it was decided that, from now on in, scripts would be specifically written for 'Laurel & Hardy.' The two screen characters which Stan Laurel and Oliver Hardy are known and loved for *were* glimpsed in earlier films, but that was by chance. In most, they had simply been playing parts from a stockpile of scripts written for just anyone. But now there was a deliberate plan to standardise the two characters, and write plots and situations to bring out the traits that were thought would work best for them. Stan christened these two screen characters "The Boys" – a term he would use in describing the premise of their films, such as: "The Boys have to deliver a washing machine to a house at the top of a steep set of steps."

Their immediate plans, however, had to be put on hold. The Roach Studios was about to close for the summer break. All there was time to do to utilise the talents of Hardy and Laurel, was to throw them into a production which was ready to roll. The idea of putting them out as a team would have to wait.

CALL OF THE CUCKOO – is a Max Davidson Comedy (another of the Roach All-Stars), with Laurel and Hardy filling a couple of minor roles. in which they appear to ad-lib the actions of lunatics playing around in a garden. After the summer break, these two lunatics would be on their way to taking over not only the asylum, but the WORLD.

New passport photo – 1927

When the Roach Studios broke on 1 July, Babe went to Cuba with wife Myrtle. Stan had already left for England, with new bride Lois. The two had married on 23 August 1926, and then made home at 3716 South Van Ness Avenue, Hollywood.

-----0-----

1927 June 29 (circa) – THE LAURELS

LOS ANGELES to NEW YORK CITY 2,814 miles

1927 July 02

'Homeric' leaves NYC for SOUTHAMPTON, England

-----0-----

1927 early July – THE HARDYS:

      LOS ANGELES, California to HAVANA, Cuba   4,100 miles

-----0-----

Stan's main reason for the trans-Atlantic trip was to see his father, Arthur Jefferson, and sister Olga Beatrice, whom he hadn't seen since leaving England in October 1912. In all, Laurel was away for almost six weeks – 29 June till 7 August – and thus missed the first week of the Roach Studio restart. It is possible that the late return meant that Stan was left out of the film "*Love 'Em and Feed 'Em*," and his part taken over by Max Davidson. We can only imagine how much better the film would have been with Laurel in the role.

As soon as Hardy was free, he **and** Laurel were able to go into the production and shooting of "*Hats Off*" – during the second week in August.

HATS OFF – finds the Boys working together as salesmen, trying to sell a washing machine to a potential buyer who lives at the top of a long, steep flight of steps.

Cementing of the partnership of Laurel & Hardy could not have better coincided with that of another one. Hal Roach had just signed a distribution deal with the film company Metro-Goldwyn-Mayer, to commence on 1 September. First to benefit from the might of MGM's publicity machine was "*Hats Off*," the launch for which was comparable to that of a major feature film. This Roach-MGM launch seemed to be announcing to the film world that "Laurel & Hardy are here – and here to stay."

Hat's Off almost stands as a metaphor for them taking their first big step on the way to the very top.

"*Hats Off*" was a great vehicle with which to promote them as a newly formed team. Almost everything which makes up the characters of the Boys can be found in this film. There's only one problem – THE FILM can't be found! Amazingly, although it probably had more prints made than any other L&H film to date, there is no known copy in existence.

The shooting script for "*Hats Off*" has survived and, coupled with extant film stills, allows us to visualise pretty well all the action in the film. And if that isn't compensation enough, one can always watch the 1932 remake, "*The Music Box*," which is much the same premise, and even the same location, but with a piano being the object delivered, instead of a washing machine.

"*Hats Off*" is not something to be mourned as "lost," as it is actually the starting point from which a further ninety-two films went on to be created, most using the same DNA profile.

In the rest of this book, I could now go on to repeat all the accepted accounts of the films and the lives of Laurel and Hardy, whereby, during their working partnership, all they did every day was go from their homes to the studio, make a film, then go home again. But to do that would be to miss out on a vast treasure-trove of recently unearthed material, which reveals that, almost from the day they had become a screen double act, Laurel and Hardy lived a double life.

o-o-0-o-o

CHAPTER 3

THE FIRST STAGE
(1927 pt2 – 1929 pt1)

In December 1927, Laurel and Hardy made their first-ever known personal appearance as a comedy team at the 'Annual Christmas Benefit,' organised by the *Los Angeles Examiner* newspaper company:

> Thursday 15 December 1927
> LOS ANGELES, Shrine Auditorium
> The 14th Annual Examiner CHRISTMAS BENEFIT
> **BIGGEST SHOW OF THE YEAR**
> A Whirlwind of Dancing, Presenting America's Supreme Stars,
> Each a Head-Liner, in Their Most Sensational Dances.
> A Pageant of Beauty and Fashion, Presenting the World's
> Most Beautiful Women in Their Richest Creations.
> 300 STARS!
> The Most Brilliant Galaxy of World-Famous People –
> Ever Assembled at One Time on One Stage.

The three hundred stars included: Tom Mix, Conrad Nagel, Joan Crawford, W.C. Fields, Marie Dressler, Mary Astor, Wallace Beery, Clara Bow, William Boyd, Gary Cooper, Myrna Loy, Ernest Torrence, Billie Dove, Edmund Lowe, Charlie Murray, Victor McLagen, Fay Wray, Loretta Young, Lloyd Bacon, and Ford Sterling.

And tucked in amongst this vast assembly of "The Most Brilliant Galaxy of World-Famous People Ever Assembled" were the names "Stan Laurel & Oliver Hardy – Two Famous Hal Roach Comedy Stars." The Examiner printed a montage of portraits of scores of the Hollywood actors in attendance; but, in the midst of this number and magnitude of film stars, Laurel & Hardy were totally overlooked.

Shrine Auditorium, LOS ANGELES

Past, present, and future associates of Stan and Babe who were also at the show included: Hal Roach's 'Our Gang,' William Austin, Fred Kelsey, Yola D'Avril, Dolores Del Rio, Thelma Todd, Clyde Cook, and Polly Moran; plus Larry Semon and Dorothy Dwan – whom both Stan and Babe had made films with individually.

With three hundred stars at the show, it is obvious that not all of them would have done stage time, but Stan and Ollie ***did.*** Their act was described as "a lively skit." Examining the content of the films they had made so far, it is hard to pick out a routine they could have lifted and performed on stage. So maybe they knocked up a quick exchange of patter at short notice.

[The show came between filming of "*The Finishing* Touch" and "*From Soup to Nuts.*"]

Just over ten weeks after the star-studded Christmas Show, Stan and Babe were again to be found on stage among another constellation of stars, but this time the luminosity was reduced by almost half – from three hundred to one hundred and seventy-five. This was still before the L.A. launch of "*Hats Off,*" but the publicity billed them as: "Stan Laurel and Oliver Hardy – screen comedy team."

Other performers of note on the entertainment programme were Hal Roach's 'Our Gang,' Marie Dressler, Ernest Torrence, and W.C. Fields.

> Saturday 25 February 1928
> LOS ANGELES, Ambassador Auditorium
> **The 7th Annual WAMPAS FROLIC and BALL**
> Great and near-great in films, social and business circles
> of the city, will be present.
> **A Cinema Fun Fest**
> 175 filmland celebrities will be on hand.
> This is a formal affair. 500 persons will contribute
> to the staging of the show.
> 13 Wampas Baby Stars of 1928 will make their debut.
> 30 feature acts comprise the schedule.
> 3,000 capacity sell-out.

[This event occurred the day after Stan and Babe finished filming "*Their Purple Moment.*"
It also coincided with the date of release of "*The Finishing Touch.*"]

On 8 March 1928 came the long-awaited first-time screening in Los Angeles of "*Hats Off,*" at the Metropolitan Theatre. Its aim in promoting the new team of "Laurel & Hardy" would have been somewhat diluted by then, as a handful of films made **after** "*Hats Off*" had been released **before** it – each one proclaiming the teaming. The film had been released in other states in November 1927, so this delayed launch was rather like advertising a marriage five months after the wedding; although, to be fair, at several outlets "*Hat's Off*" had been promoted as "A Stan Laurel Comedy," so now the emphasis was on the teaming of Laurel AND Hardy.

Laurel and Hardy weren't there in person, but a couple of look-alikes stood in during the carnival-like promotional events. However, Stan and Babe did appear at the Metropolitan just fifteen days later, but it was a tragedy, rather than a comedy, which drew them there.

At three minutes to midnight on 12 March 1928 the St. Francis Dam, located in San Francisquito Canyon, had burst. A wall of water, initially one-hundred-and eighty-foot-high, raced through San Francisquito Canyon and then down the Santa Clara River Valley, devastating the towns of Piru, Fillmore, and Santa Paula before emptying into the Pacific Ocean at Montalvo, between Oxnard and Ventura, some five to six hours later. It left an estimated six hundred people dead. So it was that the Hollywood film community gathered in support, and staged a massive benefit show:

Among those who lent their support were: Gloria Swanson, Fay Wray, Wallace Beery, Victor McLagen, William Boyd, Emil Jennings, W.C. Fields, Irving Berlin, Eddie Cantor, Jack Dempsey, Tom Mix and 'Tony,' Joan Crawford, Lupino Lane, Charlotte Greenwood, Conrad Nagel, King Vidor, Clive Brook, Buddy Rogers, Richard Arlen, Conrad Veidt, John Barrymore, Jack Benny, Charlie Murray, Edward Everett Horton, and the Wampas Baby Stars; plus stars from stage musicals.

From the Hal Roach Studios came: Stan Laurel, Oliver Hardy, Charley Chase, Viola Richard, Dorothy Coburn, and Max Davidson. Others who had earlier or later association with Laurel & Hardy films were Vivien Oakland, Charles Middleton, and Glenn Tryon.

Another Hollywood comedian whom Stan may have enjoyed meeting up with on the night was a little man by the name of Charles Chaplin, who also put in an appearance – a fact not found in any other biographies.

From the Hal Roach Studios came: Stan Laurel, Oliver Hardy, Charley Chase, Viola Richard, Dorothy Coburn, and Max Davidson. Others who had earlier or later association with Laurel & Hardy films were Vivien Oakland, Charles Middleton, and Glenn Tryon. Another Hollywood comedian whom Stan may have enjoyed meeting up with on the night was a little man by the name of Charles Chaplin, who also put in an appearance – a fact not found in any other biographies.

> Wednesday 21 March 1928
> LOS ANGELES, Metropolitan Theatre
> (Midnight Show)
> **Red Cross Relief Fund**
> for victims of the
> St. Francis Dam Disaster
> 40 Acts – 150 Stars

The show netted $12,000 to aid the refugees of the dam disaster.

[This show was on the evening of the day that Stan and Babe finished filming *"Should Married Men Go Home?"*]

-----0-----

The Roach Studios closed for its spring break on 26 March, and re-opened five weeks later on 2 May. Babe Hardy – along with brothers James and Charles Parrott, plus several other Roach employees – went on a road trip to Vancouver. One source claims Laurel went too; but, as he now had a fifteen-week-old baby, I would like to believe that he chose to stay at home, rather than go on a stag trip, the purpose of which was to evade the California prohibition laws.

[James Parrott was then working at the Roach Studios as a film director. Previously, he had been a film comic, using the name "Paul Parrott." His brother Charles is better known as comedian "Charley Chase."]

-----0-----

1928 late March (*circa*)
      LOS ANGELES, California to VANCOUVER, B.C.　1,276 miles

-----0-----

1928 April 19 (*circa*)
      VANCOUVER, B.C. to LOS ANGELES, California　1,276 miles

-----0-----

Hardy was back in time to welcome his house guests, Mr. and Mrs. D. D. Bronson, between Saturday and Tuesday 21-24 April. Hardy was now feeling particularly flush, and had recently moved into what was described as a "mansion," located at 621 North Alta Drive, Beverly Hills – an area which reflected his affluence. Laurel too had made use of his increased income, and bought a large colonial-style house at 718 North Bedford Drive, also in Beverly Hills. If you've got – flaunt it!

Fast forward through the making of *"Early to Bed," "Two Tars," "Habeas Corpus," "We Faw Down," "Liberty," "Wrong Again,"* and *"That's My Wife,"* to the third week in December 1928, and we find the film *"Big Business"* in production at the Roach Studios. There is a popular belief that the Boys were trying to sell Christmas trees in July, based on the premise that the film was made in the summer. But it is clearly the case that, though Christmas in the U.K. is celebrated in arctic conditions, in L.A. the sun is still known to shine.

On 29 December the Roach Studios closed for the holidays. Various dates were given for the proposed restart of filming – from as early as 28 January 1929, to as late as 1 April. The reason for the uncertainty was because Roach was having sound-stages and equipment installed to accommodate that new-fangled gimmick – "talking pictures." It would never last!!

Concurrently, another surprise announcement was made:

> During the closing down of the Hal Roach Studios in Los Angeles for five weeks, his comedy team Stan Laurel and Oliver Hardy will play picture house dates in person.
>
> (*Waterloo Evening Courier* – 12 December 1928)

The real surprise is that, this early on in their film careers, Laurel and Hardy were already contemplating making "live" stage appearances. However, no records of any appearances during this particular period have been found.

When the Boys went back to work the sound equipment was still not fully up and running, so they continued making "silents" – "*Double Whoopee*," "*Bacon Grabbers*," and "*Angora Love*." It was the last week in March before the first Laurel & Hardy talkie was made, "*Unaccustomed As We Are*," with the title chosen to fit the sense of occasion and not the premise of the film. Next came two more talkies, "*Berth Marks*" and "*Men O' War*," with time taken out to film cameo roles in the MGM extravaganza "*Hollywood Revue of 1929*," after which Stan and Babe finally made a public appearance – albeit for a somewhat puzzling, reason.

> Saturday 15 June 1929
> LOS ANGELES, Grauman's Chinese Theatre
> ## "BROADWAY MELODY"
> FAREWELL MIDNIGHT MATINEE
> Guests of Honor:
> Stan Laurel and Oliver Hardy – Hal Roach comedians
> Master of Ceremonies: Conrad Nagel
> Star Guests Extraordinary:
> Charles King, Anita Page, and Bessie Love – IN PERSON

The Metro-Goldwyn-Mayer film "*Broadway Melody*" had just gone into the record books for having had the longest run of any talking picture in California, and was about to go out with a bang by having a last showing, with many stars of stage and screen in attendance. Charles King, Anita Page, and Bessie Love had all starred in "*Broadway Melody*," so it was natural for them to be there on the night. However, Laurel & Hardy were not in "*Broadway Melody*" but **were** in the film coming in to replace it – "*Hollywood Revue of 1929*."

Grauman's Chinese Theatre – as it looked for the premiere of "*King of Kings*" – four weeks before the premiere of "*Broadway Melody*."

Pre-publicity for the 'Gala Midnight Matinee Show' for "*Broadway Melody*" advertised that, "Stan Laurel and Oliver Hardy, Hal Roach comedians, are to appear in impromptu presentations on the stage." Stan and Babe never did anything "impromptu." It is more likely they were about to do an act which would *seem* to be impromptu. This leads me to believe that they did a stage version of the "shirt-ripping" sequence from their then current release "*Berth Marks*" – a theory which may be backed up by reviews of a couple of events to come.

Another possibility is that they did a snippet of their magic act from the film they were there to plug – "*Hollywood Revue of 1929*" – but then, as the preview trailer was shown on the night, surely that was enough to act as a teaser.

The First Stage

A letter written by Laurel in November 1958 gives no clues:

```
Yes, I've been to Grauman's Chinese theatre many times,
Babe & I also appeared in an act on the stage there one
night, the reason we did'nt sign our names in cement was,
we were never asked - (they probably saw our act.!!)
```

And the *Los Angeles Times* (13 June 1929) provided only pre-publicity:

COMEDY TEAM AT CHINESE

Appearing as guests of honor will be Stan Laurel and Oliver Hardy, Hal Roach's famous comedians, who will unveil new tricks in their impromptu presentations on the stage.

The phrase "new tricks" might suggest the aforementioned cod-magic act, but still nothing definite. And if you feel the description of the Boys' act is unclear, how about this one?

In the roles of star guests will be the trio of stars of "Broadway Melody," including Charles King, Anita Page, and Bessie Love, who will be seen and heard in extemporaneous novelties behind the footlights.

Great to note that, even with so many "real" Hollywood film stars present, it was Laurel and Hardy who, this early in their career, gained the banner headline.

[This appearance was on the evening of the day Stan and Babe finished filming "*Perfect Day*."]

-----0-----

> Thursday 20 June 1929
> LOS ANGELES,
> Grauman's Chinese Theatre
> ## "Night of Nights"
> The World Premiere of
> Metro-Goldwyn-Mayer's Screen Extravaganza
> **HOLLYWOOD REVUE OF 1929**

The "World Premiere" of "*Hollywood Revue of 1929*" was held the following Thursday, again at Grauman's. Press details of the actual staging of the premiere of "*Hollywood Revue of 1929*," both before and after, are very scant. The only names mentioned in pre-publicity were those of the actors who were actually appearing **on the screen**, and not those there in person.

The Los Angeles Times did do a write-up, three days after the event, which informed readers:

> *"'Hollywood Revue,' in its first showing, was the last word in premieres,"* and that: *"The stars of the cast were present and were introduced on the stage."* However, amongst the list the L.A. Times gave, none were of the major stars of the film. They did excuse themselves by saying that there were just too many stars there to name, and substituted the figures *"three-fourths of the members of the profession,"* plus *"nearly all of the MGM stars."*

Stan & Ollie performing their cod-magic act in the film: "*Hollywood Revue of 1929.*"

A couple of stars who *were* in attendance, but not in the film, were Douglas Fairbanks, Jr. and new wife Joan Crawford, who were making their first public appearance since marrying a fortnight earlier. The Hollywood café 'Montmartre' boasted that, "*Hundreds of Stage and screen celebrities will entertain with dinner and after-theatre parties for this epochal event*," but the only named Hollywood stars who went there were Mr. and Mrs. Charles Kenyon, Sally Ellers, Thelma Todd, Ann Cornwall, Ben Lyon, and Charles Chaplin.

Another after-show party was held in the Blossom Room of the Roosevelt Hotel, this one for the guests of Harry Rapf – who was the producer of both "*Broadway Melody*" and "*Hollywood Revue of 1929.*" This would lead one to presume that all the MGM stars went there – although none were named.

An article by Eleanor Parker in the October 1929 issue of *The Picturegoer* places the Boys at Grauman's only:

> Two quiet unassuming gentlemen, wearing smart straw hats and their dinner coats correctly tailored, stepped up to the microphone in the lobby of the famous Chinese Theatre in Hollywood. It was one of those glaringly gorgeous openings for which Hollywood is famed.
>
> "Now we take pleasure in introducing Mr. Laurel and Mr. Hardy, the screen's funniest clowns. They will say a few words to the listeners of the air who are not with us tonight."
>
> The announcer then turned to the two gentlemen. "Say something funny," he whispered, while the standers-by listened to hear words of mirth and humour from the mouths of the two funny men.
>
> And what did the two comedians say? They looked at each other in bewilderment. The people, seen and unseen, were waiting in silent anticipation of side-splitting comedy.
>
> "Good evening, ladies and gentlemen. We are happy to be here to-night." Thus did Stan Laurel answer the call for humor.
>
> "Good evening, ladies and gentlemen. We wish that you could be here with us to-night." These were the words of brilliant wit, uttered in his turn by Oliver Hardy.
>
> "That's the reason we avoid all public appearances," Stan confided as he walked into the theatre. "People expect us to be funny all the time. We are like everyone else, with our regular business. Comedy is our business. We can't go around all the time, doing comedy falls and hitting each other."
>
> "Then, if we did try to be funny, and didn't succeed, people would say, 'Oh, they're not half so good as we thought they were'," Oliver added, "So we refuse all requests to appear in public, and keep our funniness for the screen."

The only clue as to which one of the two recent Grauman's events Ms. Parker is recounting is when she says: "It was one of those glaringly gorgeous openings for which Hollywood is famed" – the keyword here being "opening," which identifies it as "*Hollywood Revue.*"

Again the event is punctuated with some positiveness, as Laurel & Hardy's comedy sketch, in the film itself, is regarded as one of the highlights of "*Hollywood Revue*" – certainly the comedy highlight.

[This premiere landed in between the making of "*Perfect Day*" and "*They Go Boom.*"]

-----0-----

This newspaper write-up gave us details of what can only be described as a fun day-out for employees at the Roach Lot. It is dated 27 June 1928, so one must surmise it took place at least one day earlier.

> Thirty-two of the Hal Roach Studio in Los Angeles, ranging in rank from Vic president down, competed in tournament, with Oliver Hardy and Ed Kennedy tying for low gross score. Kennedy also won low net. Lou Foster, Tim O'Donnell, Charles Chase and Lew Powers got prizes. Stan Laurel won the booby (prize), without contest

The First Stage

A pictorial account of the tournament was featured in this 4 August 1929 *Moving Picture World*.

The Roach Studio Folks Go Golfing

OCCASION again arises for the presentation of filmfolk in the serio-comic roles of golf tournament players. The one before us now is the private links party of the Hal Roach studio, and doubtless this serious business offers extraordinary relief to contestants whose life is just one comedy after another for MGM's program. The tournament was held at the Riviera Country Club near Hollywood.

Charlie Chase, comedy star, with the cup he donated and also won.

What's wrong with this picture? Stan Laurel, star comedian, gets his billiards and gouf a little confused, it seems.

George Stevens, cameraman, plays the 13-ball in the side pocket—er—But let it pass!

H. M. Walker, veteran comedy title writer — and we can't think of a single gag for him!

As Robert McGowan, the veteran director of "Our Gang" comedies, looks in his togs.

Another director of long standing with the Hal Roach organization, the huge Arch Heath.

Even the adjectives were abjured for the day by Ray Coffin, studio publicity director.

And the mighty casey struck out—Oliver Hardy, star comedian, trying a Babe Ruth.

Another cameraman who reeled off a few million feet of footwork—Len Powers.

As stated, this is serious business. Hence, this "shot" of Ed Kennedy, contract player.

And finally, for space permits no more of this interesting meet James Parrott, director.

	CHARLIE CHASE Comedy star	STAN LAUREL star comedian	GEORGE STEVENS cameraman
H.M. WALKER comedy title writer	ROBERT MCGOWAN director "Our Gang"	ARCH HEATH director	RAY COFFIN publicity director
OLIVER HARDY comedian	LEN POWERS cameraman	ED KENNEDY contract player	JAMES PARROTT director

LAUREL and HARDY – The U.S. Tours

The next public appearance a few days later, and saw the Fox Film Corporation put MGM's efforts to stage a première to shame – and that's something you won't read too often.

The Fox Theatre in San Francisco, built at the staggering cost of five million dollars, opened on 28 June 1929. This was an event which was not going to pass by without Hollywood sitting up and taking notice, as no less than one hundred and fifty of its most notable stars and producers were about to make an exodus to attend.

-----0-----

1929 June 28

LOS ANGELES, California to **SAN FRANCISCO**, California 382 miles

The Southern Pacific ran a special train from Los Angeles, named for the occasion: "The West Coast Fox Special." Upon its arrival at 10.40am the stars were welcomed by the Mayor of San Francisco, accompanied by the sounds of the Municipal Band. Around five thousand devoted movie fans crowded around to get a glimpse of the galaxy of stars, before they were whisked away in automobiles, on a circuitous route around the City Hall, to the Palace Hotel. After a luncheon at the Olympic Club, at Lakeside, the stars and executives were taken back to the Palace Hotel to rest, before the evening's "Big Parade" to the Fox Theatre.

> *Friday 28 June 1929*
> *1 night only*
> Galaxy of Actors and Actresses to be here for the opening of the New Five-Million-Dollar
> **SAN FRANCISCO,**
> **Fox Theatre**

After the audience had been given two hours to gaze with awe and wonderment at the lavish interior of this movie temple, they were given more cause "to gaze with awe and wonderment" as the Hollywood stars paraded on stage. These included: Marion Davies, Janet Gaynor, Wallace Beery, Joan Crawford and Douglas Fairbanks, Jr.; Will Rogers, Loretta Young, Buster Keaton, Stan Laurel, and Oliver Hardy.

Add to this a group of actors who were to work with Stan and Babe at the Roach Lot: Lupe Velez, Polly Moran, Sharon Lynn, Charley Chase, and Harry Langdon. And in the audience was Hal Roach, with his wife Marguerite, seated in the company of Mr. and Mrs. Louis B. Mayer; Mr. and Mrs. Jack Warner, and Irving Thalberg and Norma Shearer; plus Sid Grauman.

The *San Francisco Chronicle* described what happened next:

> Then came Will Rogers to introduce the stars. Waves of laughter swept the mighty throng as he brought each dainty beauty across the big stage, or escorted each broad-shouldered man star to take his bow. His comments on each, and their smiling replies, raised chuckles to guffaws, and thunders of applause swept the theatre as the audience paid tribute to their favourites.

The line-up was followed by Fanchon and Marco's "*California Capers,*" which had a company of two hundred artistes. Then at 9.30 the audience watched the world premiere of the film "*Behind That Curtain.*" The whole presentation was enhanced by the sounds of a forty-piece orchestra, and a fifty-voice choir.

Louella O. Parsons was present at the opening, and later wrote:

> Snapshots of Hollywood collected at random: Will Rogers introducing Mayor John Porter of Los Angeles at the Fox opening. Mayor Porter asking Will Rogers for points on how to be Mayor. Polly Moran singing "Sonny Boy." Gus Edwards getting everyone to sing "Your Mother and My Mother." Buster Keaton playing the ukulele and not being arrested. Lois Wilson celebrating her birthday. Carlotta King doing her grand opera stuff at the Fox luncheon. George K. Arthur leading the parade.
>
> Stan Laurel and Oliver Hardy receiving an ovation that proved that fifty thousand people can't be wrong when they pick on them as their favourite comedians. George Jessell making a speech as usual. Charley Murray being invited to say a few words.

(*San Antonio Light* – 2 July 1929)

[This appearance landed in between the making of "*Perfect Day*" and "*They Go Boom.*"]

The First Stage

1929 June 29

SAN FRANCISCO, California to LOS ANGELES, California 382 miles

-----0-----

There wasn't long to wait for the next public event – just twenty-four hours, to be exact. From San Francisco, Stan and Babe barely had time to get back to Los Angeles to change their shirts, before dashing over to the Beverly Theatre.

> Saturday 29 June 1929
> LOS ANGELES, Beverly Theatre
> **MIDNIGHT FROLIC**
> Proceeds will go towards the $65,000 Fund to construct the Spanish mission-type home for the Beverly Hills Masonic Lodge.
> Charles King, Ukelele Ike, Laurel and Hardy Joe E. Brown, Jack Goodrich, Fanny Brice, Helen Kane, Marie Dressler, Lawrence Tibbett, Lupe Velez, Jack Benny

Sharing the bill was Metropolitan opera star Lawrence Tibbett, for whom Laurel and Hardy were shortly to do for his film, "*The Rogue Song*," what they had done for "*Hollywood Revue of 1929*" – i.e. to add some comic relief. Interesting to note that Jack Benny was at this show. One would have thought his services would have been better employed at the premiere of the latter-mentioned film, as he played the M.C. in it.

Interesting to note too that, apart from Lupe Velez, Laurel and Hardy were the only ones of all the stars from the previous evening to make this one. Makes you wonder if it isn't spotlights which attract most stars.

[This appearance too landed in between the making of "*Perfect Day*" and "*They Go Boom*."]

After the making of "*They Go Boom*," the Roach Studio closed for a four-week break, commencing 27 July 1929. A news clip from 18 July 1929 offered that: "*Stan Laurel and Oliver Hardy, the comedy team, are to make personal appearances in the east.*" However, two weeks later it would appear that no such plans were in place, and Hardy and Myrtle went off on their pre-booked cruise to Cuba.

-----0-----

1929 Aug 1 (circa) – THE HARDYS:

LOS ANGELES, California to HAVANA, Cuba 4,100 miles

HE'S GONE TO THE BEACH
Babe and Myrtle – taken during their August 1927 vacation in Cuba.

When the Roach Lot re-opened, during the last week in August, production started on the Boys' next film, "*The Hoose-gow*;" after which came another "appearance." Unlike the June 'Midnight Frolic' there were no spotlights here, which reflected in the number of stars present – TWO!

> Thursday 5 September 1929
> LOS ANGELES, Ambassador Auditorium
> The 7th Annual
> **NATIONAL RADIO SHOW**
> Thursday night will be Paramount night,
> with a number of studio stars present.
> Also on this night will be
> Stan Laurel and Oliver Hardy - Hal Roach comedians.

Note that Stan and Ollie are still being billed as "Hal Roach comedians."

[This broadcast came one week into the shooting of "*The Hoose-gow*."]

-----0-----

During a ten-day loan out, split across late September and early October, Stan and Babe filmed eight very short comedy scenes – for the MGM musical "*The Rogue Song*." Imagine if you will that the finished film, starring Metropolitan Opera star Lawrence Tibbett, was a loaf of un-sliced bread. Now imagine cutting that loaf into nine slices, and inserting very thin pieces of Laurel & Hardy cheese between the slices, in order to make it all the more palatable to the consumer. Well, that is "*The Rogue Song*."

Bread
&
Cheese

The Boys' next two ventures were also away from the Roach Studios – both of which were surprising and unusual.

o-o-0-o-o

CHAPTER 4

THE NEXT STAGE
(1929 pt2 - 1931)

The next live appearance was in a venue one would not normally associate with Hollywood stars, although at least three are now known for locating a film in one such structure – a CIRCUS TENT!

> Friday-Saturday 25-26 October 1929
> **BEVERLY HILLS**
> Beverly Hills Society Circus

The film actors who became circus acts for this two-evening event include: Clara Bow, Eddie Quillan, Eddie Dowling, Lon Chaney, Louis Dresser, Edmund Lowe, Victor McLagen, Warner Baxter, Lois Wilson, Hoot Gibson & Company, William Collier, Sr., and Ken Maynard. Plus, Stan Laurel, Oliver Hardy, Polly Moran, and Charley Chase.

We all know that Laurel and Hardy went on to make a film about a circus – "*The Chimp*" (1932) – but one of the stars present had already made his. "*The Circus*" had premiered in January 1928. Yes! It was that little man again - Charlie Chaplin. That is now three stage shows he shared with Laurel and Hardy which you didn't know about!

[These two nights of appearances came during the making of "*Night Owls*."]

-----0-----

In November 1929, some five months after the opening of the Fox Theatre in San Francisco, where they had observed first-hand the successful mixture of "LIVE" entertainment and the screening of a film, Stan and Babe chose to chance their arm and partake in such a programme themselves. They were to be featured not just as the characters on the screen, but also as live entertainers. This was an extremely risky gamble.

First question that had to be asked was: "Could Laurel and Hardy cut it as live performers?" This wasn't going to be a brief pause at the microphone, on a conveyor belt of stars. Here, they were the main attraction, and would have to justify the admission fee which the several thousand patrons would be paying to see them over the six-day, four-shows-daily appearance. If Laurel and Hardy failed, the two years of hard work they had put into building their reputation as screen comedians could be destroyed overnight.

> Friday-Thursday 22-28 November 1929
> **SAN FRANCISCO, Fox Theatre**
> LIVE – IN PERSON
> **Laurel & Hardy**
> With RUBE WOLF and 100 others
> Plus Fanchon & Marco's "Baby Songs"
> On the Screen:
> "The GIRL From HAVANA"
> Laurel & Hardy in "They Go Boom"

-----0-----

1929 November 21
    LOS ANGELES, California to SAN FRANCISCO, California 🚂 382 miles
-----0-----

The contemporary reviews inform us how they fared:

> The crowds yesterday at the Fox Theater were very probably attracted by the promise of seeing those deliciously droll fellows, Stan Laurel and Oliver Hardy, but they had much else to be thankful for. There is a good "crook and detective" picture *"The Girl From Havana,"* plus a Laurel and Hardy screen comedy, *"They Go Boom,"* which will make you laugh even if you have the toothache.
>
> But it was, really it was, Laurel and Hardy in the flesh that everybody waited for, and howled over. They are funny fellows, and they do a lot of rough-housing, so much that, when they finish, Rube Wolf is in his union suit, their director James Parrott, is minus coat, shirt, porus plaster and waistcoat: a man in the audience is stripped of his clothes in the aisle and thrown into the orchestra pit, and both Stan and Ollie have barely enough clothing to keep within the law.
>
> Their act is a riot of laughs. Perhaps they are just a bit funnier, this pair of rowdy comedians, in the picture than they are on the stage.
>
> Maybe it was a mistake to play them against themselves. "They Go Boom" is tremendously funny.
>
>   (*San Francisco Chronicle* – Saturday 23 November 1929)

A second review from the *Exhibitors Herald-World* added a little more:

> Rube introduces James Parrott, director of Laurel and Hardy in Hal Roach productions, and then the funny team of rough-necks comes on. Theirs is an act of characteristic slap-stick stuff, and it is not long before they are tearing each other's clothes until they soon have the minimum allowed by law. Their director comes in for attention and, in a twinkling of any eye, his tuxedo is ripped into shreds. A man in the audience objects, and is hauled up on the stage and transformed into a scarecrow. Rube thinks they have gone a little too far and, when Laurel and Hardy have finished with him, he has nothing on but a union suit, and is compelled to finish his directing in a dressing gown.

Fox Theatre, San Francisco, advertising Laurel & Hardy's live stage appearance.
22-28 November 1929

The Next Stage

> Yes, Laurel and Hardy are a riot, and must give employment to a lot of tailors, figuring four shows a day and five outfits ruined at every show. When they go off the stage the show comes to an end, because – THEY STOP IT!

The man in the audience who objected was of course a plant – played by fellow Roach actor Charlie Hall. Charlie, from Birmingham, England, would go on to play parts in no less than forty-seven Laurel & Hardy films; plus the films of other actors in the Roach stable. Interviewed by a journalist almost a decade after this event, he remembers the show at the Fox Theatre in rather different detail – some of which is enlightening, and some of which is told with poetic licence. He starts off by letting us in on how the sketch was conceived:

> Going along on the train I asked the boys what they intended to do for an act. "Oh!" says Babe casually, "Just go on stage and say 'Hullo' and perhaps introduce yourself as our menace, and tell the folks that you are the toughest guy in Hollywood, and so on. You know the sort of stuff, Charlie."

It was Hal Roach who had nicknamed Hall "the little menace," as his usual role in the Laurel & Hardy films was that of the little guy who gets caught up in the Boys' mayhem, and reacts with retribution.

Of the show, Charlie related that, when Laurel and Hardy walked on stage:

> It was fully a couple of minutes before the boys could open their mouths, there was such pandemonium. Then they put on a few gags and introduced me. I had done myself proud for the occasion, and had on a new suit. Perhaps I looked a bit cocky in it, for Babe glared at me and said, "So you're the little tough guy who kicks me on the shins –eh? You're the chap who pokes me in the eye?"
>
> "Yes," I answered proudly, "I am."
>
> "And you're the one who kicks me out of bed in the middle of the night, are you?"
>
> "Sure I am," I said, beaming all over my face, and getting still more pleased with myself, I added "What are you going to do about it anyway?"
>
> That crack cost me plenty. Stan gave Babe the well-known nod and grin and they started to cut the top of my hat, which I was holding, Babe tore my shirt collar and the top of my shirt. They ripped my brand new suit off my back between them and chased me off the stage, clad only in my vest and pants.
>
> When we got back to the dressing room the boys just stood laughing, mighty pleased with themselves.
>
> "What came over you guys?" I asked.
>
> Babe explained that if I hadn't looked so darned cocky and self-satisfied, nothing would have happened.
>
> "Never mind, Charlie," said Stan, "It won't happen again." That was all he knew.
>
> WE did 32 appearances that week [*sic*], which meant 32 suits, 32 hats, 32 collars, and 32 ties.
>
> (*London Weekly News* – 4-part serial commencing 3 September 1938)

The business mentioned in the on-stage dialogue was reference to some of the incidents which many audience members would have seen in the Laurel & Hardy films. "So you're the little tough guy who kicks me on the shins," is a reference to the shin-kicking-and-de-bagging business in "*You're Darn Tootin'*." "You're the one who kicks me out of bed in the middle of the night," is a reference to Hall being their landlord in "*They Go Boom;*" while the main part of the stage sketch is a re-enactment of the shirt-ripping sequence from "*Berth Marks.*"

Why they chose this crude, silent slapstick routine, when they could have done a far gentler spoken dialogue routine, like "Soda, soda, soda" from the more recent release "*Ship Ahoy*" (aka: "*Men O' War*"), is hard to reason. In fact it is hard to understand what they were doing there at all, when they should have been making films.

Having chanced their whole reputation as screen comedians, by making stage appearances, they now had to return to the Hal Roach studios to discover how they stood with Hal Roach as, unbelievably, the appearance at the Fox Theatre had not been arranged by him. Permission for Laurel and Hardy to go there had been given only at the eleventh hour, as the following letter to Roach, from Laurel (and one worded exactly the same, from Hardy), will confirm:

```
Gentlemen:                                    Nov. 20th, 1929
I desire to accept an engagement for appearance at the Fox
Theatre in San Francisco during the week commencing
November 21st, 1929 and ending November 28th, 1929,
returning to the studio on the 29th.

During the period of such engagement I request a suspension
of the terms of the contract now in existence. All terms
and conditions to become applicable again on November 29th,
1929. Such suspension to be for the purpose aforesaid and
no other.
```

So how was it that the two film stars, plus their director James Parrott and foil Charlie Hall, would risk ruining their working relationship with Roach, or even lose their jobs, just to do this one-off appearance?

Hardy is holding the representative "mum" and flower of one team, and Stan is holding those of the other team. Myrtle, meanwhile, is holding the two rivals apart.
(San Francisco – 22 November 1929)

Upon arrival, Laurel had made light of his reason for being in San Francisco by teasing a reporter with the rhetorical question: "*Queer that the booking came just at Big Game time, isn't it?*" Stan was referring to their being in San Francisco at the time of the annual football game between the University of California and Stanford University – or 'Golden Bear' and 'Palo Alto' – as Babe referred to them. However, that a college football game had any influence in their playing this break-away week in San Francisco does not, in my opinion, hold any credence.

Firstly, Laurel had no interest whatsoever in football – an opinion he was to express many times in later letters. One would also have to question Hardy's interest in two University teams, neither of which he had an affinity for. Add to this that Stan and Babe would be committed to the theatre, and unable to watch the game. And then, on the day of the game, a large number of the local populace would be at the game rather than at the show.

Hardy is now holding two "mums" – painted dollies' heads on sticks – which are used to represent the team one is supporting.

The Boys have just raided a nearby flower stall, as the colour of the flowers also signifies which team one supports.

(San Francisco – 22 November 1929)

I believe that instead of it being: "Queer that the booking came just at Big Game time, isn't it?", it would have been far nearer the truth if Laurel had said: "Queer that the booking came just three weeks after the day of the Great Wall Street Crash, isn't it?" ("Black Tuesday" – 29 October 1929). Laurel had reportedly lost $30,000 in the crash, and it is likely that his fellow performers had lost money too; so the $10,000 fee they were getting for their appearance was a quick way of recouping some of their losses. It sure beat jumping out of an upper-storey window!

[This engagement came in the period in between the filming of "*Night Owls*" and "*Blotto*."]

-----0-----

1929 November 29 (*circa*) Friday
    SAN FRANCISCO, California to **LOS ANGELES**, California 🚂 382 miles

-----0-----

The second and third weeks in December found the Boys engaged in making "*Blotto*," after which Babe made a quick visit to the 'Our Gang' studio to do a cameo in "*Barnum & Ringling, Inc.*" This took them up to the Christmas close-down at the Roach Lot. Hardy went off with Myrtle, to attend the opening day of the season at Agua Caliente race track, Tijuana; while Laurel spent Christmas at home with his wife and two-year-old daughter.

-----0-----

1929 December 28 – HARDY
    BEVERLY HILLS, California to **AGUA CALIENTE**, Mexico 🚂 138 miles

-----0-----

The racing season at Agua Caliente was to last sixty-one days. Concurrent with the first few days of racing was a professional golf tournament at a local course; and in town was a twenty-four-hour gambling Casino – three reasons why Hardy would not be leaving in a hurry. He did, however, make it back in time for the filming of "*Brats*," which commenced at the start of the third week in January 1930. On the Friday evening of that week, Stan and Babe had to leave the "Brats" with baby-sitters, so they could attend the premiere of "*The Rogue Song*."

> Friday 17 January 1930
> **LOS ANGELES, Grauman's Chinese Theatre**
> The World Premiere of Metro-Goldwyn-Mayer's
> Screen Extravaganza
> **"THE ROGUE SONG"**

Little is known about the evening's events, except that the stars of "The Rogue Song" – Laurel, Hardy, and Lawrence Tibbett – made a live radio broadcast from the forecourt of Grauman's theatre.

Stan and Babe making a radio broadcast outside Grauman's Chinese Theater. Below can be seen the cement casts of hand- and footprints of Hollywood stars. The only handprints of Laurel and Hardy kept for posterity, were in police files.

The only other piece of coverage came from an interview Erskine Johnson did with Stan and Babe, wherein they gave him their recollections of how a particular bit of business started. Remarkably, the article came some twenty-one years after the event itself (16 November 1951):

The only other piece of coverage came from an interview Erskine Johnson did with Stan and Babe, wherein they gave him their recollections of how a particular bit of business started. Remarkably, the article came some twenty-one years after the event itself (16 November 1951):

> It was at an MGM formal dinner party at the Roosevelt Hotel, after the Hollywood premiere of Lawrence Tibbett's "The Rogue Song."
>
> "The Who's Who of Hollywood were there," Hardy said.
>
> "A real snooty formal affair," Laurel added.
>
> "Suddenly a drunk walked up to me," Hardy said, "and pulled off my tie with the crack, "I can do that comedy, too."
>
> "Well, after I'd had a couple of drinks I looked up this character and grabbed his tie. It was on an elastic. It snapped back and rocked the guy on his heels. He got mad and pulled off the collar of my shirt. Then Stan started grabbing, and everybody got into the act.
>
> "Buster Keaton was in tatters, and even Louis B. Mayer pulled off a couple of ties."

However, I would challenge that this incident happened on this night. The business smacks of a toned-down version of the shirt-ripping routine in the film "Berth Marks" (ibid.), which had been released in June 1929. The story fits better if we accept the theory that Laurel and Hardy did the routine on stage at Grauman's, during the 'Farewell Tribute' to the MGM film "Broadway Melody" on 15 June 1929, and that the drunk accosted them at the after-show banquet, with the opening line: "I can do that comedy, too."

The story fits even better for the "Midnight Frolic" on 29 June 1929, which Lawrence Tibbett also attended, and which may have resulted in the mixed memories. Take your pick!

The Next Stage

-----0-----

1930 January 22 (Wednesday)   LOS ANGELES, KHJ Studios

The next event Laurel and Hardy attended was for a radio show. Joining them on "*Voices of Filmland*" were Roach co-stars Charley Chase, Harry Langdon, Thelma Todd, and child actors from Roach's 'Our Gang.' Supplying the music was the Earl Burtnett Orchestra.

[This broadcast also occurred during the making of "*Brats*"]

-----0-----

"*Below Zero*" was filmed during the last two weeks in February, after which the Roach Studios closed for the whole of February, and maybe a little longer!

"*Hog Wild*" was shot during the first two weeks after the restart then, just before production of the next film, tragedy struck. The Laurel's second child, Stanley Robert Jefferson, born on 7 May, died just nine days later. Everyone was absolutely devastated, but Stan had little time to grieve. He was in the studio just three days later to spend the last two weeks of May filming "*The Laurel-Hardy Murder Case*," which made life on set much darker than the dark overtones of the film.

Less than two weeks after losing his child, Stan again put aside all thoughts of the tragedy in his own life, to go and give support to others who had major problems in theirs. The occasion was another benefit show, with Babe. He could have so easily pulled out, and everyone would have totally understood, but Stan had a way of erasing all thoughts of death and quickly moving on to catering for the needs of the living.

> Tuesday 27 May 1930
> **LOS ANGELES**
> Olympic Stadium
> **BENEFIT SHOW**
> for the tubercular of the World War
> in the Mt. Olive, San Fernando,
> and Sawtelle hospitals.

Taking part in the entertainment were: Bert Wheeler and Robert Woolsey (acting as Masters of Ceremonies), opera star Marguerite Padulla, Cliff Edwards, the Duncan Sisters, The Hunnard Sisters, Laurel and Hardy, Frank Richardson, Harold Robert's Band, and other specialities; with hundreds of other stage, screen, and vaudeville celebrities in attendance.

[This show came just before filming came to an end on "*The Laurel-Hardy Murder Case*."]

-----0-----

Between June and the end of 1930, the following Laurel & Hardy films were shot: "*Pardon Us*," "*Another Fine Mess*," "*Be Big*," and "*Chickens Come Home*." The only known personal appearance during this period was the following:

The pre-publicity for this event ran:

> Jack Dempsey will turn his many talents into a new line today. The boy of 'iron mike' fame will raise the iron mike to call "Strike three, you're out!" at Hoot Gibson's Saugus ranch, the 17th inst.
>
> One of the highlights of the big-time affairs is a ball game, with Joe Brown heading one nine, and Mitchell Lewis the other. Laurel and Hardy, the funsters, have taken out additional life insurance, Mitchell Lewis, president of the Masquers reports, inasmuch as they are to help Jack Dempsey umpire the game.

> Sunday 17 August 1930
> Hoot Gibson's Saugus Ranch
> **THE MASQUERS**
> **MIDSUMMER REVEL**

Hardy would have been well at home as the referee of a baseball game, as he had officiated at many games in his late teens and early twenties.

Hoot Gibson wasn't just an on-screen cowboy – he lived the life of a real cowboy. In 1929 he had purchased an old ranch near Saugus, thirty-two miles north west of L.A., on which, over the next two years, he built a rodeo arena and stadium, which could hold up to twenty-five thousand spectators. The newly-named 'Golden State Ranch' then played host to annual events billed as: "The Greatest Rodeo and Wild West Show ever staged on the Pacific Coast." For those of you who would like to see for yourselves just how great these Rodeo and Wild West Shows were, you need to watch the Hoot Gibson film "*Wild Horse,*" which was storied around the one held in 1932.

A second big attraction for the spectators at these rodeos was the large numbers of Hollywood stars who attended. Meanwhile, the main attraction for the stars seemed to be the real old-fashioned feast, served up from the barbecue in front of the ranch house.

[This appearance came during the making of "*Pardon Us.*"]

-----0-----

In the first three months of 1931, Laurel and Hardy were filmed for the following: "*The Stolen Jools,*" "*Laughing Gravy,*" and "*Our Wife,*" which brought them up to the studio's spring break.

Back in December one showbiz column had revealed that:

> The Hal Roach studios plan to stay dark during April 1931, when the yearly schedule will be completed.
>
> During that siesta the hard worked team of Laurel and Hardy, now cavorting through two foreign language versions simultaneously, expect to join a studio party to Panama.

It looks like Oliver Hardy fell in with the plan, as he and wife Myrtle went to Havana, Cuba, which would have involved firstly going to Panama. However, no confirmation that they travelled in a party with other Roach employees was found.

That Myrtle was in the mood for a studio party was in severe doubt. Less than four weeks earlier, a newspaper item had revealed:

> Mrs. Myrtle Hardy, 28, wife of Oliver Hardy, film comedian, who escaped from a sanitarium late yesterday, was located in a Los Angeles hotel today [St. Paul Hotel, West 6th Street].
>
> Police reported that Mrs. Hardy refused to admit them to her room, and declared that she would jump from a window if they broke the door.
>
> The police retired and summoned a fire department squad to frustrate that possibility.
>
> Finally, according to police reports, a policewoman from the juvenile department persuaded Mrs. Hardy to allow her to enter the room.
>
> *(UP – 26 March 1931)*

Considering that Myrtle had threatened to jump to her death, one would seriously have to consider the wisdom in taking her on board a ship!

-----0-----

1931 April (date unknown) – The Hardys:

LOS ANGELES, California to **HAVANA**, Cuba 4,100 miles

-----0-----

Laurel, meanwhile, had made his own plans. Back in January, he had written to friend and film producer Alf Goulding, in the U.K.:

Jan. 19th '31

```
Dear Alf,
I was expecting to take a trip home again this summer, but
won't have time - we have a month vacation in April so may
go to Honolulu instead - we haven't been there, so should
be very interesting.
```

The Next Stage

Interesting to note that by "home" Laurel was referring to England, even though he had lived half of his life in the U.S.A.

Stan's theory re the sea voyage with wife Lois was that it would calm troubled waters within their marriage. So, just before the Roach Studios closed for the whole of April, Stan, Lois, their daughter, and Lois's mother Ella set sail for Hawaii.

-----0-----

1931 March 28 – *SS City of Los Angeles* sets sail for Hawaii.
            LOS ANGELES, California to **HONOLULU**, Hawaii   2,560 miles

-----0-----

Stan would have had some fellow Hollywood actors to talk to on the six-day voyage to Honolulu, as on board the *SS City of Los Angeles* was a company of actors and crew from 20th Century-Fox – including Mary Gordon, Joe Kerrigan, Murray Kinnell, Bela Lugosi, and Warner Oland – who were going to do some location filming for "*Charlie Chan in – THE BLACK CAMEL.*"

It's a pity Laurel's activities weren't filmed as, during his three-week stay on Hawaii (3-25 April), he made some stage appearances. These would otherwise have never come to light if it hadn't had been for his mentioning them in a letter – some three decades later:

                                                                                    Sept 25th. '62

```
I visited Honolulu in 1930 [sic] had a marvelous time
fishing, was out several times on a 'Sampan' - I too made
two or three appearances at the military & Naval Bases -
Pearl Harbor & Wheeler Field, I think that was the name -
Hardy wasn't with me, so I had requests to appear single -
naturally I wasn't prepared, but everybody seemed satisfied
just to see me, so all were happy.
```

Stan has the year wrong in this 1962 letter. The correct year is in his letter of 19 January 1931. The *Honolulu Star Bulletin* (3 April 1931) confirms it:

> Stan Laurel arrived in the city of Honolulu today, on a vacation trip. He was accompanied by Mrs. Lois Laurel, his daughter, and Lois's mother Ella Nelson.
>
> Oliver Hardy, Mr. Laurel's partner, is taking his vacation in Havana.
>
> "We took somewhat divergent paths, you see," explained Mr Laurel.
>
> He plans to spend three weeks here, and will be at the Halekulani Hotel.

Great choice of hotel by Stan! The Halekulani is a 5-star hotel, overlooking Waikiki Beach.

Many years later Stan wrote of his feelings for Honolulu:

                                                                                     July 1st. '57

```
Dear Earl:-
Re Hawaii, I spent three weeks there in 1930 [sic] enjoyed
it very much - had some wonderful fishing trips. After a
few weeks you've seen everything & you begin to feel a bit
isolated & have a great desire to get back to the mainland,
you get a bit tired of pineapple and the native goods, but
the bathing at Waikiki is out of this world - only a small
section of beach but the water is wonderful, you can stay
in for hours day & night & never feel cold.
```

In his next letter to Earl, Stan added a little more about his stay there:

                                                                             August 6th.'57

```
Dear Earl:-
No, I did'nt get any sail fish in Honolulu, mostly small
tuna, each around 70lbs in weight. You really get a fight
on light tackle.
```

The view of Diamond Head mountain from the Halekulani Hotel

Even here, in the middle of the Pacific Ocean, two and a half thousand miles from the mainland, Laurel still couldn't escape his fame, for showing at the local cinema was "*Another Fine Mess.*"

And is it any coincidence that, just two years later, in the Laurel & Hardy film "*Sons of the Desert,*" the convention the Boys attend is referenced as being in – HONOLULU!

-----0-----

1931 April 25   The Laurels set sail on the liner *Malolo*.
   HONOLULU, Hawaii to **LOS ANGELES**, California   2,560 miles

-----0-----

Stan with wife and daughter, on the *Malolo*, docking at Los Angeles. Also in the party was Lois's mother – Ella Nelson.

Laurel arrived back in Los Angeles on 30 April. On the ship's manifest of the *Malolo* he had registered under his real name, but that would be the last time he signed anything as "Arthur Stanley Jefferson" as, in July, he applied to the courts to have his name officially changed to "Stan Laurel."

Filming began again at the Roach Studios in mid-May. Between then and the end of August, Laurel and Hardy made only two shorts – "*Come Clean,*" and "*One Good Turn.*" The Boys then absented themselves for ten days or so, and went off to pursue their favourite pastimes – Laurel to go fishing, and Hardy to play golf. This newspaper cutting gives more detail:

Hardy has been at Del Monte for the past week or so, to get in some practice for the California Amateur Golf Championship, which gets under way on Monday [7th], and continues till Sunday [13th]. Every day sees Hardy out on the links, in an effort to get down his handicap.

(6 September 1931)

-----0-----

1931 September 1 (*circa*)
    LOS ANGELES, California to **DEL MONTE**, California 321 miles

-----0-----

Hardy getting the lie of the green,
by having a lie on the green.
(Del Monte – September 1931)

To cater for the vast number of participants in the Del Monte "California Amateur Golf Championship," it was being staged on two courses – Cypress Point and Pebble Beach, which are links on the Monterey Peninsula.

Down in Del Monte harbor were several craft which had sailed there specially for the tournament. Among them was Howard Hughes' $500,000 170-foot yacht. Aboard were twenty crew members, and a delegation of twenty-five Hollywood celebrities who had sailed with Hughes from L.A. It is not known if Hardy was one of them.

As for the tournament, it would seem as though Babe may have been excluded, by way of not having a handicap of seven or less, as his name did not appear amongst the hundreds of golfers named in the fixtures and results over the duration of the tournament. Maybe he caddied for someone!

Hardy would have been unable to stay till the end of the golf tournament anyway, as he was booked to be at yet another huge Hollywood event:

-----0-----

1931 September 10 (*circa*)
    DEL MONTE, California to **LOS ANGELES**, California 321 miles

-----0-----

> Friday 11 September 1931
> LOS ANGELES, Olympic Stadium
> **LA FIESTA DE LOS ANGELES**
> 'The Billion-Dollar Event'

Pre-publicity for "*La Fiesta de Los Angeles*" billed it as "The Billion-Dollar Event" – which was a tilt at the value of the hundreds of Hollywood stars in attendance. Post-publicity declared it to have been, "the most brilliant spectacle in the history of show business." The latter is subjective, but the claim that the spectacle was witnessed by "the greatest throng even assembled in the Olympic Stadium" can be taken as factual. So packed was the stadium that even two and a half thousand people who had tickets had to be turned away, and relegated to joining the amassed crowd of four hundred thousand lining the streets on the pageant route outside.

Among those appearing at the *Fiesta* were: Conrad Nagel – as Master of Ceremonies; Richard Barthelmess – as sponsor of the trick-riders of the screen, including Tim McCoy and Buck Jones; Victor McClagen and Edmund Lowe – sponsors of the rodeo winners; Wheeler and Woolsey – who introduced "The Great Lorenzo" (a "cod" escapologist); Mary Pickford – who sponsored her husband Douglas Fairbanks, in an exhibition of the popular game of "Doug;" and Laurel and Hardy – who sponsored a handicap-race, in which notables of the silver-screen ran the 100 yard dash.

Dolores Del Rio was hostess for the Wampas Baby Stars of 1931, with Ramon Navarro as her escort. These "babies" were actually starlets, destined to be the stars of tomorrow, and included: Joan Blondell, Constance Cummins, and Anita Louise. Harold Lloyd was Grand Marshal of the film event, and led the procession of stars in their beautifully decorated and illuminated cars and studio floats in the Electric Parade – termed the "Pageant of Jewels." Others occupying seats in the stars' cars were: Richard Dix, Irene Dunne, Frederic March, Billie Dove, Janet Gaynor, Charles Farrell, Joan Crawford, Carole Lombard, William Powell, Lew Ayres, Wallace Beery, and Jackie Cooper.

[This appearance came during the shooting of "*Beau Hunks*."]

-----0-----

In just four years Stan Laurel and Oliver Hardy had gone from being two unknown comedians on the bill, to being the regular attraction at Hollywood's biggest events. But their live appearances had not ended yet. In fact, they were only just warming up.

o-o-0-o-o

CHAPTER 5

HABLAS ESPAÑOL?
(1932)

October to December 1931 saw the making of "*Helpmates,*" "*Any Old Port,*" and "*The Music Box,*" followed in late January 1932 by "*The Chimp*" and late February by "*County Hospital.*" It was May before shooting started on the Laurel & Hardy feature "*Pack Up Your Troubles,*" which was interrupted one evening for a personal appearance. The reasoning behind this causes a bit of a puzzle which, hopefully, can be solved here:

Saturday 20 May 1932

LOS ANGELES, Teatro California

Gala Premiere of
The Big Mexican Film Drama

"SANTA"

All spoken in Spanish

Filmed under the direction of
actor and director

ANTONIO MORENO

Guests of Honor:

The Kings of Laughter

LAUREL Y HARDY

MEMORABLE NIGHT! A NIGHT OF EMOTIONS!
MEMORIES OF THE BELOVED HOMELAND!

N.B. The facsimile of the advert above has been translated from its Spanish wording.

Several guests of honour are named as attending this film premiere, but Laurel and Hardy are the only non-Hispanic ones. So what were they doing there? In 1930 and early 1931 the following Laurel & Hardy films had been made in both English *and* Spanish: *Night Owls, Blotto, Be Big, Hog Wild, Berth Marks, Chickens Come Home, Below Zero, Laughing Gravy, The Laurel-Hardy Murder Case*, and the feature film *Pardon Us*. But then none of these films were being shown or promoted.

In all probability Laurel and Hardy were there at the behest of the impresario Frank Fouce. Fouce operated a circuit of cinemas in Los Angeles, devoted exclusively to screening films in Spanish. Plus, in his time there, he booked pretty well every major Latin-American and Spanish performer for personal appearances. But it was a previous activity of his which may well have secured the services of Stan and Babe:

In the early 1920s, Frank (real name, "Francisco") had been assistant to "Bronco Billy" Anderson who, in 1921, had produced "*The Lucky Dog,*" with its first-ever joint on-screen appearance of Laurel and Hardy. Then, commencing January 1922, Anderson had gone on to shoot a series of seven films with Stan Laurel as the star; the last of which, "*When Knights Were Cold,*" Fouce actually directed. And so, with both halves of the partnership owing credit for some part of their early film careers to Frank Fouce, the two screen comedians were happy to pay back a little by attending this premiere.

Laurel retained a life-long friendship with Fouce, as this letter from him will show:

```
Dear Ernie [Murphy]:                    May 20th. '58
Strange that you should mention Frank Fouce, I had'nt seen
or heard of him for a couple of years & out of a clear sky,
he called me last Sunday & he & Anna came out to see us.
Yes Frank is doing very well, besides his theatres in Town
here he holds quite an interest in the Mexican area of TV &
Radio, also in South America, Argentina etc. He too
operates a small TV station in San Diego covering Lower
Calif. - really in the CHIPS. Frank looks well & prosperous
& has put on a lot of avoirdupois (that's French, meaning
BIG BELLY!). I expect to see him again soon so will give
him your message.]
```

[POSTSCRIPT: Frank Fouce was also a guest on the TV show "*This Is Your Life*" (1 December 1954), when Laurel and Hardy were the subjects.]

But then, upon checking the Masquers Club website, I discovered that actor-director Antonio Moreno was in office that year as elected "Harlequin" – the term given to the Masquers' president. As both Stan and Babe were proud Masquers, one would surmise they were also at the film premiere to support their president.

[Antonio Moreno went on to play 'Devilshoof' in the 1936 Laurel & Hardy film "*The Bohemian Girl*."]

-----0-----

The Boys' next public performance came just twenty-four hours after the Teatro California appearance, but in a different medium. Having mixed comfortably with the Hispanic community, Stan and Babe were now about to mix with a whole host of cosmopolitan stars, in a radio broadcast designed to attract spectators to the Olympic Games.

> Sunday 21 May 1932
> LOS ANGELES, Radio Station KHJ
> **INVITE TO OLYMPIC GAMES**
> Marlene Dietrich, Claudette Colbert, Tom Mix,
> Dolores Del Rio, Maureen O'Sullivan,
> Stan Laurel, Oliver Hardy, Bela Lugosi.

Here is how one newspaper described it:

> Motion-picture stars hailing from foreign lands will invite their countrymen to the Olympic Games through the medium of an international radio program, to be broadcast next Sunday from 12:30 to 1:30, from station KHJ.
>
> Will Rogers [Cherokee-American] cowboy humorist, will officiate as master of ceremonies, and will introduce the following screen luminaries, each of whom will speak in his or her native tongue: Marlene Dietrich [German], Claudette Colbert [French], Dolores Del Rio [Mexican], Maureen O'Sullivan [Irish], Stan Laurel [English], Oliver Hardy [American], Bela Lugosi [Hungarian], and Tom Mix [American].
>
> William May Garland, chairman of the Olympic Organizing Committee, will extend over the air an official invitation to the people of the world to attend the Games 30 July to 14 August.

[This appearance came during shooting of "*Pack Up Your Troubles*."]

-----0-----

Stan and Babe may well have done their bit to attract people to the 1932 Olympic Games, but they had no intention of being in Los Angeles themselves while the Games were on. They fled the city two weeks before the event even started, and didn't return until more than two weeks after it had ended. Whether or not they had had the foresight to rent out their houses for the duration has not been discovered. If not, then they missed out on earning a tidy sum.

Hablas Español?

Stan had been over to England only once since 1912, and that was five years ago; so, when it came to taking a holiday, England was an obvious choice for him. That Hardy chose to go with him, though, when he could have gone literally anywhere in the world, speaks volumes for the high regard the two partners had for one another.

Babe decided to have his wife Myrtle accompany him, in the hope of saving their eleven-year marriage. He had been having an affair with an attractive divorcee by the name of Viola Morse, so thought the vacation might help to patch things up. Stan, though, left his wife Lois at home, insisting: "She doesn't like crowds and travelling, and is not over strong, so preferred not to make the trip." The truth was that Laurel's marriage was also on the rocks, and Lois could not face the ordeal of making the trip in order to keep up appearances.

Also in the party were Dr. Golden B. Falconer (sic) and Mrs. Ethel Falconer, who were to remain with them throughout the trip. The Falconers have been quoted by one writer as being "friends of Myrtle;" whilst another claimed Dr. Falconer was "Hardy's dentist" – but, as the Falconer family resided in Santa Cruz, it is far more likely they were friends of Lois, and/or he was the family dentist. The Nelson family had been living in Santa Cruz for over twenty years, since moving from Tulare. The 1910 Census reveals the father to be Albert Nelson – a Danish labourer; the mother – Ella Nelson, from Carson City, Nevada; and three daughters – Stella (18), Lena (17), and Lois (14); all residing at 28 Bethany Circle, Santa Cruz, California.

It was to Santa Cruz that Lois Laurel went for her own holiday, while her husband went off to England. Her mother Ella was now widowed, and living alone at 85 Continental Street. One would surmise Lois went to stay with her mother, unless she went house-sitting for the Falconers.

-----0-----

1932 July 12 (*circa*)
>LOS ANGELES, California to **NEW YORK**, New York   2,814 miles

-----0-----

As Stan and Babe understood it, the trip was purely a social call to the "Old Country," where they could take in a few weeks of golfing and fishing. MGM, though, had different ideas, and organised a massive publicity campaign around the trip, in both Britain and America. Consequently, when Laurel and Hardy came to change trains at Chicago, on their three-day train journey from Los Angeles to New York City, thousands of fans and photographers confronted them.

At first they thought there was someone in an adjacent compartment whom the crowd were seeking; but, as mob's demands for attention increased, it soon become frighteningly obvious that this wasn't the case. Wanting to get away from the situation as quickly as possible, Stan and Babe fought their way through the swarm to catch their connection for New York.

The reason Laurel and Hardy couldn't believe all the adulation was for them was that, as far as they were concerned, all they had done for the last five years was make short supporting films for the main cinema features, in which were the "real" stars. The public, though, saw it differently. Little did they know that their nightmare had just begun, and the likes of the reception at Chicago were to be repeated at every stop.

Mob number two, in New York, was even bigger. On Broadway the press were out in force, and the presence of the two newly discovered stars, plus the newsreel cameras, whipped the crowd to a point of hysteria. It took more than a little subterfuge, and a great deal of assistance from members of the New York Police Force, before Laurel and Hardy were able to board the Cunard liner the *Aquitania*, and set sail for England. [**FILM**]

-----0-----

1932 July 16
>*Aquitania* leaves NEW YORK and sails for **SOUTHAMPTON**, England

-----0-----

LAUREL and HARDY – The U.S. Tours

On 23 July 1932, the *Aquitania* arrived at Southampton, England, to be greeted by the unbelievable and totally unexpected sight and sound of thousands of Laurel and Hardy fans – waving, cheering, and whistling *The Cuckoo Song*.

[Many Americans call it *The KuKu Song* – thus interpreting the actual bird call as one note, repeated; when it is so obviously two different notes. There is also an arrangement called *The Dance of the Cuckoos*, but the most favoured is *The Cuckoo Song*.]

Waterloo Station (23 July 1932)

Upon disembarking, it took Stan and Babe an hour to fight their way through the ever-demanding crowd and pressmen, before they could board the train for London. On arrival at Waterloo station, they were met by a similar scene to the one at Southampton, prompting Laurel to exclaim: "*What a reception. I never imagined anything like this.*" Neither could he have ever imagined that, over the next few days, the crowds would get bigger and bigger, to the point where he and his partner were literally in danger of losing their lives.

The next terrifying encounter came on the second night in London, during an appearance at the Empire Cinema, in London's Leicester Square. The crowd was so tightly packed that Stan and Babe, in their car, felt like they had been dropped into a scrap yard crusher. With the help of a police cordon they managed to escape, and made a rush for the cinema foyer, with the only damage being to the car – but it could quite easily have been all so different.

The next two nights in London were spent visiting theatres and attending social dinners in London, after which it was time to hit the provinces, the itinerary for which ran as follows:

Wednesday 27 July

Overnight train to the North East town of Tynemouth. Stay the night at the Tynemouth Hotel.

Thursday 28 July

Stan meets up with his father, Arthur Jefferson, then goes round to his former home in Dockwray Square, in the neighbouring town of North Shields.

Friday 29 July

A thousand fans meet L&H at Edinburgh's Waverley Station. At a later appearance at the Playhouse cinema, police on horseback are employed to keep back the huge crowd outside.

Late-Evening: Glasgow, the Scottish capital. Central Station is jammed solid with an estimated eight thousand fans. A posse of policemen ring the celebrities and try to lead them out of the station entrance, but the pressure of the crowd is such that they are pushed and shoved down a side-subway, and then all the way to the Central Hotel, where they are to stay. Both men are lucky to escape, as several people were injured - a few even hospitalised.

Saturday 30 July

Policeman and police horses are again needed to hold back the crowds congregated outside the Scala cinema. Inside, Stan and Ollie perform a short stage routine to three thousand cinemagoers.

Tour of Laurel's father's old theatre, the Glasgow Metropole, where Stan is brought to tears reminiscing about the times he spent there in his late teens.

Hablas Español?

Sunday 31 July

Hardy plays golf at Gleneagles. Laurel rests at the hotel.

Monday 1 August

Blackpool: Massive crowds await the Hollywood comedian's arrival at the Metropole Hotel on the promenade. In the evening, appearances at the Winter Gardens, the Tower Ballroom, and the Palace cinema, lead to blocked streets, outside, and rooms filled to bursting, inside.

Tuesday 2 August

Manchester: Four hundred fans are at Victoria Station to greet Laurel and Hardy. At a press reception at the Midland Hotel, Stan remarks that they came to see England but, so far, have managed to see only, "people, hotels, more people, theatres, and yet more people."

Wednesday 3 August

Leeds: Two thousand people turn up for the stars' arrival at New Station. They later address a packed City Square from the balcony of the Majestic Cinema, while inside, thousands more get to see them on stage.

Thursday 4 August

Sheffield: Following a tumultuous welcome, Stan and Babe rest at the Grand Hotel.

Friday 5 August

Birmingham: Thousands greet Laurel and Hardy at New Street Station. Their evening appearance is at the Gaumont Cinema, where they perform their usual stage routine.

Saturday 6 August

The two travel-dizzy film stars board the train to London where, upon arrival, they are-booked into the Savoy Hotel.

Having now fulfilled all the MGM press engagements, Laurel and Hardy were effectively able to disappear for a while from the eye of the national press.

Arthur Jefferson, now retired, was living in London with his second wife Venetia, at 49 Colebrook Avenue, Ealing, where on Monday 8 August Stan went to visit him. Here, in the doorway, and also on the garden path, footage was shot of Stan trying to encourage his stone-faced father to smile for the camera.

Two days later, A.J., Venetia, and Stan's sister Olga waved the two comedians off at Victoria Station, on the first leg of their journey to Paris. Hardy's farewell comment was: "*We shall stay in Paris for ten days, and hide from everyone.*" It was not to be! Reluctantly, after only two days, they gave up, and – also cancelling their planned sightseeing tour of Deauville, Berlin, Antwerp, Brussels, and Madrid – returned to London.

Sometime between 13 and 23 August Laurel paid a visit to the Elstree Studios where, it is believed, he discussed the possibility of Laurel & Hardy films being made there. At the moment all was fine at the Roach Studios, but the time wasn't too far away when Laurel would be looking for pastures new.

Come 24 August, and having pretty well achieved their objective in having a few days free from unwanted attention, Laurel and Hardy travelled down to Plymouth, to board the *SS Paris* and sail for New York. It was as close as they could make it to following in the wake of the Pilgrim Fathers.

-----0-----

1932 August 24

SS Paris, leaves PLYMOUTH, England, bound for **NEW YORK**. Arrives 30 August.

1932 September 1

NEW YORK, New York to **LOS ANGELES**, California 2,814 miles

-----0-----

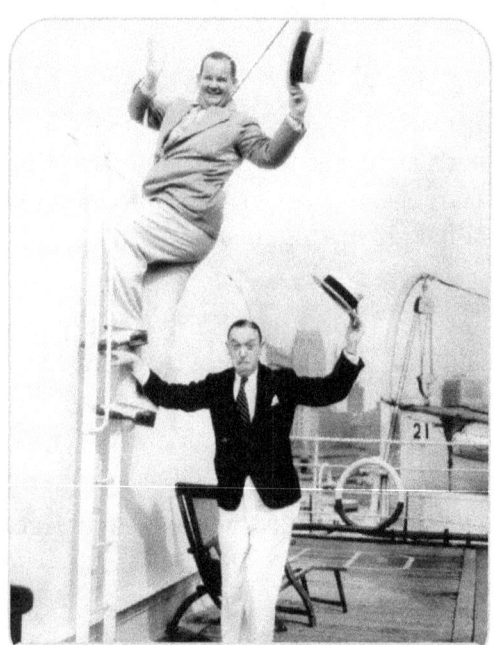
The *Aquitania* arriving at New York

The party's arrival in New York coincided with a solar eclipse, whereby the moon passed between the earth and the sun, causing a total eclipse. They were able to view the phenomenon through smoke-filtered glasses, which had been mass-produced for the event.

It is believed that it was during this 2-day in New York, when the two comedians made a short comedy film. [**FILM**]

Lois had flown to New York to welcome Stan back, but the expected hugs and kisses never materialised. During the enforced absence, Stan had given cause for Lois's feelings to cool considerably, and their relationship would never recover.

Stan and Babe were absolutely staggered by the reception they had received in Britain, and on the Continent. Let us not forget that, before visiting England, they had made only two feature films, the latest of which, "*Pack Up Your Troubles*," had not even been released yet. Having been kept in the cocoon of Hollywood, the comedy couple had no idea how widespread their films were being distributed, and how popular the films were with cinema audiences.

They had of course appeared before huge crowds in and around Hollywood, but those appearances had had full Hollywood glitz and glamour presentations behind them. The events had also been attended by a whole host of film stars, whereas, on the recent overseas tour, Laurel and Hardy had been the sole attraction. No wonder they had been totally surprised and overwhelmed by it all.

The arrangement for Laurel and Hardy to be absent from the Roach studios had been made in an agreement dated as late as 29 June 1932. The terms were that their current contracts be suspended for sixty days, and the time added on to the original termination date of their contracts.

The sixty-day period allowed for the trip, ran from 10 July to 12 September. Stan and Babe arrived back in Los Angeles with eight days to spare, but it was the fourth week in September before they were back in front of the cameras.

By the beginning of October "*Their First Mistake*" was in the can; but, before commencing on the next film, "*Towed in a Hole*," Stan and Babe broke into the pre-production schedule to play in a benefit show:

> Wednesday 26 October 1932
> **LOS ANGELES, Shrine Civic Auditorium**
> Benefit for the Mount Sinai Home for Invalids
> All 6,800 seats sold. Show starts at 8:00pm

In attendance were: Leo Carrillo, Sid Grauman, Pat O'Brien, Barbara Stanwyck, Darryl F. Zanuck, Jack Warner, Jackie Cooper, Jimmy Durante, Buster Keaton, Conrad Nagel, Lupe Velez, Cary Grant, Louis B. Mayer, Eddie Borden, Vivien Oakland, Charles Farrell, Janet Gaynor, Lew Ayres, and Mack Sennett; plus fifty stars of the Masquers Club, including: Charles Murray, Cecil B. DeMille, James Cagney, Laurel and Hardy, Bebe Daniels, Ben Lyon, and many others.

[This show came after the shooting of "*Their First Mistake*," but before "*Towed in a Hole*."]

-----0-----

The next star-studded event came just over three weeks later, and was another benefit, but with a twist. This time, the stars themselves got all the benefits:

> Friday 18 November 1932
> **LOS ANGELES, Ambassador Hotel**
> **5th Annual ACADEMY AWARDS**
> 'Academy of Motion Picture Arts and Sciences'

The Fiesta Room was crammed to bursting with practically every Hollywood film star, director, executive, and technician, plus a number of state and city officials, totalling one thousand in all. The most high-profile actors included: Helen Hayes, Alfred Lunt, Joan Fontaine, Norma Shearer, Will Rogers, Wallace Beery, Lionel Barrymore, and Fredric March; plus producers Louis B. Mayer, Mack Sennett, and Walt Disney – among others.

This was only the fifth Academy Awards ceremony, with the number of categories being just nine: Outstanding Production; Best Actor; Best Actress; Directing; Writing; Cinematography; Art Direction; Sound Recording; and Short Subjects.

The short subjects were divided into: Cartoon; Comedy; and Novelty. The Laurel & Hardy film *"The Music Box"* won the award for the "Best Short Subject: Comedy." It was the first time that short subjects had been recognised, and the award was only a certificate. So, although one can correctly state that Laurel and Hardy won an Academy Award, it is incorrect to say they won an Oscar. One could be even more pernickety and say that the award went to the Hal Roach Studios. The irrefutable fact, though, is that *"The Music Box"* won an Academy Award for "Best Comedy of the Year 1931-32."

ACADEMY AWARDS
Hal Roach clutching the prestigious certificate, awarded for *"The Music Box."* Come the camera flash – and it was gone.

When the award was announced, Hal Roach himself went up to receive it, but was trailed by his table guests – Stan and Ollie. As Conrad Nagel was handing the certificate to Roach, Hardy snatched it away, only to be trumped by Laurel, who snatched it from Hardy – leaving Roach to walk off having said nothing.

Hardy then asserted his pompous 'screen' authority and gestured to Laurel to hand back the certificate, at which he went in to a heartfelt acceptance speech. His words had little or no effect, however, as they were drowned out by the laughter as Laurel went into his crying routine.

[This appearance came between the shooting of *"Towed in a Hole"* and *"Twice Two."*]

Laurel's on-stage crying may have been pretence but, off-stage, he had cause to cry for real. Around 1 November he had been spotted dining alone in the Brown Derby restaurant, Beverly Hills. Two weeks later, the reason why became known – he and Lois had separated. She further lodged intent to ask for a divorce and to seek custody of their daughter. Even before the divorce was granted Laurel handed over their marital home (718 North Bedford Drive, Beverly Hills), plus two life trusts – totalling more than $200,000 in value.

LAUREL and HARDY – The U.S. Tours

Stan explained to a United Press representative:

> It was just one of those things. I felt badly about it, and I know that Mrs. Laurel did too. We reached a point where everything one of us did displeased the other. We got on each other's nerves, so we parted.

Meanwhile, the clown had to continue hiding his tears when December saw him back in front of the cameras, as well as in front of the public. This was Stan and Babe's second appearance at an "Examiner Christmas Benefit" – the first being in 1927, when they were almost unknown.

> **Thursday 13 December 1932**
> **LOS ANGELES, Shrine Civic Auditorium**
> **19th ANNUAL EXAMINER**
> **CHRISTMAS BENEFIT**
> The Show of Shows!

This time around they were more than able to hold their place with the likes of: Wheeler and Woolsey, Jimmy Durante, Billie Dove, Helen Kane, Claudette Colbert, Jackie Cooper, Ben Lyon, Bebe Daniels, Douglas Fairbanks, Jr., Barbara Stanwyck, Cary Grant, Tom Mix, Maureen O'Sullivan, Will Rogers, Randolph Scott, Lupe Velez, Boris Karloff, Johnny Weissmuller, Spencer Tracy, Mickey Rooney, and Ginger Rogers. After all, who is going to question the status of two comedians who have just received an Academy Award!!

Of Laurel and Hardy's contribution to the evening's entertainment, one review revealed:

> 'Browne and Willa' appeared in a fetching comedy sketch, which was immediately burlesqued a few minutes later by Laurel and Hardy, Hal Roach's comedians.

Don't ask me!!

One newspaper reported:

> The Yueltide's traditional good cheer overflowed tonight, splashing upon the thousands of spectators at the Annual Benefit for the unfortunate, held at the Shrine Auditorium. It was a great stage show, put on by favorite entertainers of the stage and screen in the name of charity – so that hungry children and destitute families would know the spirit of Christmas this year.
>
> From trained kangaroos to Will Rogers, and Johnny Weissmuller to Jackie Cooper, Hollywood turned out to fill hungry little mouths, and gladden worried mothers' hearts with baskets of food.

Backstage with Jimmy Durante — just one of the many stars attending the **"19th Examiner Christmas Benefit."** (15 December 1932) – (Corbis)

[This appearance fell in between the making of "*Twice Two*" and "*The Devil's Brother*."]

1932 ended with post-production on "*Twice Two*," and 1933 was about to start with the first Laurel & Hardy comic-opera feature film, "*The Devil's Brother*."

Everything was on the up and up.

o-o-0-o-o

CHAPTER 6

BEWARE! SAILORS

(1933 pt1)

The Roach Studios' annual break was usually just before Christmas Day, till just after New Year's Day, but for Hardy at least the celebrations seemed to carry on a little longer as, during the second week in January 1933, he was spotted among a party of ten, having a night out at the Cocoanut Grove.

Filming on "*The Devil's Brother*" (aka: "*Fra Diavolo*") started during the first week in February, and finished during the first week in March. Three weeks later, filming began on "*Me and My Pal*." A little way into shooting, the Boys gave up one of their evenings to make an appearance at a benefit show, to raise money for victims of the recent earthquake disaster.

The quake had occurred on 11 March 1933. Although classed as only "moderate," it caused serious damage from Los Angeles south to Laguna Beach. One hundred and fifteen people were killed, and property damage was estimated at $40 million.

> Hardy told the organizers: "We don't make a business of appearing outside the screen or stage, but when a party is being given for so worthy a cause, with the gross receipts going into the fund for aiding earthquake sufferers to reconstruct their damaged homes, we want to help all we can."

Considering the number of benefit shows Laurel and Hardy had done to date, and the scores more yet to come, Babe was being more than a little modest when he stated: "We don't make a business of appearing outside the screen or stage." ("Business" here meaning "habit," and not "work done for money.")

Saturday 25 March 1933
SANTA MONICA
La Monica Ballroom (on the pier)
RED CROSS EARTHQUAKE RELIEF BENEFIT

Others lending their support included: Gloria Stuart, Joel McCrea, Tom Brown, and Hardy's buddy-pal, actor Andy Devine. Music was supplied by the Max Fisher Orchestra.

Once the cameras had stopped turning on "*Me and My Pal*," there was to be no more filming for the next ten weeks, which covered the whole of April and May, and the first two weeks of June. However, there was still post-production to do on the latter film, and the previous one, "*The Devil's Brother*." Hardy was not involved in any of this, so took himself away for a bit of play. He didn't go far – just to Catalina Island, twenty-five miles off the California coast from Los Angeles Harbor.

-----0-----

1933 April 13 (*circa*)

  BEVERLY HILLS to **LOS ANGELES HARBOR**, California   34 miles

  LOS ANGELES HARBOR, California to **CATALINA ISLAND**   25 miles

-----0-----

1933 April 14 CATALINA ISLAND, Golf Club

Babe was one of many Hollywood stars who had entered the Catalina Golf Tournament, in the hope of winning the coveted Bobby Jones statuette. Other entrants were John Quillan, Eddie Quillan, Harry Langdon, Clark Gable, and Babe's pest pal – Guy Kibbee.

Hardy on Catalina (Corbis)

Charlie Chaplin happened to be taking a well-earned break on Catalina. Having handed in the first instalment of his autobiography just a few months earlier, and being between films, he was anxious to enjoy, and show off, his brand new luxury yacht, the *Panacea*. He did however promise to give the golfers some support from the gallery.

-----0-----

1933 April 18 (*circa*)
CATALINA ISLAND to **LOS ANGELES HARBOR**, California 25 miles
LOS ANGELES HARBOR to **BEVERLY HILLS**, California 34 miles

-----0-----

Barely had Hardy returned from Catalina, when the Roach Studios broke for four, or maybe five, weeks (commencing the first or second week in May, till the end of the first week in June), and off he went to Cuba for the fourth time in six years. Do you think he was smuggling cigars!

-----0-----

1933 May 12 (Friday)

LOS ANGELES, California to **HAVANA**, Cuba 4,100 miles approx.

-----0-----

The *SS Santa Lucia* left Port of Oakland, California, at noon on Friday 12 May. With Hardy was his wife Myrtle, and travelling companions Milton Bren and his wife. Bren was Production Supervisor at the Roach Studios.

The final destination would be New York, via the Panama Canal, but first would come stop-offs at Havana, Cuba; and Miami, Florida. Hardy boarded at its first port of call on its way south – Los Angeles.

The Hardys aboard *SS Santa Lucia* (Corbis)

BABE and MYRTLE HARDY'S VACATION

1933 May (exact date not known)

HAVANA, Cuba to **NEW YORK**, New York 1,309 miles

1933 May (exact date not known)

NEW YORK, New York to **CHICAGO**, Illinois 788 miles

1933 May (exact date not known)

CHICAGO, Illinois to **LOS ANGELES**, California 2,039 miles

-----0-----

Beware! Sailors

For different reasons, the Laurels' marriage too was still on the rocks, and Stan knew that a break-up was imminent. As he still loved Lois, he thought that he could win her back by showing her what he was like when all the pressures of work, and all the distractions of other people around him, were removed. His idea was a four-week motoring holiday. Bad idea! To go from hardly seeing your partner at all, to being with them 24/7 is an arrangement doomed to fail.

-----0-----

STAN and LOIS LAUREL'S VACATION

1933 early May

      BEVERLY HILLS, California to **VICTORIA**, British Columbia 1,217 miles

-----0-----

The reason offered for Lois Laurel not accompanying Stan on the 1932 trip to Britain was that she did not enjoy travel. Considering that in 1931 she had sailed over five thousand miles to Honolulu and back, and was now undertaking a two and a half thousand mile car journey, one would have to ask which part of travel it was that she didn't like. The answer was obviously "her husband" as, immediately upon their return (*circa* 20 May) they separated, and Lois filed for divorce.

-----0-----

1933 May 17 (*circa*)

      VICTORIA, British Columbia to **LOS ANGELES**, California 1,217 miles

-----0-----

Stan moved out of their home at 718 North Bedford Drive, Beverly Hills, and into rented accommodation at nearby 303 South Palm Drive. Sharing the residency were Stan's younger brother Teddy (Edward Everitt Jefferson); plus Teddy's wife Betty, and their two sons. Prior to the move to his brother's house, Teddy had been lodging with a Russian dressmaker at 4813 O'Sullivan, Los Angeles – on his own!

Teddy had come over from England in July 1920, and met up with Stan and Mae during a three-month engagement of vaudeville appearances in and around New York City. Stan and Mae continued their coast-to-coast vaudeville tour, and in September 1921 hit California. It is not known if Teddy toured with them throughout that period, but it is confirmed that they did meet up in Los Angles no later than April 1922, as Stan secured some work for Teddy as an 'extra' in at least one of the films in the series he was making with G.M. Anderson. It was then in 1923 that Teddy married Betty.

Edward Everitt Jefferson – aka: "Teddy"

And here is Teddy, as the butler, in the 1922 Stan Laurel picture "*The Egg*."

Here in 1933 he was working as a chauffeur for the manager of the Ambassador Hotel. In addition to Teddy's family, the Laurel household consisted of a cook, Tomasina, and ex-vaudevillian Pete Gordon.

In her divorce suit, heard on 25 May, Lois described Stan as "*an inattentive and unloving husband*," who insisted that he no longer loved her. The Hardys, too had separated upon returning from their holiday. A divorce application followed – the only difference here being that it was the husband filing the divorce suit. This press release will explain:

> Four weeks after Mrs. Lois Laurel sued Stanley for divorce, Oliver Hardy asked for a divorce from his wife, accusing her of intemperance.
>
> The complaint charged Mrs. Myrtle Lee Hardy with absenting herself from home for long periods and returning in "an exhausted and bedraggled condition due to intoxication." Repeated promises of reform were only idle, the comedian alleged. Such conduct, he charged, was detrimental to his motion picture career, built up by 'years of struggle and serious application.' He further charged his wife with mental cruelty.
>
> The Hardys have been on the verge of a divorce before. He said they reached a reconciliation in April 1931, but separated for the last time on June 7. He asked the community property [621 Alta Drive, Beverly Hills] be divided by the court so as to provide for the support of Mrs. Hardy in a fair and equitable manner.
>
> (*UP* and *AP* – 21 June 1933)

When the Hardys first separated in 1931, Babe had moved into a property at 3687 Freedonia Avenue, Hollywood Hills; but here in 1933 it is believed he went to stay at the Beverly Wilshire Hotel.

In her cross-complaint regarding the divorce suit, filed 6 July, Myrtle Lee Hardy told of her husband being a consistent loser both at the gaming tables, and betting on horses. She claimed Hardy lost $30,000 in one day at the Agua Caliente race track; and on another occasion, in the same Mexican resort, lost $3,000 playing roulette at the casino.

One story goes that at one session of roulette, during which Hardy was losing heavily, he noticed that the croupier would lean on the table after he had set the ball in motion. Believing this was a deliberate ploy to influence which sector of the roulette wheel the ball came to rest in, Hardy decided to change the odds in his favour. He started to lay his bets to cover the set of consecutive numbers on the sector of the roulette wheel which was on his side of the table. Standing up to do this, he would remain standing even after the croupier had called out, "Rien ne va plus," and then lean heavily on the table. Over the next series of spins there were repeated appeals to, "*Please sit down, Mr. Hardy. Mr. Hardy, please sit down,*" from the Casino manager, getting longer and more agitated each time. But the 300lb comedian stayed just where he was, and repeated his actions until he had won back his money. That's how the story goes, anyway!

Myrtle was seeking to be awarded $1,400 per month alimony, plus $4,000 in attorney's fees, and a half-share of their $100,000 property. With the charges she was bringing against her husband, she had every chance. But then on 2 August, just as the two of them were scheduled to appear in court, their attorneys announced that an amicable settlement had been reached regarding the alimony, and that a property settlement was also being drawn up. Friends of Hardy are reported to have stated there was a possibility of reconciliation, and that the couple's contested divorce suit might be dropped.

On the second and third days in August, statements were released that the Hardys AND the Laurels had patched up their differences, and were reconciled. A cynic would offer that both husbands were offering the olive branch in the hope that the courts would go easy on their respective pending property settlements. Another feasible theory is that Roach was issuing statements to clean up Laurel and Hardy's off-screen characters, so that their on-screen characters wouldn't be tarnished by association.

Between June and August 1933, while the court battles were raging on, the Boys were still engaged in regular film-making. Amazingly, they turned out some of their best work – "*Midnight Patrol,*" "*Busy Bodies,*" and "*Dirty Work*" – with a cameo in the 'Our Gang' short "*Wild Poses*" thrown in for good measure. It is hard to believe that the same two men who were undergoing such disharmony in their home life could achieve such perfect harmony in their working life.

Beware! Sailors

Just before the end of August, Laurel and his band of trusted scriptwriters started work on Frank Craven's script for the Boys' next feature film, "*Sons of the Desert.*" But then, a few days in, Labor Day interjected and broke up the party. Labor Day, which falls annually on the first Monday in September, was then a Federal holiday, on which most government offices, schools, and businesses closed. Originally granted as a day of rest (which ought to make it "<u>non</u>-Labor Day") its uses gradually diversified. For some it triggered the urge to take a trip before summer is finally out. For students, it was the last chance to party before schools and colleges restarted. Others stayed at home, but celebrated with firework displays, barbecues, or sporting events.

Oliver Hardy spent his Labor Day weekend freshwater fishing, at Lake Hodges near San Diego.

1933 September 2 Saturday (*circa*)
    BEVERLY HILLS, California to **SAN DIEGO**, California 🚗 120 miles

1933 September 4 Monday (*circa*)
    SAN DIEGO, California **BEVERLY HILLS**, California 🚗 120 miles

-----0-----

Laurel too went fishing, with fellow fisherman William Seiter. "Bill," as he was informally addressed, was a friend of Hal Roach, who had just been hired by him to direct "*Sons of the Desert.*" Seiter owned a yacht, the *Victoria*, which he had bought in May 1932 to woo his beautiful film actress wife, Laura la Plante. She, however, was currently receiving attention from another Hollywood film director, Irving Asher.

Working on the old adage "What's good for the goose," Seiter was now giving his attentions to another Hollywood film beauty, Marion Nixon. Problem was, she was still married to wealthy polo player Eddie Hillman, and had to be chaperoned whenever she visited Catalina to meet up with Seiter. It would seem, therefore, that Seiter's chaperone was Stan Laurel. Funneeeeee!

BILL SEITER – who certainly didn't qualify for the nickname Bill "Smiler." Even with Laura la Plante, one of Hollywood's most-beautiful women on his arm, his face didn't crack.

-----0-----

1933 September 2 Saturday (*circa*)
    BEVERLY HILLS to **LOS ANGELES HARBOR**, California 🚗 34 miles
    LOS ANGELES HARBOR, California to **CATALINA ISLAND** 🚢 25 miles

Route from Long Beach, Los Angeles Harbor, and San Pedro, to Avalon, Catalina Island.

[N.B. Ferries sailed from Wilmington; the giant steamships sailed from Long Beach; whilst many of the privately owned vessels sailed from San Pedro Harbor, all in close proximity.

It may well have been Roach who suggested that Laurel and Seiter spend some time together. It would be the first time Seiter had worked on a Laurel & Hardy picture, and so if he could win over Laurel he might avoid being disempowered by him on set. Roach may also have felt that Seiter was the man to sort out Laurel's head as, because he too was going through divorce proceedings, he would be able to empathise with Laurel. However, Laurel needed no empathy, as he fell for the first attractive lady who crossed his path – literally!

In "*STAN – The Life of Stan Laurel*" author Fred Lawrence Guiles details Laurel's chance meeting, gleaned from a later personal interview with the lady in question. Basically, the story goes like this:

> Virginia Ruth Rogers, an attractive twenty-nine-year-old blonde, decided to spend a week on Catalina Island with her friend Gladys. The girls sailed from Wilmington [adjacent to Los Angeles Harbor] on one of two steamships running that route [the *Catalina* and the *Avalon*]. As the steamer was coming in to berth at Avalon, Stan and Bill Seiter happened to be passing in Seiter's yacht. Both wore yachting caps, and Laurel had a megaphone, through which he shouted a greeting to the girls, followed by pulling his famous grin.

When the steamship docked, Bill and Stan were waiting for the girls on the dockside and, after a bit of chat, persuaded them to have lunch aboard Bill's yacht. While they were enjoying the meal on deck another boat passed them, on which were some children who, upon recognising Stan Laurel, mimicked the wide grin and hair-ruffle of his screen character. It was only when Stan responded to the children's antics, by doing the facial grimace himself, that Ruth realised who he was. This may seem hard to believe but, because the image of Laurel being permanently accompanied by Hardy was so engrained in the public's mind, it was often the case that, when Hardy wasn't with him, Laurel could pass by without being recognised. An incident recounted in a newspaper cutting back in October 1931, will perfectly illustrate just that:

> On his first day-off, after filming "Beau Hunks," Stan Laurel, the sad-faced little comedian hied [*sic*] himself to one of several fishing barges, anchored off the Pacific Coast, for a bit of piscatorial pastime. A pudgy [*sic*] stranger who had stood next to him, fishing in silence for some time, walked over to the barge-keeper to get some bait. When he came back, he was chuckling.
>
> "Say," he hailed the actor, "Can you beat it? That dumb cluck," jerking his thumb toward the barge-keeper, "thinks you're Laurel, of Laurel and Hardy. Keep at it, and we'll have a lot of laughs."

Although Laurel and Seiter bumped into the girls on further occasions over the September 1933 weekend, there was to be no advancement in a relationship. Bill was totally stonewalled by Gladys; while Ruth, following the rules laid down by her mother's teachings on single girls and morality, kept Stan at a distance. [End of précis of Guiles' account.]

1933 September 4 (*circa*) Monday

> CATALINA ISLAND to **LOS ANGELES HARBOR**, California 25 miles
> LOS ANGELES HARBOR to **BEVERLY HILLS**, California 34 miles

-----0-----

Stan, however, did obtain Ruth's contact details, and would soon pay her a surprise visit, with an even more surprising offer.

o-o-0-o-o

CHAPTER 7

NO TIME FOR LEVITY

(1933 pt2 - 1934 pt1)

Stan tracked down Ruth at the boutique she owned – the "Rosemarie" in Hollywood. She was serving another customer when he entered, but was aware that he never took his eyes off her. When it came his turn Stan told Ruth he wanted a tie, and took thirty minutes of her time in looking. He eventually bought four and, as she was ringing up the sale at the checkout, said to her: *"Next time, I'll take you home with me. Working in a boutique is not for you."* Upon expressing her reservations about his married status, Ruth was assured by Stan that his divorce was imminent and, as soon as it went through, he would bring her the papers to prove it.

After the Labor Day weekend, Stan rejoined the writing and production teams working on *"Sons of the Desert,"* which brought them up to mid-September. It was here that Hardy came into the frame to team up with his partner – but it wasn't at the studio.

Eighteen months ago the Boys had been guests of honor at a film premiere at the Teatro California. Now back there, they had been elevated to "patrons!" The film this time was *"La Llorona,"* and was an even bigger affair than the premiere of *"Santa."* When the other guests of honour are the Consul of Mexico, and the Consul of Spain, you know you are in good company.

A report of the premiere in *La Opinion* revealed that: *"Stan and Ollie improvised a sketch, which caused great amusement."* [AJM: You'll get no guesses from me!!]

Note the presence of Antonio Moreno again, and also Sol Wurtzel – two men who would become involved in Laurel & Hardy films within the next few years.

> Thursday 14 September 1933
> **LOS ANGELES, Teatro California**
> Grand Premiere of
> **"LA LLORONA"**
> Totally spoken in Spanish
> JOSE MOJICA
> STAN LAUREL
> OLIVER HARDY
> Patrons of this Big Function
> GUESTS of HONOR
> El Sr. Consul de Mexico – D. Alejandro
> El Sr. Consul de Espana – Don Alejandro Torres
> Antonio Moreno, Sol Wurtzel.

While *"Sons of the Desert"* was still in pre-production, Roach loaned out Laurel and Hardy to MGM for a four-day shoot on some comedy snippets for the film *"Hollywood Party"* (Friday-Sunday 22-24 September). *"Sons of the Desert"* was then shot between the first and fourth week in October, back at the Roach Studios.

Just before filming commenced, a story came out that the Hardys were getting back together again (*AP* – 3 October 1933):

> After four years of intermittent marital troubles, Oliver Hardy and his wife have become reconciled. Through his attorney the comedian said:
>
> "We are making a new start realizing that we owe each other the duty of taking our just share of blame for any past misunderstandings with the acknowledged determination to achieve and preserve our new-found happiness."

This wasn't reconciliation in its true sense, whereby the Hardys were about to try and live together as man and wife, but more the case that Oliver Hardy was not about to desert his wife. He knew that to do so would only accelerate her decline into chronic alcoholism. So, abiding by the part of the wedding vows where both bride and groom promise to take one another "for better, for worse, in sickness or in health," Hardy again had Myrtle admitted to the Rosemead Lodge Sanitarium, in Temple City, where she would be treated for her alcohol dependency.

As for Lois Laurel, on 11 October 1933 she finally got her day in court – where she told the superior court judge:

> Living with a motion picture comedian isn't just a life of giggles. He was forever leaving home, staying away for two or three days at a time. He refused to explain where he had been when he returned.
>
> He frequently told me that I could not get a divorce fast enough to suit him. I decided life with a film comedian is anything but funny.
>
> (*Associated Press* – 11 October 1933)

Stan should have heeded the cautionary saying; "*Be careful what you wish for.*" He had promised Ruth that he would bring her the divorce papers as soon as he had them, but his projected joy at receiving them instead triggered an extreme reaction.

Laurel had known since June that the divorce was imminent, and had begun to soften the coming loss of Lois in his life by getting much closer to Ruth. As well as seeing Ruth in private, he had been taking her to the Roach studios during filming of "*Sons of the Desert.*" He even got her a small part as an extra, in the scene in the booking hall of the steamship company. So why Laurel was so grief-stricken when the divorce was finalised, almost as if it were a court-case verdict he had never anticipated, is difficult to comprehend.

Ruth Laurel looking every inch the glamorous star, as she turns up at the Roach Studios to pick up her husband in her new car.

Filming on "Sons of the Desert" finished at the end of the third week in October, five days ahead of schedule. However, before filming commenced on the next short, "Oliver the Eighth," time was taken out to celebrate. On Wednesday 6 December, Hal Roach threw a party at the Roach Lot, to celebrate his twenty years in the picture business. A handful of photos from the evening would seem to indicate that only Hal Roach and his wife, along with Thelma Todd, Patsy Kelly, Stan Laurel, and Oliver Hardy were present. However, somewhere must be a stack of photos which show a far greater number of Hollywood stars in attendance.

The extant photos too are deceiving, in that they show the only decoration in one room to be a huge anniversary cake and, in another, just a potted plant, whereas the huge sound stage on which the party was held, was more elaborately decorated than a Hollywood nightclub.

Pleased to say this beautiful cake, made for Roach's 20th Anniversary, didn't end up being deposited on Laurel or Hardy, but was sent to a local children's home.

-----0-----

Mr. Laurel and Mr. Hardy with a change of partners. Stan is with the boss's wife Marguerite Roach, while Babe is with glamorous co-star Thelma Todd. — (Corbis)

KINGS OF COMEDY MEET KING OF CARTOONS
Stan Laurel, Walt Disney, Hal Roach, Babe Hardy
This photo has appeared many times before, with the source claiming it to have been taken at the 1932 Academy Awards. Compare it with the previous photo and you can see it was shot in the exact same place, and that Stan and Babe have barely moved.

The guests came under three different categories. First was "Current Roach employees." In this category were the four aforementioned comedy stars, plus 'Our Gang' producer Bob McGowan, and comedian Charley Chase, who acted as Master of Ceremonies throughout the event.

Second were "Past Roach employees" – who included Jean Harlow, Janet Gaynor, Harold Lloyd, Lupe Velez, Bebe Daniels, Martha Sleeper, Sally Rand, Polly Moran, Louise Fazenda, and Will Rogers. Lupe Velez was accompanied by her husband of less than seven weeks – Johnny Weissmuller. Jean Harlow too was with her new husband – Harold Rosson. Lionel Barrymore, Theda Bara, Mary Pickford, and Fay Wray were on the guest list, but their attendance could not be confirmed.

The third set of guests were those who liked Roach, and/or liked to party. Some surprising names in this category were: Wallace Beery, Groucho, Zeppo, and Chico Marx, Raymond Griffith, Constance Cummings, Ruth Roland, Pete Smith, Ben Bard; and English actress Pat Paterson escorted by Frank Orsatti.

The fourth category contained some of Hal Roach's peers who came to pay him tribute, and included producers Darryl F. Zanuck – from 20th Century-Fox; Jesse Lasky – from Paramount Pictures; Louis B. Mayer – from Metro-Goldwyn-Mayer; and Walt Disney – from the Disney Studios; plus Sid Grauman – owner of Grauman's Chinese Theater, in Hollywood.

Hal Roach receiving special thank-yous from three of his greatest discoveries: Harold Lloyd, Jean Harlow, and Stan Laurel – in this recently discovered rare photo.

NBC covered the event in a thirty-minute radio slot, which was broadcast the following evening, and featured contributions from the "Current Roach employees" plus Louis B. Mayer – who paid a personal tribute to Hal Roach.

On the night, four orchestras played in different venues, which Will Rogers described as: "*One to get out of your car to; one to check your hat by; and one to dance to*." The fourth was a Hawaiian Orchestra playing, so Rogers said, "*The Last Round Up*." [Shouldn't they have been playing "*Honolulu Baby*"?]

Will Rogers getting flirty with Marguerite Roach, while the boss is doing his rounds.

Funniest scene of the night was Hal Roach standing at the bar, trying to get served, while shouting at the barman: *"Don't you know who I am?"*

Christmas should have brought further cause for celebration in the Laurel household but, in the lead up, tragedy struck. On Friday 15 December, Stan's brother Teddy went to the dentist to have a tooth extracted, and reacted badly to the nitrous oxide gas used to anaesthetise him. He died two days later. He was just thirty-three.

It was inappropriate for Teddy's widow, Betty, and her two sons to remain in Stan's apartment after Teddy's passing, so he set them up in alternative accommodation.

To allow Laurel to grieve in private, Roach ended shooting on "*Oliver the Eighth*" a few days before the scheduled Christmas break kicked in. It would seem rather insensitive therefore that, on Christmas Day, Stan held open-house at his residence, to celebrate the release of "*Sons of the Desert.*" One must accept that different people have different ways of controlling their grief.

With two bedrooms now vacant in Laurel's four-bedroom apartment at 304 South Palm Drive, Stan was able to persuade Ruth to move in. The proviso was that Alice and Baldwin Cooke, Laurel's former vaudeville partners, also move in to act as chaperones. Chaperoning was the done thing in those days, for unmarried couples.

According to one newspaper report, Laurel then went on vacation: "… *doing snow sports in the High Sierras.*" Meanwhile, Babe and Myrtle Hardy were said to be: "… *enjoying their yuletide festivities at Palm Springs.*"

-----0-----

1933 Dec. 24 (circa) (**HARDYS**)

      BEVERLY HILLS, California to PALM SPRINGS, California 🚗 106 miles

1933 Dec. 27 (circa) (**LAUREL**)

      BEVERLY HILLS, California to YOSEMITE PARK, California 🚗 310 miles

-----0-----

[Yosemite Park runs along the California-Nevada border for around 360 miles. As it is not known which part of the High Sierras Laurel went to, the mean-average distance has been used.]

-----0-----

1934 Jan 4 (circa) (**HARDYS**)

      PALM SPRINGS, California to BEVERLY HILLS, California 🚗 106 miles

          (**LAUREL**)

      YOSEMITE PARK, California to BEVERLY HILLS, California 🚗 310 miles

-----0-----

A news snippet released 4 December 1933 revealed:

> A record-breaking production schedule lies ahead for the Hal Roach Studios. The schedule, announced today, calls for the production of at least twenty-four short comedy subjects, and two feature-length films in the first six months of 1934. Laurel and Hardy will be among the first to start work.

Indeed they were, and got the 1934 schedule off to a great start by completing "*Oliver the Eighth*" during the second week in January. But then Laurel and Hardy's contribution to the quota came to a dead stop. Work should have begun on the feature film "*Babes in Toyland,*" but Laurel had major reservations about the premise of the story, and refused to work with it. Hal Roach, though, was more than happy with the storyline – seeing as he himself had written it.

Back in December 1933 Roach had obtained backing to the tune of $1.5 million to produce the feature "*Babes in Toyland,*" for release through MGM. For their money, MGM had been promised the following stars from the Roach Lot: Laurel & Hardy, Charley Chase, Thelma Todd, Patsy Kelly, and the "Our Gang" kids. Roach would also get to pick out some MGM stars. Top of Roach's wish list was either Ramon Navarro or Rudy Vallee for one of the leading roles.

Roach had been fired up into making this "All-Star Musical" after viewing the recent release of the Paramount musical fantasy "*Alice in Wonderland*," whose stars included Richard Arlen, Gary Cooper, Leon Errol, Louise Fazenda, Cary Grant, W.C. Fields, Edward Everett Horton, Jack Oakie, Polly Moran, and Ford Sterling – among many others.

ALICE in WONDERLAND
The film which inspired "*Babes in Toyland.*"

Playing the eponymous role of "Alice" was Charlotte Henry, who had secured the part against competition from seven thousand hopefuls. Striking while the iron was hot, Hal Roach secured Miss Henry on a loan-out to play the female lead in "*Toyland*."

The problem with having so many stars in one picture is that their individual screen time is limited, as the pie has to be cut so as to give each one a decent share. In the storyline Roach had come up with, he had Stan and Ollie cast as Simple Simon and the Pieman. "*You know the story*," he told one reporter, "*Simple Simon meets the pieman, and buys a pie from him.*"

Laurel would not have been slow to add something on the lines of: "Yeh! And then they're never seen again." Roach visualised the film as an: "All Singing – All Dancing – Star-Studded Musical Spectacular," whereas Stan was looking at it as: "LAUREL & HARDY in *Babes in Toyland*."

"*Fra Diavolo*" had been the biggest grossing Laurel & Hardy film to date, and there was every reason to be confident that adapting "*Babes in Toyland*" to carry the characters of 'Laurel & Hardy' would repeat that success – which is why Laurel so rightly questioned why all the other stars were needed. But Roach had sold the idea of the "Musical Spectacular" to MGM. For Roach to go back and tell them he had totally changed the original concept was a step too far, and might well have lost him the $1.5million deal. So, in order to remove what appeared to be the "immovable object" in the equation, Roach, the "irresistible force," suspended Laurel (effective as from 24 January) on the grounds of "*... his inability to continue the rendition of services in accordance with the contract in existence dated January 7th, 1930.*"

To give Laurel further cause to realise he wasn't 'immovable,' Roach threatened to bring in Wallace Beery and Raymond Hatton to take over from Laurel and Hardy as the lead comics. Now Roach was faced with an even greater climb-down if he decided to scrap his own storyline, and go along with one supervised by Laurel.

Hardy used the break in filming to play golf. On Friday 9 February, he partook in a golf tournament at his local club, the Lakeside, which was solely for males from within the Hollywood star system. They would be playing for trophies courtesy of Bing Crosby, plus the 'Ernest Torrance Memorial Cup.' The following pairs had been drawn:

Raymond McCarey with Jack Oakie; Bing Crosby with Duke Hinnau; W. C. Fields with Gregory Lacava; and Oliver Hardy with Frank Craven. Other participants were: Wallace Ford,

James Dunn, Leon Errol, Ralph Morgan, Harry Langdon, Wesley Ruggles, John Ford, Conway Tearle, Eddie Quillan, Guy Kibbee, Richard Arlen, Mack Sennett, Frank Lloyd, Edgar Kennedy, Robert McGowan, Andy Clyde, and George Bancroft.

For those who simply need to know: Oliver Hardy and Frank Craven beat Jack Oakie and Ray McCarey, 3 and 2. As for Round 3 – you are on your own!

In this earlier photograph, Hardy has chosen less-challenging opponents, with the other three players being drawn from his fellow Roach Studios employees. Next to Hardy is Bob McGowan (Director of the 'Our Gang' series); actor James Finlayson; and prolific gag writer and Director — Leo McCarey.
This round of golf may well be the occasion which inspired McCarey to come up with the premise for "*Should Married Men Go Home,*" filmed (possibly here) in March 1928.

[The photographer's embossed stamp locates him at the Biltmore Hotel."]

Being suspended, here in early-1934, also gave Laurel some free time – too much free time! So much so that he too decided to play games away from home – but it wasn't the kind of games he ought to have been playing!

o-o-0-o-o

CHAPTER 8

SPLIT MILK

(1934 pt2 – 1935 pt1)

Relationships between Stan and Ruth continued to deteriorate when Stan began drinking more and more. Ruth put this down to his way of filling the void he always felt whenever a film had been finished. But it went far deeper than that – he was still heartbroken over losing Lois.

Stan was always remorseful after a drinking bout, but remorse does not always go hand in hand with good judgement. Laurel, especially, was never lacking in heaping one bad move upon another. His next one was to phone up Ruth, propose marriage, and giver her just a couple of hours to prepare for the ceremony – in MEXICO. When you are terribly upset because the love of your life has left you, throwing yourself upon someone you don't love is hardly the remedy. But Laurel did – and off he and Ruth went to Mexico. With them went chaperones Baldwin and Alice Cooke.

After a car drive to the train depot; a train ride to Tijuana; and a short taxi ride; the 'Laurels' and the Cookes arrived at the suburb of Agua Caliente. The literal translation of the Spanish name Agua Caliente is "hot water," which ought to have been a sign of what Laurel was getting into.

-----0-----

1934 April 03 (Tuesday)

BEVERLY HILLS, California to AGUA CALIENTE, Mexico 🚂 138 miles

-----0-----

Fred Lawrence Guiles (*ibid.*) interviewed Alice Cooke in later life, and obtained the following insider-view of what happened next:

> Stan reserved two rooms with connecting bath at that gorgeous big hotel down there. And that night [Tuesday 3 April 1934] Stan had the Justice of the Peace come over, a Mexican, and the man brought five others with him. They all had such long faces, so sober, that Baldy broke up. Then the Mexicans started to laugh, too. They laughed right through the ceremony.

-----0-----

1934 April 06 (circa)

AGUA CALIENTE, Mexico to BEVERLY HILLS, California 🚂 138 miles

-----0-----

The following newspaper article gives a commendable explanation of some of the technicalities of the marriage:

Comedian Laurel is Single – Though Wed.

> Divorced last fall, Stan Laurel has remarried in Mexico, but he was back in the United States today [7 April 1934] – a single man. Being married and single at the same time may not sound possible, but this is the way Laurel accomplished it:

> Last October [1933] an interlocutory decree of divorce was entered, separating him and Mrs. Lois Laurel. Under California laws, the final decree is not awarded for a year after the interlocutory decree is entered. During that time, a person may not live legally in California in wedlock.

> Early this week, Laurel and Mrs. Ruth Rogers, society widow of Los Angeles, made a trip to Agua Caliente, Mexico, and were married in that country. They returned here, and will live apart until next October 11 [1934] when, Laurel said, a second ceremony will be performed in California.

Stan and Ruth's wedding photo.
(11 April 1934)

The divorce settlement had a second clause weighted against Stan, which was that Lois was entitled to one half of his earnings until the divorce became finalised in October. Rather than work for half-money, Laurel had decided not to work at all, and had remained unavailable throughout the whole of March and April. However, on 7 May, after the five-week Roach Studios' spring break, he returned to work. It was good work, too, with "*Going Bye-Bye,*" and "*Them Thar Hills*" being filmed on schedule.

Stan's decision to return to filmmaking had almost certainly been influenced by his having to pay for the newly acquired property at 10353 Glenbarr Avenue, Cheviot Hills. California. It was a small Mediterranean-style, four-bedroom villa, in a fairly new development of luxury homes located west of Culver City, just minutes from the Roach Studios.

Around this time, the Laurels also acquired a second "home," in the form of a trailer – which boasted hot and cold plumbing, and electric refrigeration from its own generator. It is not known whether the film "*Them Thar Hills*" (in which the Boys buy a trailer) was influential in Laurel buying a trailer, or whether the purchase of the trailer inspired the writing of the film.

Come the summer break at the Roach Studios, and the newly-weds went off on holiday in it.

-----0-----

1934 June 25 (circa)

    CHEVIOT HILLS to LAKE ARROWHEAD, California   77 miles

Near San Bernadino.

    CHEVIOT HILLS to BEAR LAKE, California   102 miles

Near San Bernadino.

    CHEVIOT HILLS to PALM SPRINGS, California   106 miles

[The above are just distances from the Laurels' home, and not meant to convey the actual route]

-----0-----

Going to the "high multitudes" and drinking water – "lots of it" – certainly seemed to work wonders on the Laurels' relationship as, within a short time of getting home, they were off again.

The Hardys' relationship too had greatly improved and so, with their newly-found spirit of summer loving, the Laurels and the Hardys actually joined up to enjoy what was effectively a second honeymoon for both couples, on Catalina Island.

-----0-----

1934 July 23 (circa)

    CHEVIOT HILLS to LOS ANGELES HARBOR, California   30 miles

    LOS ANGELES HARBOR, California to CATALINA ISLAND   25 miles

-----0-----

Stan had been to Catalina in March 1925, when filming "*Half a Man*" for producer Joe Rock, and again in 1933 with Bill Seiter. Hardy too had been there in 1933, to play golf, so both were well acquainted with its topography and attractions.

The residents of Avalon (which, just to remind you, is the one and only town on Catalina) were so used to seeing Hollywood stars that the stars were left to wander around without hindrance; whereas on the mainland they would have been surrounded by a huge crowd within seconds. This freedom obviously played a great part in Catalina becoming "Little Hollywood." The Laurels and the Hardys certainly enjoyed their right to roam as, in all the extant photos of them in Avalon, there is not a single fan in shot.

Two screen partners and two marriage partners in perfect bliss. Hold that image. (Avalon Pier – circa 2 August 1934)

On two of the days during the Catalina holiday, Stan took Babe out fishing. Stan just loved fishing, and was actually on the lookout for his own boat; but, at the time, had to content himself with hiring a small fishing boat named the *Avalon* – not to be confused with the ferry of the same name.

After Hardy had joined in with Stan's favourite hobby of fishing, Stan reciprocated, and played a round of golf with him. Their opponents in a golfing foursome were Philip K. Wrigley, and Jan Garber. The latter was an orchestra leader, who was playing a two-month residency at the Casino; while the former OWNED most of the island – including the golf course.

All seems well, with Hardy spending time trying to improve his relationship with his real-life partner.

The girls even accompany the Boys on a fishing trip,
but how long would it be before the Boys ditch them?

-----0-----

All we need is a couple of fish-poles.
What! For a million dollar idea like that?
We're going to get ourselves a boat.

Capt. Mills about to gaff Hardy's giant catch and haul it on board, while Laurel stands by ready to stun it if it puts up a struggle.

After a hard day fishing, Hardy enjoys a hardy meal. (Mind you, I can't see any fish on those plates.)

Philip Wrigley (in the next photo) was the heir of the Wrigley millions, made by his father (chewing gum manufacturer William Wrigley, Jr.) who had died in January 1932. Wrigley was also owner of both the 'Chicago Cubs' and the 'Los Angeles Angels' baseball teams (hence both stadiums being named 'Wrigley Field').

And I bet he still made Stan and Babe pay for their round of golf.

Back Row: Myrtle Hardy, Mrs. Wrigley, Ruth Laurel, Jan Garber.
Front row: Philip Wrigley Stan Laurel, Oliver Hardy. (Catalina - August 1934)

2nd right is graphics designer Otis Shepard, among whose designs, during a 30-year working relationship with Wrigley, were the wrappers for the chewing gum packs.

CATALINA ISLAND to LOS ANGELES HARBOR, California — 25 miles

LOS ANGELES HARBOR, California to CHEVIOT HILLS — 30 miles

Split Milk

On 6 August the male section of the honeymooners returned to work at the Roach Studios, where "*Babes in Toyland*" finally went before the cameras. Following all the quarrels and rewrites which had delayed filming for several months, everyone was going to be relieved to get this one in the can. But then Mr. Murphy (he of the well-known law) stepped in. On 14 August, while filming, Laurel tripped over and fell awkwardly. The cast and crew initially laughed, until they realised Stan was not writhing in agony as a joke. He had torn muscles in his right leg, which necessitated his having his leg put in a cast, and being kept in hospital for two weeks. It was a further two weeks before he could walk about freely, and one or more before he could recommence filming. Hardy was able to stave off his own hospitalisation until film was completed, and then went in to have his tonsils removed.

In November, it was back to making another short, "*The Live Ghost*," followed by a second, "*Tit For Tat*," produced and filmed in the first three weeks of December, just in time for everyone to make the studio holidays. But firstly, for the Boys, came a Christmas radio broadcast:

-----0-----

1934 December 23 (*Oakland Tribune*)

IN YULE BROADCAST

Hollywood's contribution to NBC's schedule of Christmas broadcasts will be heard over an NBC-KGO network tonight, when the film capital goes on the air between 11.05 and midnight. Directed by New Zealand-born actress and Broadcaster Nola Luxford, the 1934 air greeting will include such screen celebrities as Stan Laurel and Oliver Hardy, Warren William, and Francis Lederer; plus a 60-piece orchestra and a 40-voice choir.

Babe had spent Christmas 1933 with Myrtle, but this year he was off on a stag break. Along with his two best pals, Guy Kibbee and Frank Craven, went fellow-actors Douglas Dumbrille, Grantland Rice, Frank Lloyd and, rather surprisingly, the boss – Hal Roach.

Their destination was Calexico, just on the California side of the Mexico border ("Cal" and "Exico" – get it?) one hundred and twenty-two miles east of San Diego, near Mexicali. (You probably worked out the last name by yourself.)

-----0-----

1934 late December (circa)

BEVERLY HILLS, California to CALEXICO, Mexico 🚗 238 miles

-----0-----

The stag party stayed at the De Anza Hotel. Opened in 1931, it had rapidly established itself as the place of choice for Southern California business barons and the Hollywood set. Its main outdoor attraction was the desert, plus it was just two blocks away from the California-Mexico border.

HOTEL DE ANZA – CALEXICO
Note the covered porch to the left, leading to the main entrance.
That is where our subjects are standing in the next picture.

The boys' main entertainment was taking daily walks in Imperial Valley, and killing as many ducks and quail as their double-barrelled 12-bore shotguns allowed them. In England, we just buy a turkey for Christmas!

-----0-----

1935 early January (circa)

        CALEXICO, Mexico to BEVERLY HILLS, California 🚗 238 miles

-----0-----

January 1935 began with production and filming of "*The Fixer Uppers.*" February should have seen similar treatment given to "*Bonnie Scotland*," but production was halted before January was even out, by Laurel contesting the storyline. If you are now experiencing déjà vu, that is because 1934 had started in the exact same way, only with the "*Babes in Toyland*" script.

L-R: unidentified, Hardy, Kibbee, and Dumbrille.
The kid accosting Kibbee is a local, trained in the art of pick-pocketin'.

Again, Laurel was correct in his reasoning, but poor in his execution. In Roach's storyline of "*Babes in Toyland*" he had the Stan and Ollie characters just popping on between the main story and love interest, doing a comic sketch, and popping off again – rather like a front-of-cloth comic who fills in between scene changes in the theatre. This had been acceptable for the snippets they had done for the "*The Rogue Song,*" as the film was all storyline and needed breaking up with comic relief. The difference with "*Bonnie Scotland*" was that the Stan and Ollie characters were the stars, and the storyline needed adapting to reflect this. Again the "irresistible force" had come up against the "immovable object."

With his film career on hold because of his partner's stand-off, Oliver Hardy saw no reason why his social life shouldn't benefit, and again set off to indulge himself in his favourite sports and pastimes. Having participated in the bloody sport of quail shooting, he next became a spectator at the bloody sport of boxing, where he took a ringside seat alongside best friends Guy Kibbee, Frank Craven, and baseball player Ty Cobb.

-----0-----

1935 February 14 (circa)

        BEVERLY HILLS to SAN FRANCISCO, California 🚗 382 miles

-----0-----

The $10,000-plus proceeds of this benefit fight went to the widow of boxer Frank Campbell, as the latter had died after a bout with Max Baer five years earlier.

Split Milk

> Friday 15 February 1935
> DREAMLAND AUDITORIUM
> San Francisco
> Benefit Bout
> MAX BAER v STANLEY POREDA

Seems a strange way of making amends! If someone dies in a car crash, you don't go and stage another one and ask the widow to watch it, do you – and especially not with the same offending driver!!

Dreamland Auditorium – venue for the Max Baer fight.
(15 February 1935)

Many other celebrities and sports stars were in attendance, but Stan Laurel was not named as being among them. It is surprising therefore to learn that, on Wednesday 20 February, when Babe Hardy and Guy Kibbee were on their way back to Los Angeles, they were spotted having lunch at the El Tejon Hotel in Bakersfield, along with – STAN LAUREL. Rather than take this reported sighting at face value, I tend to believe that it was actually Ty Cobb, who was spotted, and mistaken for Laurel by virtue of his being with Hardy.

-----0-----

No! this isn't Laurel and Hardy. It's baseball players Babe Ruth and Ty Cobb. Now you can see how mistaken identities occurs.

What Hardy and company did in San Francisco during the five days following the fight is not known, but it is a sure bet that they now wanted to get back to Los Angeles to watch Thursday's boxing match between Joe Louis and Lee Ramage – live at Wrigley Field stadium. You may also want to place a double bet that Babe was at the Santa Anita races on the Saturday.

-----0-----

1935 February 20 (Wednesday)
    SAN FRANCISCO, California to BAKERSFIELD, California   281 miles
    BAKERSFIELD, California to BEVERLY HILLS, California   101 miles

-----0-----

Upon returning to the studio, to resume production on "*Bonnie Scotland*" (aka: "*McLaurel & McHardy*" and "*Laurel & Hardy in India*") Laurel continued showing his unhappiness with the script. On 15 March, unable to get his way over a rewrite, he walked out. A press-release was immediately issued:

LAUREL & HARDY SEPARATE

> Motion picture 'team' of Laurel & Hardy, oldest and best-known comedy duo in the industry, has been broken up.
>
> Hal Roach announced today that Stan Laurel had not signed a new contract. "Inability to agree on screen stories" was the reason given..
>
> The producer said Oliver Hardy would remain at the studio as the star of a series of domestic comedies with Patsy Kelly as his wife, and little Spanky McFarland as their troublesome off-spring.
>
> (*Associated Press* – 15 March 1935)

Laurel's version, as given to a reporter was: "We were working on the story and although there had been differences, these were all ironed out and settled. I was amazed when I was notified the picture had been called off and my contract terminated."

Since 7 January 1930 Laurel had been on a five-year contract, the termination date for which was originally 7 January 1935, but which with add-ons was now 13 April. This should have given ample time for "Bonnie Scotland" to be completed; but, as Laurel's contract was now about to expire before the completion, Roach decided to stop production all together, rather than have four weeks of further arguing and nothing to show for it.

Louella Parsons, who was usually quick to champion the Boys, then did them a total disservice by grabbing hold of the wrong end of the stick:

> Oliver Hardy and Stan Laurel have definitely parted. The two boys have been battling for a long time. Hal Roach always stepped in as the great pacifier. Now their troubles have reached such a stage that Stan Laurel stepped out today.
>
> Roach, in verifying the story, said Babe and Stan couldn't get together on stories, so it seemed better for them to separate.
>
> (*US* – 18 March 1935)

Roach had sold her a massive feint here, which placed him as the innocent party and Laurel and Hardy as the two who couldn't agree. Laurel was quick to defend himself and his partner.

> Babe and I have never had a word in the world. I thought everything was all right when I was called into Mr. Roach's office and told they wished to terminate my contract and that our picture had been called off. Of course we had a bit of trouble on story, but who doesn't?
>
> (19 March 1935)

Hardy also wired the news office to say that he and Stan were still pals and the trouble was between Stan and Roach, at which Parsons printed a retraction:

> So often the members of successful teams, who decide to travel the single path, have found the going rough and stony. So those of us who have watched the Laurel and Hardy comedies, and consider them top-notch entertainment, were ready to editorialize on two people who couldn't bury their personal differences when they had so much at stake.
>
> Both deny they have ever fought. When he talked to me yesterday Stan said: "Please don't say Babe and I have ever had a word. Babe is one of my best friends, and the only arguments we have had have been on stories. There isn't an actor in the world who doesn't want to discuss a story idea and give his own personal viewpoint."
>
> I might have thought that Stan was trying to cover outbursts of temperament which, I had been told, were the cause of the break, if Oliver Hardy hadn't been just as vociferous in his denial that he and Stan had ever had a serious quarrel.
>
> (*US* – 24 March 1935)

Parsons then revealed that the grief Laurel was suffering, over alimony claims from ex-wife Lois, was manifesting itself in various forms in the studio. He insisted that, unless his alimony claims could be settled satisfactorily, he would never make a film again.

Regarding the fallout over the storyline, Louella recalled an interview she had had with Laurel several years ago, wherein he said that he would never be willing to accept another writer's stories, as he knew exactly what was best for their two screen characters.

Meanwhile, in order to quash the rumours they had fallen out, Stan and Babe came up with a little ruse. On Saturday 27 March, accompanied by their wives, they turned up together at one of their favourite haunts – the Cocoanut Grove, in the Ambassador Hotel, Hollywood.

Stan and Babe, at one of their favourite haunts, the Cocoanut Grove, in the Ambassador Hotel – cocking a snook at the Hollywood press. (27 March 1935)

They later repeated their tactics at another venue – the Trocadero, on Sunset Strip. It was a clever move, which had the desired effect of hitting the gossip columns. Under the banner headline "NO RIFT," the *Daily Variety* of 29 March 1935 informed its readers:

> Laurel and Hardy showed up at one of the late spots the other night making a very gay foursome. Resplendent in dinner jackets and broad grins they denied by their appearance together that there had been a rift.

On 1st April came yet another press release stating that Laurel had broken up the partnership because of story dispute with producer Hal Roach. At least they got that bit right. But then the article went on to say that Hardy had announced he had chosen Patsy Kelly and Spanky McFarland as his "new screen pals," and the three of them would start a new picture soon – as "*The Hardy Family.*"

Like an April Fool joke, Hal Roach's bluff was soon exposed and, on 4 April, he actually gave Laurel a one-year extension on his contract. Roach further capitulated by allowing Laurel to work on a rewrite of the script for "*Bonnie Scotland,*" for which filming began on 1 May. Come the middle of June, and it was in the can. Hurrah!

Anyone watching the earlier Laurel & Hardy film "*The Fixer-Uppers,*" filmed in January 1935, might notice that Oliver Hardy has lost a significant amount of weight. One newspaper reporter even commented on it:

> Oh, Oh! Here's something which looks like the beginning of a major disaster. Stan Laurel has GAINED 18 pounds during the last three months, while Oliver Hardy has LOST 45 pounds.
>
> If they keep on, it's apt to play havoc with them as a comedy team. First thing we know: Laurel will have to play Hardy's roles, and vice versa.
>
> (1 March 1935)

This train of thought had obviously set the comedy cogs in motion as, in July, the Boys began filming "*Thicker Than Water,*" the premise of which was based on that very outcome – Laurel and Hardy switching roles.

Shame to say, "*Thicker Than Water*" would prove to be the last ever short Laurel and Hardy made. Because of the decreasing demand for short subjects, plus the fact that features made more money, Hal Roach had decided that from now on in all the Laurel & Hardy films would be feature-length. It was a move that would stretch not only the plot-lines, but everyone involved in their making.

o-o-0-o-o

CHAPTER 9

GONE FISHIN'
(1935 pt2)

The Roach Studios closed for its summer vacation from 27 July till 26 August 1935. On or just before 20 July, Stan's father Arthur Jefferson and step-mother Venetia had arrived in L.A. for an extended stay. Laurel put them up in an apartment, in the Beverly Wilshire district. On 2 August Stan and Ruth went to Long Beach, to look over Stan's new $9,000 acquisition, a fishing boat named the *Ida May*. This wasn't just any boat. It was a Sportfisher-type yacht, which the previous owner had had custom-built to house every facility for the serious angler. At 35-knots, it was even boasted to be the fastest boat on the water.

The 'RUTH L'

The name "Ida May" was a dedication to the first owner's sister "Ida Mary Campbell." How strange a coincidence that "May" was the name of Laurel's first (common-law) wife, and that "Ida" was the name of the lady who would become his last wife. However, a couple of weeks later Stan had it rechristened *Ruth L*, after his current wife. Later in its history, Laurel would have the boat renamed after his NEXT wife – making Stan Laurel the only man in history to have one boat named after his FOUR wives.

The day after Stan took ownership of the *Ida May*, he and Ruth took "A.J" and Ven to see it, and gave them the honour of being the first to sign the Visitors Book. Captain Chester Mills, who would be skippering Laurel on all future sailings, then gave the four of them a test-run, with a quick trip around Los Angeles Harbor. The following day Mills piloted them to Catalina Island, where they would be staying for the next twenty-four days.

-----0-----

1935 August 04

CHEVIOT HILLS to LOS ANGELES HARBOR, California 🚗 30 miles

LOS ANGELES HARBOR, California to CATALINA ISLAND 🚢 25 miles

-----0-----

Stan and Ruth went fishing every day, leaving "A.J" and Ven to enjoy the attractions and views on this beautiful island; although they did join Stan on a couple of fishing expeditions. Fellow employees from the Roach Studios would also be coming along.

First of these were brothers James and Charles Parrott (*ibid.*), who arrived on 6 August. The next day Stan, Ruth, Ven, Charley and Jimmy all went out on the *Ida May*. Joining them was Jan Garber, who was again playing a two-month residency with his orchestra at the Casino.

Stan may have regretted taking Jimmy along, as Stan's prized target, a giant marlin (aka: swordfish) chose Jimmy's line instead of his. On return to the Catalina Yacht Club, the poor sailfish was hauled up onto the landing stage via a jib and pulley system, weighed, and then left hanging for display and photograph opportunities. Even though it was Jimmy Parrott's catch, there are those who still display the picture and credit the fish to Laurel. It is not what he would have wanted. The idea is to catch your own!

On 14 August actor Charlie Hall and his wife-to-be, Foxie, joined the Laurels' party. In the L&H films Charlie was Stan and Ollie's nemesis, but the very next day he proved to be a good luck talisman, as Stan caught his first giant swordfish – a 171lb marlin. The poor thing was played on the end of a hook for forty-five minutes, left to die, then hung upside-down on the yacht club's landing stage. Still, maybe the fish didn't mind sacrificing itself for the grand cause – Laurel being awarded a Tuna Club Badge. [I didn't get a badge when I ran over a rabbit once – just a horrible sickly feeling!]

THE DEAD PARROTT FISH SKETCH
James Parrott proudly holding the fish-pole on which HE caught the marlin pictured. Charles Parrott, Ruth and Stan Laurel, and Jan Garber bask in the reflected "glory."

STAN LAUREL and 'JIMMY FIN.'
Laurel's first catch from the *Ruth L* – a 171lb marlin. Charlie Hall, Ruth Laurel, and Foxie join in at the weigh-in ceremony.
15 August 1935 — (Courtesy of Ray Andrew)

Over dinner on 16 August the Laurels, Jeffersons, and Halls received the tragic news that actor Will Rogers had been killed in a plane crash. It is hard to describe just how well-loved Rogers was by the American public – not just for his films, but also as a comedian, raconteur, humourist, sportsman, philosopher, and humanitarian. If Rogers had ever stood for President he would have won by the largest margin in American history.

All Roach employees would have been especially upset, as Rogers had made some of his early films at the Roach Studios (October 1923 – August 1924). Stan and Babe had also met Will at social functions, including the opening of the Fox cinema in San Francisco in June 1929; the Academy Awards ceremony in 1932; and Roach's 20th Anniversary Party in December 1933.

Gone Fishin'

Hal Roach was a very close friend of Rogers. Both were keen polo players, and had popularised the sport with the Hollywood film crowd, at the Midwick Country Club, before forming their own team, 'The Uplifters,' based at Rustic Canyon, Santa Monica. It was a sad day for all.

The Halls went home on the 18th, but two days later Stan was joined by Roach film director James Wesley Horne, his wife Cleo (nee Ridgely) and actress daughter June; who were to socialise, fish, and dine out with them over the next seven days.

HORNE-A-PLENTY
Mrs. Cleo Horne, Ruth and Stan Laurel, June Horne, James Horne.
St. Catherine Hotel, Catalina Island. (circa 24 August 1935)
In 1944 June married former "Little Rascal" Jackie Cooper. [inset]

On the Laurel party's last night on Catalina, 27 August, they were dinner guests of millionaire chewing-gum magnate Philip Wrigley, Jr., at his beautiful home over-looking Avalon Bay.

The following morning the Laurels, their two servants, and friends sailed back to the mainland in the newly-named *Ruth L*, while the Jeffersons were relegated to taking the regular passenger steamship *SS Catalina* to Wilmington, Long Beach.

Stan may have been wishing that his father and stepmother, after having been treated to a five-week holiday, would now be happy to return to London. But Arthur Jefferson was not ready to go home – not by a long chalk.

-----0-----

1935 August 28

CATALINA ISLAND to SAN PEDRO, California 25 miles
SAN PEDRO to CHEVIOT HILLS, California 30 miles

-----0-----

"And what of Oliver Hardy?" I hear you say. Well, originally, the big plan had been for the Hardys to join the Laurels and the Jeffersons on a trip to Hawaii, with their hosts being no less than Hal Roach and his wife Marguerite.

Roach was going there to play polo. But the plan fell apart. The Hardys were by now separated, and Hardy didn't wish to be in Myrtle's company while she was still hitting the bottle.

As for the Laurels, Stan had chosen to spend time on his newly-acquired boat, and so the other three had had to fall in line. So Roach was upset that his kind gesture had been snubbed; Myrtle was upset that Babe wouldn't be accompanying her to Hawaii; and Ruth, A.J and Ven were upset because they had wanted to go the real Hawaii, and not Catalina Island – even though it was billed as "the nearest thing to Hawaii, without going to Hawaii." Still! Stan got what he wanted – or at least he thought he had. Within days of getting back from Catalina, he deserted Ruth.

Babe was having a happier time. After the Parrott brothers left Laurel, they teamed up with him and went on a motoring holiday along the Pacific coast, enjoying the comforts of Babe's new 8-cylinder roadster car.

-----o-----

1935 August 10 (circa)
> BEVERLY HILLS, California to DEL MONTE, California 🚗 323 miles

-----o-----

Along the way Babe, Charley and Jimmy stopped off at various golf courses and freshwater fishing spots. First stop-off was Del Monte, on the Monterey Peninsula, which had both a golf course and a fishing lake within a couple of miles of each other. Hardy had attended a golf tournament there in September 1931, so knew the area. It may have been something he had enjoyed on his first visit, which attracted him back there.

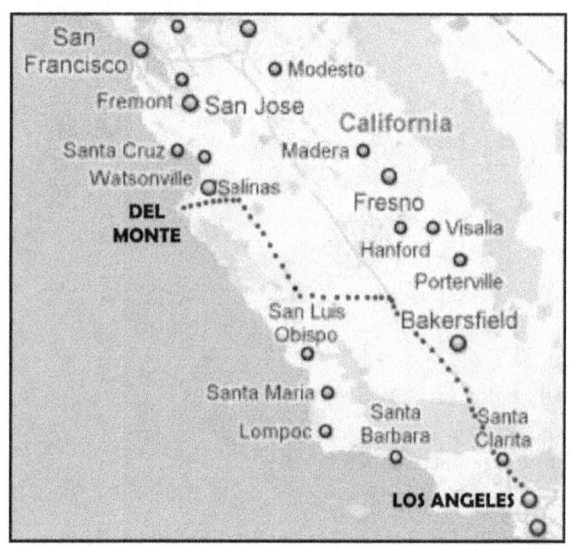

ROUTE MAP
Los Angeles to Del Monte

EL SOMBRERO Y LA SENORITA BONITA
At the hotel, Hardy somehow got dragged into the preparations for the forthcoming Bal Masque (Masked Ball), by committee members of the Carmel Artists and Writers, who were about to stage the event there in late September. — [Newspaper scan]

Gone Fishin'

-----0-----

1935 August 12 (circa)
         DEL MONTE, California to SEATTLE, Washington 🚗 909 miles

-----0-----

Of other stops on the journey, author John McCabe reveals in one of his books:

> Hardy spent two days in Seattle, seeing friends and visiting the local race track. At the track the judges invited him to come up and see the races from their stand. "No thanks," he said. "I'm on my vacation and I'm having fun right where I am."

After Seattle he left for a fishing trip at Diamond Lake, near Crater Lake [Oregon], then back to Los Angeles.

-----0-----

1935 August 17 (circa)
         SEATTLE, Washington to DIAMOND LAKE, Oregon 🚗 439 miles

1935 August 19 (circa)
         DIAMOND LAKE, Oregon to BEVERLY HILLS, California 🚗 746 miles

-----0-----

Upon returning to L.A., Babe spent each and every day of the remaining holiday playing golf at Lakeside with his best friends – actor Guy Kibbee, and writer Frank Craven.

The Laurel & Hardy unit were back at the Roach studios by early September, at which time Laurel got some disturbing threats from an anonymous source:

> A "bodyguard racket," which reputedly aimed to fleece such film celebrities as ZaSu Pitts and Stan Laurel under threats of kidnapping, was investigated today. The scheme was exposed by Miss Pitts, who said she had received threatening letters, demanding money and "suggesting" that she employ bodyguards to protect herself and her family.
>
> The authors apparently sought to frighten intended victims by threats of kidnapping or death, and followed this up by applying for jobs as bodyguards at high prices.
>
> Laurel said he flatly refused to hire guards, and the threats ceased.

(*UP* – 6 September 1935)

Whether the incident had a ripple effect, and delayed production at the Roach Studios while the matter was sorted out by the police, is not known. It would, however, be the second week in October before shooting began on "*The Bohemian Girl.*"

So with time to spare before filming commenced, the Boys went off for one last fling. Hardy went to the Los Angeles County Fair, being held in Pomona, forty-two miles west of Beverly Hills.

-----0-----

1935 September 28 (Saturday)
         BEVERLY HILLS, California to POMONA, California 🚗 42 miles

-----0-----

It was the last day of the sixteen the County Fair had been running, and was all the more attractive to Hardy as horse racing had been added to the programme. However, his time in the stands at the track was ruined by a constant demand from autograph hunters, as was his companions' – comedy actors Joe E. Brown and ZaSu Pitts. Good to see the latter unperturbed by the recent threats.

Meanwhile, on that same weekend, Laurel's final fling would prove life-changing. After having committed an act of extremism at one end of the marital scale (in this case – desertion), he flipped to the opposite extreme and proposed that he and Ruth get married again. It reminds one of the puppet character, Mr. Punch, whereby, no matter how bad his choice of action and/or reaction is, he believes it was the right thing to do, and crowns it with the line: "That's the way to do it." Unbelievably, Ruth went for it – and off they set for Arizona.

1935 September 27 (circa)
        CHEVIOT HILLS, California to FLORENCE, Arizona 434 miles

-----0-----

The ceremony took place on 28 September 1935, in the law library of the Pinal County Court House, Florence, Arizona – near Phoenix. Present was a party of close friends who had travelled with the bride and groom to witness the ceremony, plus members of the bride's family, who actually resided in Florence. Stan's father and step-mother are believed to have stayed behind in California; the reason for which, if so, seems to have remained within family circles.

Laurel's raison d'être for the second marriage ceremony was two-fold: One was to remove the technicality of his first marriage to Ruth having come before his final divorce from Lois. The final divorce had been granted earlier than the expected date in October, hence the reason for the timing of this second ceremony with Ruth. The second reason was Stan's way of trying to convince Ruth that this time he would put Lois behind him, and commit himself totally to her. But before the honeymoon had even started, the two-folds folded.

The plan had been for the honeymoon couple to travel to New York City by train, spend a few days there, and then return home. But eleven hundred miles out, at Kansas City, Stan got cold feet, jumped train, and returned home.

On the train journey back he bumped into Charlie Hall's mother, who was on the last leg of her journey from England to be at her son's wedding. Good to report that Charlie and Foxie's marriage lasted somewhat longer than Stan and Ruth's.

Charlie Hall's mum, on the set of "*The Bohemian Girl*"

-----0-----

1935 September 29 (circa)
        FLORENCE, Arizona to KANSAS CITY, Kansas 1,100 miles
1935 September 30 (circa)
        KANSAS CITY, Kansas to CHEVIOT HILLS, California 1,615 miles

-----0-----

Laurel later told Ruth that he thought marrying her again would have eliminated all his feelings for Lois. But it hadn't. He still loved Lois.

1935 September 05 (circa)
        CHEVIOT HILLS to LOS ANGELES HARBOR, California 30 miles

        LOS ANGELES HARBOR, California to CATALINA ISLAND 25 miles

On or just before 5 September, Stan took Ruth over to Catalina, so he could get in some fishing from the *Ruth L*. But maybe he felt that spending too much time with her, without a distraction, might test their relationship a little too much. So, he invited along an old acquaintance – Fred Quimby. Their last known meeting was back in 1932, when the Boys had arrived back from the British tour, when Quimby was based at the MGM offices in New York.

Gone Fishin'

Fred Quimby, writer Dorothy Hope, Ruth and Stan, posing on the open deck, atop the main cabin of the *Ruth L* – anchored just off Catalina Island.

Dorothy Hope had first met Laurel in England, during the 1932 tour. Then, in September 1934, on a visit from London to California, she got herself invited to Fort Laurel, where she combined the hospitality of the Laurel household with making notes for an article for *Film Pictorial* (29 December 1934 issue).

A few days after her day with Stan, she met both Laurel AND Hardy on the set of "*Babes in Toyland*." What acquaintanceship she had with Fred Quimby, if any, during this 1935 trip, could not be determined.

Ruth sat at the stern of the boat, in what is known as the "fighting chair."

I hope Stan used it only for fighting with the fish.

(Photo taken on a previous trip).

At least the falling out with Ruth hadn't caused a scandal, and so Laurel was able to return to work at the Roach Studios without any egg on his face. It was then that a surprising announcement came out, with a questionable heading:

HAVE PLENTY OF WORK

Their heavy production schedule has forced Stan Laurel and Oliver Hardy to turn down an offer to appear in a London stage production of "The Better 'Ole." The two are now working in Roach's full-length production of "The Bohemian Girl."

(27 October 1935)

It is quite ironic that Laurel and Hardy were looking for "a better 'ole." The expression comes from an incident in WWI, when a soldier was reputed to have refused to leave his current shell hole, until a better one was found. The phrase then entered the English language to express the intent of remaining in one bad situation, until one can move to where the conditions ought to be better, without knowing that will be the case – a kind of alternative to moving to where "the grass is greener," or, "Better the devil you know."

One must suspect that Arthur Jefferson, who was still visiting Stan, had had a hand in getting Stan and Babe considered for the parts, as for a few years past he had run his own theatrical agency in London, and would still have had contacts in the theatre world.

A.J and Ven on the set of *The Bohemian Girl* (circa late October 1935)

On 7 December, while post-production of *"The Bohemian Girl"* was in progress, the Boys made a radio broadcast, but not the usual Christmassy one.

GALA PROGRAM WILL FEATURE STUDIO OPENING

Something different in the way of Hollywood openings is promised tonight, with the opening of NBC's new Hollywood studios. The ceremonies will be broadcast coast to coast, and will be heard here on KPO and KGO 7.30 to 9.30.

At the microphones in the new studios in Hollywood will be Jack Benny and Company, Anne Jamison, Nelson Eddy, Marion Talley, Edgar Guest, Irene Rich, Clark Gable, May Robson, Bing Crosby, Irvin S. Cobb, Wallace Beery, Ginger Rogers, Phil Regan, Joe Penner, Al Jolson, Stan Laurel, Oliver Hardy, George Jessel, Jan Kiepurs, and Martha Eggerth.

"The Bohemian Girl" took far longer than scheduled to complete; mainly because of illness among the cast, but by the end of November it was finally in the can. It didn't stay there long. On 16 December, the Roach Studios, and indeed the whole of Hollywood and far beyond, was rocked by news that screen actress Thelma Todd had been found dead.

Gone Fishin'

The circumstances surrounding her death were never established, and conspiracy theories exist to this day. Those who worked at the Roach Studios were especially shocked and saddened. In April 1929 Ms. Todd had signed a five-year deal with Roach, and subsequently made an impressive start with a leading role in Laurel & Hardy's first talking-picture "*Unaccustomed As We Are.*" She went on to co-star with the Boys in "*Another Fine Mess,*" "*Fra Diavolo,*" "*Chickens Come Home,*" and then "*The Bohemian Girl.*"

Thelma in costume for *Fra Diavolo*.

Thelma's body lay in state in a glass casket, and an estimated fourteen thousand mourners came to pay their respects. On the 19th a private service was held in the Wee Kirk O'Heather chapel, at the Forest Lawn Memorial Park, after which the body was cremated. Sharing her mother Alice Todd's grief were Thelma's former screen partners Patsy Kelly and ZaSu Pitts, plus Mr. & Mrs. Stan Laurel, Mr. & Mrs. Oliver Hardy, Charley Chase, and Hal Roach.

It had been hoped that "*The Bohemian Girl*" would be a great follow-up to "*Babes in Toyland,*" but now it was felt that having Thelma Todd up on the screen, while audiences were still full of shock and grief, would totally overshadow the enjoyment factor of the film. So, immediately after the funeral, Roach had most of her scenes deleted and then re-shot them with other actors.

Two days after Thelma Todd's funeral saw the commencement of the 'Southern California $3,000 Open Golf Championship.' This three-day event was the first open golf tournament to be staged by Oakmont Golf and Country Club, Glendale, California. More than sixty of California's leading amateurs had entered, including the following motion-picture stars: Harold Lloyd, Richard Arlen, Randolph Scott, Bing Crosby, and Oliver Hardy.

-----0-----

1935 December 21
BEVERLY HILLS, California to OAKMONT, California
12 miles
-----0-----

Two days before the tournament, Hardy had met up with fellow-members of the Lakeside Country Club – Bing Crosby, Guy Kibbee, Frank Craven, Harold Lloyd, Richard Arlen, Randolph Scott, and Humphrey Bogart – for extra tuition from the Lakeside instructor. However, over the days of the actual tournament, 21-23 December, Hardy's name did not appear on the results sheets, nor in any write-ups.

I did originally surmise that Hardy had withdrawn from the tournament in deference to Thelma Todd, coupled with his being needed for re-shoots of "*The Bohemian Girl*" — but that theory was scotched when I came across this newspaper clip of Hardy actually at the tournament.

It can be confirmed though, that Babe didn't come in among the winners. Pity! The prize money would have come in handy, as Myrtle Hardy had just been awarded $1,000 per month alimony.

It was not the kind of award Mr. Hardy had been hoping for.

-----0-----

Grantland Rice, sports writer, and Oliver Hardy, at the Southern Californian Open Golf Championship at Oakhampton.

1935 December 23
> OAKMONT, California to **BEVERLY HILLS**, California — 12 miles

1935 December 25
> BEVERLY HILLS, California to **SANTA ANITA**, California — 25 miles

-----0-----

Christmas Day may mean a lot to millions of religious people, but to thirty thousand horse-racing fanatics it meant just one thing: the '$5,000 Christmas Stakes' at the Arcadia Track, Santa Anita Park. Not only was this a big event in its own right, but the start of fifty-eight days of racing, culminating in February with the "$100,000 Santa Anita Handicap" – the world's then richest horse-racing prize.

Race-mad Hollywood was represented by such stars as Bing Crosby, Mae West, Joe E. Brown, Al Jolson, Ruby Keeler, Ann Harding, and Clark Gable. The name Oliver Hardy was missing from the newspaper reports, but it is worth a fair-sized bet that he was there; and a 'double' that he was accompanied by Viola Morse, a mistress he had been seeing for a number of years now, and who was so frequently with him on such occasions that many thought her to be Mrs. Hardy.

A letter of intent written by Hardy to his real wife, Myrtle, gives away his next "sporting" event – a hunting trip. (dated 23 November 1935)

```
I don't think it is advisable to see you as it would make
matters worse. For that day, I am going to the desert
hunting.
```

Daddy

At the time of writing, Myrtle was back in Rosemead sanitarium – having yet more treatment for alcohol addiction. If Hardy did go hunting, it is a fair guesstimate he went across the California border into Mexico – maybe a repeat of his 1934 trip – although this could not be confirmed.

-----0-----

1935 late December (*circa*)
> BEVERLY HILLS, California to **CALEXICO**, Mexico — 228 miles

1936 early January (*circa*)
> CALEXICO, Mexico to **BEVERLY HILLS**, California — 228 miles

-----0-----

I suppose Hardy was entitled to some play. Remember the old adage: "All work and no play – makes Jack a dull boy." Unfortunately, for six out of the next twelve months it was going to be, for Laurel *and* Hardy, a case of: "No work – and all play."

o-o-0-o-o

CHAPTER 10

TWO GOLFS AND THREE FISHES

(1936 pt1)

With no Laurel & Hardy films in prospect at the Roach Studios, Babe entered yet another golf tournament.

-----0-----

1936 January 15 (circa)

   BEVERLY HILLS, California to SACRAMENTO, California 🚗 384 miles

-----0-----

   Sacramento Golf – Starts Thursday 16 January 1936

   2 days of qualifying – 2 days to conclude

Among the one-hundred-plus entrants were several golf aces; a handful of big league ballplayers; a world heavyweight boxing champion – Max Baer; Eastern sportswriter and friend of Babe Hardy – Grantland Rice; plus film stars Richard Arlen, Andy Devine, Randolph Scott, Johnny Weissmuller, and Oliver Hardy.

Reporter Lee Dunbar said of the latter group:

> Grant Rice and Dick Arlen are the two best golfers, the former particularly being a consistent shooter in the 70s. Arlen shoots a pretty fair game, and may squeeze in among the low 10 amateurs. Oliver Hardy seldom if ever breaks 80, but has a lot of fun and is getting to be quite a follower of the California golf circuit.

                  (*Oakland Tribune* – 10 January 1936)

Wednesday was a practice round, and Thursday's pre-qualifying round was abandoned because of adverse weather conditions. Hardy is not mentioned in reports of the first day of play proper on 17th. On the 18th all the players who had scored under 100 were named but, again, Hardy was not among them. Maybe he got teed off – and left!

-----0-----

1936 January 20 (circa)

 SACRAMENTO, California to BEVERLY HILLS, California 🚗 384 miles

-----0-----

Previous reports of Hardy's golfing prowess would have us believe that he was the best the Lakeside crowd had to offer, and that it was a waste of time any of the other members of the acting fraternity turning up to challenge him.

The following article confirms that, in the mid- to late-1920s, Babe Hardy was indeed the one to beat, but whether he had been able to maintain his status through to the mid-1930s was not discovered.

GOLF CHAMP URGES STUDIO COMPETITION IN ATHLETICS

> Motion-picture people are not sufficiently bound together by any interest outside of the actual making of pictures, and have very little common interest in social and sporting activities, in the opinion of one person at least. This one person is Oliver "Babe" Hardy, 285 pound personality of Hal Roach comedies.
>
> Mr Hardy has been appearing in Roach comedies as a featured player for a year or so ... but he steps out of character ever so often to defend the title he won two years ago in a tournament, that of golf champion of the film industry.
>
> *(Los Angeles Sunday Times* – 6 March 1927)

While Hardy was chasing golf balls on the green fairways of Sacramento, Laurel was chasing fish in the blue waters off San Pedro. However, in Laurel's case, the "fish" decided to chase back.

> Stan Laurel, mariner-comedian, went out for a pleasure voyage yesterday, and ran his cabin cruiser into a school of ocean leviathans.
>
> Captain Chester Mills, Laurel's skipper, averted disaster and damages when one of the whales contacted the 46-foot craft a mile off Point Fermin, San Pedro, Ca.
>
> The school of nine, measuring 50 to 60 feet in length, was described by Mills as the largest he had seen in 20 years sailing on the Californian and Mexican coast.
>
> *(Bakersfield Californian* – 24 January 1936)

The whales had probably heard how Laurel treated marlins, and had come to warn him off future persecution.

Laurel still inviting friends aboard, to avoid being left with Ruth 24/7.
Ruth is in the spotted dress. The man behind her is skipper Chester Mills.

[Hands up if you started singing: "Fresh fish, caught in the ocean this mor-or-ning," when you saw this photo.

Between early February and early May, all of Laurel's AND Hardy's energies should have been concentrated on writing, production, and filming of "*Our Relations*," but it would appear they were still working on "Our Relaxations." It's an odds-on bet that, on 22 February, Babe was back at the Santa Anita racetrack to watch the aforementioned end of season race, the '$100,000 Santa Anita Handicap.' He wasn't actually named in press releases as being among the fifty-thousand-strong crowd, but then nor were any of the "many movie celebrities and famous sports figures" said to be in attendance.

As for Laurel, on 27 February, he was again noted as being out fishing.

> Stan Laurel was all smiles today as he reported catching eight yellowtail [a member of the 'jack' family of fish] averaging 25 pounds each, while fishing from his yacht, the *Ruth L*, in Catalina channel yesterday.
>
> (28 February 1936)

Also around that time, Laurel was passing *HMS Skeena* and *HMS Vancouver* on the *Ruth L* when he was spotted, and invited aboard. He was given such a rousing welcome, that he invited the officers and men to visit the set during making of the next Laurel & Hardy film. Consequently, those allowed to go had the thrill of being shown over the elaborate "pirate ship café," when filming began a few weeks later on "*Our Relations*."

Hal Roach was more than happy for his two prized-comedians to be absent from the studios to attend the next event, although he would have preferred a happier ending:

-----0-----

5 March 1936

Biltmore Hotel, LOS ANGELES – Academy Awards

On 5 March 1936, Laurel and Hardy attended the Academy Awards at the Biltmore Hotel, Los Angeles. At their table were Myrtle Hardy, and Roach producers Gus Meins and James Parrott, with Mrs. Parrott. The Boys were hoping to repeat their success of 1932, when "*The Music Box*" had won the award for 'Best Short,' but the latest nomination, "*Tit For Tat*," came only third to "*How to Sleep*" (MGM) and "*Oh, My Nerves*" (Columbia).

-----0-----

Mid-March finally saw the commencement of filming of the Laurel & Hardy feature, "*Our Relations*." This was punctuated one day in mid-April, when the Boys took a short walk over to the Charley Chase unit, to film a cameo appearance for "*On the Wrong Trek*." Filming on "*Our Relations*" then ended during the first week in May. This coincided with a press release, which indicated that one of Oliver Hardy's hobbies was getting to be rather expensive. After losing tens of thousands of pounds betting at the racetrack, Babe had decided to cut out the middle man by buying into a racecourse:

> Spokesmen for a group of Hollywood and San Diego sportsmen, headed by Bing Crosby, screen star, said today plans were underway to establish a horse racing track near San Diego.
>
> Formal articles of incorporation for the organization, the Del Mar Turf Club, were filed at Sacramento, with capital stock of $250,000.
>
> Directors named are Harry L. Crosby (Bing); his brother Everett N. Crosby; Pat O'Brien, Oliver Hardy, and Lloyd Bacon – film director.
>
> Application for a permit will be filed shortly with the California Horse Racing Board, it was said.
>
> (*Associated Press* – 6 May 1936)

A second article revealed the names of more Hollywood investors, including one rather surprising one:

> The Hollywood film colony has organized its own turf club, the Del Mar, which plans a 25-day meeting next winter – several miles north of San Diego. Bing Crosby is president, and the board glitters with the names of stars and directors – Gary Cooper, Joe E. Brown, Pat O'Brien, Stan Laurel, Oliver Hardy, David Butler, and Leo McCarey, among them.

While the comedy couple were waiting for all the formalities and legalities to be sorted, Laurel may have made a coast-to-coast trip to New York and back. The only evidence is another letter of intent, written by Laurel to a friend in New Jersey, back on 7 December 1935:

My Dear Duncan Boss:
I am expecting to be in New York around the end of May next
[1936] and will advise you upon my arrival as I would very
much like to meet you again and swap experiences.

Stan

-----0-----

If Laurel did make the trip, then these are the probable travel arrangements:

-----0-----

1936 May

       CHEVIOT HILLS, California to **NEW YORK**, New York 🚂 2,814 miles

       NEW YORK, New York to **CHEVIOT HILLS**, California 🚂 2,814 miles

-----0-----

Hardy, meanwhile, took himself off to Mexico with Guy Kibbee, to do some fishing.

-----0-----

1936 May (*circa*)

       BEVERLY HILLS, California to **MEXICO** 🚗 .??? Miles

Guy Kibbee waving his cap and revealing a bald pate. As the boat is identified as the *Avalon* (sic), we can safely assume they are in Catalina waters.
(Date unknown)

-----0-----

1936 May (*circa*)

       MEXICO to BEVERLY HILLS, California 🚗 ??? miles
(N.B. It is not known whereabouts in Mexico Hardy and Kibbee went to.)

-----0-----

With no filming during the whole of July, the Boys showed up on the radar only when they appeared at a huge benefit show:

Two Golfs and Three Fishes

> Wednesday 1 July 1936
> Pan-American Auditorium, Hollywood
> ## NIGHT OF 1000 STARS
> The 55th Annual Actors' Fund
> of America – Benefit Show.
> 8.30 – 11.30pm
> 2000 Players; 5 Bands; a 100-piece Orchestra;
> a Ballet of 1000
> Stars re-enacting best-known scenes of their film careers

Between the many musical numbers were to be found the following screen stars: Olivia de Havilland, Billie Burke, David Niven, Walter Pidgeon, Eddie Cantor, Al St. John, Mack Sennett, Eleanor Powell, Lew Ayres, Leo Carrillo, Bela Lugosi, Bette Davis, Pat O'Brien, Mae West, Joan Crawford, Robert Montgomery, Claudette Colbert, Clark Gable, Frank Capra, Edmund Gwenn, Joe E. Brown, Frank Morgan, and Mary Pickford.

Added to these were the following actors who had past, present, or future connections to the films of Laurel & Hardy: Patricia Ellis, Eric Blore, Lionel Belmore, Minna Gombell, Herbert Rawlinson, Jean Harlow, William S. Hart. Oh! And, er … Stan Laurel and Oliver Hardy.

And then there was that little silent clown again. What was his name? Oh yes! Charlie Chaplin. (That's the FOURTH appearance with Stan and Babe you didn't know about.)

Writing and pre-production of the next Laurel & Hardy feature, "*Way Out West*," had begun in May; but, come August, the Roach studio closed for its summer vacation with not a single frame of footage having been shot. Laurel didn't seem too concerned. He jumped on his fishing boat with Ruth, and Captain Mills took them to Catalina for an extended stay.

Around 12 August, Hollywood columnist Erskine Johnson spent several hours aboard the *Ruth L*, observing Laurel as he cruised the waters of Catalina hoping to catch a swordfish.

> The 'Ruth L', a 50-foot cabin cruiser, is one of the fastest on the Pacific coast. Hits around 35 knots, wide open. There's a galley, sleeping room for eight, and a pair of comfortable fishing chairs at the stern.
>
> There's a captain, too, a lanky gent with a frozen face. Laurel wouldn't know what to do if the engines sputtered and died, and he seldom takes the wheel himself. The skipper also baits Mr. Laurel's hooks, rules the galley, and keeps everything amazingly ship-shape.
>
> The captain would wash dishes, too, if Laurel didn't like that chore himself, but Stan doesn't wash 'em in approved manner. He grabs a plate, leans overboard, and lets the rushing water lick the plate clean.
>
> Ruth Laurel, the comedian's pretty blond wife, also likes to fish. Like all good anglers, she didn't moan because the fish wouldn't bite. She dozed off occasionally, but otherwise her fishing deportment was class AAA.
>
> The amount of fishing tackle on Laurel's boat is astounding. Two lockers are jammed full of leaders, feathered lures, hooks, canned bait, assorted rods, and a dozen reels ranging in size from 50 to 500 yards. There's even a live bait tank, hidden beneath an otherwise swanky leather chair. Laurel knows exactly what everything is for, and he handles a rod like an expert.
>
> He caught a 171 pound swordfish last summer, but hasn't been able to hook another since. He catches lots of sharks and smaller fish, though.
>
> If his swordfish luck doesn't improve, however, Mr. Laurel is going to ship his boat by steamer to the gulf of Lower California. "There are hundreds of 'em down there," he says. "They say it's terrific." That's just how nutty Mr. Laurel is about fishing.
>
> (*NEA – circa* 15 September 1936)

If only Erskine had gone along a couple of days later he would have witnessed the historic moment when Stan caught a marlin weighing in at 258lb, which proved to be the biggest catch of the season by a Yacht Club member.

The sacrifice of this creature earned Laurel a signed certificate from the Catalina Tuna Club, and a 'gold button' which he was to wear wherever there might be another angler ready to hear his tale. The swordfish, meanwhile, got a signed copy of the weigh-in photograph, with the dedication: "*I was caught by Stan Laurel.*" If only!

A few days later, Laurel wasn't so jubilant.

> Stan Laurel's face was red, and it wasn't from sunburn either, when he established a new fishing record off Catalina last week. Hooking what he believed to be a marlin swordfish, the comedian gave battle, while dozens of glasses [binoculars] were trained on him from nearby boats.
>
> Then Stan's face began getting red. For, at the other end of the line now appeared a partly submerged packing case.

Laurel didn't see the funny side. He wrote to the newspaper company, complaining that they were being unfair in making him a laughing-stock, when only a few days earlier he had landed a record 258lb marlin. He could have looked on the bright side. All he needed for the second catch was a piece of glass, and he had a case in which to display the first catch!

Laurel with the love of his life – a giant marlin. Ruth Laurel dresses the scene.

Of all the major works on Laurel & Hardy, and/or Charlie Chaplin, only one contains the occasion when Stan Laurel chanced to meet Charlie Chaplin on the high seas. In "*STAN – The Life of Stan Laurel*" Fred Lawrence Guiles recounts:

In the Catalina waters, Chaplin recognised Stan and had one of his crew toss him a line. Stan chose to forget the times he had tried to talk to Chaplin by phone "just for a get together" when Chaplin could not be reached.

There followed a hearty reunion at sea, and as first one, then the other recalled incidents from their early days with Karno, the awkwardness of the years of separation fell away. Ruth and Paulette became a delighted audience for a couple of hours as the men competed with each other in dredging up the hoariest of music-hall ballads.

Chaplin accepted a gift of freshly-caught blues and they parted, vowing to keep in better touch. But their lives were running on different tracks, and years would go by before they would meet again.

Guiles places the encounter in October, which can't be correct. Chaplin was at Catalina from 6 to 8 June inclusive, with his two sons – eleven- year-old Charlie, Jr. and ten-year-old Sydney. He took the boys there again on 13 June, but that was aboard John Barrymore's yacht, the '*Infanta.*' The next recorded visit was 24 July to 2 August. None of these fits Laurel's known movements, but the next one does: Chaplin was in and around Catalina from 22 to 29 August inclusive. Laurel was confirmed as being there throughout most of August, but no later than the 26th, as he reported to the Roach studios on the 27th.

So, the best bet for their meeting was between 22 to 26 August. If Guiles is correct that it was on a Saturday, that gives us just the one possible date – Saturday 22 August 1936.

Chaplin caught mooning the sun, on a previous visit to Catalina (September 3, 1933) on board Joseph Schneck's schooner *Invader*:
His shipmates are: L-R: Mrs. Harry Greene, Harry Greene, Grace Poggi, Joseph Schneck, Margaret LaMarr, Paulette Goddard.

The lady identified by Guiles as 'Paulette' was Paulette Goddard, Chaplin's beautiful leading lady in the recently released Chaplin film, "*Modern Times.*"

Note how Guiles makes out that Laurel and Chaplin hadn't met for years, and yet we have already identified four social functions which they both attended. It is hard to believe that Stan would not have sought out Charlie to say "Hello!" on at least one of these occasions.

Ruth wasn't happy during her time on Catalina. She complained, among other aspects of Stan's behaviour, that he booked the two of them into cheap and tatty accommodation, when he could have afforded better. Just days later, 1 September 1936, the relationship changed again – when they separated.

Production of "*Way Out West*" had begun just before August was out. Four weeks later came a press release in which Hal Roach revealed that Laurel and Hardy were scheduled to make a western picture. The term "scheduled" would seem to be a little late in the day for a film this far into production.

Just two days after the first press release came another, this one putting a dampener on any immediate follow-up to "*Way Out West.*"

Ruth had done her best to always appear attractive and attentive to Stan, but that wasn't all that he wanted. What he did want, he couldn't have – Lois.

> The splitting of Stan Laurel and Oliver Hardy, after one more picture at Roach's, brings forth much speculation. Mr. Laurel states that he is only taking a three months' vacation, and that when he comes back, he will listen first to Mr. Roach's offers before signing elsewhere.
>
> It is a well-known fact that the last time a contract was signed at the studio, Mr. Hardy signed first, without consulting his co-partner, and as a result, Laurel was forced to sign at a figure lower than he expected. So maybe this is the finale of his pique.
>
> (*King Features Syndicate Inc.* – 26 September 1936)

Here we go again with news that Laurel and Hardy have fallen out. If they had, how does one explain this other contemporary article:

> Oliver Hardy, the 250 pound member of the team of Laurel and Hardy, loves to eat, according to Mrs. Stan Laurel, who calls him "Babe." Ruth and Stan Laurel have "Babe" over to dinner at their house once a week.
>
> The morning of the day "Babe" is to dine with them, Mrs. Laurel tells Lillian, their colored cook, that Mr. Hardy is coming to dinner. Lillian beams, and rolls up her sleeves even higher than usual, and sets to work with gusto. Hardy, you see, is an Atlanta, Ga. product. Mrs. Laurel, a modern wife, who goes tuna and swordfish angling with her husband, thinks "Babe" is very funny.
>
> (23 September 1936)

As Ruth and Stan had separated three weeks before this article, one must conclude it had being doing the rounds for some time. However, it does disprove the theory that Stan and Babe always went their separate ways once they left the studio.

And here is yet another evening they attended together: The event was described as:

> Stan Laurel and Oliver Hardy are just so glad. They have been invited to the Hollywood Press Photographers Frolic, which will be held at the Biltmore Hotel on October 7. The cameramen will park their equipment for the evening, but others will carry the torch for them.

What that means, I have no idea. I also have no idea when or where this mystery photo was taken. Maybe it was a bit of "Frolic" which the Stan and Babe added to the evening.

> Another unanswered question: "Is Laurel impersonating Hardy, or sending up Chaplin?"
> [Answers on a £20 note to the author, please.]

"*Way Out West*" took till early November to complete, and then the Boys filmed two five-minute cameos for the forthcoming Roach musical "*Pick a Star.*" It was now time for Laurel to take the three-month break he had given notice of. What neither he nor anyone else could have predicted was that it would actually be **thirteen** months before Laurel faced the cameras again.

o-o-0-o-o

CHAPTER 11
THERE'S GOING TO BE A FIGHT
(1936 pt2 – 1937 pt1)

If Stan thought he was about to have three months respite, now the pressure of filmmaking had been released, he couldn't have been more wrong. In fact the pressure was about to increase, as he was about to be squeezed from two different sides.

The problem had started on 14 October 1936, when Ruth Laurel issued a maintenance suit, charging that her husband had told her, "*he did not love her, never did love her, and married her to spite his first wife.*" Ouch! She asked for $1,235 per month alimony from Laurel's estimated earnings of $200,000 a year.

In court on 22 October, Stan Laurel made a cross-complaint that, "*On one occasion she told me she no longer loved me, but that it was up to me to support her the rest of her life.*" He further denied he received a movie salary, and declared his pay as $65,000 for each picture.

In court again on 24 October, Laurel was asked for a breakdown of his annual income. Journalist's notes taken in court showed that:

> Although his income is $167,500 a year, he was unable to explain exactly what happened to it all.
>
> "My hotel room costs me $175 a month, but my bill is about $500 before the month is over. I pay out $1,500 a month in salaries, too."
>
> Laurel further explained that his manager and booking agent received around $16,000 a year from him, and his boat captain $175 a month. His wife also gets $172 a month from an annuity policy.

[Amusing to note that Laurel's boat captain got more than his own wife.]

While Stan was still wrestling with Ruth, an opposing tag-partner from a totally unexpected quarter jumped into the ring. It was none other than Mae Dahlberg, Stan's former vaudeville partner, whom Joe Rock had encouraged to return to her native Australia way back in 1925. Mae made her claim for separate maintenance on 31 October, in Los Angeles, when she sued Stan for $1,000 per month, plus costs, and a share of the property she contended they had accumulated together.

The property included the Laurel house, the furnishings, Laurel's boat, and $2,000 worth of motor cars. Her claim was based on their living together as man and wife, from 1919 to 1925. To strengthen her claim she alleged that she and Stan Laurel had entered a contract of common law marriage, on or about the 18th day of June 1919, in New York City.

[Mae had her years wrong here. It was June 1920 when Stan & Mae Laurel were appearing in New York].

Mae Dahlberg presents her scrapbook of early photographs, in court, in an attempt to prove she was "Mrs. Laurel."

With evidence of their touring coast-to-coast together for over fours, Mae would have had no problem in convincing the court that they had lived as man and wife. But then …

Ruth wouldn't be too happy about Mae claiming the marital home at 10353 Glenbarr Avenue, Cheviot Hills, as she was currently living there. Stan, meanwhile, had moved into an apartment at 'La Belle Tour,' on Franklin Avenue, Hollywood, after deciding he and Ruth could no longer live under the same roof – hence the $500 per month hotel room bill.

On 5 November, the tag-team did a switch, and Ruth got back into the ring to continue her fight. In court, Stan Laurel's lawyer asked the judge to compel Ruth to pay the $9,000 attorney fees out of the $20,000 Stan had already given her, and here is the reason:

Ruth Laurel had tied up Stan's boat, the *Ruth L*, with an injunction which stopped him from disposing of it, or even boarding it. This was to prevent him sinking it, setting fire to it, or giving it away – the kind of things marriage partners do in such acrimonious disputes. Coincidentally, the boat was valued at $9,000; so, if Laurel had to pay the attorney fees, the only way to raise the money would be to sell the boat.

Laurel trying to work out if his monthly payments to ex-wives are going to be greater than his earnings.

There's Going to Be a Fight

The judge had no sympathy for Laurel's priorities and, the following day, awarded Ruth Laurel $750 monthly payments, plus Stan would have to pay her $2,000 to cover outstanding household bills, and her attorneys' fees of $9,000. So now he would have to say "Goodbye" to his house, his wife, and his boat. As Stanlio says in the film *Fra Diavolo*: "Come easy – go easy."

While Stan was waiting for the next bout with Mae, Hardy next stepped into the ring to take on his wife, Myrtle. Babe had deserted Myrtle a year ago, but then taken her back in May. But now they were living apart again.

In her suit for separate maintenance, heard over 10 and 11 November, Myrtle commented that her husband, *"treated her almost as badly in real life as he did Laurel on the screen;"* and of, *"once confining her to a sanitarium against her will."* A further charge was that, *"he gambled frequently, and lost large amounts from their community property."*

Hardy himself was in court on the 17th and 18th to counter the claims. He admitted locking his wife out of their Beverly Hills home on 6 June, but said he did so because of her alleged intemperance, charging that she drank frequently. The judge found in favour of Myrtle and awarded her temporary alimony of $1,000 per month. He also ordered her husband to pay her attorneys' fees of $7,500, plus $500 court costs.

If Myrtle Hardy were looking to get $1,000 per month out of her husband, she'd be better-advised to become a bookie.
Here, Hardy is tearing up yet another losing betting slip.

Ding! Ding! Round 3. Re-enter Mae "Laurel." There was a better outcome for Stan in this battle. On 18 and 19 November he was in the same Los Angeles court as Hardy to hear the judge rule that, as he and Mae had not lived together since 1925, Mae would have to wait until the trial to learn if she was entitled to any allowance. But it wasn't looking good for Mae. She had married after breaking away from Laurel, and her association with him was not listed on the marriage license.

Laurel AND Hardy's court battles fought on into December 1936. On the 15th Myrtle was granted attorney's fees to fight her husband's appeal against the fees the court had ordered him to pay; and Laurel lost his attempt to halt the filing of an amended complaint by his wife Ruth.

On Christmas Eve, Laurel got his present early when the judge granted him an interlocutory divorce decree. He immediately wrote, in a letter to Ruth:

```
                                            24 December 1936
I don't think I could ever love again like I loved Lois.
She killed all my illusions. I tried to get over it, but I
can't. I am unhappy even after all you've done to try to
make me happy, so why chase rainbows.
Babe, meanwhile, spent Christmas Day watching horses chase
one another.
```

-----0-----

1936 December 25

BEVERLY HILLS, California to **SANTA ANITA**, California 🚗 25 miles

-----0-----

Yes, it was the opening day of the season at the Santa Anita race track. One reporter described Hardy as: *"running interference between the crowds for Jack Haley and Frank Morgan."* Other stars of the movie colony on parade in their Christmas finery included: Edmund Lowe, Ricardo Cortez, Eugene Pallette, Wallace Beery, Lee Tracey, William Frawley, Al Jolson and Ruby Keeler; plus scores of jewel-bedecked wives and escorts.

For Laurel, the New Year didn't so much as "ring in the new" as "ring to start Round 4" when, on 17 January 1938, he filed a formal answer in court denying he had ever been the husband of Mae Laurel. Mae was told, therefore, she would have to prove, in trial court, that she was Laurel's wife.

Finally came an article covering new films to be made by Laurel and Hardy, but even that was bad news:

```
Oliver Hardy and Stan Laurel have parted gain, and this
time, according to our Hollywood reporter, the split is
definite. Hardy has just signed for a solo part in the Hal
Roach produced picture "Road Show" while Laurel is said to
be going to England to make pictures.
```
(30 January 1937)

Two days after the announcement that Laurel and Hardy were going their separate ways, came that of a public appearance. But it differed somewhat from others Laurel and Hardy usually made. Firstly, it was on the radio and, secondly, Hardy did not accompany his partner Laurel.

1937 February 01 (Monday)

Scores of the brightest stars of radio, stage, and screen will be heard in a two-hour program, in behalf [*sic*] of the American Red Cross drive for funds to relieve suffering in flood-stricken areas, over NBC-WSYR, starting at 10 o'clock.

Among those participating in the program will be (from New York) Kitty Carlisle, Billy House, Jane Froman, Mary Small, and Jack Pearl: (from Hollywood) Irwin S Cobb, Will Hays, Carole Lombard, Bing Crosby, Amos 'n' Andy, Marion Talley, Stan Laurel, Bob Burns, and Lum 'n' Abner: (from Miami, Fla) Morton Downey, Ted Lewis, Wayne King, Russ Morgan, Sheila Barrett, and Harry Richman.

What kind of comic scenario Stan scripted for himself as a solo performer would be hard to predict. Stan always had to do set or scripted pieces, and use a feed. It is highly likely that he got the radio presenter to do Hardy's lines.

Coincidently, 1 February was also the day when Laurel got back together with Ruth. Yes! You read it right: "Laurel got back together with Ruth" – just thirty-nine days after their interlocutory divorce decree. Laurel's way of effecting the reconciliation was to take Ruth to New York City; which, although it is a long way, is a little short of "going to England, to make films."

-----0-----

1937 February 03 (Wednesday)
HOLLYWOOD, California to CHICAGO, Illinois 2,039 miles

The couple left Los Angeles on Wednesday 3 February. On 10 February they were reported as having stayed at the Blackstone Hotel, in Chicago. Just how old the report was, or how long they had stayed in Chicago could not be determined.

Before leaving home, Stan had told the press that he and Ruth intended to remarry. The ideal place en route would have been Las Vegas, but that option lay unexplored. Maybe Stan was postponing his decision until *the end* of the trip. Maybe he wasn't as dumb as he looked!

-----0-----

1937 February 10 (Wed)
CHICAGO, Illinois to NEW YORK, New York 788 miles

-----0-----

There's Going to Be a Fight

Blackstone Hotel, Chicago.
[It's a long distance from Atlanta, Georgia.]

The Laurels would have arrived in New York around the 11 February, where they were to stay seven or eight nights. Ruth thought they would be having a typical honeymoon, but soon found to her disappointment that Laurel was about to show her no affection whatsoever. What she didn't know at the time was that she was being used in a piece of subterfuge Stan was employing to cock-a-snook at Roach.

When she realised what the game was, she returned home on her own. But Laurel stayed on, believing that Roach would soon be begging him to return to the studios.

When this didn't happen, Laurel decided to extend his time away, and booked on a cruise ship, which would be calling at Havana, then sailing trans-Panama canal, via Cristobál and Balboa, back to Los Angeles – taking a total of twenty-one days.

-----0-----

1937 February 19 (Friday)

NEW YORK, New York to **HAVANA**, Cuba   1,309 miles

-----0-----

Also on board the liner *President Taft*, for the first leg of the voyage, were seven members of the New York Giants baseball team – bound for Cuba. The rest of the team were to fly from Miami the following day. The Giants were going to Havana to set up their Spring training camp, and play pre-season warm-up matches, the first one being against the Cuban All-Stars. When the *President Taft* docked at Cuba, on Sunday 21 February, the passengers had only a twelve-hour window in which to enjoy its sights, sounds, and people. Laurel spent part of his limited time under a blazing Cuban sun, watching the New York Giants at batting practice.

-----0-----

1937 February 21 (Sunday)

HAVANA, Cuba to **LOS ANGELES**, California   4,100 miles (est.)

-----0-----

While Laurel was on his way home from Havana, press releases revealed his real reason for going to New York – (*UP* – 3 March 1937):

Won't Sign Contract

Hollywood, Mar. 3—A reported "sit down strike" by Stan Laurel carried the threat today of a breakup of the famed team Laurel and Hardy.

Hal Roach, who produces their films admitted Laurel is staging a "holdout." Laurel's new contract is minus his signature here while the funny man remains in New York.

Roach professed to be puzzled by Laurel's actions in filing incorporation papers in Sacramento for his own company 'Stan Laurel Productions' with capitalization at $100,000, for "general amusement purposes."

Hardy is still under contract with Roach.

Ruth was already mad, after having to return from New York on her own, but when she saw the press cutting, exposing that she had been strung along by Stan on the pretext of the New York trip being a reconciliation – she was livid. Her embarrassment at the world now knowing it was nothing but a ruse to get at Hal Roach, turned to absolute rage.

Many wives in comparable situations have been known to cut up all their husband's clothes, but Ruth took it to a whole new level. She stripped their Glenbarr home bare. When Stan got back from the cruise, he found just an empty shell. His reaction, as told by Ruth to Fred Guiles, was to sit on the front terrace and weep.

The reason Laurel was refusing to sign with Roach was that, though his contract had expired, Hardy's still had two years to run. The two contracts ran *independently*, so what Laurel wanted was a contract which ran *concurrently*, and was for the team of "Laurel & Hardy" and not the two individuals. Stan also wanted far more control over every aspect of the making of their films.

Instead of going to New York when he did, Stan could have stayed nearer home and then quickly returned to the studios if Roach had decided to negotiate. But, by putting himself out of communication, Laurel was making it blatantly obvious to Roach that there were to be no negotiations, and the only thing that would get him to return to the studios was his every demand.

As the press release announcing that Laurel was in New York had been issued when Stan was actually in his twelfth day aboard the *President Taft*, one must conclude that Hal Roach was unaware Stan had extended his self-exile and put himself totally out of reach.

To further scare Roach into giving him his every demand, Laurel had drummed up some press coverage of his own. Firstly, he had let it be known that he was going to New York to find a filmmaker who would back him, via 'Stan Laurel Productions,' to the tune of $2,000,000. After leaving New York he had let it be known that:

> Stan Laurel is on the way from New York to Hollywood with plenty of money to finance the project. He plans to break from Oliver Hardy and team with various funny men.
>
> (6 March 1937)

"Plenty of money" does not exactly describe the $2 million Laurel had set out for. Thank goodness he was full of wind and peas, otherwise the number of Laurel & Hardy films in existence would be missing some classics.

o-o-0-o-o

CHAPTER 12

FIFTY-SIX DAYS AT THE RACES
(1937 pt2)

In April 1937, still smarting from the way Stan had used her as a female escort on their trip to New York, Ruth filed for divorce.

Mrs. Stan Laurel Has One Divorce, But She Wants Another

Stan Laurel was knee-deep in domestic litigation tonight, when his second divorced wife hinted she wanted to divorce him all over again. Mrs. Virginia Ruth Laurel obtained an interlocutory divorce decree last Christmas, but the score was run up again when she filed a motion to have the decree set aside.

Her husband, she complained in an affidavit, failed to "treat her with the kindness and affection" as promised when they kissed and made up on Feb. 1.

(27 April 1937)

Meanwhile, Hardy had again forsaken his wife's company for that of the horses. After being at the first race of the Santa Anita season on Christmas Day 1936, Hardy had made sure to be there for the last one, on 27 February 1937.

-----0-----

1937 February 27

BEVERLY HILLS, California to **SANTA ANITA**, California 🚗 25 miles

-----0-----

The movie crowd was again well represented with the likes of Doug Fairbanks and his wife – Lady Sylvia Ashley; Charlie Chaplin and Paulette Goddard, Mae West, Ann Sothern, Edmund Lowe, Charley Chase, George Burns and Gracie Allen; Victor McLaglen, and Joe E. Brown; plus movie directors Jesse Lasky and Todd Browning.

> One article said of Babe: "Only Oliver Hardy could wear a sea blue suit with cap to match. Hardy looks funnier off the screen than he does on."

The question is now: "Just how many of those days between the first and last race did Hardy also attend?"

From the races, it was back to the cases. On 17 February Hardy had filed an appeal against the separate maintenance Myrtle had been awarded in December. Then, during the fourth week in April, he filed a sealed divorce complaint to supersede the separate maintenance suit – charging "mental cruelty." On 18 May, Hardy was back in court to hear the judge grant him an interlocutory divorce decree. But it was a bitter-sweet victory. Babe did love Myrtle, but just couldn't live with her alcoholism, and left the court in tears.

May brought promising news for Hardy on the film front. Roach was making a genuine effort to launch him as a solo actor, now that Laurel was literally out of the picture. Since the idea of starring him in "*Road Show*," back in January, Roach had had writers building up Hardy's allocated role of the blustering Southerner, Colonel Carraway. Roach had also brought in a totally unknown actor to be the leading man – one Vincent Price, an actor who was yet more than a decade and a half away from finding his niche as a master of horror. Patsy Kelly and Lyda Roberti were earmarked as the two leading ladies.

Alas, "*Road Show*" failed to hit the road until 1941, with Patsy Kelly retaining her role, but Adolphe Menjou taking over Hardy's part. Perhaps it was a blessing that Hardy didn't try to relaunch his career with this film, for reviews would suggest that, as a "Road Show," it should have been run out of town.

With Hardy's film career still in abeyance, there was one activity bound to keep him happy – his beloved horse racing. On 3 July 1937 came one of the biggest events not just in Hardy's life, but in California horse-racing history, when the brand new Del Mar Racetrack and Turf Club opened its gates.

-----0-----

1937 July 03

BEVERLY HILLS, California to **DEL MAR**, California 🚂 110 miles

-----0-----

Del Mar is in Southern California. For Hollywoodians it's a one hundred and ten mile ride south, pulling up twenty miles short of San Diego, and just a furlong from the sea.

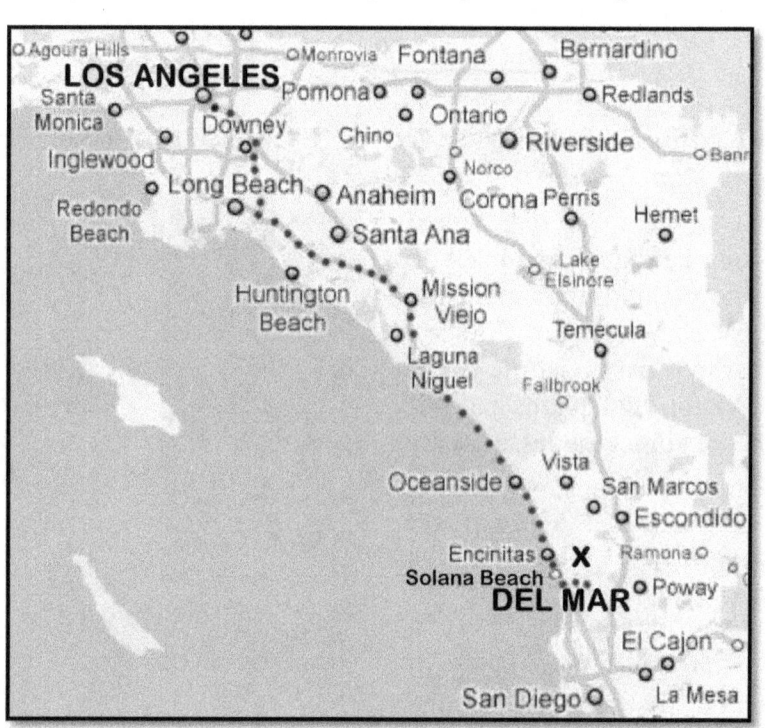

LOS ANGELES to DEL MAR

One report said of the event:

> Hollywood took the day off and moved to Del Mar for the opening day's races of the Del Mar Turf Club.
>
> Scores of co-workers and golf-playing friends of the club's crooning president, Bing Crosby, were seen in the crowd. They included Claudette Colbert, Bob Burns, George Burns and Gracie Allen, Shirley Ross, Gary Cooper, Martha Raye, Gail Patrick, Fred Astaire, Pat O'Brien, and Bert Wheeler.
>
> Between races the clubhouse took on the aspects of a comedians' convention, with such well-known wits in evidence as Joe Penner, Parkyakarkus, Charles Butterworth, Tom Kennedy, and Oliver Hardy.

(*AP* – 3 July 1937)

| Hardy and Crosby making the recording at the pre-opening party on the Thursday. | And here broadcasting 'live' on what would become a regular slot for Crosby on race days |

The opening day was Friday 3 July, with the season about to go on until 5 September. On the eve of the event, Bing Crosby performed the opening ceremony, which was recorded for broadcasting in a thirty-minute insert to go out on *Kraft Music Hall* for WJZ-NBC on the Friday.

With the ceremony over, and the microphones packed away, Crosby hosted a grand party for his Hollywood pals, which lasted until the blue of the night met the gold of the day!

[The Del Mar Turf Club had been set up in May 1936, with a board consisting of Bing Crosby (President); Bob Crosby (Vice President) ; Pat O'Brien and Oliver Hardy as officers, and other prominent stars on the executive committee.]

Crosby spared no efforts to attract Hollywood stars, even to the point of handing out personal invites during visits to different film lots. Thus Del Mar became what was termed "Playground of the Stars," with celebrities filling all the hotels, bars, restaurants, and beaches previously filled by regular holidaymakers and locals. And, inside the racecourse grounds, he had an ornate Clubhouse built, with lavish interior decoration and furnishings.

Opening day was as extravagant an event as a film premiere. Crosby, himself, unlocked the gates, and welcomed the first horde of spectators. For this opening, and all subsequent race meetings, special trains were run, to carry the celebrities. The Press, too, were well catered for, and put up at the Del Mar Hotel.

Bing's parties in the Clubhouse ran through the night, and became legendary, thanks to many of the big stars giving impromptu acts, and making "Playground of the Stars" a well-chosen name.

| Babe gives that burned-up look to camera … | … then tears up his losing ticket in disgust. |

News-reel footage of the opening day's events also reveals Robert Taylor and Barbara Stanwyck, and Una Merkel to be in attendance. [**FILM**]

-----0-----

1938 July (date not known)

BEVERLY HILLS, California to **DEL MAR**, California 110 miles

-----0-----

The months were rolling on, with Roach and Laurel still at an impasse. The way Laurel viewed the changing situation is revealed in two contemporary letters:

```
Dear Ruth,                                    Jun. 30th. '37
   I am perfectly aware of all that's going on and am not a
bit worried of the outcome. I will win out. It is tough
sledding now but it won't be long. If Roach wants me, he
will pay my price, if not, that's that. I have waited long
enough and intend to go to work elsewhere, so you will soon
be receiving your five percent.
   Take care of yourself and have a good time.
                                              Stan
```

One month later, Laurel's confidence in getting Roach to pay his price had totally evaporated, and he had resigned himself to breaking all ties with Roach.

```
   Miss Ethel [Stanley],                      Jul. 26th. '37
I haven't worked since "Way Out West" picture (8 months) -
having contract trouble at the Studios - Roach deciding to
split up the team & keep Hardy. So it looks like I start
out all over again from scratch - It will be tough going
but I think I'll make it again alright.
                                              Stan
```

August became September, and September became October. With "*Road Show*" now side-lined, Hardy was still looking for a suitable role. Golfing and racing buddy Bing Crosby tried to help out, by offering Babe the part of the policeman in "*The Badge of Policeman O'Roon*" – originally paged for Victor McClaglen. Hardy turned down the part, which then went to another good friend of Babe's – Andy Devine. Hardy had good cause to let the part go – he was about to get back with Stan Laurel.

On 9 October Hal Roach announced that Stan Laurel and Oliver Hardy had teamed up again, under a two-year contract, calling for two feature films per year. The terms of the new contract were aired by *Boxoffice* – 23 October 1937:

> With its organizational papers having been received from Sacramento, officers of the 'Stan Laurel Corp.' have disclosed that the contract recently signed by Laurel with Hal Roach was with the corporation, and not with Laurel personally – thought to be the first such arrangement ever negotiated in the picture colony.

> The corporation is a production unit which is not bound exclusively by the Roach contract and can make any number of pictures outside, starring Laurel, if it so desires. Laurel is president, L.A French vice-president, and Vincent A. Marco legal counsellor. Erman Pessis is publicity director.

> At the same time Roach officials announced that the budget on "*Swiss Miss*," first feature-length Laurel-Hardy comedy to be made under the new contract, has been set at $700.000 – much higher than on the comedy team's previous pictures.

> John Blystone has been signed to direct, and shooting scheduled to start Oct. 25.

You would have thought that Oliver Hardy, not having been in front of a camera for eleven months, would have run all the way to the studios to get started on the film about to go into production. But, no! He was too busy enjoying his enforced one-year sabbatical, and was miles away – watching horse racing.

Fifty-Six Days at the Races

-----0-----

1937 October 18 (*circa*)

        BEVERLY HILLS, California to **SAN MATEO**, California   376 miles

-----0-----

San Mateo is in northern California, just nineteen miles before one reaches San Francisco. Babe booked into the Hotel Benjamin Franklin, in time to watch the second week's racing of the fall season at Bay Meadows, which began on Tuesday 19 October. Hardy told a *San Mateo Times* reporter: "*I don't bet much on the horses. I just like to watch them.*" As the old challenge goes: "Tell that to the judge!" His ex-wife Myrtle would certainly have challenged his claim.

Babe went on to inform the reporter that one of the two horses he owned, 'Tedsim,' had run the previous day, and the other, 'Mannie,' was running the following day (22 October). 'Mannie' went on to do very well. In an extremely close run race, he came within a nose of not being last!

Hardy's buddy Bing Crosby did rather better when his horse 'High Strike' won Tuesday's 'Alameda Handicap.' Crosby's horse though had an unfair advantage over Hardy's horses – it had four legs.

-----0-----

1937 October 24 (*circa*)

        SAN MATEO, California to **BEVERLY HILLS**, California   376 miles

-----0-----

The Laurel & Hardy film "*Swiss Miss*" remained in production all through November, with the original shooting date having been rescheduled for 13 December. But, just before then, there was some old business to attend to.

On 6 December "Stan Laurel vs Mae Laurel" was brought to trial, but then immediately dismissed when the attorneys explained that a settlement had been effected out of court.

A statement was read out which confirmed Stan's previous one, which was that Mae Laurel had never been his legal wife.

Stan did of course feel sorry for Mae. At an earlier hearing he had told a court reporter: "*It was just one of those things. She told me she had been deserted by her husband, and was struggling to support herself and a child.*" The settlement Stan made was therefore more by way of assisting Mae, than of buying his way out of a case he thought he might lose.

While Laurel was in court, Hardy was holding court with Henry McLemore – racing correspondent and sports writer for United Press. At the Hardy home, Babe confessed to McLemore:

> A man's troubles do not begin until he becomes a race horse owner. If worrying made me thin, I wouldn't weigh a pound over fifty.
>
> A horse is worse than a baby for getting things wrong with him. The first time Mannie ran, his feet got all tangled up, and he cut one of them. The next time out he ran last, and the trainer said he couldn't have missed winning if I hadn't fed him so much sugar. He was last the next two times, too, but the trainer said I shouldn't be discouraged, as it was obvious that these two efforts were just what Mannie needed to get him in shape.

When McLemore asked if Hardy found operating a stable an expensive business, he replied:

> Yes, even a comparatively small one such as mine. As well as oats, hay and grass, Mannie eats everything, apparently—lettuce, tomatoes, carrots, spinach, onions, potatoes, radishes, and chicken à la king!
>
> And keeping him in proper clothes costs plenty too. He has to have a blanket to wear out to the track, a blanket to cool off in, and a blanket to wear after he's been cooled off. Then there are saddles, bridles, stirrups, whips, combs and brushes.
>
> But I still believe that some day Mannie will show his gratitude for all the fine things I've done for him, and win a race.

Hardy with friend and fellow-actor Andy Devine, pointing the way towards the knacker's yard.

Hardy comments show how little he was aware of his total expenditure. Just paying for stables and staff wages is a huge, continuous expense – far in excess of the cost of food, and one-off items like blankets.

If he wished to keep his stables, his rate of filmmaking would have to increase somewhat. One would have thought, therefore, that Hardy would have been quick to make filmmaking his priority; but, when the cameras did finally start rolling on "Swiss Miss" on 13 December, he was miles away playing the horses – AGAIN!

-----0-----

1937 December 13 (*circa*) Monday
BEVERLY HILLS, California to **TANFORAN**, California 🚗 374 miles

-----0-----

Tanforan Race Track was situated in San Bruno, south of San Francisco. The week's racing was Tuesday to Saturday (14-18 December). It can't be confirmed that Hardy was there for all five days, but it's a heck of a long way to drive for just a one-day visit!

Here at Tanforan, Babe again met up again with racing correspondent Henry McLemore, who later revealed to his readers that Hardy had backed a 51-1 outsider named 'Quick Look' and bagged himself a $500 payout.

SPOT THE JOCKEY
Hardy is the owner – Ralph Reeves is the jockey. Going off the results, some believed it was the other way around.
(from the Jack Scagnetti "Laurel & Hardy Scrapbook")

Fifty-Six Days at the Races

It comes to something when Hardy has to let the world know when he has a winner. What he didn't reveal was that if he had won $40,000 he might be close to getting back all the money he had bet over the years. Add to that the thousands of dollars Hardy had spent buying his own stable of horses, and you qualify to ask whether Hardy should be celebrating a $500 win at all.

It was at this exact moment that the realisation of all the money he had poured into his horses finally struck home with Babe. Deciding that enough was enough, he sent off the following telegram:

```
Wire: Dec 16, 1937
JULIUS REEDER=SECRETARY TANFORAN=SAN BRUNO CALIFORNIA=
WILL YOU PLEASE INSTRUCT SAM HOSKINS MY TRAINER TO DELIVER
HORSE AND ALL TACK TO MANNIE KELLER AS I AM DISPOSING OF
SAME AND WITHDRAWING FROM FURTHER RACING … OLIVER HARDY
CALIFORNIA …
```

-----0-----

1937 December 16 (*circa*) Wednesday
    TANFORAN, California to **BEVERLY HILLS**, California to 🚗 374 miles

-----0-----

Just over one week later, and Hardy was off again.

-----0-----

1937 December 25 (Saturday)
    BEVERLY HILLS, California to **SANTA ANITA**, California 🚗 25 miles

-----0-----

Hardy may have issued intent to cease being a race-horse owner, but he never said anything about ceasing to become a spectator – or gambler.

Hardy reading "Horse Racing Form."
What he should have been reading was "Horse Retirement Farm."

Babe's best pal, Guy Kibbee, behaved like one of Hardy's horses at the races. He just stopped everything – and ate!

Also present at this, now obligatory, first race of the season at the Arcadia Track were: Alice Faye, Carole Lombard, Gail Patrick, Claudette Colbert, Robert Montgomery, Jeanette MacDonald, Don Ameche, Bette Davis, Al Jolson and Ruby Keeler, Richard Arlen, and Warner Baxter; plus a host of film directors and producers. Some of the motion picture stars in attendance were also stable owners. These included: Joe E. Brown, Raoul Walsh, Bing Crosby, AND Oliver Hardy – who hadn't yet sold off his stable of horses.

Newsreel footage further reveals Virginia Bruce, Adolph Menjou, Mr. & Mrs. Spencer Tracy, and Guy Kibbee, to be present. [**FILM**]

Crosby's horse 'High Strike' went on to win again – Hardy's horse 'Mannie' didn't! At least Hardy didn't have two losers this time around, but only because he had sold his horse 'Tedsim.' Maybe some removal men had bought it, to pull their cart!

With Christmas Day falling on the Saturday, and no racing at Santa Anita on Sundays or Mondays, Oliver Hardy may possibly have reported to the Roach studios on those two days; but then, on the Tuesday, he was off again to visit his substitute family at the track.

-----0-----

1937 December 28 (Tuesday)
>BEVERLY HILLS, California to **SANTA ANITA**, California 25 miles

-----0-----

The other birds of a feather flocking there were: W.C. Fields, Edward G. Robinson, George Raft, Spencer Tracy, and the ever-present Bing Crosby.

With just three days of December remaining, Hal Roach might well have been screaming, "NOW can we start filming?" Well, sorry to say, but "No!" It was now Laurel's turn to go to the place he was spending a lot of his free time – court.

Laurel was actually getting ready to celebrate one huge imminent event, but first there was one huge obstacle to be removed before he could go ahead. The judge did that for him when, on the day of New Year's Eve, he granted Stan a final divorce decree from Ruth. Although she had previously filed an affidavit seeking to prevent issuance of the decree, she finally gave up all thoughts of a peaceful reconciliation with Stan. And who could blame her!

So 1937 came to a close, with not a single Laurel & Hardy film having been made. At least it had ended with peace and harmony restored, and all battles with wives past or present seemingly resolved. So 1938 was promising to be a good year. But then, before the clock struck midnight on 31 December, Laurel did something that would make the next twelve months the most traumatic in the lives of not only himself, but also Hal Roach, and Oliver Hardy. Many others around him would also feel the effects of the fallout.

o-o-0-o-o

CHAPTER 13
HELLO VERA
(1938 pt1)

On 31 December 1937, before the ink was even dry on his divorce papers, Laurel announced that he was about to fly immediately to Yuma to get married again – not to Ruth, but to a completely new woman in his life. Laurel's latest love interest was a statuesque, buxom Russian named Vera Ivanova Shuvalova. Her family background was as a member of the Georgian Shuvalovas, compatriots of famed Georgian Family Mdivani, if we are to believe her account.

Laurel had set his eyes upon her just five weeks earlier, when she attended an audition at the Roach Studios for the female lead in *"Swiss Miss."* She was turned down for the part, which Della Lind eventually secured, but Stan was captivated by her looks and wanted to see more of her.

Prior to coming to Hollywood, Ms. Shuvalova had been earning a living singing in the Biltmore Hotel and the Versailles Café, in New York, under the name of "Illiana" – a name she will be referred to by, from now on in. Here in California she had found work singing in the 'Balalaika,' a Russian nightclub in Hollywood, where Laurel began showing up to date her. She was around twenty-eight, Stan was forty-seven. All the signs were there, but Laurel couldn't see them.

-----0-----

1938 January 01

HOLLYWOOD, California to **YUMA**, Arizona 282

-----0-----

True to his impulse, although swapping the plane for a train, Laurel whisked Illiana off in the very early hours of New Year's Day morning, to Yuma, Arizona, just a few miles east of the California-Mexico border. The wedding venue was Del Ming Hotel, in a district known as 'Eden of Hollywood' – a common choice for Hollywood stars wanting to get married quickly, and with little publicity.

Accompanying the bride and groom were two witnesses, later identified as Roy Randolph – occupation given as "dance director;" and Illiana's friend, Sonia Belikovich, who claimed to hold the title of "Countess."

A local journalist reported on the ceremony:

> *First wedding of 1938 was that of Stan Laurel, comedian, and Illiana, singer. Justice of the Peace Ed. M. Winn married them at 5a.m. Saturday [1 January]. Laurel had only received his final divorce decree from Virginia Ruth Rogers Laurel on Friday.*
>
> *Mrs. Virginia Ruth Rogers Laurel, who contended the divorce decree Laurel obtained in Los Angeles last week was invalid, because they had lived together as man and wife between the time of filing of the suit and the final decree, came to Yuma from Phoenix when she heard of the comedian's intention to marry for the third time, but arrived too late to halt the wedding.*
>
> *While the short ceremony was being performed, Mrs. Ruth Laurel telephoned police and said her husband, if he married, would be a bigamist. Mr. Justice Winn informed her that he had proof the California courts had stated the divorce final, he said, and she became infuriated.*

In the hours between the wedding ceremony and their catching the return train, Stan and Illiana retired to the Del Sol Hotel. At 8.30am, Ruth, having missed Stan at the wedding venue, also booked herself in at Del Sol, and informed the manager that she had come to consult her husband. Her consultation consisted of banging on the door of the bridal suite, ranting: "Bigamist!"

But Ruth's tirade didn't end there. When the newly-weds left the hotel to go and catch their return train, she trailed them to the railway station and continued her verbal assault:

> They [Stan and Illiana] came by train and left for Los Angeles on the 10.50a.m. train. In order to prevent a scene at the railroad station, police advised Laurel and his second wife to hide on the wrong side of the train and board the train through the baggage car.
>
> The first Mrs. Laurel [Ruth] stood by, indignantly protesting the marriage, police reported.
>
> (*Yuma Daily Sun* – 3 January 1938) [Abridged]

The "new" Laurels must have heaved a sigh of relief as the train pulled out, leaving Ruth behind, and praised the heavens they hadn't booked their honeymoon in Yuma.

-----0-----

1938 January 01

YUMA, Arizona to **HOLLYWOOD**, California 282 miles

-----0-----

As it happened, the honeymoon would have to wait as, on Monday 3 January, Stan reported in at the Roach studios. Maybe "Swiss Miss" was about to start filming! But wait! Where's Hardy? He wasn't back at the Santa Anita race track was he? No! That's closed on Sundays and Mondays. But Babe had found a race track where the Sunday restrictions didn't apply – in Mexico.

-----0-----

1938 January 02 (Sunday)

BEVERLY HILLS, California to **AGUA CALIENTE**, Mexico 138 miles

-----0-----

> The $3,000,000 Agua Caliente Turf Club will become the mecca for the elite of Hollywood's movie colony Sunday, when the winter race meeting is inaugurated here.
>
> Included in reservations for boxes were those of: Al Jolson and Ruby Keeler, Bing Crosby and party, Oliver Hardy, Chico and Zeppo Marx; Harry Cohn, who will be accompanied by many of the Columbia Picture Studio stars; and many others. Special Santa Fe trains will bring hundreds of fans from Hollywood and Los Angeles.
>
> (*UP* – 31 December 1937)

-----0-----

1938 January 02 (Sunday)

AGUA CALIENTE, Mexico to **LOS ANGELES**, California 138 miles

-----0-----

With both comedy stars back at the Roach Studios for 3 January, the way was now clear for uninterrupted filming of "*Swiss Miss*" – or was it? Even though Stan had divorced Ruth, she was proving harder to lose than chewing-gum on the sole of his shoe. Since Stan had tied the knot with Illiana, Ruth had been doing everything she could to untie it, as the following newspaper cutting will explain:

> Stan Laurel met a new crisis in his love life today [11 January], by asking superior court for an injunction to keep his second wife away from his apartment, where he is having a honeymoon with his third wife.
>
> Wife No.2, who refuses to give him up and has been pestering him for months [*They've been married for only ten days.] has resorted to ringing his telephone and

pounding on his door in the middle of the night, he charged. The landlord at the apartment house has also been disturbed by the commotion.

Besides, Mrs. Virginia Ruth Laurel has been threatening him with unfavourable publicity, and has generally obstructed his movie work. By her conduct, he said, she has violated their property settlement and has forfeited her right to the five per cent of his earnings that the court told him to pay her. Otherwise, the comedian and his Russian bride informed the world, they are supremely happy in their new found romance.

(UP – 12 January 1938)

It may seem as though Ruth was the woman scorned here, and was venting her fury because another woman had taken her man. Time would soon reveal, however, that Ruth was actually trying to protect Stan, as she had seen in Illiana something which others had not yet picked up on. Meanwhile, Stan felt that she was all sweetness and light:

```
                                              Jan. 13th. '38
My Dearest Vera,
Here are the pictures I took - Didn't they turn out good! I
think you will like the house Dear and am sure you will be
very comfortable there. We start to move in on Sunday.
Sonya called me a couple of times last night. She is
working today at the Studio. I may have to work this
afternoon and again on Friday. I hope you are having a good
rest Dear and enjoying yourself with Bobby. I went to bed
right after I talked to you last night and had a swell
sleep - didn't wake up till 8:30 this a.m.
I do miss you my Baby and am eager to see you again. It
won't be long now so don't get lonely Darling - have a real
good time and be happy like I want you to be. I will call
you this evening, Dear, as soon as I get back home. Bye bye
my Sweetheart. I love you more and more each day and am
thinking of you always and now that I have Julius to drive
I don't have to worry about red lights or what road I have
to take!!
    Fondest Love, Ever My Vera.
        Your affectionate Husband,
```

Stan

[N.B. "Bobby" is Illiana's eight-year-old son.]

[Note that Stan addresses his wife by her real name of Vera, whilst most journalists and biographers refer to her as "Illiana." When writing her stage-name, Laurel would spell it "Illeana," in order to emphasise that the second 'i' was pronounced as an "e" (as in "illegal") and not like the second "i" in "illicit." Subsequently, others picked up on the misspelling.]

The letter should have contained a "P.S." saying: "*By the way, I can't stand your singing voice, so please don't ever sing in the house while I'm at home,*" as this is one of the actual rules Stan imposed on Illiana.

Stan was still in temporary residence at La Belle Tour Apartments, on Franklin Avenue, Hollywood; but, since marrying Illiana, had purchased a property at 20213 Strathern Street, Canoga Park, in the San Fernando Valley. The property came with some land, but the only accommodation was a tiny stone cottage – hence Laurel's reserved comment in the letter to Illiana that she would be "comfortable." Stan had grand plans to build a new house on the site, plus other out-buildings – but first he would need to earn some money.

Note, too, the references in the letter to Stan now having a driver. The full implications of just why would soon emerge.

The letter also reveals that working hours at the Roach Studios weren't exactly "every morning at daybreak, till light's gone in the evening," but were a far more casual "come when you are called upon" arrangement. Analysing the letter we see that on Thursday 13 January Laurel "may have to work" in the afternoon; on Friday he again "may have to work," and on Sunday he was about to move into his house.

"Ebony and Ivory – living in perfect harmony." But not for long!

Nor would there be any filming of the two Laurel & Hardy characters on the Monday as, on that day, Hardy was once more at the Santa Anita race track.

1938 January 17 (Monday) BEVERLY HILLS, California to **SANTA ANITA**, California 25 miles

There was no racing at Santa Anita on Mondays, but then Hardy wasn't going there to watch some horses win – he was going there to win some horses. At this mammoth horse auction, at which forty-three thoroughbreds were sold, Hardy purchased 'Marv,' 'Miss Chase,' and 'Rare Ben,' for a combined total of $3,100. So much for the telegram he had sent just twenty-eight days ago, telling his trainer to dispose of his horses, as he was withdrawing from racing.

Weight of evidence would suggest that Babe had been a regular visitor at the Santa Anita races, since the season started on Christmas Day. On 9 January one newspaper commented:

> Oliver Hardy, the only cap wearer at the track—except the jockeys, is another regular. As guest handicapper for a newspaper, he picked two winners had had 10 in the money [sic]... he isn't always so lucky.

The article goes on at length, to comment on the betting habits of the Hollywood regulars, but contained one surprise entry: "*Stan Laurel is the long-shot addict.*"

Laurel isn't known for betting on the horses, but the term "addict" would suggest it was a regular vice. Hardy picked up on this and, in the comedy by-play between him and Bing Crosby in footage shot at Del Mar race track, Babe delivers the line: "*You're dealing with 'longshot' Hardy.*" (31 July 1937) [**FILM**]

The article covering the Santa Anita auction (18 January 1938) further revealed:

> 'Marv,' a horse who not more than a year ago was beating $5,000 horses, was bid-in by Oliver Hardy for $700. An hour afterward he was offered $1,500—and refused it.
>
> Some horsemen friends, however, thought that Hardy played a sucker role when he bid in a selling plater named 'Rare Ben' for £1,700, when the same horse only a month ago at Tanforan was running in $1,200 claiming races.
>
> "Maybe I was a sucker," Hardy admits, but I owe the hoss [sic] a couple of free eats, for I had $500 on his nose that day last week, when he came home in front and paid 35 to 1."

"Longshot" Hardy collects his winnings from "Bookie" Bing ...

... then blocks Crosby's shot to camera.

'Rare Ben' ran at Santa Anita on 31 December, and the 6 and 13 January. One must presume Hardy was at the race track on all three days to watch it run, and to place bets – making yet more days when he wasn't filming. Before you offer that Hardy could have placed his bets by phone, read this paragraph from the same article:

> Hollywood has to go to the track now to do its betting. The district attorney clamped down on the bookies just before the current season opened. In previous years, studio's switchboards were swamped with calls to the bookies. One studio clocked 186 'race' phone calls from one set, in one day, last year.

As the new owner, Babe would also have done his best to watch 'Marv' run on the 18th and 'Rare Ben' run on the 22nd, when it again came in second – although his attendance could not be confirmed at either. The bigger question is: "Just how many days in December and January were the two film comedians on set at the Roach studios?" These two seemed to work fewer days per annum than Santa Claus.

As for Laurel, even when he *was* filming, his head must have been full of the domestic strife happening with his new bride, plus the chore of firstly house-hunting and then moving house. There was also the trauma of having to cover every legal technicality so that he didn't lose out in any forthcoming court cases with both Ruth *and* Illiana.

Ruth was actually back in court on 25 January. She was trying to have the final decree set aside – claiming that, in the year elapsing between the interlocutory decree and the final divorce decree, she and Mr. Laurel were reconciled. As evidence, she produced in court letters written to her by Stan between June and August 1937, which were then read out in court:

At the hearing held 12 February, the court found against Ruth Laurel by validating the final divorce decree issued on 31 December 1937, meaning that she *was* legally divorced from Stan, and that his marriage to Illiana was valid. With that weight off his mind, Laurel was able to concentrate on finishing the film "*Swiss Miss*," which wrapped just before the end of February.

Just to make doubly-doubly sure that their marriage was legal, on 28 February 1938 Stan and Illiana had another ceremony performed, this time a civil one performed by a town clerk. For the honeymoon, Stan took Illiana to Catalina Island. He had the services of a boat, but it wasn't the *Ruth L*, it was one that he chartered. You may feel that Laurel was being sensitive and caring towards Illiana, in not taking her on a boat which held so many memories of his former wife, Ruth. But get this: Stan's big surprise for this honeymoon cruise was that his first wife, Lois, was actually on the boat and GOING WITH THEM. You couldn't make this up!

Having totally messed up the honeymoon arrangements, and caused Illiana to split, Laurel tried to win back favour with her, by entering her seedy world. Firstly he tracked her down at the Café Lamaze, where she was having a night out with friends, and wheedled his way into the party. Ten days later he went with her to a Masquerade Party at the Balalaika Café. This was not a world he should have been in.

> In the words of the Chaplin song:
> *Smile though your heart is aching.*
> *Smile, even though it's breaking.*

It was Hardy's turn next to sort out his marital problems. On 15 March 1938 he attended court to try to get his alimony payments to Myrtle reduced. She was looking for twenty-five per cent of his average monthly income. The following day, Hardy attended court again, but discovered his wife had been taken to hospital.

Maybe it was the shock of having discovered that her husband had just spent a fortune having a new swimming pool built. It would be hard to take twenty-five per cent of that.

While Hardy was battling Myrtle in court, Laurel still was trying to make it up to Illiana for the disastrous honeymoon trip he had organised on board the boat. This time, to ensure Lois didn't pop up, or Ruth didn't come banging on their door, they travelled miles away from L.A. – although not far enough away for Illiana's liking.

In order to appease Illiana, Stan had told her that when the court case was over he would take her to Russia and they would honeymoon on "the Russian river." True to his promise, Stan stuck her in the car and drove her to – SAN FRANCISCO!

-----0-----

1938 March 24 (*circa*)
        CANOGA PARK, California to **SAN FRANCISCO**, California   382 miles

-----0-----

While the Laurels were away, word hit the papers that Laurel and Hardy were planning to make personal appearances:

> On Stan Laurel and Oliver Hardy will trek to Mexico City some time in April, for three weeks of personal appearances.
>
> Contracts have been signed, with dates left open until after completion of editing on Hal Roach's "Swiss Miss," their newest picture.
>
>   (*Variety* – 23 March 1938)

The same day came a similar report, in Harrison's Carroll's 'Hollywood' column, but with one very dramatic difference:

> Columns ago, I told you not to be surprised if Stan Laurel and Illiana do a personal appearance tour together. Well, the deal is now to the contract stage, though nothing is signed as yet. The tour they are discussing would be in this country.
>
>   (*King Features Syndicate* – 23 March 1938)

So! was this tour for the Laurels only, or was Hardy included? The answer came a week later.

> Are Stan Laurel and Oliver Hardy fighting over the script for their personal appearance tour because of the big part Laurel wanted to give Illiana? So the story goes anyway. The odd part of it is, George Jessel also would like to sign Illiana for his personal appearance act.
>
>   (*King Features Syndicate* – 31 March 1938)

Hardy must have been praying Jessel would take Illiana. Having just divested himself of his own uncontrollable wife, he sure as heck didn't want to a have Laurel's troublesome wife in tow.

On the day this report came out, the Laurels were on their way back to Los Angeles when, between Paso Robles and King City, California, their car ran off the road and into a ditch. Thankfully, they were able to continue, with Stan suffering only bruising. You can bet your bottom dollar the accident occurred because the two of them were arguing, and the reason why didn't take much finding.

That San Francisco had been chosen as their holiday destination had little to do with having a holiday. Having been such a phenomenal draw back in 1929, when Laurel and Hardy played a week at the Fox theatre, Stan thought he could rely upon the San Franciscans to come out in their numbers to support this latest, proposed, personal appearance. However, Illiana changed the agenda, and negotiated an offer to appear in a San Francisco supper club as a solo act. He should have let her. That way he may well have won back his comedy partner.

-----0-----

1938 March 31 (*circa*)
        SAN FRANCISCO, California to **CANOGA PARK**, California   382 miles

-----0-----

Hello Vera

In January it was all hugs and kisses.
In March, it was all tiffs and tantrums.

The rift between Stan and Illiana remained for weeks after their return from San Francisco. During the second week in April, Stan was reported as being a lonesome figure on a night out:

Stan Laurel, a sartorial symphony in light blue tweed sport coat, with darker blue trousers, at a night spot – between matrimonial battles with Illiana.

What is disturbing about this comment is it showed that the Laurel's domestic battles were already public knowledge in Hollywood. Soon, the world would know!

But battling with wife No.3 was only part of Laurel's war: — [(*UP* – 12 April 1938)

Stan Laurel, who has had so many wife troubles that he regards King Solomon as a happy-go-lucky playboy, told today Tuesday [12 April] how the laws of Hollywood economics permit a man to be broke while earning $160,000 a year.

He was whistled into court on orders of wife No.1, who demanded a $1,355 check [cheque] each and every month. His present wife, who recently threatened to leave Laurel but changed her mind, accompanied him to court. She squeezed his hand frequently to show him he had her moral support. But his voice was mournful, and his face long when he finally climbed into the witness-box to tell how a movie star can be down-at-heel on a salary that would take a Keokuk tourist 160 times around the world.

Income tax, federal and state, has taken a big bite out of his earnings. Agent fees, clothes, automobiles, insurance bills, haberdashery, household expenses and other incidentals will take care of the rest, leaving nothing with which to pay wife No.1 the amount she asks, he explained.

Anyone in court on 13 April, for the second day of "Stan Laurel v Lois Nelson," must have thought they were attending rehearsals of Stan's next comedy film. In court were his first wife, Lois, who was suing him for child maintenance, and his second wife, Ruth, who had already sued him for maintenance. His third wife, Illiana, would have been there, except that she was in hospital after running her car into a tree!

Continuing with the theme of why, when his salary was double that of President Roosevelt's, his outgoings were even greater, Laurel explained that the main trouble was he not only had to give his wives alimony, but also had to pay their income taxes – and added:

All I have left out of the thousands I have earned is the income from an endowment that pays me $217 a month. My wives can sue all they want, but they can't touch that. I can always live like a king in Tahiti on it.

(*UP* – 13 April 1938)

He then told the judge that he expected to be "broker than ever," as soon as he collects the rest of the $160,000 his studio has contracted to pay him this year. *"I am not only insolvent now, you honor,"* he said, *"but I will end the year with a deficit."*

On 15 April, Lois lost her claim. The judge ruled that she had quite enough to support her, as a result of a settlement made five years ago. The property was worth an estimated $274,000, which was ten times more than her former husband's current bank balance. The judge then criticised Laurel for throwing a good deal of his money away, and letting too many people chisel him.

With Lois removed from the scene it is now time to catch up with Illiana who, last we heard, had used a tree as an emergency braking-system.

> Illiana, Russian singer, and present wife of Stan Laurel, movie comedian, was in hospital today following a hectic escapade with police.
>
> According to police records, she led officers a merry chase in her husband's roadster automobile through the streets of Hollywood. She struck two parked cars on Beverly Drive, then continued to within a block of her home, where she crashed into a tree.
>
> Taken to the Hollywood jail, she was booked on suspicion of drunken driving, and held there until Laurel arrived and posted $500 bail for her. He then took her to the hospital where she was treated for bruises and a cracked rib.
>
> (*INS* – 13 April 1938)

Illiana is the accident victim, but it's Stan who is feeling the pain.

It was only now, just three and a half months into Stan and Illiana's marriage, when news of the fiery existence led by Stan and Illiana started to come out. One article revealed:

> Maybe Laurel's marital adventures have kept police squad cars, process servers, and even ambulances buzzing around his house at intervals.
>
> Last month, wife No.3, Mrs Vera Shuvalova Laurel fled from his home, to a hospital. Later they kissed and made up. Her smash-up last night made her husband's financial future no brighter. The worried Stan bailed her out, took her to the hospital in an ambulance, and said he tried in vain to keep her from behind the steering wheel. She was arrested in Beverly Hills, and held in $500 bail on hit-and-run misdemeanour charges.
>
> (*UP* – 13 April 1938)

By now you are getting an idea of Illiana's dark side. If not – read on!

o-o-0-o-o

CHAPTER 14

THREE'S A CROWD

(1938 pt2)

Stan had hoped to earn a few thousand dollars by making personal appearances with Babe in Mexico City, and/or appearances with Illiana, but the on-going court cases, for both men, had put paid to that.

> The reason why Stan Laurel and Illiana haven't started on a personal appearance tour is that he had to make a court appearance to answer the suit of a former wife. Oliver Hardy also goes to court that day.
>
> "Isn't that's cute that the both of them have to go?" says Illiana.
>
> (*Evening Independent*, Massillon, Ohio – 13 April 1938)

On the up side, the court cases prevented what would undoubtedly have been an unmitigated disaster if Illiana had gone along on any tour. So you would have thought that Stan's priority now was to ditch her, and concentrate on getting in some money by making films.

The latter was achieved when, after retakes had been shot during the fourth week in April, "*Swiss Miss*" was completed. But then Laurel's next move was staggering! Instead of pushing Illiana away, he attempted to bring her closer – by MARRYING HER – AGAIN!!

This THIRD ceremony took place on Monday 26 April 1938 – a day that is traditionally part of the weekend when Russians celebrate Easter. The theme was continued with a Russian-style ceremony, conducted by a Father of the Russian Orthodox Church. It seems rather ironic that the one word you could not apply to Laurel's marriages to Illiana was "orthodox."

[Three different newspapers state that the wedding ceremony was performed at the Laurels' home, while one modern-day source claims it was at 455 Beverwell Drive, Beverly Hills.]

After the ceremony Stan is reported to have said: "We'll do it again, when we get around to it. It's one way of throwing a party."

So what of their honeymoon destination? Well on 22 April, when both attended the Los Angeles License Bureau, Stan had told one attentive reporter:

> *We'll combine our honeymoon with the personal appearance tour I'm making with Oliver Hardy. And we may get married in every state.*

Stan, Sergei Temoff, Illiana, Serge Malavski, Father Leonid Znamensky. Why is everyone so solemn? Maybe they knew how it would all end.

If Oliver Hardy was still going along with plans to tour with Illiana in tow, he should have either been made a saint, for his patience and understanding with the mismatched couple, or been condemned to the nuthouse. Mercifully, the tour didn't go ahead; but Hardy was still in danger of having Illiana's presence forced upon him, when Laurel came up with another hair-brained idea for keeping his little angel happy:

> The unpredictable Illiana-Stan Laurel plans take another turn. Cancelling their personal appearance tour, the pair will appear together in Stan's next comedy with Oliver Hardy for Hal Roach. Illiana will be leading woman. Stan is producer.
>
> (Harrison's Carroll's "Hollywood" – 10 May 1938)

They say "There's no fool, like an old fool." Had Laurel learned nothing from his experiences with having Mae in his early solo films?

So, on 23 May 1938 when writing and production of the film "*Block-Heads*" commenced, "The Lot of Fun" had become "A lot of unhappiness." Hardy was unhappy with Laurel, for losing them their personal appearance tour; Illiana was unhappy with Stan because, for the second time running, he hadn't got her a part in one of his films; Laurel was unhappy with Roach, as he still hadn't been given the joint contract he had set his mind on; and Hal Roach was unhappy with Laurel's life on *and* off set.

Of them all, Illiana seemed the least happy. Just five days later, Louella Parsons announced in her column:

> The thrice married Illiana and her chronic bridegroom, Stan Laurel, have parted. The Russian singer has left Stan's bed and board and gone to live with her good friend, Countess Sonia.
>
> Illiana said: "No, there is no chance of our ever making up. It is too serious this time. I don't even want to tell why I am leaving him."
>
> (28 May 1938)

In mid-June, it was reported that Laurel was about to get back with his working partner, Hardy, but it wasn't to make a film:

> Convincing testimony that the popularity of Stan Laurel and Oliver Hardy is something to shout about is supplied in the fact that the two comedians are to be paid $7,500 per week for the start of their personal appearance tour, at least.
>
> The pair are to visit France, England and Germany, and the initial engagement at the Cirque Madrona [in Paris] for two weeks is to be the high-paying one, but what with percentages and all, may be matched at various other stages.
>
> Laurel and Hardy will undertake the jaunt following "Just a Jiffy," and it will last eight weeks. The two comedians are assured of an audience in Europe, even though their pictures may not be liked so well here.
>
> (*Los Angeles Times* – 16 June 1938)

It is hard to believe, looking back some seven decades, that anyone would write that the Laurel & Hardy pictures weren't liked in the U.S. – especially as the journalist is referring to the ones made at the Roach Studios, the bulk of which are now considered to be classics.

The announcement re the proposed European tour had actually come way back in March, some two months before production began on "*Block-Heads*" (working title "*Just a Jiffy*"), which may well show that Laurel had a premeditated intention of rocking the Roach boat if he did not get his own way.

Laurel was going all-out to break the terms of the current *individual* contracts he and Hardy had with Hal Roach, in order to obtain just the one contract for the partnership of "Laurel AND Hardy." It may have been that Laurel had galvanised his attorney, Ben Shipman, into using the proposal of a tour as a device to lever Roach towards issuing a new contract rather than have his prized comedy duo desert him.

Whether the tour was part or wholly fiction, it didn't do the trick. Nor did it materialise.

Three's a Crowd

There was little reason for revelry during the making of "*Block-Heads*," except for 16 June, when there were four reasons. These prompted a cake presentation on set, and a bigger celebration at Laurel's house, in the form of a combined birthday party for Stan himself; Milton Bren – production manager; Harry Langdon – gagman; and Hal Roach, Jr. – producer; whose birthdays were as follows: Milton Bren – 14 June; Harry Langdon – 15 June; Hal Roach, Jr. – 15 June; and Stan Laurel – 16 June. How many candles do you put on that cake!

Stan Laurel is spoon-fed birthday cake by Hal Roach, Jr., while "*Block-Heads*" co-star Patricia Ellis looks on with amusement. Babe Hardy, meanwhile, uses the distraction to help himself to Harry Langdon's piece of cake.

Once the day's filming had ended, it was everyone over to the Laurels' house, where was Stan given a raucous chorus of "*Happy Birthday*."

The singers are Babe, and Harry Langdon, while songwriter Lew Porter bashes out the notes on the piano. Even Illiana returned to the fold, to join in.

Despite Stan absenting himself from the studios on several occasions, "*Block-Heads*" was actually shot on schedule, and managed to emerge without obvious chisel marks. However, when it came to doing re-shoots, to replace some of the bits which didn't work so well, Stan was nowhere to be found.

Back in February 1937, when Roach had failed to cater to Laurel's demands, Laurel had done a runner to New York, and then taken a leisurely cruise back to L.A. Unbelievably, because he still hadn't been given the new joint-contract by Roach, he repeated his tactics and, on or around 14 July, went off to New York again, but stopping off first at Kansas City. This was Stan's usual middle-ground for meeting up with Ruth, but on this occasion he was actually there to meet Illiana. [Me smell dirty trick!]

-----0-----

1938 July 14 (*circa*)
        CANOGA PARK, California to **KANSAS CITY**, Kansas 1,615 miles

On 5 July Illiana had been sentenced to five days in jail, with twenty-five days suspended, fined $100, and banned from driving for six months, after pleading guilty to reckless driving during the incident back on 12 April, when she had lost an argument with a tree. She immediately submitted her intent to appeal. Anyone in their right mind would have accepted blame, but then this was Illiana. Back in court, on 14 January 1939, she offered the following defence:

> The Bixel System, Inc. has filed suit for damages against Illeana Laurel, dancing wife of Stan, the comedian, charging she rented a car last April, drove it at excessive speed and finally wrecked it. In reply, Mrs Laurel declared it was the plaintiff's fault, saying nobody asked if she had a driver's licence and she didn't know how to drive anyway.

Meanwhile, here in July 1938, in an effort to gain a little sympathy after her misdemeanours, Illiana announced she was pregnant. Stan fell for it. She then left for Kansas four days ahead of her husband to prepare for his arrival, and … wait for it! … their FOURTH wedding ceremony.

They told the local press they had planned the fourth marriage, "just because we love each other." No corroboration has been found that the re-marriage went through.

Next stop – New York!

-----0-----

1938 July 16 (*circa*)
    KANSAS CITY, Kansas to **NEW YORK**, New York 🚂 1,195 miles

-----0-----

Illiana had obviously been influential in New York City being the chosen destination. She still had contacts and friends there, in the Russian community; and insisted that she and Stan stay at the Waldorf, close to the theatre district, so she could visit her old haunts. One could well imagine Illiana going to the Biltmore Hotel, and the Versailles Café, where she used to sing, to show them the catch she had landed in Hollywood. The couple were also snapped in Sardi's restaurant, along with Illiana's friend, Sonia, who had travelled with them.

It would seem that Stan and Illiana then headed south, for some glitz, glamour and gambling.

-----0-----

1938 July 23 (*circa*)
    NEW YORK, New York to **ATLANTIC CITY**, New Jersey 🚂 127 miles

-----0-----

It is not known how long the Laurels stayed in Atlantic City, but two pieces of ephemera place them there. On 23 July Laurel sent a telegram from Atlantic City to the Roach studios, enquiring how the preview for "*Block-Heads*" had gone. If this was meant to pacify Roach, it was badly misjudged. Roach wanted Laurel at the studio, doing the retakes, and was being driven frantic by his absence. But Laurel was in no hurry to return home.

Ventnor City Pier

Laurel telling angler David Etheridge: "Call that a fish. See that! That's for catching a 258lb fish, that is" – pointing to his gold tuna badge. Mayor Hodson looks on..

His next recorded sighting was on the fishing pier in Ventnor City, New Jersey, just three and a half miles down the coast from Atlantic City. He was snapped there with no less than the Mayor of Ventnor, Harry Hodson, who may have been showing Laurel around. The said press photo was date-stamped 'August 1, 1938,' but other evidence would seem to indicate that the Laurels may already have been on their return journey to the coast by then.

This photo has previously been billed as having been taken in Omaha, whereas it is actually Laurel receiving the ceremonial key to Atlantic City from Mayor W. Bennett Cramer, here, some two years earlier (27 July 1938). The "lady" looking on is Illiana Laurel.

-----0-----

1938 July 25 (*circa*)
        ATLANTIC CITY, New Jersey to **NEW YORK**, New York 🚂 127 miles
1938 July 27 (*circa*)
        NEW YORK, New York to **CANOGA PARK**, California 🚂 2,814 miles

-----0-----

Little is known of Oliver Hardy's movements since filming ended on "*Block-Heads*." One would presume he continued to enjoy golfing and horse racing, with the emphasis on the latter now that he had extended his stable of horses. One event that wild horses could not have dragged him away from was the opening of the second season at Del Mar Turf Club.

-----0-----

1938 August 10
        BEVERLY HILLS, California to **DEL MAR**, California 🚂 110 miles

-----0-----

Hardy was back at Del Mar on 10 August 1938. It was said the race promised to attract a crowd which was "expected to include every motion picture and radio celebrity from the Hollywood colony." That's a lot of celebrities, but the only ones named were:

Dorothy Lamour, Mary Carlisle, Ralph Morgan, Lucille Ball, Minna Gombell, Wesley Ruggles, Charles Ruggles, William LeBaron, David Butler, Howard Hawks, Raoul Walsh, and Frank Morgan.

Mind you, even someone as big as Oliver Hardy can hide among a crowd of ten thousand racegoers.

This charming (unidentified) lady appears to have a notebook in her hand, so perhaps she is a journalist. Then, again, it could be a very large autograph book.

So what of Stan? Well, on 1 August 1938, the *Los Angeles Times* ventured the news that, "*There is talk that Stan Laurel, England's favourite comedian, is coming up for knighthood next year.*" The people who vet nominees must then have been sent copies of the Hollywood gossip columns for the last eight months, as the subject was never mentioned again.

On that exact same day, Laurel finally reported to the Roach Studios. If he was expecting to see a big "WELCOME HOME" banner suspended across the studio gates, he was soon to get a rude awakening.

o-o-0-o-o

CHAPTER 15
INTO THE BREACH
(1938 pt3)

Instead of being given hugs and handshakes, when he walked into the Roach Studios on 12 August, Laurel was told to "go take a walk." This was followed by legal papers being issued, threatening litigation:

Studio Sues Stan Laurel For Breach of Contract

Stan Laurel was accused of breach of contract today by Hal Roach studio, in a legal squabble that threatened to end his long screen partnership with Oliver (Babe) Hardy. Differences between Laurel and Roach executives arose over his absence from Hollywood at a time when several re-takes were to be made for his latest picture, "Block-heads."

(*Associated Press* – 17 August 1938)

A second article was targeted to let Laurel know he wasn't calling the shots.

STUDIO BOOTS STAN LAUREL

To Team Harry Langdon With Oliver Hardy

After 11 years, Stan Laurel was handed his walking papers yesterday by the Hal Roach studio. They came, according to the film company, in a letter informing the star that his two-year contract, with two pictures yet to go, was being terminated by his employers.

At the same time, the studio revealed that plans are under way to make a series of pictures teaming Oliver Hardy with Harry Langdon, who will don make-up again after a four and one-half year absence from the screen.

The Roach company charges Laurel breached his contract on two counts—by leaving before the picture, "Block-heads," was finished, making retakes impossible, and by not reporting in time to start his new picture.

(*INS* – 17 August 1938)

It would seem that the last two press releases had been deliberately held back, until after the press preview of "*Block-Heads*," so that the reviewers would concentrate on the on-screen action, rather than Laurel's off-screen actions. It was only once the reviews were out that Roach threw Laurel to the dogs. But an immediate response from the Laurel camp made it obvious he was going to fight back:

Film producer Hal Roach announced today that he had signed Harry Langdon, comedy star of silent pictures, to replace Stan Laurel in a series of films opposite Oliver Hardy.

Roach previously contended Laurel had breached his contract, which calls for two more pictures with Hardy.

Laurel contended he obtained permission to leave the city. He said that if the suspension continues he will go to court.

(*Associated Press* – 18 August 1938)

Meanwhile, Harrison Carroll had tracked down Laurel, and interviewed him for his "Hollywood" column. Over a cocktail in a Hollywood late-spot, Laurel and Illiana cheerfully told him of their newest predicament.

"I got back to Hollywood two days ago," said the comedian, "and I find the studio has docked me several weeks' salary. I hear they are even thinking about teaming Babe Hardy with Harry Langdon in the future."

Illiana and Stan revealing only cheerful countenances for the camera.
"When she was good, she was very very good, but …"

A spokesman for the Roach studio later confirmed the news of the trouble with the comedian.

Studio Claims Comedian Broke Pact.

"We needed Stan for several scenes on his last picture," he said. "We couldn't find him, so we had to write around him. We haven't paid his salary since he left, as we feel that Stan has breached his agreement with us."

However, the studio denied there is any thought of teaming Hardy with Langdon. "Harry is just employed here as a writer," said the spokesman.

And there you have both sides of the story. Hollywood awaits the outcome with interest.

(*King Features Syndicate* – 18 August 1938)

Harrison Carroll's column was printed daily, so one would think his Hollywood gossip was always up-to-date. If this one was, it would indicate that Laurel had returned to Hollywood a good sixteen days later than first thought – unless, again, the article had been held back. This would then explain why the Roach Studios denied any thoughts of teaming Hardy and Langdon, while saying, on what appeared to be the same day …

Harry Langdon Takes Laurel's Film Role.

Hal Roach studios announced Wednesday night (17th] that Harry Langdon, pantomimist of the old silent screen would replace Stan Laurel as a movie team-mate of Oliver Hardy.

Executive Producer Milton H. Bren said Laurel had been dismissed because of "wilful disregard in failing to report" to the studio for retakes on a recent picture.

(*Associated Press* – 18 August 1938)

The follow-up article even named the film:

STAN LAUREL IS SUSPENDED

> Stan Laurel's screen future was a question mark today, his comedy partnership with Oliver Hardy dissolved by order of Producer Hal Roach.
>
> Harry Langdon, slapstick star who lost out with the advent of talking pictures, a decade ago, was selected by Roach as Hardy's new team-mate.
>
> The first picture for the pair is "Zenobia's Infidelity," from a novel by H. C. Bunner.
>
> Laurel's attorney, Ben Shipman, said he would go to court for redress if the suspension continues.

(*Associated Press* – 19 August 38)

HARRY & HARDY – HARDLY!
Harry Langdon – "the new Stan Laurel."
I don't think so.

Another press release added more chronological disorder:

> If it's true that Stan Laurel called off the European personal appearances just to be with Illiana on her tour, the comedian will have made his most expensive gesture to love. For the continental bookings would have netted him in the neighbourhood of $100,000. European managers were even willing to pay his income taxes over there. Of course, by staying at home, he can make a picture.

(15 August 1938)

Another press release, some six weeks later, was the cause of more questions regarding whether a tour was on or off, and just ***who*** was touring with ***whom***:

> Latest idea of Stan Laurel and Illiana is to go on a personal appearance tour. First she'll lose some weight,

(29 September 1938)

Maybe if it had said: "First she'll lose the bottle," it would have been more feasible.

Laurel had threatened to quit pictures many times, but now that Roach had sent him packing, he was doing all he could to get back in. And just to show that his was a promise, and not just a threat, Roach did go ahead with making the film "*Zenobia*" with Langdon and Hardy – although one could hardly call it a "teaming." But that was yet a few months away.

While Roach's film intentions weren't a bluff, Laurel's next call must have been – either that, or very naïve:

> Mack Sennett, the boy who invented slapstick and made the world custard-pie conscious, is returning to the movies. This time it isn't hearsay, but a definite organization to be known as the 'Sennett Pictures Corporation.' Mack's first will be "The Problem Child," starring Stan Laurel.
>
> The role is that of a normal-sized child of midget parents. Jed Bluell, who recently made the all-midget western, will join Mack as associate producer.

(Louella O. Parsons (*INS*) – 13 September 1938)

Mack Sennett, too, was kidding himself if he thought that he could possibly revive his filmmaking career, which had been at its zenith in the SILENT era. But Hal Roach wasn't faring much better with Langdon. A press release informs us:

> Midway in production of "It's Spring Again," formerly "Zenobia's Infidelity," Hal Roach has discovered that the Stan Laurel role isn't entirely suitable to Harry Langdon, his successor. The picture has been withdrawn from production pending revision.

(1 November 1938)

This didn't signify that Roach was eager to get Stan back to work, especially while Laurel was attracting such negative publicity. One newspaper bitingly commented:

> One of these days we are expecting to pick up a newspaper in which the name of Stan Laurel is NOT on Page one. That will be news!

(4 November 1938)

Meanwhile, Harry Langdon *seems* to have come out of it very well.

> The story of Harry Langdon, his rise, his fall, his return, is to me one of the greatest human interest stories in Hollywood. A few short months ago he was still just another 'has been'.
>
> Today he is secure at the Hal Roach studios, with a seven-year contract in his pocket, to star opposite Oliver Hardy in a series of important features, with casts that sound like "Who's Who".

(*San Antonio Light* – 13 November 1938)

The above sounds less like "Who's Who," and more like "Who's KIDDING Who?" Why would Roach give a twenty-one film contract to Harry Langdon (seven-year contract – three films per year) before anyone could even gauge whether he would be a success in just ONE? Langdon had recently been "greeted warmly" for his part in the Roach comedy *"There Goes My Heart,"* but only by the few who saw the preview. AND – it was a very minor role at that.

No! this was Roach playing mind games to break Laurel's stand against the studio. But it backfired. Instead of trying to work his way back into the Roach camp, Laurel decided to position himself outside, and fire off the heavy guns:

> Los Angeles, Cal. Dec 6. – Stan Laurel came into another court today to file a $700,000 civil damages action against "Hal Roach Studios Inc." asserting a breach of contract. The screen comedian sued as an individual and as "Stan Laurel Productions Inc." because Roach studios teamed Hardy with another veteran comic, Harry Langdon, leaving Laurel out in the cold.
>
> Laurel charges that he signed a contract with Roach Oct. 8, 1937, calling for four pictures. Hardy already was under contract to Roach. But, Laurel alleges, Roach repudiated the agreement last Aug. 12, after the pair had made "Swiss Miss" and "Block-heads," and signed Langdon for the rest of the series. Laurel says Roach's action reacts to his (Laurel's) detriment as an actor, writer, director.

(*Associated Press* – 7 December 1938)

With such sums being contested, it was now open season. On 18 November the Laurels had separated, and Illiana had executed a maintenance claim against Stan. Now she was going in for the kill – and the money:

> Life with Stan Laurel was just one sleepless night after another, with his two former wives disturbing her slumbers at "ungodly hours," blonde Illiana Laurel charged today. The Russian dancer, who married Laurel three times during 1938, demanded $1,500 monthly in a separate maintenance suit.
>
> Climaxing a hectic marital life which began last New Year's Day with an elopement to Yuma, Ariz., continued with frequent tiffs and as many reconciliations, including solemnization of the two extra marriages. Illiana's suit asked ejection of the comic from his Canoga Park home, title to all community property, and $25,000 attorney's fees.

Into the Breach

> She claimed that "by reason of his attitude toward his former wives," they annoyed her by having police and firemen visit the house, and by causing persons to write her anonymous letters.
>
> (*Associated Press* – 29 December 1938)

What a difference a year makes. Exactly one year ago Illiana had stood in front of a Justice of the Peace and been pronounced married. Now, on 31 December 1938 she stood in front of a judge, as an estranged wife, and was sentenced to five days in prison for the reckless driving offence back in April. Some might say the judge was doing the Laurels a favour by keeping them apart.

Following an appeal, and some tears in court, Illiana's sentence was reduced to just one day in jail, or to be precise – nine hours! On 5 January, Stan took her to Beverly Hills jail, and gave her a goodbye kiss as she was locked up. He was back five hours later, and spent the next four hours waiting for her. Upon her release she said: "*I will tell the judge that the suit is off,*" and added: "*All I want is my Stan.*" Laurel contributed: "*This is the real thing this time—we love each other.*" So how long would it last? Place your bets!

Hardy needed no prompting to do the latter. During the last week in November he had been visiting the Agua Caliente race track.

Agua Caliente Race Track. (24 November 1938)
Babe Hardy not welcoming the intrusion into his private meal time.
Next to him is Viola Morse, and next to her is Mrs. Frank Childs.

[N.B: As a racehorse trainer, Frank Childs' successes included winning the Hollywood Oaks, the California Oaks, and the Del Mar Oaks. He was inducted into Racing's Hall of Fame in 1968. Childs must have been a very honest man, as Hardy obviously never benefited from any insider tips.]

On 31 December, Hardy was at Santa Anita Race Track for the opening day of its winter racing season. The sky was blue and the sun was shining, highlighting the $500,000 refurbishment of the clubhouse. Caught on camera, doing their bit to brighten the day, were Mr. & Mrs. Bing Crosby, Mr. & Mrs. Spencer Tracy, Virginia Bruce, Arthur Treacher, Oliver Hardy, and Guy Kibbee. [**FILM**]

First, Hardy checks the race positions …   … and seems happy with the placings.

Till he realises something has gone wrong …   … and throws up his arms up in surrender.

But the camera missed some of the biggest stars: Joe E. Brown, Constance Bennett, Louis B. Mayer, Carole Lombard, Clark Gable, and Dorothy Lamour.

The season was scheduled to run till 11 March 1939. With over $910,000 being handed out in prize-money the lure to Hardy was irresistible, and it would be hard to believe he did not make several more visits in those next ten weeks.

o-o-0-o-o

CHAPTER 16

WAR AT HOME

(1939 pt1)

Considering all the conflict between Stan and Illiana during 1938, this billing from the Roosevelt theatre in Oakland, California, takes some believing:

Two previews of the forthcoming shows on Saturday and Sunday 21 and 22 January 1939, mentioned only Stan.

> Making a personal appearance for two days only, Stan Laurel, famous screen comedian of the team of Laurel and Hardy comes to the Roosevelt, Saturday, to head the all-star vaudeville revue.
>
> (19 January 1939)

And No.2

> Today the Roosevelt Theater presents an outstanding stage attraction in the personal appearance of Stan Laurel, formerly of the team of Laurel and Hardy.
>
> Laurel offers a comedy act in the manner that has made him so popular with millions of people who have seen him in numerous pictures.
>
> (22 January 1939)

But then, in the main advertising block, there was the name "ILLIANA" – almost as big as that of "STAN LAUREL," with the bill matter: "Singing Russian Ballads."

During Illiana's act, Stan came on stage to join her in a duet. The song they chose is not known, but a good song for Laurel to sing to Illiana would have been the one Hardy sang in the 1930 Laurel & Hardy film "*Blotto*":

"The Curse of an Aching Heart"

> You made me think you cared for me,
> And I believed in you.
> You told me things you never meant,
> And made me think them true
>
> I gambled in the game of life,
> I played my heart and lost.
> I'm now a wreck upon life's sea,
> Alone I pay the cost.
>
> You made me what I am today,
> I hope you're satisfied.
> You dragged and dragged me down until,
> The soul within me died.
>
> You shattered each and every dream,
> You fooled me from the start.
> And though you're not true, may God bless you.
> That's the curse of an aching heart.

-----O-----

Interesting to note Eddie Borden and James Morton on the bill. Borden was a bit player from the Roach Studios who had appeared as the "foppish nobleman – with lorgnettes" who was robbed by Ollie in the Laurel & Hardy film "*Bohemian Girl*." He would go on to appear in the next three Laurel & Hardy films, most memorably in one film as a student, dressed in a white sheet, pretending to be a ghost.

James C. Morton, on the other hand, was a well-known character actor who had played in several Roach 'Our Gang' films, and at least ten Laurel & Hardy films – most notably as a grouchy a cop in "*Tit For Tat*," and as the bartender in "*Way Out West*." As these two actors weren't stage comedians as such, one can safely presume that they were there as foils to Stan Laurel, whose act would no doubt have been a sketch he had knocked up. Sorry to say, nothing is known about the sketch, and there are no known reviews to assist.

What you *can* guarantee, re this live appearance, is that there would have been more goings-on off-stage, than on. It will also come as no surprise that the Laurels had a major bust-up during these two nights, which prompted Illiana to leave Stan and go into "seclusion."

The Laurels' stage show should have been the first on a tour. Two further known bookings were scheduled for February – in Seattle, Washington; and in Vancouver, British Columbia – but these were now pulled out, resulting in a loss of earnings for the Laurels of $1,500 per week.

Over the last eight months Stan Laurel's battles at home, at the studios, and in the courts, had made for more newspaper headlines and more column inches than Laurel and Hardy's filmwork; and Stan was spending more time in front of the judge than he was in front of the camera. Hal Roach, for one, had had enough. He decided to use the activities in Laurel's private life as ammunition to counter Laurel's monetary claim against him.

> Hal Roach studio answered today actor Stan Laurel's $700,000 breach of contract suit by saying he was discharged for violating the "morality clause." The studio charged in its superior court answer that Laurel incurred unfavourable publicity through numerous squabbles with his wife.
>
> (*UP* – 4 February 1939)

Considering that Laurel was now fighting to overturn the "morality clause," what his wife did next was not exactly helpful:

> Illiana Laurel was arrested today [Thursday 9 February] by sheriff's deputies and held in the county jail on a charge of being drunk on private property. Officers took her in custody at a Russian café on the "Sunset Strip," just over the city line from Hollywood. She faced arraignment later today in Beverly Hills justice court.
>
> (*Associated Press* – 10 February 1939)

Of the court hearing, a second report added:

> Illiana Laurel tapped an impatient foot, and hummed Russian songs in the county jail today. The Russian songs were of the old regime, and distinctly not filled with patriotism for Communist Russia.
>
> She was taken into custody Thursday night, when her distaste for the present regime in Russia caused her to sing anti-Communist songs; and to orate loudly against the Soviets, which annoyed other guests at a party given jointly by the chief state liquor law enforcement officer, and an official of the state motor vehicle department.
>
> The blonde and shapely Illiana was booked on suspicion of intoxication, a charge she denied. She will be arraigned in court Feb.14.
>
> (*INS* – 11 February 1939)

The oration she made was about the Bolsheviks, of whom she was alleged to have said: "*The Bolsheviks killed my brother, and that man over there is a Bolshevik*." At this, she pointed at George M. Stout, head of liquor law enforcement in California. You would have thought that the last person Illiana would want to upset was the man in charge of the liquor laws.

War at Home

At the arraignment on 14 February she pleaded "not guilty" and demanded a jury trial, which was set for 23 March. When a sheriff's deputy demanded she give him her jewellery to satisfy a $2,000-plus judgment which had been granted against her husband, she told the deputy: "*My jewellery is all in hock*."

The answer to "how long would the marriage last?" (posed after Stan had picked up Illiana from jail on 5 January) can now be given. It was fifty-nine days. On 6 March, Illiana was at the Superior Court to resubmit the separate maintenance suit against her husband, for $1,000 per month.

On 23 March Illiana was due for another court hearing regarding the drunken outburst in the Russian café, the Balalaika, but she failed to appear. Her attorney claimed she was in hospital, being prepared for an operation.

She was scheduled to appear in court again on 4 April, but again failed to do so. Consequently, the judge ordered her bail be forfeited, and issued a bench warrant for her arrest.

On 6 April she was taken to jail prior to coming up before the judge, who then pronounced her "guilty," and put her on probation.

Meanwhile, over at the Roach studios, cracks were beginning to appear in the Langdon & Hardy film partnership. One gossip columnist offered:

> Nothing has happened (cinematically!) to Stan Laurel since he quit Babe Hardy. Babe and Harry Langdon have since been teamed, but their initial contribution to fun is said to be no laughing matter.
>
> (*Associated Press* – 9 April 1939)

In fact the crack was big enough for Laurel to walk through, right back into the Roach studios.

> Hollywood April 8. For a long time, life has been nothing but troubles for Stan Laurel, but the comedian will greet Easter morning with a big smile.
>
> He has signed a peace pact with the Hal Roach studio, and reports back on salary April 15 to make another series of pictures with his old screen partner, Oliver Hardy.
>
> Settlement of the difficulty between Laurel and Roach is expected to result in the withdrawal of the comedian's $620,000 suit against the film company, which he charged with breach of contract.
>
> An unofficial spokesman said Laurel would receive a significant sum, to be held in trust pending disposition of the separate maintenance action brought by Mrs. Laurel.
>
> (*Associated Press* – 9 April 1939)

The new contract was also dependent upon Laurel breaking all ties with Illiana:

> Illiana, tempestuous wife of Stan Laurel, stepped aside Saturday to allow what appeared will be a reunion of Laurel with Oliver Hardy in filming of comedies for producer Hal Roach.
>
> Following a conference of attorneys, Judge Gould approved a stipulation dissolving a court order under which Illiana had prevented Laurel from settling his $700,000 damage suit against the Roach studio.
>
> Illiana had sued for separate maintenance, and Laurel's damage suit [with Roach] could not be adjusted until [Illiana's] maintenance suit was heard.
>
> Laurel filed his damage suit against the studio after his contract was cancelled on the grounds he had violated one of its provisions by refusing to work last May for retakes on "Swiss Miss."
>
> Reports had been current for some time in Hollywood that both Laurel and Roach were anxious to settle their differences so the team of Laurel and Hardy could resume work in a series of short comedies.
>
> Mrs. Laurel's plea for temporary alimony is to be heard next Thursday.
>
> (*UP* – 9 April 1939)

Here are the circumstances which brought Laurel and Roach back together:

After the release of the dreadfully unfunny Harry Langdon-Oliver Hardy film "*It's Spring Again*" (aka: "*Zenobia*") Hal Roach knew he simply had to get Laurel back with Hardy in front of the camera. But getting him there would be the least of Roach's problems, as working with him had become nigh on impossible. It was going to take a catalyst to get Laurel to play ball – which is exactly what happened.

Enter Boris Morros, a Russian composer, whose film work to date had been mainly as musical director, but who was now endeavouring to make his first ever film as producer. Morros had acquired the American film rights to the French comedy hit, "*Les Aviateurs*," and wished to re-film it – provided he could get Laurel and Hardy to play the lead roles. When Morros approached Roach about acquiring the services of the two comedy stars, he would have learned that Roach was in a position to loan out Hardy, but that Laurel had an arrangement whereby he could work for his own company – 'Stan Laurel Productions.' There was no way, however, that Roach was going to release Hardy, unless Laurel came back and worked under the Roach banner.

As Messrs. Roach, Morros, Hardy, **and** Laurel were all enthusiastic about making the Morros' film – newly titled "*The Flying Deuces*" – attorneys started work on the fine print of the agreement, which worked out like this:

Laurel would dismiss his breach of contract suit against Roach, and sign a new contract, which was ***concurrent***, though not ***joint***, with Hardy's. Laurel and Hardy would then make the two Roach films which were still outstanding from their earlier contracts. In between the making of the Roach films, Roach would lend out his two reunited comedy stars to Morros's company.

The man Rodin was known for "The Kiss."
The man from Rolin – wasn't!

The new agreement was signed on 14 April 1939. At the press call, held in a Beverly Hills venue, the first thing Babe did was to plant a big kiss on the side of Stan's face, as a show of affection for his return. No photos exist of Roach doing the same!

All that was needed now, to ensure that Laurel was able to fully commit himself to the making of the three films, was to remove all threat of Illiana.

She was back in court on 13 April, to strengthen her claims for separate maintenance against Stan. In her evidence she charged that Laurel insisted on taking his first wife, Lois, with them on their honeymoon cruise aboard a chartered yacht, and spent long hours below deck with her. She also told that he often invited Lois to their home, where they would sit and reminisce on the intimacies of their former married life.

Despite Illiana's many faults, she does seem to have a really good case in this instance. However, the judge didn't see it that way:

> Los Angeles, Cal.—Opposing counsel filed a dismissal notice Saturday of the $1,000 a month separate maintenance suit of Vera Illiana Laurel, against Stan Laurel. Laurel's lawyer, Ben Shipman, said the couple had reached a property settlement, and that he contemplated filing a divorce suit for Laurel soon.
>
> (*Associated Press* – 16 April 1939)

The divorce suit came just ten days later, during which Stan Laurel charged his wife with mental cruelty against him. He accused Illiana of staying away from home for days on end, and returning intoxicated (which was the exact same line Hardy had used against Myrtle). When they went to film colony nightspots together, Illiana was so loud and boisterous that they were often asked to leave.

Now with Illiana out of the way, maybe Laurel, Hardy, Roach, and you the reader, can get back to Laurel and Hardy making comedy pictures. Maybe!!

The Boys reunited on the set of "*A Chump at Oxford*" on 1 May 1939. But then, just as things were getting back to how it used to be on the Roach Lot, a dark cloud appeared which threatened to ruin the reunion. On 10 May, Illiana was re-arrested on the drunkenness charge in the Russian café. Two days later she was fined and ordered to spend five days in jail, but was then released – pending an appeal. The judge told her:

> This should be an ordinary drunk case, but evidently you want to focus attention on yourself for publicity purposes, and your attitude has not only been that the whole thing was a huge joke, but it has been an attitude of disrespect for American courts.

(INS – 12 May 1939)

What the judge failed to add was that Illiana's antics had been a huge contributory factor in almost wrecking her estranged husband's continuing film career. Plus, it was her husband's name which had made the headlines, even in cases where she was the miscreant. She had to go! So, on 17 May, Stan obtained an interlocutory decree of divorce from her. Illiana was not in court to defend herself, as she had agreed to let the divorce go through by default.

Good news for Stan was that Illiana was planning to leave for the East – i.e. New York. Better news was that the terms of her probation on the drink-driving charge were that, if she should return to Hollywood, a fine of $100 and a five-day jail sentence awaited her. It wasn't going to be enough!

In July 1939, with Laurel and Hardy officially back together, and with a film tucked under their belts to prove it – "*A Chump at Oxford*" – Stan and Babe were now confident enough to put in their first known public engagement for over three years.

> Saturday 15th July 1939
> LOS ANGELES, Wrigley Field
> Shirley Temple, Buster Keaton (Captain),
> Jimmy Durante, Edgar Kennedy,
> Stan Laurel, Oliver Hardy

The event was a charity baseball match, which thirty-five thousand spectators paid to watch. For their money they got to see not only a game between the two teams, but guest appearances by Buster Keaton, Jimmy Durante, Edgar Kennedy, Stan Laurel, and Oliver Hardy; plus Shirley Temple who announced the line-ups.

Next under Laurel's new contract came the making of "*The Flying Deuces*," which was filmed by Morros's production company during August, at the General Service Studios, in Hollywood. The airplane sequences were shot at a local independent airport; and the laundry scenes were done on location in San Fernando Valley.

Mid-way through the filming, a press release was made to the effect that: "Laurel and Hardy are dickering to make a film in South America, after '*The Flying Deuces*,' and keep some personal appearances in the East." In addition, those plans on the back-burner, for Laurel and Hardy to make stage appearances in Europe, were simultaneously re-heated. Author Randy Skretvedt tells of Stan's admiration for the work of Roach cameraman Art Lloyd, and quotes Lloyd's wife Venice on an offer Stan made to Art on the set.

The two comedy stars having a breakfast meeting with Eddie Sutherland, who was about to direct them in "*The Flying Deuces*" – or so he thought. Laurel had other thoughts.

We were going to go to Europe for a three-year deal with Stan and Babe – they were going to make films at the Elstree studio in England; they were also going to make stage appearances there and in France.

So, according to Venice Lloyd, the stage tour originally announced in June 1938 had, in just fourteen months, grown from a proposed two-month run to one of THREE YEARS, and with the addition of making future films elsewhere.

It was now almost ten years since Laurel and Hardy had performed their actual stage show (during the week at the Fox Theatre in San Francisco), so to take up stage work on a full-time basis was a bit of a leap of faith. An even greater leap would be in making films in England.

It is doubtful that a move to a film studio in England would have gained Laurel the freedom he so desperately craved. It is also extremely doubtful that the Elstree studios could have come close to making the kind of films Laurel wished to produce. We do know that Stan visited Elstree in August 1932, but whether or not he had received an open invitation to "come and film here anytime you like" was not recorded. As to committing himself and Hardy to a three-year period in England and France, they might as well have said "for good" – as, after three years away from the U.S., there would have been no open door for them to return.

If there was indeed a serious intention to spend three years touring, then the following booking, announced just days after the completion of "*The Flying Deuces*," takes a bit of explaining:

RKO Palace in Cleveland To Resume Stage Shows

Nat Holt, RKO Great Lakes division manager, has just returned from New York where it was determined stage shows will be resumed at the RKO Palace on September 8. The opening stage attraction will be Artie Shaw.

Holt is more enthusiastic over the forthcoming stage attractions this season than for several season's past. The reason is that he has already signed such well-known headliners as Rudy Vallee, Rochester, Betty Grable, John Boles, Patsy Kelly, Sammy Kaye, and Laurel & Hardy.

The key phrase here is that Holt "has already signed" Laurel & Hardy. If the Boys had already been signed to play the Cleveland RKO Palace, why all the talk of their going to England and the

Continent for three years? This Cleveland booking was surely to be only one, in a series of theatre shows.

But then any plans for going anywhere overseas – whether confirmed, intended, bluff, or just delusional – had to be shelved when, on 3 September 1939, came the dreaded announcement that Britain and Germany were at war.

With the U.S.A. not yet called into the war, Laurel and Hardy were able to spend September rehearsing and filming new material for two reels to be added to the four already in the can for "*A Chump at Oxford.*"

Come 2 October the following press statement was released:

> Laurel and Hardy have just finished "A Chump at Oxford," and there's talk these two will organize a company of their own when they leave Hal Roach's. The comedians have been presented by various producers in the past, but have reached the point where they believe they can do better with their own company and producing staff.

Three weeks after the above announcement, Laurel and Hardy did indeed form their own production company – "*Laurel & Hardy Feature Productions*" – which begs the question: "If Roach didn't have the clout to continue producing Laurel & Hardy films, what chance did they have?"

"*The Flying Deuces*" was released on 20 October 1939, and received good reviews. Laurel and Hardy decided to strike while the iron was hot, regarding future films with their company, and almost immediately released details:

> Laurel, Hardy Form New Movie Company
>
> SACRAMENTO October 25: Laurel and Hardy Feature Productions, with comedians Stan Laurel and Oliver Hardy listed as two of three directors, has filed articles of incorporation.
>
> The corporation asked authorities to issue only one class of shares of stock, with the number set at 1000, and all shares to be without par value.
>
> The corporation's third director is Benjamin W. Shipman of Los Angeles. Its principal office will be in Los Angeles [523 West Sixth Street].
>
> (*Associated Press* – 26 October 1939)

ALICE ARDELL
Always the bridesmaid – never the bride.

Thanks to "*The Flying Deuces,*" not only had Laurel and Hardy regained credibility as film comedians, but they had also found happiness in the courtship of new partners. Holding on to Stan Laurel's hand most days on set during October, was another lady from Stan's past – long-running friend, Alice Ardell.

On 14 November, news had leaked out that, "*Stan Laurel expects to marry Alyce Ardell as soon as his divorce from the tempestuous 'Roosian' is final – sometime in June* [1940]." But Stan's relationship with Alice would prove to be yet another gap-filler, with more to come – as and when there was a gap.

However, the new girl in Babe Hardy's life would turn out to be special. The girl in question was one Virginia Lucille Jones, who had worked as script-continuity girl on "*The Flying Deuces.*" After the initial courtship, the romance was able to blossom when Babe secured further work for Lucille on the Roach Lot during additional shoots for "*A Chump at Oxford,*" and then for the forthcoming Roach-Laurel & Hardy film "*Saps at Sea.*"

But then, just as the Boys were about to "put to sea," the waters began to churn and boil, and it was a case of, "Batten down the hatches Boys, there's a storm a-comin.'" Emerging from the murky depths came "The Creature From the Blue Danube," who was going to transfer the '*Prickly Heat*' from the studio to the courts, and "*Saps at Sea*" was about to be retitled: "*Spats at C*" – the 'C' standing for "Court."

The storm had been brewing since July, when Illiana had instructed her lawyer to find a way of preventing the courts from jailing her if she returned to Los Angeles. The reason for her wishing to return was made clear in October.

> Stan Laurel and Illiana, his buxom blonde ex-wife, appear due for another trip to the courts. Illiana, from a hospital bed where she was recovering from a "temporary nervous disorder," announced she would seek to set aside the divorce and property settlement he won by default last May.
>
> Her attorney made the statement: "Illiana contends that Laurel got his divorce fraudulently, and through collusion."
>
> Laurel sighed as a reporter told him of the impending new action. "I've tried to do my best with that woman," he remarked. "Oh well, if she wants to go to court and battle it out, I will tell the whole truth about it all. I'm just being persecuted."

Over the next few days, more muck was dredged up from the sea bed (See how we are keeping up the analogy!). Laurel charged that Illiana was, "*attempting again to profit by fraud and deceit,*" and asked that the superior court uphold his divorce. Laurel denied all charges, adding that he had had to employ a bodyguard to protect himself against Illiana, who weighs 170lb and towers half-a-head above him; and against her former manager, who weighs 240lb.

Laurel wasn't lying when he said he had hired a bodyguard. The man in question was "Tonnage" Martin, a man-mountain who, at 396lb, almost equalled the combined weight of Illiana and her manager. Laurel was genuinely physically scared of Illiana, and felt threatened by her very presence. Martin, therefore, was to be an ever-present at Laurel's side for the next nine months, while the battles in court were fought out.

Tonnage, an ex-seaman, said of his ordeal:

> I've been through hazardous experiences in the four corners of the world. During the last war I was torpedoed twice. But I'd rather face more torpedoes any time than go through another nine months like those I did with Mr. Laurel. It was up to me to protect him, and that meant mixing it with Illiana. I'll take torpedoes – you can have the 'battling Russian.'

It had been all smiles when Illiana and Stan applied for a license to marry. Now they were applying for a "license to kill" – EACH OTHER!

During Illiana's attempts to criminalise Laurel, it was one of her own criminal acts which caught up with her. The judge ordered her to serve out the five-day jail sentence she had been given back in May, after the drunk and disorderly episode in the nightclub. However, on 9 November, just as she was being processed ready for her internment, there was time only for her to be fingerprinted before a writ of habeas corpus arrived, and she was released pending her next hearing in court. When the case picked up again, the judge gave his verdict on the many stories Illiana had given to the court defaming Stan's character (*UP* – 25 November 1939):

> "This court," he said, "believes the witness has committed perjury, and recommends that the District Attorney investigate the matter, and that prosecution be carried out."

Filming of "*Saps at Sea*" had been going on throughout November, concurrent with the trial, for which every credit must be given to Laurel for his ability to cope with the outside pressures, and be FUNNY! "*Saps at Sea*" was completed in early December, and came through the voyage with no sign of the stormy seas it had weathered. Let us hope it had been the storm before the calm!

o-o-0-o-o

CHAPTER 17

DROP THE LOT

(1939 pt2 – 1940 pt1)

With Illiana having moved out of Laurel's life, and Lucille having moved in to Hardy's life, all was well in the Boys' private lives. Relationships, too, were much improved on the film front. With the three films under the last contract now completed, Roach went as far as to begin planning an additional film:

SCREEN NEWS HERE AND IN HOLLYWOOD

By Douglas W. Churchill

> An untitled comedy of the Roman era will serve Stan Laurel and Oliver Hardy with a spring vehicle at Hal Roachs. The comedians will be seen as gladiators. Harry Langdon and Jack Henley are working on the script.
>
> (*New York Times* – 26 December 1939)

The scriptwriters must have been thrown to the lions, as the "*Gladiators*" never entered the arena. Meanwhile, "*Saps at Sea*" was previewed on 29 December, under its working title "*Two's Company.*" However, it was the presence of one of Laurel's former wives who stole the reviews:

> HOLLYWOOD – Stan Laurel knocking Hollywood cold by showing up at the preview of his latest, "Two's Company," with Ruth Laurel, who was wife No.2 in the long parade of Laurel fraus.
>
> (29 December 1939)

So Alice Ardell was out, and Ruth Laurel was back in – AGAIN. Would Ruth ever learn? And what about Alice? She had been strung along now for some fourteen years as his mistress – but never his missus!

Gearing up to make Lucille Jones his missus, was Oliver Hardy. Since his divorce from Myrtle, Babe had been subconsciously using horses as his surrogate family. Now that he was receiving the partnership and love he needed from Lucille, he wisely decided to let them go – this time for real. The sale of the horses, and the cessation of the expense of their upkeep, would also help to finance a better lifestyle for Hardy and his bride-to-be bride.

Friend and sports journalist Henry McLemore (*ibid.*) went to interview Hardy, when the sad deed had been done:

> Americas biggest racing owner is through. No longer will the unfamiliar green and white silks come tearing across the finish line last. Oliver Hardy has disbanded his stable because of jealously – his horses became funnier than he was.
>
> Mannie, pride of the Hardy stable and the only horse ever to be quoted at 10,000 to 1 in the Kentucky Derby, has been sold. Gone is Crete, who only lacked blanket disqualification to win in several big races. And gone, too, is Schoolmom who taught plenty of betters sad lessons, and Miss Chase, who went to the post six times and loving it so well, stayed there six times. [Gone also were 'Marv' and 'Rare Ben.']
>
> Sitting in his Hollywood home today Oliver Hardy nibbled on the sugar he had hoarded for the use of his thoroughbreds, and kept plying me with old carrots. "If the carrots arent to your taste," Oliver said, "help yourself to a saddle, or have a bite on a bit, or wrap yourself up a blanket. There is only one thing you can't have. That is my racing silk."
>
> Then, like a man exhibiting a great treasure, Hardy unlocked three doors, twirled the dials on a safe, took a peek to see that the burglar alarm was in order, and tenderly, carefully lifted out a bit of green and white silk. There was a suggestion of tears in his eyes as he unrolled the silk.

I made a move as if to handle it, and he looked at me as if I were Stan Laurel.

"Careful," Hardy said, "Careful! What is left of this shirt cost me $18,000. That runs to almost $9,000 a yard, and no one in the world but me has ever paid such a price."

Actually, the silk jockey shirt cost Hardy more than that, because the $18,000 he put into his stable during two years of sensational failure does not include the wagers he made on his own horses as a proud owner.

Hardy insists that the phrase "Also ran" was invented just because of his stable, and that the only thing that kept his horses from holding their own with the greatest thoroughbreds on the turf was the starter. "If they had done away with the starter." he says. "I would have done all right. My horses were the equal of any until the time came to run."

(*UP* – 5 January 1940)

With 1940 having witnessed a complete turnaround in the on- and off-screen lives of Laurel and Hardy, the New Year brought continued peace and serenity. January passed without incident, and February contained only one hiccough – Illiana!

Illiana Laurel was in jail again today as she faced banishment from California upon her release, 14 days hence.

The judge told the Russian night club singer, and former wife of comedian Stan Laurel, that Hollywood police were "fed up" with her intoxicated antics, that they disliked the continual job of dragging her to jail from her apartment, taxi cabs, and night clubs, from whence came complaints that she disturbed the peace.

Twice in a week she had been jailed for intoxication, and twice in a week the 175-pound buxom blonde singer had mauled police, some of them smaller than she.

Judge Holland agreed to suspend 45 days of the sentence he imposed yesterday, if she agreed to leave the state for at least a year. When Judge Holland said it was "for the safety of our police," members of the brawn squad nodded their heads. Hefty policemen who have had midnight and sunrise skirmishes with the Russian singer stepped warily about her. Some of them claimed she mauled them on numerous occasions when they attempted to take her into custody. The court observed she had "no respect" for law or police.

(*UP* – 11 February 1940)

Reports that one man in the court house shouted out: "Ain't ye goin' to hang her?" could not be confirmed!

After being released from jail on 23 February, and with the judge's warning still ringing in her ears that, if she should return to California within twelve months, she would face forty-five days imprisonment, Illiana was put aboard the Streamliner train, bound for Pittsburgh, on the first leg of her exile to New York to take up an engagement at a nightclub.

And that is the last I shall write on the subject of Vera Illiana Shuvalova. Everybody now: "Hip-hip hooray! Hip-hip hooray! Hip-hip hooray!"

Good news too on Hardy's marriage lines. On 7 March 1940 Babe married Lucille Jones. The ceremony was performed by a judge, at the home of an attorney, in Las Vegas, Nevada.

-----0-----

1940 March 7 (*circa*)
    VAN NUYS, California to **LAS VEGAS**, Nevada   275 miles

1940 March 8 (*circa*)
    LAS VEGAS, Nevada to **VAN NUYS**, California to   275 miles

-----0-----

Upon their return from Vegas, Babe and Lucille went off on a one-month motoring holiday. For Hardy, the marriage signalled the end of marital strife, and he was to enjoy peace and happiness with Lucille to the end of days.

Upon returning from their honeymoon, they were able to start off married life in a new house on a three-acre estate at 14227 Magnolia Boulevard, Van Nuys, California.

The future in the film world, though, wasn't looking quite so bright. In mid-March it was announced that Laurel and Hardy were: *"... expected to join the star roster at Universal when they complete their present contract with Roach."* But this came to nought. So, on 5 May 1940, just two days after the release of "*Saps at Sea*," both Laurel *and* Hardy's contracts, and all associations with Hal Roach, were terminated.

They had made some wonderful films with Roach, in three different formats: silent, short, and feature – most of which can rightfully be termed "classics." Laurel thought they could do better. Laurel was wrong.

To keep their public profile high while waiting for film offers to come flooding in through 'Laurel & Hardy Feature Productions,' the Boys attended a huge event at the L.A. Coliseum.

Saturday 18th May 1940
LOS ANGELES, Coliseum
CHAMPIONS of 1940 – Aid to Finland

The show was under the auspices of the "National Finnish Relief Commission and the Southern California Committee for Olympic Games." Fifteen thousand Southlanders turned out to witness the presentation, which boasted champions in the world of entertainment and sports.

Other Hollywood stars supporting the Finns included: Eddie Anderson ('Rochester' – from "*The Jack Benny Show*"), Mary Martin, Sonja Henie, Roy Rogers, Ronald Regan, Jane Wyman, and Jean Hersholt. Several of the stars and starlets presented awards to the winning athletes.

A couple of days later, with 'Laurel & Hardy Feature Productions' seemingly a company in title only, Laurel and Hardy sought to approach another film producer who might take them on – Boris Morros. For that, they needed to chase him down – in New York.

-----0-----

1940 May 20 (*circa*)
    LOS ANGELES, California to **NEW YORK**, New York 2,814 miles

-----0-----

Boris Morros had recently teamed with Robert Stillman, to form the Morros-Stillman Company, trading as 'National Pictures.' In May 1940 they were about to put two films into production: "*Second Chorus*" – for which Artie Shaw and his wife Lana Turner had been short-listed for the lead roles; and "*The Life of O'Henry*" – with Douglas Fairbanks, Jr. in the eponymous role.

Where Laurel and Hardy came in to the picture (pun intended), is hard to figure, and so the comedy couple returned to L.A. with nothing but the usual line, "Don't call us, we'll call you," for their trouble.

-----0-----

1940 May 27 (*circa*)
    NEW YORK, New York to **LOS ANGELES**, California 2,814 miles

A worrying exposé hit the newspapers while Laurel was in New York: "*Liens, claiming additional Federal income taxes due, have been filed against comedian Stan Laurel for $3,586 for 1937.*" It is to be hoped that Laurel had put enough by to pay off his tax to date (1937 to 1940) – but it is doubtful.

It was the necessity to pay off their tax bills which finally committed both Laurel and Hardy to doing live stage shows. Having been threatening to transfer from film to stage work for more than two years, Stan and Babe finally put together an act which they considered would be suitable, and chose to do a try-out at the *Golden Gate International Exposition*.

The International Exposition Park, on Treasure Island in San Francisco Bay, had taken three years to complete, as most of the island had had to be man-made, before all the Exposition venues, roads, attractions, and infrastructure could be put in place. Its eventual cost would reach the staggering sum of $60 million dollars. (Using the GDP Deflator, thus would equate to $1,097 million in 2019 – i.e. over a US billion).

Laurel had visited the Exposition during the third week in June, probably as a birthday treat to himself, which is when he would have instigated plans to perform there. Laurel then returned on 21 August, with Hardy, and the two of them booked in at the famed Sir Francis Drake Hotel, on Union Street in San Francisco, close to the causeway which takes one to Treasure Island.

The day before the event, the comedy couple opened the new Beauty Parlour within the hotel, then went to visit the acting Mayor of San Francisco.

-----0-----

1940 August 21

        LOS ANGELES, California to **SAN FRANCISCO**, California 382 miles

-----0-----

Their performance at the Exposition was on Thursday 22 August 1940, which had been designated a "Benefit Day" – with the gate receipts from the twenty-five thousand attendees going to the American Red Cross "Campaign of mercy for the war sufferers of Europe."

At 8pm in the Federal Plaza, the resident "*Treasure Island Varieties*" show was complemented by three major Hollywood stars: Charles Laughton delivered Abraham Lincoln's "*Gettysburg Address*," between singing spots by Morton Downey, Benay Venuta, and Linda Ware; The music in the show was provided by the 50-piece Exposition Band. If that weren't enough, a 20-piece orchestra backed the artistes. The master of ceremonies was Art Linkletter.

Laurel and Hardy's contribution was a sketch written by Stan, titled: "*How to Get a Driver's License.*"

ABOVE: Stan and Babe sheepishly trying to attract the attention of Acting Mayor Warren Shannon, to get him to sign their certificate.

BELOW: Acting Mayor Shannon swears in Stan Laurel as "Honorary Acting Mayor," while Oliver Hardy is elevated to "Chief of Police."

Gloria Dea from the 'Billy Rose Aquacade," holding the paperwork to prove that Laurel and Hardy have been officially certified.
Both are unsure as to what "being certified" actually means.
(Mayor Angelo Rossi's Office, on Treasure Island (22 August 1940)

The name acts at the benefit show were giving their services for free, so that the whole of the proceeds could go towards the Red Cross. In typical generous fashion, Stan and Babe wanted to raise even more money, and so, at the end of the show, auctioned off all their props – including their Derbies, plus THE CAR they had used in the sketch. Whether this was a car from one of their films, which they had somehow managed to commandeer from the Roach Lot, or whether it belonged to either Stan or Babe personally, was not forthcoming. Then again, it may have been just a mock-up.

The Hollywood stars' gesture in giving their services for free, seems to have gone somewhat unappreciated. Firstly, Oliver Hardy had TO PAY at the gate to get in to the Exposition. And then Charles Laughton, in trying to get there in time for the show, was fined for speeding. Sometimes, Karma takes a day off!

-----0-----

1940 August 23 (*circa*)
    SAN FRANCISCO, California to **LOS ANGELES**, California 382 miles

-----0-----

Our two screen comedians had taken a real gamble in performing a 'live' show at the Exposition. The Federal Plaza was an open-air rectangular venue, with most of the 10,000-capacity audience that night having had free entry. They weren't a regular theatre audience, in a regular theatre, but were day visitors, mainly families, in a carnival-style atmosphere, and not trained as to theatre etiquette. If it went wrong, Laurel and Hardy could so easily be branded as "has-been film comedians" who couldn't hack-it on stage, and their future in live entertainment could have effectively been ended before it had even begun.

Although no reviews are known to exist, it would seem that the booking agents were happy with what they saw as, on the back of it, a tour was arranged.

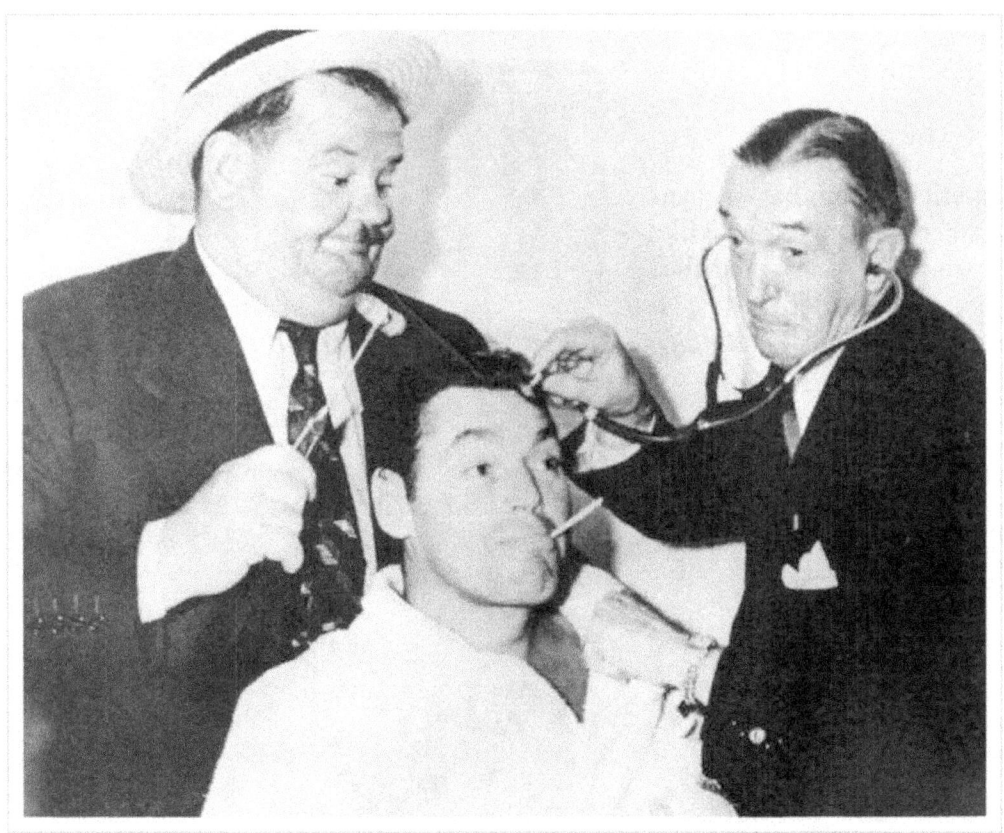

Actor Johnny Weissmuller was starring in 'Billy Rose's Aquacade,' at the Expo's pool. He had by then played Tarzan in 4 films (1932-39), but would go on to play the role a further 8 times, between 1941 and 1949.

Just seven weeks later, our comedy subjects set off to sample the delights of more live shows, playing "*The Driver's License*" sketch. Laurel and Hardy's first thought, following confirmation of the tour, might well have been: "Can we have our props back, please?"

-----0-----

-----0-----

Weissmuller swimming in sync with Esther Williams, whose film career started in 1941, and then ascended rapidly after the release of her fifth film –"*Bathing Beauty*" (1944)

Weissmuller
Hardy
Ginny Hopkins
Morton Downey
Laurel

Also present, was Morton Downey's valet, Jimmy Murphy, who was shortly to transfer his allegiance to fellow Lancastrian – Stan Laurel.

o-o-0-o-o

CHAPTER 18
LIFE BEGINS AT 1940
(1940 pt2)

Prior to the Exposition gig, Stan and Babe had done all their rehearsing at the Hardys' new home at 14155–14227 Magnolia Boulevard, Van Nuys, which he had purchased in March 1940, for $20,000. The grounds of the house featured a swimming pool, guest-houses, and stables.

In mid-October, Hardy staged a play at his home: "*Methods in His Madness*," a humorous mystery drama, written by Dick T. Street, adapted from a Sherlock Holmes story. Street was the publisher of the "*Eye-Opener*" – a weekly newspaper in San Gabriel, near Los Angeles; but he also did publicity for, among others, Laurel and Hardy.

Most of the thirty-strong audience on the night of the play were well-known Hollywood residents, including Herbert Marshall, Douglas Fairbanks Jr., Alan Mowbray, and 'Trixie' the dog – aka: 'Toto' from "*The Wizard of Oz*" (I guess he wasn't in Kansas anymore!). Proceeds went to the 'English War Relief Fund.'

[Hardy is known to have had a theatre in the grounds, which he named "Laurel and Hardy's Fun Factory;" but, for reasons which will become clear later, I believe it had not yet been built. Hardy may well have used the stables as a make-shift theatre.]

After the play, it was back to rehearsals for Stan and Babe, and then on with the theatre tour. Just before the Boys left, Hollywood columnist Jimmie Fidler gave his readers much to consider on what the heck Hollywood was doing letting them go:

> Today, my good friend Oliver "Babe" Hardy and partner Stan Laurel, open a personal appearance tour in Omaha, Nebraska. Their act, which had a try-out at the Golden Gate Exposition, is especially funny, and will make them many new friends.
>
> But frankly, it's my opinion they should not be on tour. I'm speaking, of course, from a selfishly Hollywood point of view. While their presence in various cities will bring enjoyment to thousands who will see them, it's far more important that comedians of their calibre remain right here in Hollywood, making screen fun for audiences totalling millions.
>
> Midst of all the groaning of producers about poor business, it's appalling how few of them realize that, if theatre receipts are down, it's their own fault. The one thing the public demands to see is good pictures—and when I say "good pictures" I mean clean comedy, music, romance and exhilaration.
>
> Instead of sitting idly back and permitting Laurel and Hardy, two of our best comics, to make an extended p.a. tour, studio heads should be sitting up nights, seeking new laugh vehicles in which to star them. At a time when the world is filled with horror and sorrow, most men seek mental relief in laughter.
>
> I say "lucky you" to residents of those cities in which Babe and Stan will dispense their comic antics in person. In the same breath I say "silly you" to film chiefs who, even as they bemoan hard times, allow their best box office assets to wander into other fields.
>
> (*Lebanon Daily News*, Pa. – 27 September 1940)

The venues Laurel and Hardy were about to work were cinemas, which had the dual facilities to stage live shows. The programme would therefore have three main attractions: the latest film releases; a five- to seven-strong troupe of vaudeville acts performing a full-blown variety show; and the big name act of "Laurel & Hardy." At some venues, further insurance was being taken by booking local acts to bring in the local crowd. Some theatre managers were to go even further, and organise a talent show as a mid-week draw. To introduce all these additional attractions would seem to indicate that the bookers had no faith whatsoever in the box-office power of Laurel & Hardy. Time would tell.

Although Stan and Babe too would have approached the stage tour with both trepidation and reservation, they must have known that their talent alone would more than justify their billing. The experience gained from their many personal appearances over the last thirteen years would also stand them in good stead, and the try-out they had done at the San Francisco Exposition was still fresh enough in their minds to give them added confidence.

Something else Stan had acquired at the Exposition was a personal valet. During a backstage conversation there with singer Morton Downey, Stan had learned that Downey's valet was looking for a new "master." The said valet, Jimmy Murphy, was not only an Englishman, but was actually from Stan's home county of Lancashire – so the two hit it off right away. Jimmy's first task was to act as gofer on the forthcoming tour, but the job was to stretch into the next few years, in residency at the Laurel home.

Babe was pleased to have his wife Lucille accompanying him throughout the tour; while Stan had Ruth along on parts of it. The choice of Ruth seems a strange one, as Laurel was still seeing Alice Ardell. Just before leaving L.A., he and Alice had twice been spotted out on the town – once in the Cocoanut Grove, and then dancing together in the Bali. If Stan Laurel were a dog, he would have had two tails.

-----0-----

1940 September 24 (circa)
        LOS ANGELES, California to **OMAHA**, Nebraska 1,550 miles
-----0-----

This thirteen-city tour commenced on 27 September, with a seven-day run in Omaha, Nebraska. Upon arrival at the Union Station, Laurel and Hardy were met by the Mayor, who presented them with the "Key to the City." However, taking them to one side, he then asked them in confidential tones to let him have the key back, as he needed it to repeat the ceremony with presidential candidate Wendell Wilkie. Wilkie was on his campaign trail to get to the White House, and his campaign route was to follow Laurel and Hardy's tour route closely.

LAUREL: Ollie. Every time I take a sip of tea, I get a pain in my eye.
HARDY: "Try taking the spoon out, Stanley." (Omaha 27 September)

Further insult was added when a gold badge pinned on Laurel by the fire chief, making him an honorary member of the fire department, also suffered the snatch-back treatment, so that it too could be presented to Wilkie.

In the evening, the two comedians performed "*The Driver's License*" sketch which, since its debut at the San Francisco Exposition, had been rewritten to include a "cop" – played by James C. Morton. It may be remembered that Morton had supported Stan on the ill-fated show with Illiana, back in January 1939, along with Eddie Borden. There is a good probability that the three of them actually played "*The Driver's License*" sketch on that occasion, with Borden taking over Hardy's role because the latter had pulled out.

-----0-----

Life Begins at 1940

Samples comparing "*The Driver's License*" sketch as a 2-hander and a 3-hander.

```
DRIVER'S LICENSE SKETCH
Page 3.

COP:   ↑ What's your address?
BABE:  ↑ We used to live at 254 South
         Main Street.
       ↑ But that was before we moved.
COP:   ↑ What did you move for?
BABE:  ↑ Well, you see sir, we
         couldn't get the landlord to
         raise our rent.
COP:   ↑ What on earth did you want
         the landlord to raise your
         rent for?
STAN:  ↑ Well we couldn't raise it,
         could we Ollie?
COP:   ↑ Listen to me very carefully.
         Have you ever been
         apprehended for contravening
         a traffic regulation?
BABE:  ↑ Oh yes sir, for speeding.
COP:   ↑ Speeding? How fast were you
         going?
BABE:  ↑ Ten miles an hour.
COP:   ↑ Ten miles an hour? That's not
         speeding, my dear boy. You
         can go ten miles an hour any
         place
STAN:  ↑ Not on the sidewalk, could
         you Ollie?
```

```
DRIVER'S LICENSE SKETCH
Page 3.

BABE:  ↑ What's your address?
STAN:  ↑ 254 South Main Street.
BABE:  ↑ 254 South Main Street ......
STAN:  ↑ That was before I moved.
BABE:  ↑ What did you move for?
STAN:  ↑ Well, I couldn't get the
         landlord to raise the
         rent.
BABE:  ↑ What on earth did you
         want the landlord to
         raise your rent for?
STAN:  ↑ Well I couldn't raise it.
BABE:  ↑ Ohhhhh.... Were you ever
         arrested for violating
         the traffic laws?
STAN:  ↑ Once - for speeding.
BABE:  ↑ Speeding? How fast were
         you going?
STAN:  ↑ Ten miles an hour.
BABE:  ↑ Ten miles an hour? Why
         that's not speeding! You
         can go ten miles an hour
         anywhere.
STAN:  ↑ Not on the sidewalk, I
         couldn't.
```

[The in-joke here is that the Hardys did actually use to live at South Main Street (in Covington, Georgia 1899-1900).]

LAUREL and HARDY – The U.S. Tours

(Friday 27 September – Thursday 3 October 1940)
OMAHA, Nebraska - Orpheum Theater (3,000)

ON THE STAGE
ORPHEUM

HOLLYWOOD'S FAMOUS COMICS
WITH THEIR OWN STAGE REVUE

IN PERSON
Stan LAUREL
Oliver HARDY
With Their STAR STUDDED
HOLLYWOOD
STAGE REVUE

30 MADCAP MERRY MAKERS
LEW PARKER
and Company
CASS, OWEN and TOPSY
DANNY DARE'S
Glamor Girls
MAXINE CONRAD
THE FREDRICOS
ON the SCREEN

"Dr. KILDARE GOES HOME"

A local newspaper reviewed the show as follows:

> Laurel and Hardy are a couple of showmen who weren't satisfied with the usual personal appearance sandwiched between three or four variety acts. They wanted to give the customers a real show, styled along zippy revue lines with some elaborate production numbers.
>
> On the Orpheum stage this week they have assembled all the pieces. They [the support acts] glitter and explode and are very nice. Then again they fizzle and drop like skyrockets in the rain. The show has variety and the blessing of star names. It also has a master of ceremonies for whom the 1907 files of Whizband must have been combed for gags.
>
> It has a couple of sparkling routines, particularly a "Three Musketeers" number that is a knockabout of color and precision, and the pretty Danny Dare Girls brightening up the stage.
>
> The Fredericos are a smooth dance team good enough for any stage, and Maxine Conrad knows how to sell a ballad. Cass, Topsy and Owen, comedy acrobats, need a swifter pace for their act, which starts out in too leisurely vaudeville style, works into some difficult twists, and closes on an hilarious piece of slow-motion pantomime.
>
> Sid Gold, gum-chewing comedian, rates a flock of laughs, and I think there would be just as many if the act were kept perfectly clean. The same goes for some of Lew Parker's gags, which somehow don't fit into my idea of a show starring two comedians who gained their reputations via clean movies.
>
> As for the boys themselves, they're swell. They have just one skit, a scene involving an application for a driver's license, with L. and H. driving a poor cop frantic with their nonsense. It's the sort of hokum you want them to display.
>
> (Keith Wilson – newspaper not known)

The review names Sid Gold as one of the acts, but he wasn't billed in any of that week's adverts. The reason is that Gold was part of the company in the "Lew Parker and Co." billing. His role consisted of pretending to be a member of the audience, and heckling Lew Parker from the stalls. Another act who appeared but wasn't actually billed in the newspaper adverts was singer-dancer Darlene Garner, a local girl who, it is believed, must have been brought in late in the day to attract her local supporters. But just how many fans, friends, and family did Miss Garner have? Her contribution was, though, deemed worthy enough for her to be retained for the rest of the tour, at the expense of any future local acts being brought in.

A pretty lady greets Babe and Stan as they get off the train in Omaha.
It may well be singer Darlene Garner, one of the acts from their show.

A second review ran:

> Laurel and Hardy themselves pace the whole colourful affair with a smart idea. Instead of doing the customary Hollywood palaver, they take a quick introduction by the m.c. – Lew Parker – then swing directly into the kind of stuff that has won their fans.
>
> After one of those stumbling cross-purposes arguments, the pair go into a full-stage police station scene, basis of their comedy resting on efforts to get a driver's license for Hardy. Both are made up as accident victims, which in itself is a big laugh. Hardy having his arm in a sling and Laurel getting a lot of belly laughs via some business with a bandaged thumb, by flipping off the bandage every few minutes and replacing it from a stock of spares in his coat pocket. While not exactly grotesque, the make-up is a strongly emphasized version of their familiar screen appearance.

Variety said of Stan and Babe's first giant step into this new medium:

> Only once or twice does Laurel run his fingers through his hair, and he breaks into his comedy sob just three times—enough to give the customers an identification mark. Their argument with a burly desk-sergeant, their belligerent attitude followed by a quick back-down after he glares at them, are the familiar pattern of L-H screen stuff. It got big laughs from fairly big audiences opening day Friday (27). The two comics make only one appearance, being showered with applause by the adult as well as the juvenile portions of the audience, and had to take several bows.

-----0-----

| IN PERSON |
| ON THE STAGE |
| HOLLYWOOD'S FAMOUS COMICS |

Stan LAUREL
Oliver **HARDY**
With Their STAR-STUDDED

STAGE REVUE
30 MADCAP MERRYMAKERS

LEW PARKER and Company
Famous Broadway Emcee

DANNY DARE'S
Gorgeous Line-Up of Glamor Girls

CASS, OWEN, and TOPSY
Movements Eccentric

Maxine CONRAD
Blonde Songstress of the Trocadero

James MORTON
The FREDERICOS
Direct from Cocoanut Grove

Although all the other variety acts on the bill were billed separately, they were also billed under the umbrella title of "Thirty Madcap Merrymakers." This led other biographers to believe that Laurel and Hardy joined a show which had already been touring under this title, but no trace of "Thirty Madcap Merrymakers" was found before or after this tour. In one Omaha newspaper the show was advertised as, "Stan Laurel & Oliver Hardy in person with their 'STAGE REVUE'," while in another it was promoted to "Star-studded Hollywood Stage Revue."

Variety, in its section dealing with box-office takings for Omaha theatres, noted:

> Only downtown house doing anything this week is the Orpheum with Laurel & Hardy on its stage, and "*Dr. Kildare Goes Home*" on the screen.

The box office takings were $18,000, which was $8,000 up on the previous week's film show only takings. Let us hope the managers of the theatres on the rest of the tour had been given notice of the takings, and would then resist swamping the stage with amateur acts to prop up the two old-timers. Umphh!

In 1938 Omaha had been put on the map with the release of the film "*Boys Town*," starring Spencer Tracy and Mickey Rooney. Tracy had won an Academy Award for his role of 'Father Flanagan' – an immigrant Irish priest who runs a boys' home. The film was based on the true story of Father Edward J. Flanagan, who came to Omaha in 1917, and quickly opened a boarding house for transient and homeless boys. Then, in 1921, again using borrowed money, Father Flanagan purchased Overlook Farm, outside Omaha. This was to become a permanent site, known as "The Village of Boys Town." It continued to grow: with a school, dormitories, and administration buildings being added. By the 1930s, the hundreds of boys calling the village their home were electing their own government – including a mayor, a council and commissioners. In 1936, the community became an official village of the State of Nebraska.

Here in October 1940, Father Flanagan was still running the home, and Babe Hardy, who knew him, had promised to visit – along with Stan. However, by a bad stroke of luck, Flanagan happened to be out of town and so, not wanting to turn up there on the off-chance, for fear people would think they were after some cheap publicity, the Boys did not visit Boys Town. However, fate would relent, and the Boys would soon meet up with their "Father." Read on!

o-o-o-0-o-o-o

CHAPTER 19

BLEW IN – BLOWN OUT

(1940 pt3 Oct)

The railroad was indispensable as a means of getting from venue to venue on this tour. Before they had even played their first show, Stan and Babe had clocked up over fifteen hundred miles from Los Angeles to Omaha. Their city-to-city journeys would now be much shorter, as they were mainly across bordering states, and on direct service lines at that.

-----0-----

1940 October 04

OMAHA, Nebraska to **MINNEAPOLIS**, Minnesota 300 miles

-----0-----

(Friday 4 – Thursday 10 October 1940)

MINNEAPOLIS, Minnesota - Orpheum Theater (2,800)

In Los Angeles and New York City "celebrity is king" and, in the history of show business, always has and always will generate headlines and column inches. In cities less celebrity-oriented though, the acts, actors and film stars have to fight to dislodge articles like: "Man Steals Bananas from Shop," or "Pig Wins Rosette in County Fair." Stan and Babe knew the value of alerting the media that they were in town, and were always up for whatever it took. One of the first things they did to attract the media was to give a cocktail party for newspaper and radio men.

Next, they personally paid for radio announcements to be played during the week, advertising the show – the inception of which gives them the distinction of being the first ever performers to do so.

They were staying at the Minneapolis Radisson Hotel where, on the Saturday night, a Cabaret–Dinner–and–Supper Dance was held in the Grand Ballroom. Stan and Babe were never slow to attend any event which included food, drink, and a late bar – and this was no exception.

The Radisson Hotel happened to be the headquarters of the Nebraska Football Club, so they tried to win over readers of the sports page, by being featured dressed as American football players – Babe donning a Minnesota Jersey and helmet, and Stan putting on the team strip of rivals Nebraska.

Sometime during the week they also did a photo-shoot for "Fire Prevention Week."

Calling all Citizens
FIRE PREVENTION
WEEK: October 6-12

No! This isn't "*Air Raid Wardens*." It's Stan and Ollie proudly wearing the badges presented to them by the Fire Chief

It would take a few days to discover if the publicity had any effect. When the results did come out, it didn't make for good reading. (*Variety* – 9 October 1940)

> It behoves [the film] "Strike Up the Band" to cop a plea of guilty to the charge of grand larceny for stealing the box-office spotlight currently. Taking into consideration various cost factors involved, it relatively even has pilfered the play away from Laurel and Hardy 'in person.' This proves again to the picture-minded that a strong, straight film offering can give box-office cards and spades to most stage shows, even when the latter boast names, as in this instance.
>
> Both of the town's stage shows—the Laurel and Hardy unit at the Orpheum and the Alvin's Follies—are failing to come up to turnstile expectations.

The local paper, however, came down on the side of the live entertainment:

> The ponderous Mr. Hardy and the mild Mr. Laurel make it comparatively easy for themselves in their personal appearance on the Orpheum stage. For all intents and purposes they have rustled back through their movie scripts, found one sufficiently clownish to meet their purposes, and transformed it bodily to the theatre. The sketch they present to the evident delight of Orpheum audiences is a travesty in a police office, with Mr. Hardy trying to get his driver's license renewed, a situation that enables both comedians to demonstrate by word, act, grimace, and gesture why they have endeared themselves to millions by their screen antics.
>
> (*Minneapolis Morning Tribune* – 6 October 1940)

A week later, *Variety* revealed the takings as:

> Laurel and Hardy and their revue on stage, $15,700, pretty good, but under expectations and considerably less than original estimate ($17,500)

The above seems a little bit harsh. The actual takings are only a fraction over ten per cent less than the estimate, which is hardly "considerably less." The previous week the film-only programme had taken just $7,100, so the Variety show had more than doubled the gross takings. So even when you subtract the cost of the show, it still gives a nice nett profit.

Maybe the estimates were too optimistic. The logic behind incorporating a live show with a film show is that you have the potential to attract both theatregoers AND cinemagoers. But then one cannot always apply logic to the public's taste. There would be those who did not wish to sit through a series of live acts, when what they really wanted to see was a film; and those who did not want to sit through a film, when what they really wanted to see was a revue show.

So, again, putting two struggling entertainment forms together does not guarantee doubling the takings; and yet – thanks to Stan and Babe doing everything they could to publicise the event – Laurel & Hardy's addition to the programme had realised just that.

It was totally unfair to label Laurel & Hardy as a disappointing box-office draw, when it was quite evident to one-and-all that vaudeville was on its last legs.

Later in the week, the comedy couple got involved with another event at the Radisson, this one billed as the "Town 'n' Gown Plantation Party" which included Southern music and a dance presentation. That was good enough for Stan and Babe, who gladly lent their support – in person.

Under normal circumstances, an end of evening wind-down at the hotel for our two stage stars must be considered a good thing. But the Plantation Ball was held on the Thursday night, which signalled the end of their having played five shows a day for two weeks, without having had a single day of rest. Consider, too, that the next full week of shows would be starting the following day, in Milwaukee. To make it in time, Stan and Babe had to make a six-hour train journey, plus all the time, effort, and inconvenience of relocating to another hotel. Oh! and ... er ... get some sleep. Another couple of weeks at this rate and it wouldn't be only vaudeville which was on its last legs.

-----o-----

1940 October 11

MINNEAPOLIS, Minnesota to MILWAUKEE, Wisconsin 🚂 335 miles

-----o-----

(Friday 11 October – Wednesday 16 October 1940)
MILWAUKEE, Wisconsin - Riverside Theater (2,550)

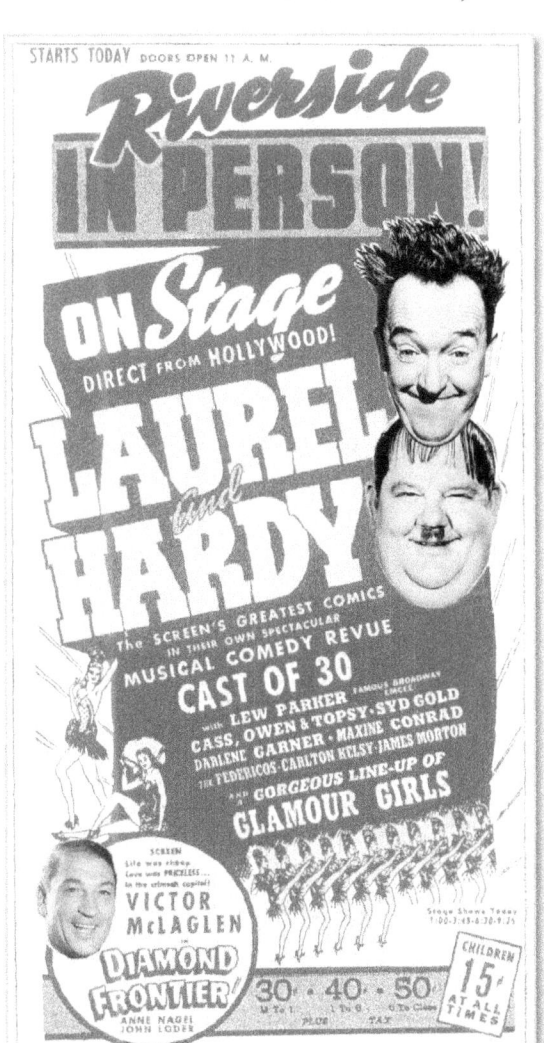

One Milwaukee reporter wrote up some comments the Boys fed to him, about how demanding they were in getting their show up to standard:

If Laurel and Hardy were a couple of green youngsters desperately striving for a foothold in show business, they could not be more ambitious or more earnest in their efforts to put on a good show than they are this week at the Riverside theatre. Up to the time of this chronological dissertation, not one of their stage performances satisfied them.

Moreover, they are far more critical of their own act than of the rest of the show. They frequently change bits of comedy business, throw out gags, and add new ones, Omaha was the first stop on this tour but something tells us the current attraction at the Riverside is considerably different to the Omaha presentation.

(*Milwaukee Sentinel* – 13 October 1940)

The bit about Stan and Babe being self-critical, throwing out gags which didn't work, and writing new ones, was indeed true. But they were also aware of weakness in the other acts on the show. In Minneapolis, when the revue dancers failed to click as L&H had wanted, they summoned the director, Danny Dare, to fly in from Chicago to polish up the routines.

The *Milwaukee Sentinel* article continued:

> The war has been a terrific blow to the box-office receipts [for the films] of these two comedians. Their pictures played in almost every country on the globe up to September last year, and the European receipts were the greater part of their revenue.
>
> With the inception of talkies, Laurel and Hardy went through the incredible chore of making their films in five different languages – English, French, German, Spanish, and Italian. They spoke their own lines in the different languages, too. Today, all foreign tongues are dubbed in by other actors, but Laurel and Hardy are keeping only the Spanish speaking actors busy these days. There is no market for the other versions.
>
> For that reason the two are searching for stories that will please Americans primarily, also Latin-Americans. They have always been a big draw in Mexico, Central and South America.
>
> Over a telephone interview the previous week, Laurel told a Milwaukee journalist that he remembered playing Milwaukee, at the Empress in 1911 with Fred Karno's London Comedians.

[Actually, he had played it THREE times: March 1911, February 1912, and November 1912.]

Stan then enquired if the Empress was still there and added that it held fond memories for him. Let us hope he still had cause to retain fond memories of Milwaukee audiences after this latest visit, as the local papers didn't choose to tell us.

Eerily, fans some seventy years later are able to bring back memories of Laurel & Hardy's appearance there, as parts of one evening's show were captured on home-movie footage, snippets of which reveal our two comedy heroes performing "*The Driver's License*" sketch.

The footage is mute, but then "LIVE and COLOUR" images of Laurel and Hardy on stage are still wondrous to behold. [**FILM**]

-----0-----

1940 October 17 [may have left Milwaukee on the Thursday]
MILWAUKEE, Wisconsin to CHICAGO, Illinois 🚂 94 miles

-----0-----

(Friday 18 October – Wednesday 23 October 1940)
CHICAGO, Illinois – Chicago Theater (3,500)

STAN LAUREL & OLIVER HARDY
with their own company of 30 in their own merry
"HUGE STAGE REVELS!"
Laurel and Hardy, with James C. Morton
Lew Parker & Co. (Paul Remos, Sid Gold)
"Laurel & Hardy Beauties" – Maxine Conrad
Gonzalo & Cristina – Darlene Garner
-----0-----
On the Screen: "Knute Rockne All American"
Pat O'Brien, Ronald Regan

The press coverage for Laurel and Hardy's appearance in Chicago was abysmal to non-existent. There were of course the usual advertising blocks, but then the newspaper companies had been paid to include these. They didn't even bother to send along someone to review the show. It was left to Stan and Babe's enterprise to get their faces in the paper, by doing some shots at the '*Ivanhoe*' – a city-centre restaurant famed for its medieval décor.

IVANHOE RESTAURANT
Clark Street, CHICAGO

A GOOD KNIGHT OUT
The medieval-themed *Ivanhoe Restaurant*, located a few blocks south of Wrigley Field, was one of the finest restaurants in the city, and was dubbed "The Seventh Wonder of Chicago."

After trying to sneak out, without paying their bill, Stan and Ollie are put in chains.

They are released only after settling the bill, and making a donation to the Ivanhoe's "Wishing Well" charity. The owner looks on, to make sure that more money goes in than comes out.

The theatre management too seemed to have no faith in the draw of the two comedians. Firstly, a name change had been made on the bill from the "Danny Dare Girls" to the "Laurel & Hardy Beauties" – which many may have thought was a spoof, rather than a promise of glamour girls. Next, they felt a need to offer an autographed photo of Laurel & Hardy to the first one thousand patrons to attend. When you think that, for just thirty-five cents, the patrons where getting to see the first release of a major film, PLUS a variety show consisting of thirty entertainers, why was there a need to give them more? The theatre management might as well have scrapped the entertainment, and given one-dollar to anyone who handed over thirty-five cents at the box office. Madness!

Stan and Babe added some sanity to the publicity process, by doing guest spots on two radio shows: Bobby Hal Tate's "*Movie Tattler*," plus a children's show at WLS, hosted by presenters 'Aunt Rita and Uncle Charlie.'

WLS STUDIO – CHICAGO
Seated, is 'Aunt Rita.' Standing, can be seen 'Uncle Charlie.' Behind the glass-screen are some wide-eyed children, watching the comedy idols at play.

Come the Wednesday, an event happened which explained why Laurel and Hardy's presence in Chicago had virtually been ignored. And then, on the Thursday, an escalation of that event culminated in our two comedy heroes getting blown out of 'The Windy City.' This is how the events unfurled:

Chicago's State Street Council had secured the rights to host the premiere of the Cecil B. DeMille film "*North West Mounted Police*." Up till then, premieres had been held almost exclusively in Hollywood, where all the stars, lights, and razzmatazz were on tap. The monopoly had been broken the previous year, when the premiere of "*Gone With the Wind*" had been held in Atlanta, Georgia. But then, Atlanta had historical significance to the film's storyline. Chicago had no such significance, so to wrest the film out of Hollywood was a great coup.

Cecil B. DeMille himself arrived at Chicago's North Western Station on the Wednesday afternoon of 23 October, along with a huge entourage of stars, technicians, musicians, and publicists. In complete contrast to Laurel and Hardy's stage appearance, the publicity machine for the premiere of "*North West Mounted Police*" had been rolling for weeks, which resulted in a crowd of over ten thousand waiting to see the likes of Gary Cooper, Madeline Carroll, Preston Foster, and Paulette Goddard as they got off the train.

First stop for the stars of the film was the City Hall, where they were officially welcomed to Chicago by Mayor Kelly. Later that evening a banquet was held at Palmer House, with DeMille and company as Guests of Honour. At 11am on the Thursday morning, the film stars took part in a parade along State Street in open-top convertibles. In the evening DeMille and his cast members made a nationwide broadcast from the WGN radio studios, in the Tribune Tower. This was immediately followed by another parade, billed as "The Bridge of Stars" – so named because it stretched across the bridge from the Chicago Theatre on State Street, to the State Lake theatre. The premiere of the movie was then screened simultaneously at both venues. On the Friday the DeMille party returned to Hollywood, whilst the film went on to complete an eight-day run.

So what of Laurel and Hardy's movements during this invasion of Hollywood-style glitz? Well, on the Thursday, they and their show had been driven out of the theatre a day earlier than usual. However, they had been allowed into the party at Palmer House on Wednesday night; but, for that, they had had to perform an act in a show, along with three singers and comedian Red Skelton.

If only one-tenth of the publicity directed at the film premiere had been directed at Laurel and Hardy, then the city and people of Chicago could have been credited with showing them some respect. As it was, the two great comedians were leaving the Second City a day early, having been papered over by publicity advertising other stars; having been pushed out of their theatre; and having had to sing for their supper.

At least they would get a much-needed break before the next stop-over – Indianapolis.

-----0-----

1940 October 24 [May have left Chicago on Thursday]
CHICAGO, Illinois to **INDIANAPOLIS**, Indiana 275 miles

-----0-----

(Friday 25 October – Thursday 31 October 1940)
INDIANAPOLIS, Indiana – Lyric Theater (1,900)

LYRIC
On Stage
Those Happy Hooligans of Humor–
Hollywood's Greatest Comedy team
LAUREL and HARDY
In Person
and Their Own Original
MUSICAL COMEDY
Revue
Direct From Hollywood
Featuring
DANNY DARE GIRLS
From the Famous Cocoanut
Grove, Hollywood
-----0-----
Melody, Madness and
Hollywood's Gorgeous
Dancing Girls

[Note that James C. Morton, Lew Parker & Co.(Paul Remos, Sid Gold), Maxine Conrad, Cass, Owen and Topsy, Gonzalo & Cristina, Darlene Garner, and Carlton Kelsey were still with show.]

One local paper said of the show:

Now it can be told. When Stan Laurel and Oliver Hardy walk out on the stage, in person, they look exactly as they do in the movies. This great truth dawned on the capacity audience at the Lyric yesterday afternoon, as the fabulous funsters of film fame began a week of personal appearances here—the first they have ever made in our town.

Besides their reputations, the stars bring with them a good show of supporting acts. Laurel and Hardy, we repeat, are the living images of their screen selves, and, in Hardy's case, the similarity is all the more complete when he begins to talk. Laurel, somehow, doesn't sound quite like we thought he would. The boys put on a comedy sketch in which Oliver, aided and seconded by Stan, applies at police headquarters for a renewal of his driver's license. It's good clean fun.

(*Indianapolis Star* – 26 October 1940)

OMAHA – MINNEAPOLIS – MILWAUKEE – CHICAGO – INDIANAPOLIS

Having already done five shows on Friday, the day of arrival (that arrival being at 4am), and with even more performances to make on the Saturday, one would have thought Laurel and Hardy would have tried to grab a little rest between shows. But no! not these Boys. Instead, they sneaked out to go and have a look around the Chamber of Commerce Flying Cadet Exhibition, on North Pennsylvania Street. Whilst showing them around, the Chairman of the Defense Committee rather foolishly gave Hardy a machine gun to inspect. One can only surmise that he had not seen what happens when Hardy is handed a tommy-gun in the film "*Pardon Us,*" otherwise he would have kept it safely locked away.

On Sunday, too, the comedy duo left the theatre – this time to go "live on air." Laurel and Hardy's piece on the show "*Sunday Noon Wire*" went out between 12.15 and 12.30pm over what appears to have been the College Circuit, after which our subjects had to dash back to the theatre for the first afternoon show.

Variety (30 October 1940) gave a much warmer summary of the show than was their norm:

> Laurel and Hardy, making their first trip to this town, prove that comedians can be as funny in person as they are in their pictures. In their closing 12-minute skit of their own revue, in which they have a mix-up in getting Hardy a driving license, they wear familiar picture outfits and use dumb routine which has the audience in stitches all the way through.
>
> With them is a talented company which puts on a well-rounded 50 minutes. Many times, top names neglect the rest of the bill, apparently in an effort to cut down expense. But Laurel and Hardy have surrounded themselves with a company which would have a good show without the principals. With the film comedians as a marquee draw, it's a cinch for good business. Unit is nicely costumed and well lighted.

"But then," as in the words of the song: "they go and spoil it all, by saying something stupid like …"

> With 18,000 schoolmarms in town for annual convention to help swell opening day grosses, biz got off to a flying start here this week with the impetus carrying through for the seven days. Two flesh shows in the downtown area are splitting the heavy coin, with Lyric topping the collections with Laurel & Hardy. Circle meantime is also running in heavy sugar with "George White's Scandals." Pix at both houses are just fill-ins between stage shows.
>
> (*Variety* – 30 October 1940)

I think the above 'review' was written in code, just in case the enemy intercepted a copy.

Sometime during their stay in Indianapolis, presidential candidate Wendell Wilkie, still on his campaign trail, paid a whistle-stop visit, of which Laurel later told a reporter.

> He was very swell to us when we finally met him in Indianapolis, and waited five minutes so he could have his picture taken with us.
>
> (*Pittsburgh Press* – 16 November 1940)

It's great to know that Wilkie respected them enough to hold the train so he could meet them, and also satisfying to know that audiences appreciated the presence of Laurel and Hardy in their theatre; but one would have to question if the theatre management showed them enough respect. Hardy said of the Lyric Theatre in Indianapolis:

> It had an underground dressing room, and the minute I walked into it, I said, "This place smells like a Turkish bath." And sure enough, we came to find out it **had** been a Turkish bath, still had the tiled walls and floors. I told them, "You can't fool an old Turkish bath man."

> "Yes," Laurel agreed, "every time we got a breath of fresh air, we'd faint. Even the alley smelled good. Ah, those garbage cans!"
>
> (St. Louis Post-Dispatch – 5 November 1940)

Well, at least the reviews in Indianapolis didn't stink. That would have been a lot harder to bear.

o-o-0-o-o

CHAPTER 20

THE OTHER MONKEY

(1940 pt4 Nov)

At their next stop-over, Laurel and Hardy were finally about to receive the press interest their presence commanded.

-----0-----

1940 November 01

INDIANAPOLIS, Indiana to **ST. LOUIS**, Missouri 245 miles

-----0-----

(Friday 1 November – Thursday 7 November)
ST. LOUIS, Missouri – Fox Theater (5,500)

FOX! Today
ON THE STAGE
In Person
HOLLYWOOD'S No.1
COMEDY TEAM
Stan
LAUREL
Oliver
HARDY
DANNY DARE GIRLS
LEW PARKER
CASS, OWEN & TOPSY
DARLENE GARNER
Sid Gold - James C. Morton
Maxine Conrad
On the Screen: *"Meet the Wildcat"*
and *"Little Bit of Heaven" (U)*.
Shows at: at 2.43, 6.16, and 9.49pm

One local reviewer opined:

> Laurel and Hardy change their medium, but not their style as the headline attraction on the triple bill which arrived at the Fox yesterday. As the featured members of the cast of a Revue which includes the usual variety of entertainers, the comedians cavort in precisely the manner they have in their numerous starring screen comedies.
>
> In fact, their big scene might have been lifted from one of their films, so typical is it of their particular brand of slapstick. In the scene, Stan and Oliver go to the police station to renew Oliver's driving license, and wind up by slapping each other around a bit; also a policeman, one of those bald comical kind they often encounter on the screen. He's James C. Morton, who, when not touring with Laurel and Hardy is a film cop. With his assistance, the comedians had the audience in a few stitches, proving, if anything, funnier in the flesh than in the flickers.
>
> (*St. Louis Daily Globe* – 2 November 1940)

James C. Morton as 'the cop' in *"The Driver's License"* sketch

A second local contributed:

> Not too blue, not too funny to outshine the stars, the [supporting] show keeps the audience well occupied until Stan and Ollie get a chance with their stuff.
>
> Just to see Stan Laurel scratching the top of his head, or watch him tune up for a whimper, has always been genuine pleasure. Hardy's flick of the necktie, his greasy [*sic*] daintiness, and impatience with Laurel, make the fun complete.
>
> On the Fox stage this week, the two comedians appear in a hilarious skit having to do with getting a driver's license for Ollie at police headquarters. That poor officer of the law.
>
> (*St. Louis Post-Dispatch* – 3 November 1940)

But, surprisingly, it was *Variety* which put the two local reviews to shame, and gave away snippets of the on-stage business, which proved they had not just compiled a feeble review from the stock publicity notes:

> Fanchon & Marco is taking another fling at stage shows in this midtown 5,000-seater and, if it can maintain the calibre of the current offering, which got away to a nice box-office start, the latest try should be a profitable one. Surveys, polls, etc., have indicated that natives want more than talkers, but for some unexplainable reason they usually shy away from the stage shows when they get 'em. At supper show caught, lower floor seating 2,860 was almost filled and payees seemed to like the fast action of this 55-minute offering. Of course it was Laurel and Hardy who drew 'em in and the talker comedians didn't pull any punches as they spend 15 minutes on the boards and wind up with a slapstick skit.
>
> It's their first p.a. [personal appearance] here and in the garb they wear in the talkers, score right off the bat. After their dumb stuff they join James C. Morton in a skit anent an altercation with a cop. They swipe the latter's lunch, ignore his questions and wind up the guffaw with a bunch of rough house stuff in which they daub Morton's nose with ink, bang him on the dome with a tin platter, tear his breakaway coat and pour water down his pants. Then the entire troupe parades across the apron to bring festivities to a finale.
>
> (*Variety* – 6 November 1940)

The two comedians were interviewed over a cup of coffee, after breakfast, at the Hotel Coronado where they were staying the week. Clarissa Start from the *St. Louis Post-Dispatch* revealed: "*It seems that every place the comedians have gone they've run into 'Conventions, Food Shows, and [Wendell] Wilkie'.*"

When the subject of their partnership and their style of comedy came up, Hardy credited Laurel with being the brains behind their films, as far as plot and gags are concerned, adding:

> I'm just the moral support, but we need that too. Making comedy is a serious business. We have to rehearse over and over so our timing is perfect. Then we have to be sure all our actions are within the capabilities of the two characters we've created. We never wise-crack, never use suggestive material. We get letters from ministers and Deans of schools, complimenting us on that.
>
> <div align="right">(<i>St. Louis Post-Dispatch</i> – 5 November 1940)</div>

As St. Louis was only a small city, fewer shows were needed to cater for the theatregoing members of the local populace, so the number was cut to three per day. The running time of each house was, however, longer – as two films were screened instead of the usual one. This allowed our subjects sufficient free time to actually get away from the theatre, and pursue leisure activities. Normally, when not working, they would stay well away from public places, but in this instance both visited the St. Louis Zoo – Stan once, and Babe twice.

Describing himself as a "zoo person," Hardy told a reporter:

> I was bitten by a big panda. That gives me some distinction, I guess, as the only man ever to be bitten by a $20,000 panda. I was getting along fine with it, playing with the pretty beast, when suddenly Stan popped around the corner. The panda took one look at him and got hysterical. I don't know what it is about me that animals like—to bite. But that's alright, we got even. Stan bit it back.

Before this rare pleasure trip, the two stars had done their bit to promote the show. Upon arrival on the Friday they had gone from the railway station straight to the KXOK Radio station, to announce their arrival in town, and advertise the show via "*The Woman's Page.*" Then, after the last house on the Saturday, they shot over this time to KMOX, to speak to listeners of Uncle Dick Slack's "*Old Fashioned Barn Dance*" program. (You can make your own jokes up about Dick Slack!). Meanwhile, you have to give credit to Laurel and Hardy, whose first visit to the radio station came after a tiring journey from Indianapolis, and whose second came after an exhausting day of Saturday performances.

Through no fault of theirs, Laurel and Hardy's next show on the schedule was cancelled, and a last-minute replacement venue had to be found.

(Thursday 7 November – CANCELLED)
CLEVELAND, Ohio – State Theatre (Loew's)

The following news article reveals just why the cancellation occurred:

Loew's Pulls Laurel-Hardy Unit Out of Cleve. in Tiff with Musicians

Laurel and Hardy stage unit which had been set to open Thursday (7), was cancelled by Lowe's State and all its negotiations with the musicians local were called off by the New York office last Friday (1) after a heated, epithet-throwing battle here, in which theatre execs accused Lee Repp, union prez, of double-crossing them.

Booking of the two film comics at Loew's deluxer was clinched a fortnight ago, but then they demanded a guarantee of 20 weeks of work for musicians during 1940-41 season. Loew's execs feel there's no need for anything more than five or six stage shows per year.

It's now stated that the State is abandoning all vaude negotiations for this season. Instead of playing the Laurel and Hardy unit, which had its Nov. 7 date shifted from Cleveland to the Loew's Ohio in Columbus.

-----0-----

1940 November 08

ST. LOUIS, Missouri to COLUMBUS, Ohio 420 miles
-----0-----
(Friday 8 November – Thursday 14 November 1940)

LAUREL and HARDY – The U.S. Tours

COLUMBUS, Ohio – Ohio Theater (aka: Loew's) (2,800)

> **Laurel and Hardy,** with James C. Morton
> *Lew Parker & Co. (Paul Remos, Sid Gold)*
> *Danny Dare Girls; Maxine Conrad*
> *Cass, Owen and Topsy; Darlene Garner.*
> On the Screen: *"Arise My Love"*

Barring the odd personal appearances, rallies, style shows and other such one-day functions, the "Laurel & Hardy Revue" was the first live show to play at the Ohio Theatre for five years.

> The revue brings with it some diverting moments. Top of the lot comes along when the lean Mr. Laurel and the chubby Mr. Hardy put in their appearance. Briefly and comically they greet their audience and then go into a skit in which Oliver applies for a driver's license. It's all typical Laurel and Hardy slapstick and that is something that is able to draw fervent response from even a typical Columbus Friday afternoon audience. James C. Morton holds still for plenty of violence in the skit with the stellar comedians.
>
> *(Columbus Dispatch – 9 October 1940)*

Of future plans for the team of Laurel & Hardy, now that they didn't have a film contract, Stan mentioned they would soon be starring in a Technicolor film titled *"The Red Mill"* – a statement which deserves a bit of analysis. Firstly, no official press statements regarding the proposed making of the film seem to have been released, which leaves Stan and Babe as the sole source. MGM had previously made *"The Red Mill"* in 1927, starring Marion Davies and Owen Moore, but that was a silent film, and a romantic comedy at that, so the screenplay held little merit for the characters of Laurel & Hardy.

Stan and Babe would have had far more interest in the stage version which, between 1906 and 1907, had played close to three hundred performances on Broadway. *"The Red Mill"* was an operetta written by Victor Herbert, from a book by Henry Blossom. Laurel and Hardy's obvious intention was to do a treatment of it, whereby they would write in the comedy parts of "the Boys," as they had done in their film *"Babes in Toyland"* – coincidentally based on one of Victor Herbert's slightly earlier works. This is exactly what the comedy double-act Montgomery and Stone had done for the 1906-7 Broadway production.

What had more than likely raised Stan and Babe's current interest in this vehicle is that, as recently as June 1940, *"The Red Mill"* had played on the light operatic stage in Los Angeles – with Charles Collins and Sterling Holloway in the lead roles. There is a distinct possibility that Stan may have gone to see it, or at the very least read the reviews, and thought that he and Babe could do a better job. However, getting MGM to commit to a film version, or getting a backer for a stage version, probably got no further than Laurel's personal wish list.

As a postscript, *"The Red Mill"* was actually revived, and ran for over five hundred performances at the Ziegfeld Theatre, New York, commencing 16 October 1945. It was also filmed, in 1958, but for TV only. Both productions came too late for Laurel and Hardy to be considered for the parts, but Laurel's confidence in the potential of *"The Red Mill"* had been vindicated.

Back to the stay in Columbus, where the subject of visiting zoos came up again. But this tale has a bit of a twist. Instead of going to the zoo to see animals, Stan and Babe were actually taking one *to* the zoo. Sounds like the old joke, doesn't it:

First man: "Where are you taking that penguin?"

Second Man: "I'm taking it to the cinema."

First man: "Shouldn't you be taking it to the zoo?"

Second man: "I took it to the zoo, yesterday."

The Other Monkey

The two men in this tale were handing over a Garo Hill ape to the Columbus Zoo. Hardy described it as: "*A lovely little pet. It bites anyone on any provocation, but it prefers biting either Stan or me. Affectionate little beastie,*" and added that he intended to visit the zoo at least once during their week in Columbus.

So! "Just what were Laurel and Hardy doing in possession of an ape?" is a question you might well be asking.

According to the *Columbus Dispatch* the pair had acquired the ape in St. Louis, and kept it as a combination pet-mascot during their coast-to-coast personal appearance tour. If the ape had indeed been acquired in St. Louis, this would mean Stan and Babe had had it for no more than one week; which doesn't match the above description that the ape had been "kept as a combination pet-mascot during their coast-to-coast personal appearance tour." Further investigation in other quarters turned up another mention of the ape and its antics as early as the first week in October, when the Boys had been in Minneapolis: (*Boxoffice* – 12 October 1940)

> Manager Bill Sears of the Minneapolis Orpheum, is nursing some nasty scratches, and has a few more gray hairs from worry, as the result of a publicity stunt for Laurel and Hardy, who appeared at his theatre recently.
>
> The stunt contemplated the gift of a live monkey, on the comedy pair's behalf, to the winner of a [local newspaper] contest. Sears had the monkey delivered to the Orpheum Theatre, and then the trouble started. Without any warning the animal began to cut capers and made an effort to escape. Sears was scratched when he tried to grab the monkey, which succeeded in getting away and dashed through the opening into the rafter space above the balcony.
>
> All efforts to coax the monkey out were unavailing. It was necessary to post a guard at the opening to prevent the animal from running out into the auditorium. Though it had no food or drink, it waited three days before it finally ventured out, and was then captured.

One would have to surmise that the winner of the monkey declined it as a prize, which would explain how "The Three 'Dumb' Monkeys" came to be together in Columbus.

Hardy was the probable "brains" behind adopting the monkey, as my good friend Mr. Louvish informs us (in his book "*STAN and OLLIE – The Roots of Comedy*") that in 1917, when Hardy was living in Jacksonville, his little playmate was a capuchin monkey. Hence why Laurel later became "the other monkey."

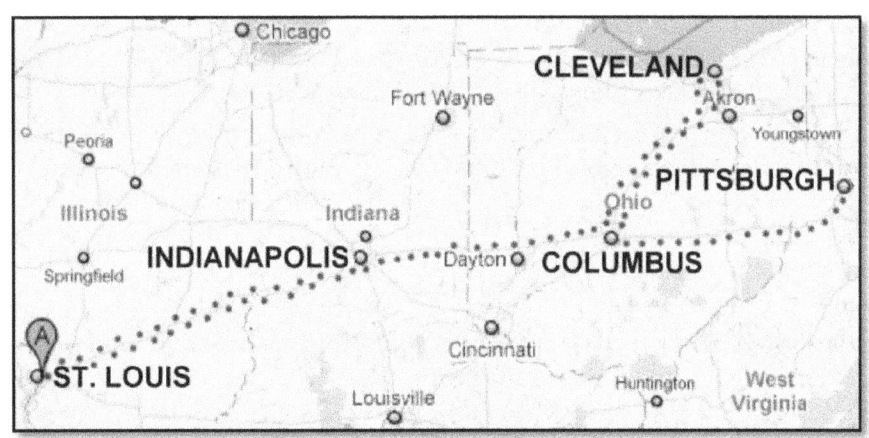

INDIANAPOLIS – ST. LOUIS – CLEVELAND – COLUMBUS – PITTSBURGH

-----0-----

1940 November 15

COLUMBUS, Ohio to **PITTSBURGH**, Pennsylvania 🚂 184 miles

-----0-----

(Friday 15 November – Thursday 21 November 1940)
PITTSBURGH, Pennsylvania – Stanley Theatre

HOURS OF LAUGHTER
ON STAGE – IN PERSON
Laurel & Hardy
With Their Own Spectacular
Live Revue
Featuring
LEW PARKER
CASS, OWEN AND TOPSY
MAXINE CONRAD
SID GOLD
JAMES MORTON
DARLENE GARNER
The DAZZLING Dancing
DANNY DARE GIRLS
Max Adkin Orchestra.
ON THE SCREEN:
"DULCY"
Shows at:
11.50; 2.20; 4.45; 7.10; and 9.40

From Columbus, Hardy and "the other monkey" travelled west to Pittsburgh, where one reviewer rather over-zealously classed their act as a …

SCREWBALL FESTIVAL

Stan and Oliver have mixed up some new and old gags into a very funny skit, which is good for more laughs than their recent movie endeavors. The boys clicked strongly with the first day audiences, and seem to have much more than the camera catches.

(*Pittsburgh Press* – 16 November 1940)

A second reviewer was less zealous, but still complimentary: (Variety – 20 November 1940)

Film comics Laurel and Hardy have cooked up an okay revue for their personal appearance jaunt. Unlike most Hollywood units, this one isn't composed of deadwood names, but is peopled chiefly by vaude standbys who know what it's all about. Result is a show that's fast, funny, good-looking and well-routined.

Laurel and Hardy confine their doings to a 10-minute skit at the close of the show and it's tailor-made for silly Stan and opulent Ollie. Chief complaints about team on the screen is that there's usually too much of them; that can't be made of their current p.a. and it's reacting to their advantage. Their style is well-known, and police station sketch, which winds up in a slap-stick melee, fits them accurately right down to the vest buttons.

Introduction brings them to the downstage mike in one for some pantomimic skills and when Hardy suggests that Laurel make a thank you speech, latter says he hasn't time because they have to go to City Hall and renew Hardy's driver's license. That leads them into a half-stage set and the body of their act, with Lew Parker doing the beleaguered sergeant in absence of ailing James Morton. Parker foiled them well, and comedy team doesn't need any apologists for either their material or execution.

Note that Lew Parker stood in for James C. Morton, who was unwell – which is not surprising. Having a jug of water poured down your trousers four to five times a day, does not exactly promote good health.

o-o-0-o-o

CHAPTER 21

COP OUT

(1940 pt5 Nov-Dec)

On Sunday, the third night of Laurel and Hardy's booking in Pittsburgh, a unique event happened. Instead of performing the show at the local Stanley Theatre the whole kit and caboodle was transferred thirty-five miles west to the Capitol theatre in Steubenville, Ohio – for just the ONE NIGHT.

-----0-----

1940 November 17

PITTSBURGH, Pennsylvania to **STEUBENVILLE**, Ohio 🚂 34 miles

-----0-----

(Sunday 17 November 1940 – 1 night only)
STEUBENVILLE, Ohio – Capitol

SUNDAY ONLY
ON THE STAGE
HOURS OF LAUGHTER
ON STAGE – IN PERSON
**LAUREL &
HARDY**
With Their Own Spectacular
Live Revue
Featuring
LEW PARKER – CASS, OWEN and TOPSY
MAXINE CONRAD – SID GOLD
JAMES MORTON
DARLENE GARNER
The DAZZLING
DANNY DARE GIRLS

Local by-laws in Pittsburgh prohibited Sunday performances, but the state of Ohio didn't. This explains "how" they were allowed to stage the show – but not "why?" Why go to all that time, trouble and expense for just one night? It's not even as if the people of Steubenville appreciated it. It certainly wasn't reflected in the coverage the press gave. They made not the merest mention of Laurel and Hardy's visit to their fair city before, during, or afterwards. The only evidence to show that Laurel and Hardy went there at all is from two unimpressive advertising blocks.

-----0-----

1940 November 17

STEUBENVILLE, Ohio to PITTSBURGH, Pennsylvania 🚂 34 miles

-----0-----

Monday found everyone back in Pittsburgh, staying at the William Penn Hotel, and returning to shows at the Stanley Theatre. Having done a minimal review of Laurel and Hardy's actual stage performance, the *Pittsburgh Press* somewhat made up for it by printing an interview with the two comedians. Firstly Babe and Stan expressed relief that Wendell Wilkie's presidential campaign was over, as his schedule had clashed with theirs and, in their words, *"almost broke up their tour across the continent."*

The last statement is a little exaggerated, whereas the next one is pushing the bounds of credibility.

> The famous comedians, now appearing at the Stanley Theatre, have been on a personal appearance tour for eight weeks, and will stay on the road until next May, just four weeks short of the top run vaudeville stretch of "forty weeks on the boards." Next week they go to Philadelphia, and expect to be in Toronto for Christmas.

No confirmation was found that this tour had been planned for anything longer than the number of weeks it actually ran; which was, including Steubenville, thirteen cities in twelve weeks. A run of thirty-six weeks would have been nigh on impossible to have pulled off. The tour had only gone into planning in late August/early September, so to have placed the show in as many theatres as they had, at such short notice, was an admirable feat in itself. One would have also had to factor in the physical limitations of the two stars being able to keep up that many performances, plus all the travelling involved for thirty-six weeks.

A few snippets of information emerged, which did seem to be factual: It was Hardy's first visit to Pittsburgh, but Laurel remembered appearing at the Kenyon Street Theatre there, in 1915. This would have been late February-early March, when he was playing "*The Nutty Burglars*" with the Keystone Trio. He had also played the Harris Theatre in 1916, with the Stan Jefferson Trio. A first for Mrs. Hardy was seeing snow. As she had been born and raised in Texas, snow was not something that had ever come Lucille's way.

The subject of "*The Red Mill*" came up again, although this can be put into the section marked "Laurel & Hardy would *like* to do," rather than, "Laurel & Hardy *are going* to do."

> Laurel and Hardy have their own producing company, and when the tour is over they plan to produce Victor Herbert's "The Red Mill." They will play the parts originally done by Montgomery and Stone, of two American tourists who go broke in Holland, and have a series of extremely engaging experiences.
>
> <div align="right">(<i>Pittsburgh Press</i> – 16 November 1940)</div>

For Laurel, a story of going broke in Holland would seem almost autobiographical, as he had actually done just that (see Chapter 1). You can bet your bottom guilder that Laurel had ideas of incorporating aspects of his real-life experiences in Holland, into the proposed new script for "*The Red Mill*" – if and when it were to happen.

Let us see how healthy the box-office returns were for the Pittsburgh show:

Picture Grosses.

"Escape," at Penn, and "Mark of Zorro," at Fulton are still doing pretty good, while at Stanley, Laurel-Hardy unit, with "Dulcy," isn't going to wind up any better than just fair.

Stanley (WB) "Dulcy" (M-G) and Laurel-Hardy on stage. Comedians are on their own, film being of little or no help. Notices for their show OK, but boys have never been particularly hefty here in pix and obviously interest in them in person is only slight. Present pace indicates $16,500, just fair. Last week, George Jessel unit and "Moon Burma" over $18,000, finishing strong.

(Variety – 20 November 1940)

In questioning Laurel and Hardy's box-office appeal, *Variety* had failed to factor in one very important reason why many people stayed out of the theatre that week; a reason that only came to light in a letter written by Laurel — some seventeen years later:

Aug. 5th, '57

```
Dear Earl:-
Interesting to hear re the improve taking place in
Pittsburgh in the clean up dept. It sure was a dirty place,
last time I was there in '40. I think we played at the
Harris [sic] theatre with our revue show. Incidentally,
during that week, the roof of the Stanley Theatre caved in
```

- fortunately the place was empty at the time & don't think
anyone was hurt, but it certainly put a scare into
everybody there. Theatre business suffered through it,
people were afraid to come in. I noticed during our
performances that many people kept looking at the ceiling &
were'nt paying much attention to what was going on with the
show.

Though it is every comedians desire to "pull the roof in,"
that is not exactly what they mean!

-----0-----

1940 November 22

PITTSBURGH, Pennsylvania to **PHILADELPHIA**, Pennsylvania 🚂 304 miles

-----0-----

(Friday 22 November – Thursday 28 November 1940)
PHILADELPHIA, Pennsylvania – Earle Theater

IN PERSON
Stan **LAUREL** &
Oliver **HARDY**
With Their Own
HOWL-ARIOUS REVUE
LEW PARKER
CASS, OWEN and TOPSY
MAXINE CONRAD
DARLENE GARNER
SID GOLD
DANNY DARE'S
10 GLAMOROUS
HOLLYWOOD GIRLS
On Our Screen
CHARTER PILOT

Evidence would suggest James C. Morton had left the show for good, so Lew Parker stood in for the rest of the tour. The change did not seem to have affected the quality of the sketch.

> The leap from screen to stage has tripped more than one visiting luminary. But not Stan Laurel and his plump partner, Oliver Hardy. In fact, they are funnier in their personal appearance now at the Earle than they've been since the very early days of their two-reelers. The script never lets the Boys down – nor are there any of those awkward moments experienced by too many Hollywood folk on their personal appearance jaunts
>
> Even without Laurel and Hardy, the stage show hits a new high for breeziness and for the pleasant people it presents.
>
> (*Philadelphia Record* – 24 November 1940)

A review from a second newspaper didn't agree that Laurel & Hardy were funnier than in their films, but then – how could they be!

> They bite into a bandaged finger in place of a banana, they kick and slap-stick exactly as you would expect of Stan Laurel and Oliver Hardy.
>
> Seems a contradiction in terms to call this goofy pair 'modest,' but they actually appear only for the final ten minutes of their long personal appearance stage revue.

They do a small bit before the mike and a skit in which Hardy attempts to renew the out-dated driver's license his grandpap gave him.

Less funny behind footlights than on the screen, but yesterday's enthusiastic audience gave them a big hand.

(*Philadelphia Bulletin* 24 November 1940)

The local press laid on a party for the Boys, which one would think would have led to some great write-ups on Laurel and Hardy's thoughts, movements, and stories about their current tour. What did emerge, however, was old or recycled inaccurate garbage regarding their early careers, plus cookie stories from their off-screen lives, the likes of which merit no inclusion in this book.

Backstage at the Earle Theatre, Laurel tries to keep Hardy away from the platter of hospitality sandwiches.

The only current information to surface was that Stan and Babe enjoyed some refreshments at O'Donnell's Bar, and that they had been lent a Studebaker car for the week, in return for posing for pictures with it. Hopefully, they didn't drive back from O'Donnell's in it. It had been "that kind" of refreshment.

The local press also failed to cover Stan and Babe going to a children's party to entertain the kids. Most of the children were British, who had been evacuated to the U.S. to escape the bombings in Britain. Others were the children of Warner Brothers employees, and all had Uncle Stan and Uncle Babe joining in their party games. The details of the visit only emerged two weeks later, and that was in newspapers in other states.

Variety's customary column on the box office returns for the Philadelphia Earle theatre revealed in its "Picture Grosses. Estimates:"

Earle: "*Charter Pilot*" with Laurel-Hardy unit on stage. Will show profit with $22,500. Not in same class, however, with last week's socko $27,000 for combo of "*East River*" and Cab Calloway orchestra.

Maybe Laurel and Hardy were *too* classy for Philadelphia.

-----0-----

1940 November 29

PHILADELPHIA, Pennsylvania to **NEWARK**, New Jersey 81 miles

-----0-----

(Friday 29 November – Sunday 1 December 1940)

NEWARK, New Jersey – Adams Theater

ON STAGE – Starting TODAY
AMERICA'S No.1 COMEDY TEAM
BIGGEST LAUGH SHOW
EVER IN NEWARK
Direct from HOLLYWOOD
**LAUREL
and HARDY**
In Person
with their own
HOLLYWOOD Musical COMEDY Revue
30 MERRY MAKERS 30
featuring LEW PARKER
SID GOLD – CASS, OWEN
TOPSY – MAXINE
CONRAD – DARLENE GARNER
Hollywood GLAMOR GIRLS
On the Screen:
"MEET THE MISSUS"

Variety said of the Boys' show:

> The jackpot has been hit with the importation of Laurel and Hardy's streamlined unit into Adams this week. Lobby ropes are up for this first time this fall.
>
> Show belongs to Laurel and Hardy, however, and they have wisely reserved final spot for their comedy antics. Unlike some other big-name comics who have played this house, they do not rely on their reputation but get out there and work for their plentiful laughs. Police station skit, with Lew Parker helping out as straight, gives Laurel chance to display his familiar set of frustrations, and Hardy opportunity to demonstrate his slow-burn technique. Act is foolproof, even to non-fans, and is just the right length to sell effectively.

While the *Newark Star Ledger* (30 November 1940) offered:

> Laurel and Hardy offer an original skit in which gags and pantomime, familiar to movie-goers, call for laughter and repeated applause. The near-capacity crowd at yesterday's matinee exhibited its pleasure by long and loud hand clapping, and waited until long after the final curtain for encores that did not come.

It would appear that Stan and Babe had Monday to Wednesday off. If so, let us hope they were able to spend the time recharging their batteries, as by now they must have been drained. Come Thursday, the Boys were back at work.

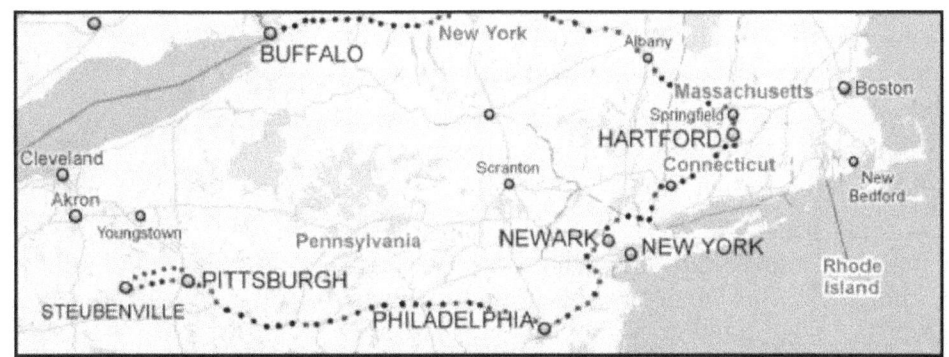

PITTSBURGH–STEUBENVILLE–PHILADELPHIA–NEWARK–HARTFORD–BUFFALO

-----0-----

1940 December 04

    NEWARK, New Jersey to **HARTFORD**, Connecticut 🚂 133 miles

LAUREL and HARDY – The U.S. Tours

(Thursday 5 December – Wednesday 11 December 1940)
HARTFORD, Connecticut – State Theater

> **Laurel and Hardy – with Lew Parker**
> *Lew Parker & Co. (Paul Remos, Sid Gold)*
> *Danny Dare Girls; Cass, Owen and Topsy*
> *Louis Prima and his Gleeby Rhythm Orchestra.*
> On the Screen: *"Phantom of Chinatown"*

Laurel and Hardy are even better in person than they are on the screen. The two zanies, now at the State Theater, are the same funny, befuddled cut-ups the film world has loved for years. But what delighted us tremendously is that they refuse to trade on their screen "reps." Instead of doing what several Hollywood stars do, they have brought to Hartford a complete revue-unit of which they are only a part—the comedy part. Two smart boys, they are far ahead of the Hollywood-to-Broadway trend, and with proper appreciation and evaluation of themselves to know that it takes many types of "acts" to please the large audiences they hope to gain.

So, ladies and gentlemen, they give you not only their own precious selves, but a great eccentric trio – Cass, Owen, and Topsy – two girls and a man who clinch in unheard of ways which make you wonder how they bring themselves back alive from such "holds." Then, for the eyes, Maxine Conrad, an eyeful! And, for good measure, fast snappy patter between her and Lew Parker, a boy with plenty of personality, but too many Joe Millers. And a great, novel audience participation angle.

There are seven really beautiful girls, with their lovely pastel flowing gowns. Their dance routines are simple, but their costumes (especially in 'The Three Musketeers' number) are fetching enough to meet Broadway night-club competition.

And of course the boys, Laurel and Hardy, in their own skit, which is well-written and well-acted. Rollicking, slap-stick, nit-witty and witty, they tear through the process of getting an automobile license, co-operating with neither the 'officer' in charge nor with themselves in their genius for bungling. Oliver, the pompous; and Stan the out-of-this-world fellow. They were great and the audience loved them!

(Hartford Courant – 6 December 1940)

On the Tuesday afternoon, the two comedians paid a visit to the *Daily Courant* offices, where they took particular interest in another of its publications, *"Parade of Youth,"* and left the following message for its young readers:

> The secret of any success is hard work. Nothing is more important than that you finish your schooling. Get as much education as you can. Often, young people don't realize this until it is too late. And when I say this I am not speaking as a comedian. I am very serious.

Asked why Laurel & Hardy films are favourites among boys and girls, as well as grown-ups, Hardy offered:

> Good comedy has to be clean comedy. Youth likes clean fun. And there is no doubt that people prefer clean comedy. Some may laugh at smut. Even though critics may sometimes laugh at it, they are usually the first to condemn smut.

You can tell that BOTH comments came from Hardy. It would have been a bit rich for Laurel to give advice about getting a good education, as he had spent more days playing hooky from school, than he had attending.

Hardy typing his message for the *Courant* readers, on a Lintotype machine – a skill he had learned as a youth.

The previous Thursday, Stan and Babe had been photographed outside the State Theater in Hartford, putting money into a Salvation Army 'kettle' – aka: a collecting pot. It would seem that, whenever they weren't on-stage giving out laughs, the Boys were off-stage, giving money to charity.

-----0-----
1940 December 12
HARTFORD, Connecticut to **BUFFALO**, New York 🚂 398 miles
-----0-----
(Friday 13 December – Thursday 19 December 1940)
BUFFALO, New York – 20th Century Theatre

> **Laurel and Hardy** – with Lew Parker
> *Lew Parker & Co. (Paul Remos, Sid Gold)*
> *Danny Dare Girls; Maxine Conrad*
> *Cass, Owen and Topsy*
> *Caroline Swan* [replaced Darlene Garner]
> On the Screen: "*Stranger on the Third Floor*"

Laurel and Hardy revue shapes up as an out-and-out, variety show. It's a fancy package for picture house trade, hits the bull's eye with its comedy values, and should coax heavy wampum from the vaude-starved natives. Name comics wisely refrain from overdosing the admiring payees, holding down the next-to-closing spot only, but gathering tumultuous response with familiarity seems to have bred increased appreciation.

> The enthusiastic salvos elicited by the perspiring efforts of these film comics is only proper payment for the earnest comedy labours. This de-luxe barnstorming tour should gain them new followers. They have the kind of personality—and what they might do with a good musical comedy book is something to think about.

> Final quarter-hour brings on the two stars, who found high favor immediately with this crowd. After some appealing comedy around the mike which establishes them solidly, they fade into full stage for their driver's license test skit. Here Parker, working straight, again furnishes invaluable assistance. The comics run the gamut of their familiar gags, ending up with the messy but socko food and water tag, practically out of the burley barns, but sapolioed [*sic*].

Lew Parker, admirably fitting into the role of the Cop, vacated by James C. Morton.

For the finale, their manipulation of finger bandages, fruit, sandwiches, soda crackers and water, with Laurel pouring the pitcher into Parker's pants for the climax, proves plenty uproarious. These boys have developed the comedy slow-timing technique to an art, and in this, as in everything else they do, they emphasize their seasoned trouping.

(Variety – 13 December 1940)

Estimates for this Week: 20th Century: *"Stranger on the Third Floor"* and Laurel & Hardy revue. Looks like over $12,000, plenty good. Last week "Laddie" and Woody Herman orchestra, so-so, under $10,000.

Here the tour ended, putting paid to the earlier statement that Laurel and Hardy "will stay on the road until next May." But what they had learned, and what they had earned, would stand them in well for the future.

-----0-----

1940 Dec 20

BUFFALO, New York to **LOS ANGELES**, California 2,584 miles

-----0-----

The Boys got home just in time to make a contribution to a radio broadcast:

Christmas Day Broadcast – Alan Mowbray Show

Scores of notables in the entertainment world have accepted Alan Mowbray's invitation to participate in the scheduled 'Christmas Greetings' broadcast to England on Christmas morning.

Lined up to date are Charles Boyer, John Garfield, Rupert Hughes, Adolph Menjou, Robert Montgomery, Laurel and Hardy, Edward G. Robinson, James Cagney, Basil Rathbone, Laurence Olivier and Vivien Leigh, Nigel Bruce, Douglas Fairbanks, Jr., and many others.

(Boxoffice – 23 November 1940)

It was almost certainly a goodwill message and thank you to all their fans in England for their continued support of the Laurel & Hardy films over the years. There is a strong possibility that Stan and Babe also informed listeners that they were coming to Britain to play their show, as plans were afoot to do just that.

While the Boys' had been playing Boston, press snippets had revealed their next two proposed projects. Firstly that:

Stan Laurel and Oliver Hardy are mentioned for the new Ziegfeld Follies, which J.J. Schubert plans to present later this season.

(Syracuse Herald Journal – 14 December 1940)

And the following day:

Stan Laurel and Oliver Hardy are scheduled for comedy leads in 'The Little Dog Laughed,' Eddie Dowling's stage production.

Neither of these stage bookings materialised – which may have been because of the aforementioned plans to tour Britain.

So, as 1940 closed its doors, Laurel and Hardy found the doors to both the film world and the theatre world had closed too. Where to next?

o-o-0-o-o

CHAPTER 22

COAST to COAST

(1941 pt1)

Laurel tried to start off 1941 with the tradition of "ringing in the new," but, for a second time, succeed only in "ringing in the old" – when his *new* marriage partner turned out to be his *old* marriage partner, Ruth.

> Las Vegas, Nev, Jan 11 (AP) – Film comedian Stan Laurel, 50, remarried the second of his four wives, Virginia Ruth Laurel, 41, of Beverly Hills, Calif., in a surprise ceremony today.
>
> They were re-wed at the Hitching Post Wedding Chapel by the Rev. Melto of Immanuel Community Church, using an old-fashioned gold ring.
>
> Each of the couple voiced "thrills" at trying matrimony together again. The couple will remain here until Monday before returning to Hollywood.
>
> (*Associated Press* – 12 January 1941)

Laurel told a *Los Angeles Times* reporter:

> It happened suddenly, like heart-failure, or strike one. We hadn't seen each other for a year when Virginia called me up a few nights ago. I invited her out to the Fort, and first thing we knew we had decided to do it all over again."

So, Stan had now married Ruth for the THIRD time – well, second time, but three ceremonies. So how long would it last this time around? Time to place another bet!

-----0-----

1941 January 11 (Saturday)
        LOS ANGELES, California to **LAS VEGAS**, Nevada 🚂 275 miles

1941 January 13 (Monday)
        LAS VEGAS, Nevada to **LOS ANGELES**, California 🚂 275 miles

-----0-----

Ruth now moved in with Stan at 20213 Strathern Street, Canoga Park, which had been substantially modified since Stan and Illiana first moved in there, in 1938. September 1940 had seen the completion of a seven-foot-high brick wall around the entire perimeter. Access was by a huge wooden gate, similar in design to those seen on medieval fortresses. Subsequently, Stan christened the property "Fort Laurel" – giving the reason for erecting the wall as: *"To ensure peace from process servers, newsmen, and the curious, as a result of tangles with ex-wives."*

If you found the idea of Stan marrying Ruth astounding, how astounded would you be if an unknown film of Laurel & Hardy were found? Intrigued?

> George McCall, who has achieved radio prominence as the CBS West coast film columnist, will appear on the Kearse theatre stage with his "Glamor Girl Revue" Wednesday through Friday. McCall, also noted for the "Man About Hollywood" revue, has gathered several on-and-off-the screen personalities for his new show, "Glamor Girl Revue."
>
> Actor Gary Cooper introduces McCall from the screen—as the man who knows everything about Hollywood and the movies. While the film, which was especially produced for the revue, unwinds McCall is at the microphone to take the theatre audience on a personally conducted tour of Hollywood and the studios, relating anecdotes about the stars, and giving various movie low-downs.
>
> Laurel and Hardy stooge in and out of the film for comedy purposes, and other stars are 'shot' in company with McCall.
>
> (*Charleston Daily Mail* – 2 February 1941)

Stan and Ruth trying to gain entry through the strong-door, at Fort Laurel, following their latest marriage. (See entrance above!)

Once inside, things get cosy. But, like a tea-cosy, what's inside can soon go cold.

Upon the film's cinema release, the review ran: (*Altoona Mirror* – 16 May 1941)

A very novel introduction is used in the opening of the show ["*Inside Hollywood*"] McCall, who is master-of-ceremonies of the show, is introduced by Gary Cooper – from the screen. McCall then makes an entrance [on to the 'live' stage] and explains to the audience that he has produced an interesting little film before he left Hollywood, in the form of a travelogue tour of the movie capital, with himself as the host. He calls it "Inside Hollywood."

The 10-minute picture is then flashed on the screen, with McCall commentating on the side lines. He takes the audience to the Paramount and Universal Studios during the production of pictures.

From there he takes you to the home of Jack Benny, Myrna Loy, and George Raft.

During the showing of the film there are many interruptions by the famous comedy team of Laurel and Hardy, in which McCall's commentates with them from the stage, while they reply from the screen. The film portion winds up with a heated argument between McCall on the stage and Laurel and Hardy on the screen.

After considering all the facts, one can be pretty certain that Stan and Babe shot new footage specially for this film – most probably in February or March, at either Paramount or Universal studios, or both. And so dear readers, to the list of films which Laurel and Hardy made together you can now add film No. 107 – "*Inside Hollywood*."

But now, with no work, Stan and Babe had lots of time to play. But playing didn't pay their enormous bills. Between them, Stan Laurel and Oliver Hardy owed over $127,000 in back taxes and alimony. The bigger part of this bill was Hardy's, who owed the U.S. Treasury $75,755 in income taxes – and that was just for 1934 to 1937. Once he had cleared them, there would be 1938 to 1941 to find the money for. That's a tough task when you are out of work.

Immediately after the hearing, Laurel and Hardy made an appearance at a show-business event. Let's hope it paid money.

LAUREL and HARDY – The U.S. Tours

(Monday 17 March 1941)
LOS ANGELES, California – Cocoanut Grove (Ambassador Hotel)
Screen Actors Guild – "Gambol of the Stars"

George Murphy, Master of Ceremonies. Eddie Cantor, Jack Benny, Frank Morgan, Stan Laurel and Oliver Hardy, and a number of other actors – still more to be added.

A self-appointed "business committee" includes James Gleason, Humphrey Bogart, James Cagney, Bela Lugosi, Boris Karloff, Edgar Kennedy, and Brian Donlevy.

Hardy is so hungry he starts to eat Laurel's fingers, which still smell of the barbecue he burnt them on a few days earlier.

The only known write-up on the event revealed:

At $11 a plate, the event included a lengthy floor show, singing, dancing and comic antics of numerous comedians. Master of Ceremonies was George Murphy, who was chairman of entertainment.

In analysing the guest list, along with the phrase "numerous comedians," one would have to conclude that Laurel and Hardy were part of the entertainment.

The comedy couple's next participation in live appearances proper came in April 1941, when they accepted an invitation to the three-day 'Mexico City Government's Motion Picture Industry Festival' – an event organised around Pan-American Day (14 April). The trip was sponsored jointly by the 'Motion Pictures Producers Association' and the 'Rockefeller Committee on Pan-American Cultural and Business Relations.'

One would have thought that, after their experiences during the 1932 visit to Britain, Stan and Babe would have avoided going where vast crowds would be there to greet them. Maybe they thought there was safety in numbers, as they were to be only two of forty-five Hollywood luminaries. But more stars meant more fans – which turned out to be the case. However, the fifteen hundred officers on duty would be sufficient to control them. Or so they thought!

Before leaving Hollywood for Mexico City, the stars had been divided into two parties: those who wished to fly, and those who didn't. To the latter belonged Mickey Rooney, Johnny Weissmuller, Brenda Joyce, Mary Gordon, Mr. and Mrs. Stan Laurel, and Mr. and Mrs. Oliver Hardy. This flock of flightless birds would be making the sixteen-hundred-mile-journey by rail and by road.

Johnny Weissmuller, Oliver Hardy, Lucille Hardy
Mary Gordon, Brenda Joyce, Stan Laurel, Ruth Laurel,
Mickey Rooney

Meanwhile, those flying on the three chartered planes included: Joe E. Brown, Norma Shearer, Mischa Auer, Frank Capra, David O. Selznick, Wallace Beery, Lucille Ball, Desi Arnaz, Sabu, Esther Fernandez, Brenda Marshall, Brenda Joyce, William Holden, Susan Hayward, Veronica Lake, Lady Ashley [Where was her husband, Doug Fairbanks?], Kay Francis, Patricia Morrison, Charles Winneger, and Frank Morgan; plus Hollywood columnist Louella Parsons.

-----0-----

1941 April 9 (Wednesday)
    LOS ANGELES, California to **GUADALUPE**, Mexico 283 miles
1941 April 10 (Thursday)
    GUADALUPE, Mexico to **MAZATLAN**, Mexico 983 miles
1941 April 11 (Friday)
    MAZATLAN, Mexico to **GUADALAJARA**, Mexico 295 miles
1941 April 12 (Saturday)
    GUADALAJARA, Mexico to **MEXICO CITY**, Mexico 330 miles
    Total = 1,891 miles

-----0-----

The train passengers left on Wednesday 9 April, two days ahead of those on the planes, so that their arrivals would coincide at noon on the Saturday. Those on the train would have been glad they had made the decision not to fly, as the flyers had a rough time. Leaving Los Angeles at 9am Friday, their target was Mazatlan, where they were to stay the Friday night before continuing their flight, via Guadalajara, on Saturday morning. However, strong headwinds prevented at least one of the planes from reaching Mazatlan. Louella Parson reported her plane as being forced down at Brownsville, Texas. After a hastily rearranged overnight stay, the plane safely made Guadalajara on schedule.

It is believed that the train passengers stayed overnight in Guadalupe on the Wednesday; stayed in Mazatlan on the Thursday; and in Guadalajara on the Friday; before joining up with the flyers at Mexico City airport on the Saturday – although this itinerary could not be confirmed.

SENOR THIN & SENOR FAT as they're affectionately called by Mexican fans, Laurel & Hardy, who'll make *Forward March* for Fox were on hand to lend their gift of gag to gay proceedings.

The Celebration of Easter Saturday in Mexico was traditionally in the form of an enormous spring show, but all past and future celebrations were to be eclipsed by the introduction of these "Hollywood Ambassadors" into the proceedings. Several thousand fans were there to greet them, and thousands more lined the route as the stars, and their escorts, made a triumphal procession to the Reforma Hotel.

The police struggled vainly to hold back the crowds, but were finally overcome when the buses pulled out of the airport, as almost everyone in the airport then ran after the buses and pitched into the throng lining the streets. Members of the massed throng shouted the names of their favourites; threw flowers; pleaded for a touch of their hands – and yelled, and yelled, and yelled.

The progress of the motorcade was impeded at every turn of the wheel. The mounted policemen, the motorcycle squad, and the hundreds of guards from both the army and the police force seemed unsympathetic to the revellers, and actually injured many of those who insisted upon pressing themselves against the sides of the buses. Within seconds of the motorcade finally arriving at the hotel, the streets became jammed in all directions; with Mexicans yelling, and jumping up in the air to gain a height advantage, in the hope of getting just a glimpse of these screen idols.

After being allowed an hour to check in at the Reforma Hotel, the visitors were taken to the City Hall, where they were officially welcomed as guests of honour. The journey to, and the arrival at, the municipal building was a near repetition of the earlier hotel scenes; but with even greater crowd numbers, exuding even greater enthusiasm. The mayor's office was so jammed tight with people that he could barely pick out the visitors in the crowd, and they in turn could barely hear his words of welcome.

From the mayor's office the throng moved like one giant colony of ants over to the American Embassy, where a state of decorum was finally achieved during tea with Ambassador Daniels. At 5pm the serenity inside the Embassy had to be abandoned, as the stars once again had to run the gauntlet of around two hundred thousand spectators, on the journey back to the Reforma Hotel.

(Saturday 12 April – Sunday 13 April 1941)
MEXICO CITY, Mexico – various cinemas
"Mexico City Government's Motion Picture Industry Festival"

Stan Laurel, Oliver Hardy, Mary Gordon, Mickey Rooney, Johnny Weissmuller, Joe E. Brown, Norma Shearer, Mischa Auer, Wallace Beery, Lucille Ball, Desi Arnaz; Sabu, Esther Fernandez, Brenda Marshall, Brenda Joyce, Sylvia Fairbanks, William Holden, Susan Hayward, Veronica Lake, Lady Ashley, Kay Francis, Patricia Morrison, Charles Winneger, Frank Morgan, and Louella Parsons; plus film producers Frank Capra, and David O. Selznick.

In the evening it was time for the guests to pay for their meal ticket, by making walk-on appearances at four of the leading cinemas: the Chino, Olimpia, Magerit, and Alameda – at 7, 8, 8:30 and 10pm. The cinemas were packed to capacity as the audiences were there not just to see the Hollywood stars, but to watch the films which had been entered in the Film Festival. But the streets too were packed with revellers and, though the Mexican army and the city's police force were present in huge numbers, the crowds at times again overpowered them. It was gone 11pm before the party of "Goodwill Ambassadors" could be bundled through the quarter of a million festivalgoers, and into the safe refuge of their hotel – glad to be in one piece.

Saturday may have been one heck of a tiring day for the visitors, but Sunday was not going to lend any respite. First event of the day was Mass at the Basilica of Our Lady of Guadalupe, the holiest shrine in Latin America, on the outskirts of the city. Next was luncheon at the Rancho del Charro, where "the watched" became "the watchers" at a traditional open-air rodeo, staged by the National Charros Association (elite cowboys). In the afternoon a typical old-time Mexican barbeque was held at the Rancho Blanco, where direct descendants of Aztecs and allied tribes entertained the diners. Some of the Aztec Indians had walked in excess of one hundred miles to be there, having chosen the primitive mode of transport over the modern motorised form.

In the evening, the stars – with their numbers now added to by the presence of Claudette Colbert and Paulette Goddard – had to repeat the battle plans of Saturday night when they visited five more cinemas: the Rex, Palacio, Iris, Olimpia, and Alameda. The visitors then ended their evening as honoured guests at a Grand Ball presented by the Mayor, Javier Rojo Gomez, and his wife, which two thousand governmental and military dignitaries also attended. The Ball was held at the Palace of Fine Arts – claimed to be "the most beautiful opera house in the world." The full beauty of the decor may not have been seen through totally appreciative eyes though, as some of those eyes would have been bleary from fatigue and others from drink, seeing as how the party was to start at midnight and go on until dawn.

Those from the Hollywood contingent who had stayed up late might have regretted their actions, as Monday morning contained a heavy schedule of events – dedicated to what had been named "Pan-American Day." The stars breakfasted at Chapultepec Castle. Built in 1725 by the commander-in-chief of the Spanish colony, this historic castle had had many uses in its chequered history, including being the official residence of Emperor Maximilian I. At the time of this visit it was a Natural History Museum.

Joe E. Brown thinks he's doing a passable impression of Stan Laurel's famous grin. Oliver Hardy doesn't agree. (Mexico City circa 12 April 1941)
[Picture from "The Laurel and Hardy Scrapbook," by Jack Scagnetti.]

Leaving the former residence of Emperor Maximilian, the American entourage was summoned to the residence of the current President of Mexico, Avila Camacho, who offered them his hospitality at the town Palace. Next, it was the turn of the Mexican Minister of Foreign Affairs, Ezequiel Padilla, to be the host – during a buffet luncheon at a venue in the beautiful "Floating Gardens of Xochimilco." The gardens don't actually float. They are artificial islands, made of silt dredged from the canal beds, on which plants, flowers and vegetables are grown. The system had been started centuries earlier by the Aztecs, who also built fifty miles of irrigation canals, some of which are still navigable today. No doubt the visitors would have taken a short boat ride on the colourful "trajineras," the Mexico equivalent of the gondolas in Venice.

Before bidding the Hollywood party farewell, Señor Padilla told them:

> Life is hard here in Mexico, and you have brought into the life of our people much happiness. For a long time they have laughed at Laurel and Hardy and Joe E. Brown. They have known the beauty of Norma Shearer. They have watched the antics of Mickey Rooney. Now you have given them a chance to see those faces in actual life. And we shall not forget you.

The press hailed this – "the greatest number of Hollywood stars to visit Mexico City" – as, "an historic event, which further demonstrates the excellent relations between Mexico and the United States," and, "That it has been the greatest thing that has ever happened to motion pictures, goes without saying."

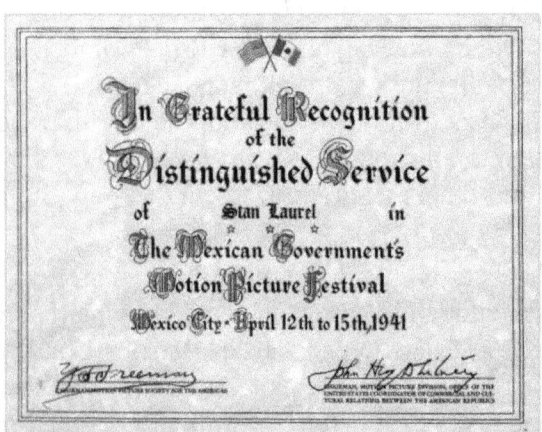

In Grateful Recognition
of the
Distinguished Service
of Stan Laurel in
The Mexican Government's
Motion Picture Festival
Mexico City April 12th to 15th, 1941

Certificate awarded to Laurel (and one to Hardy) being a part of the Film Festival in Mexico.

-----0-----
1941 April 14 (Monday)
    MEXICO CITY, Mexico to **GUADALAJARA**, Mexico 🚂 330 miles
1941 April 15 (Tuesday)
    GUADALAJARA, Mexico to **MAZATLAN**, Mexico 🚂 295 miles
1941 April 16 (Wednesday)
    MAZATLAN, Mexico to **GUADALUPE**, Mexico 🚂 983 miles
1941 April 17 (Thursday)
    GUADALUPE, Mexico to **LOS ANGELES**, California 🚂 283 miles
-----0-----

It is thought that the all the Hollywoodians, whether travelling by train or plane, travelled only as far as Guadalajara on the Monday, where they stayed the night. The following day, en route for Mazatlan, it was the train passengers who this time had the shock of their lives–LITERALLY–when an earthquake struck.

The earthquake was centred fifty miles inland from Acapulco, but was felt for hundreds of miles around. In Mexico City the quake lasted just five seconds, and no fatalities were reported, although buildings did collapse and fires destroyed others. One day earlier President Avila Camacho of Mexico had been entertaining Hollywood stars – the next day he was mobilising planes, trains and lorries to supply emergency relief to the affected areas. That's how quickly life can change – in Mexico's case, just seconds!

Hardest hit was Colima, just two hundred and seventy-five miles west of Mexico City, where half of the city's residents were reported as homeless, and many were either injured or dead. Casualties were sustained too by residents of Guadalajara, which is located just one hundred and twenty-two miles north of Colima. Louella Parsons was to say:

We left Guadalajara just an hour before the earthquake hit Mexico, and we knew nothing about it until we arrived in Hollywood.

Those travelling by terrestrial means would not have fared so well. Near Colima, a half-mile stretch of track on the Southern Pacific Railroad was blocked by a gigantic landslide, which was almost forty foot high in parts. Thankfully, there were no reports of any trains being struck. If the big guy in the sky had not been looking after the Hollywood stars that day, film history could have so easily been rewritten. It had come very close!

The whole Hollywood-Mexico event had started off merely as Jimmy Roosevelt's intention to promote his new picture "*Pot O' Gold*" in Mexico City, but the plans had somehow just grown and grown. President Avila Camacho of Mexico was so honoured that the son of President Roosevelt should open his picture there, he had declared the event an official holiday. Jimmy though, didn't actually make it, as he stayed behind to finalise his wedding plans. However, the event was such a success that it led to plans for future "goodwill motion picture pilgrimages" to be made to the capitals of Latin America.

Nice to see that Laurel and Hardy gained first credits on the Minister of Foreign Affairs' list of the stars who had given laughter to the people of Mexico; but just why Stan and Babe volunteered to be precipitated into this three-day maelstrom is hard to reason. As self-promotion, the whole event did not offer much. No Laurel & Hardy films were shown; nor did the two comedians get to perform. During their stay, all forty-five stars had lived, eaten, and moved in one cluster, and none were singled out by the press for special treatment.

The question may have been answered a few weeks earlier in the show business gossip column "Hollywood Keyhole," in which the columnist Ken Morgan revealed:

Laurel and Hardy will be the next film luminaries to gather in some of the folding money to be picked up around the theatre circuits. The funny men leave shortly for an extended tour of Mexico. The pair haven't made a picture for some time, and their decision to tread the boards again hints of a possible film deal. They [their films] were sensational grossers in Europe, and now, with that market a negligible quantity, they will try the Latin Americas in search of a new [film] audience.

Their manager thinks enough of them to demand a $2,500 advance before the train leaves from the Los Angeles station.

(22 March 1941)

The proposed "theatre circuit" mentioned here, does not refer to the trip Laurel and Hardy had just been on, but one whereby they would return as a solo stage act. But then, even if they were to receive a $2,500 advance, with more to come from appearance fees, it would obviously come nowhere near to clearing their outstanding debts. It would seem a safe bet, therefore, that the underlying objective in grooming Mexico was to secure some form of film deal. And so it would prove to be – although the film company which surfaced first was not based in Mexico.

Louella Parsons, who had been championing the Boys for some time, revealed in her Hollywood column:

> I couldn't be happier that Laurel and Hardy, who have been away from the screen too long, are booked to do "Forward March," an army comedy for 20th Century-Fox. They were so popular in Mexico City, that it opened all of our eyes to what these two comics mean to moviegoers all over the world.
>
> The Mexican Foreign Minister, Ezequiel Padilla, in greeting the stars said, "The wit of such artists as Laurel and Hardy, Joe E. Brown and Mischa Auer has brought smiles to faces frowning under the weight of care and worry of life itself."
>
> On the heels of this glorious Mexico City welcome, Oliver and Stan were given a new five-year contract at 20th Century-Fox, and it's the intention of Darryl Zanuck and all concerned to make some typical Laurel and Hardy pictures—the kind that make you laugh and forget your troubles.

(*INS* – 24 April 1941)

The more likely scenario is that the approach made by 20th Century-Fox had **nothing** to do with the recent display of popularity shown to Laurel and Hardy in Mexico, and **everything** to do with the popularity of the newly emerged screen comedy team of Abbott & Costello.

In her round-up of show business events in 1941, Louella Parsons was to say:

> The most sensational success in Hollywood was registered by a comedy team—plump Lou Costello and his lean sidekick, Bud Abbott. The two boys came here from radio, and after their first picture it was evident that the public wanted to laugh and that comedy was king. Not since Charlie Chaplin's day have any comics been as enthusiastically received as these two Universal funsters.

(*INS* – 28 December 1941)

It would seem pretty safe to suggest, therefore, that the "old Boys'" were being brought in as direct competition to the "new Boys." The deal being offered by Fox was for Laurel and Hardy to make one picture, with the option of a further nine over the next five years. The two actors would be free during this term to make films with other companies, and do radio and stage appearances. It was an offer that was too good to refuse – but for financial reasons, rather than artistic ones, as hindsight would soon reveal.

The agreement was signed on 23 April, followed by a binding contract on 29 May, with filming scheduled to start in mid-July. With two months to kill before Stan and Ollie became born-again comedians, they filled a little of it by taking part in another star-studded event – a three-day convention in Atlantic City, New Jersey, on the East Coast. It would turn out to be like a "*Sons of the Desert*" convention – only in real life.

o-o-0-o-o

CHAPTER 23
HAVING THE TIME OF OUR LIVES
(1941 pt2)

Thursday to Saturday 15-17 May 1941 was the "Variety Club Seventh Annual Convention," which twelve hundred of its members (known as "Barkers") would be attending.

> This city will be filled for three days beginning today with men wearing high silk hats, false noses and phoney handle-bar moustaches.
>
> The occasion will be the annual convention of the Variety Clubs of America; made up of actors, theatre managers, and others in "show business."
>
> Silk hats and flowing black moustaches are symbols of the old-time circus "barker," and all delegates to the convention are supposed to wear them.
>
> The convention will be a continuous round of private parties and shows, at which theatrical people who earn their bread by amusing others, are expected to "get even" by entertaining themselves for a change.
>
> *(Atlantic City Press* – 15 May 1941)

The convention was billed as: "The biggest and best ever." For just a $20 registration fee the conventioneers got admission to boxing and wrestling matches; a "monster" show; a theatre show; a cocktail party; a lobster dinner; entry to a nightclub; and a formal banquet. It might seem that the members of the Variety Club were simply using the society to feather their own nest but, to be fair, the twenty-two tents involved had, during the 1940 financial year, raised the colossal sum of $800,000 for charitable causes.

-----0-----

1941 May 14 (circa) Wednesday
    LOS ANGELES, California to **ATLANTIC CITY**, New Jersey 2,784 miles
-----0-----

With the business part of the Convention having been gotten out of the way on the Thursday, it was time to party. So, on the Friday, a whole host of Hollywood stars were brought in to add some sparkle to the high-jinks to come. Among them were our old buddies, Stan Laurel and Oliver Hardy, who came in by train from Hollywood. Others flew in.

Stan and Babe arrived at 10.10am with travelling companions Ronald Reagan and his wife Jane Wyman – which meant that Mrs. Regan had shared a carriage with a future President, a President, and a Vice-President. (Before you ask: Stan Laurel and Oliver Hardy were respectively President and Vice-President of 'Laurel & Hardy Feature Productions.')

After dropping off their bags at the Claridge Hotel, our comedy twosome went to registration at the convention headquarters in the Traymore Hotel. The afternoon's main activities were sailing and fishing parties; so, as Laurel no longer had his own fishing boat, he may well have gone to see if his old fishing rod, and his old sea legs, still worked.

-----0-----

(Friday 16 May – Saturday 17 May 1941)
ATLANTIC CITY, New Jersey – Traymore Hotel
"Variety Club Seventh Annual Convention"

Friday evening started off at 7.30pm with a dinner party in the Chelsea Hotel's Westminster Hall suite. Visiting officials joining the conventioneers included Mayor Taggart of Atlantic City; FBI Chief J. Edgar Hoover, and six senators. After dinner the ladies were asked to retire, and the rest of the evening, billed as "The Night of Nights," became a strictly "stag" affair.

Part of the entertainment ran as follows:

> A learned group of showmen known as "The Committee on Gags" will delve deep into the filing cabinets in search of jokes and wise-cracks, in an all-out effort to make even tired comedians roll in the aisles.
>
> *(Atlantic City Press* – 15 May 1941)

Although a clean comedian on film, Laurel's choice of jokes told in private often strayed into the "blue" area, so he may well have contributed to the gag session. Hardy, though, was totally against any off-colour humour, and was known to reprimand anyone who aired such jokes in front of ladies. However, as no ladies were present, one would surmise he kept his objections in check.

Whatever went on in that room – stayed in that room. There were uniformed guards at every doorway, and Pinkerton men in plain clothes patrolled the hotel corridors to ensure that neither newsmen nor other non-delegates gained entry.

After sparring and assaults of the verbal kind, came those of the physical kind, with two wrestling matches, and six bouts of boxing to watch over in the ballroom of another venue – the Convention Hall. As both Babe and Stan were keen boxing fans, they would have been willing spectators. It was then on to a nightclub where the main activity, namely "drink yourself silly," went on until daylight. Just as well that no duties were planned for Saturday morning.

Saturday afternoon, however, started off in a BIG way, with the stars coming out from behind locked doors and parading in front of the public – literally. The parade started off at Massachusetts Avenue at 12 noon, with the route taking it over the Boardwalk on the Steel Pier, and finishing at the Convention Hall.

The line-up had an advance guard of motorcycle officers and the U.S. Navy Color Guard. Second in line came the Parade Marshal, the Chief Barker, the Mayor and the City Commissioners. Next were three hundred men from the 44th Division at Fort Dix. Sandwiched among the carnival floats came a real circus parade, consisting of a clown band, elephants, bears, and Bengal tigers. Music was provided by a bugle corps of boys fronting more carnival floats carrying "Miss America 1940" and the Ziegfield Girls, to name but two.

Immediately behind the Variety Club float was a motorcade of open-top cars carrying the likes of Hollywood stars Dorothy Lamour, Ronald Reagan and Jane Wyman, Walter Pidgeon, Robert Young, Laraine Day, Lew Ayres, Jean Hersholt, Fay Wray, Phil Regan, Wayne Morris, Andy Devine, Eddie Norris, Helen Parrish, Frank Morgan, Carol Landis, Marjorie Weaver, and Charles Lang.

BUT! leading the WHOLE parade were comedy legends – STAN LAUREL and OLIVER HARDY – who, just to emphasise their role, were given the position of "Grand Marshals." Nice to see their status being fully recognised among some of Hollywood's finest film stars.

Leading the parade, along Massachusetts Avenue. Atlantic City 17 May 1941

The termination of the parade was in the Auditorium, at the Convention Hall, where a few hundred children, with what today we would call "special needs," were given their own private parade. They were then joined by over one thousand local schoolchildren, who filled up the seats around a three-ring circus, for their own free show. The adults would have to wait for the evening performance – and PAY!

The sign on the Steel Pier Theatre reads:
"STEEL PIER
AND ATLANTIC CITY
WELCOMES
VARIETY CLUBS
OF AMERICA"

For the Variety Club members and guests, Saturday evening was the main event of the Convention – a formal banquet in the Traymore Hotel. The toastmaster was former Governor General of Texas, William McGraw; and among the guests was an assortment of ambassadors and statesmen, not only from America, but also from foreign countries. Part of the evening's programme was the "Humanitarian Awards" for which a former winner of the award, Father Flanagan of Boys Town, had been invited to partake. His presence enabled Stan and Babe to finally say "Hello" after missing him in Omaha nine months earlier. [**FILM**]

On Sunday the city returned to sanity, when the delegates took their leave by whatever transport they had arrived by. For anyone, then or now, who thinks that it was a disgraceful state of affairs for these people to be out drinking and partying for three days, while good men and true were preparing to protect the country from invasion, we will let Mayor Taggart have his say. In his welcoming speech he had paid tribute to the guests by declaring:

> The fact that the American people retained their ability to laugh was largely due to the leadership of the Variety Clubs in the amusement and entertainment field.

> The morale of the American people must remain on its present high level. No such undermining of government and people must prevail here as did in the fall of France. In this respect the Variety Clubs, through their sponsorship of amusement and gaiety, are making a vital contribution by helping to overcome internal agitation upon which unfriendly parasites feed.

That's his excuse – and he's stuck with it!!

-----0-----

1941 May 18 (Sunday)
　　　　ATLANTIC CITY, New Jersey to **LOS ANGELES**, California 🚂 2,784 miles
　　　　-----0-----

When you add together the time Stan and Babe spent in Atlantic City, plus the six days of train travel from L.A. and back, this was an awful lot of time and effort to donate to a charity event. But then, that was Stan and Babe for you. Thankfully, the next request for their services was a little nearer to home.

On Friday 6 June 1941, an emergency call went out for entertainers who could get their act together at short notice, and perform for the troops at Camp Roberts, Paso Robles, on the coming Sunday. With filming still some weeks away, Laurel and Hardy accepted the invite and quickly packed their bags.

-----0-----

1941 June 08 (Sunday)

LOS ANGELES, California to **SAN MIGUEL**, California 214 miles

-----0-----

Stan and Babe's fellow passengers aboard the bus which ferried them from Los Angeles to San Miguel were:

> Red Skelton, Jane Withers, Helen Parrish, Martha O'Driscoll, Margaret Whiting, Dorothy Lovett, Natalie Thompson, Dorothy Morris, Sidney Miller, Peggy Morse, Virginia O'Brien, Borrah Minnevitch, Elaine Moray, Berry Brothers, Joan Leslie, Chico Marx, Buddy Pepper, Ella Logan, Jimmy Durante, and harmonica virtuoso Larry Adler.

(Sunday 8 June 1941)

PASO ROBLES, San Miguel, California – Camp Roberts

"USO Camp Show" – for the U.S. Army Field Artillery Troops

Laurel and Hardy were the headliners at this, the first show promoted by the newly formed "United Services Organization" – for the U.S. Army Field Artillery Troops. It was a fund-raising event, but the audience consisted solely of soldiers, who numbered fifteen to twenty thousand. They were at Camp Roberts for training, where parachuting was one of the main skills being learned.

Being the first show held there, not everything was in place to stage such an event. As the stage lighting system had not yet been installed, the show had to be held in daylight hours – hence an afternoon being chosen.

As for the normally pampered Hollywood stars, they had to rough it in dressing rooms which had not yet been completed.

Stan and Babe performed their now customary sketch: *"How to Get a Driver's License"* – with "cop." The cop has not been identified.

Both photos from the Camp Roberts show.

1941 June 9 (Monday)

SAN MIGUEL, California to **BAKERSFIELD**, California 115 miles

-----0-----

Returning to Los Angeles the next day, the Boys broke their journey at Bakersfield, and called in for a meal at the Padre Hotel, at 1702 18th Street. There they met up with two actor friends, Jack and Kay Baxley. Mrs. Baxley was better known to Stan and Babe as Kay Deslys, a blonde statuesque actress who had appeared in a handful of Laurel & Hardy films – most notably as Mrs. Hardy in "*Perfect Day*." [Surprising to note that Kay (née Kathleen Herbert) was English.]

-----0-----

1941 June 9 (Monday)

BAKERSFIELD, California to **LOS ANGELES**, California   112 miles

-----0-----

One week later, it was Stannie's birthday (16 June) which was always celebrated with something special. The *Los Angeles* Times thought this one, his fifty-first, special enough to do a write-up on it.

LAUREL AND HARDY JOIN THE FOUR-PURPOSE PARTY

Last week a group gathered for an outdoor barbecue in the Canoga Park home of the Britt Woods to celebrate Stan's birthday and the return to films of the Laurel and Hardy combination who are doing "Great Guns."

After the barbecue the guests drove to the Hardy home in the valley to inaugurate the new Spanish-type theater behind the gardens and citrus orchards and to honor the Woods who left the following day for a personal appearance tour.

-----0-----

1941 June 16 (circa) (LAUREL)

CANOGA VALLEY, California to **VAN NUYS**, California   14 miles

The *Los Angeles Times article* (13 July 1941) article continued:

Since the Hardy theater is fully equipped with screen, sound equipment, projection machines, stage and footlights, an impromptu program was in order. First, a hilarious old Laurel and Hardy picture was run off, then the old time vaudevillians in the audience staged a 30-act show, made up of impromptu acts and some that have appeared on a number of stages.

Charlie Irwin was master o' ceremonies, ably assisted by Eddie Kane and Wally Ford. Britt Wood did his banjo and singing act. Ames and Arno showed off their acrobatic stunts, Lasses White stirred the audience with the Southern preacher's eulogy to a colored boy's death, and Alphonse Berg and his trained pony 'Midge' performed.

The reporter's phrase: "...to inaugurate the new Spanish-type theater" seems to confirm my belief that, when Hardy first-started laying on entertainment at his home, it must have been in one of the old out-buildings, or the stables. Strange that the reporter failed to mention the theatre was named "Laurel and Hardy's Fun Factory." The name was almost certainly suggested by Stan, as "The Fun Factory" was what Fred Karno nicknamed the four adjacent buildings he ran his empire from in London, England – and which Stan would have been to many times during the UK engagements he had with Karno between 1909 and 1912.

Immediately prior to this inauguration, Laurel had visited Hardy to help get the place ready. [See photos on next page!]. As has been noted, the Fun Factory doubled as a cinema, where old Laurel & Hardy films, and ones yet to be made, would be shown. There would be no problem finding a projectionist to run the 35mm projector which had been installed, seeing as Babe's profession in his late teens to early twenties was that of a projectionist.

But – as well as for the showing of films, and staging plays – Stan and Babe would be using it to rehearse their film roles, plus work-up their stage sketch. There was also the more sentimental usage of the theatre which was that of a social meeting place; and an outlet for friends, old vaudeville acts, and film actors, who wished to continue performing.

[The Hardy's lived here from 1940 till 1955. The property was then bought by bandleader Horace Heidt who, in 1962, had the Fun Factory torn down to make room for expansion of his development of Country Club Apartments, which he named "Magnolia Estates."

What was probably the farewell show in the Fun Factory was in 1961 — attended by a gathering of old time (silent) movie actors, including: Lucille Hardy, Jane Darwell, Dorothy Gish, Joyce Compton, Francis X. Bushman, Rosetta Duncan, Beatrice Kay, Babe London, and Chester Conklin.

(Compiled by the author, from information supplied by fellow-author –Randy Skretvedt)].

-----0-----

1941 June 16 (*circa*) LAUREL
       VAN NUYS, California to **CANOGA PARK**, California 14 miles

-----0-----

THE FUN FACTORY

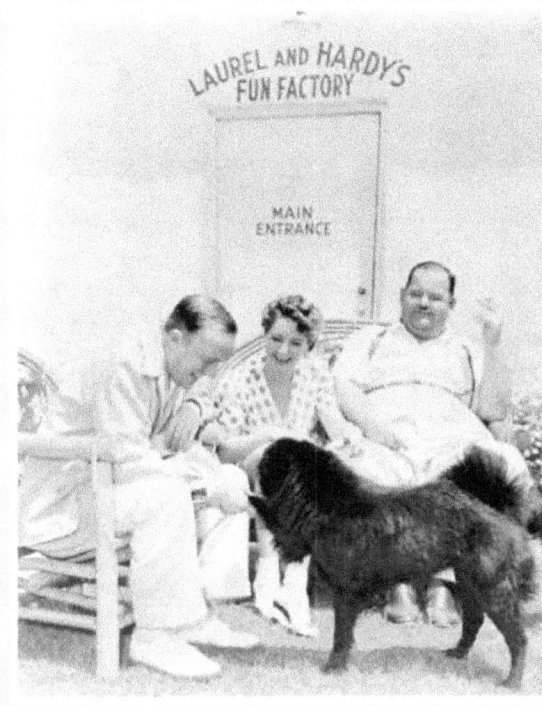

Lucille and Babe's dog eating the steak which Laurel had in his sneaker to cover the hole.

Those two workmen putting up the Laurel & Hardy poster sure look familiar.

Laurel asking: "Is this where the projectiles come out?"

Looks like Stan's been down the basement to get some globes.

[All eight images are thought to have been taken on the same day, but I have never been able to confirm the date. My guesstimate is on, or just prior to, Stan's birthday on 16 June 1941.]

HARDY GARDEN

Laurel asking Hardy how many omelettes he's going to cook for the two of them.

Hardy singing the line from "*Oklahoma*": "The corn was as high as an elephant's thigh."

During Laurel's visit, Hardy finds a little time to spend with his wife Lucille, relaxing by the swimming pool.

My wife says I think more of you than I do of her.
Well you do, don't ye?
Well we won't go into that.

So the two had been seeing a lot of each other of late, and would soon be seeing each other a whole lot more.

With the June show at Camp Roberts show having been rated a success, the U.S.O. committee decided to make the audience of the next fund-raising event a split between non-paying members of the Army and Navy, and paying members of the public. The show was held at the Hollywood Bowl, on Sunday 29 June 1941. The five thousand invited for free entertainment were soldiers from Camp Haan, who were ferried to Los Angeles on a loop of eighty Army trucks.

The money from the fund-raising half of the audience would be going to provide recreational facilities for U.S. servicemen. Reports of the attendance varied between fifteen and twenty thousand. Let us hope the people counting up the receipts were more accurate with figures!

-----0-----

Sunday 29 June 1941

HOLLYWOOD, California – Hollywood Bowl

Stars of Screen and Radio – for the U.S.O. (7.30pm)

The entertainment programme was broken into four categories: actors and actresses who sang, danced, or participated in a dramatic sketch. These included: Tyrone Power, Robert Taylor & Barbara Stanwyck, Rosalind Russell, Cary Grant, Loretta Young, Charles Boyer, Irene Dunne, Nelson Eddy, Melvyn Douglas, Norma Shearer, and Edward G. Robinson.

On the comedy side were: Jack Benny, Mary Livingstone, George Burns & Gracie Allen, Bob Burns, Laurel & Hardy, Jane Withers, Fanny Brice, and Hattie McDaniel.

The Musicians were under the leadership of Jackie Cooper [orchestra leader – not the child actor], who played for the following singers: Nelson Eddy, Rudy Vallee, and Carmen Miranda.

There were also dance specialities by Miss Miranda, plus George Murphy and Eleanor Powell. Additional routines featured Gene Autry, Charles Boyer, Irene Dunne, Orson Welles, John and Lionel Barrymore, Edward Arnold, Frank Morgan, and Judy Garland.

The *Los Angeles Times* reviewed the show, and revealed what many of the acts performed on the night. One omission was whether or not 'The Wizard of Oz' got back together with 'Dorothy.' But the most disappointing omission from the review was a lack of mention for the greatest comedy team of all-time.

-----0-----

After being the host for Stan's birthday celebrations, Babe next became the visitor, when he went to spend some time with him at Ft. Laurel, just three days before Stan paid a dreaded visit to the dentist to have some major extractions.

-----0-----

1941 July 01 (*circa*)

    VAN NUYS, California to **CANOGA PARK**, California 14 miles

    CANOGA VALLEY, California to **VAN NUYS**, California 14 miles

-----0-----

A visiting journalist caught the two of them together:

> Laurel and Hardy have a script now, called "Great Guns," which they are going to start putting on film for 20th Century-Fox. It's their first picture in a year, and one which they hope will put an end to stories of a personal disagreement, stories which started when they ended, one at a time, their long-standing association with Hal Roach studios.
>
> The comedians brought us up to date on these developments during a visit to "Ft. Laurel," the country home of Stan Laurel, at Canoga Park in the San Fernando Valley.
>
> Ft. Laurel, incidentally, is entirely unlike a movie star's home. There is not a single swimming pool, no tennis courts, and no station-wagons sitting around. The space is taken up with Laurel's unpretentious home, workshop, an outdoor barbecue, vegetable gardens, a duck pen, greenhouse, and fruit trees.

Posing in front of the Gallery of Stars, friends, and self-portraits which Stan has the biggest affection for. Note Babe and Hal Roach above Stan's head. The Den – Fort Laurel.

-----0------

Babe discussing the cartoon drawing of Laurel & Hardy which Harry Langdon drew for them. They later had small stickers made of it, which they would stick onto the pages of autograph books, either side of which they signed their names.

Having the Time of Our Lives

The plums were just getting ripe, and Hardy, who lives on a country place of his own a few miles away, had picked a bucketful which he said he, himself, was going to make into preserves.

Inspecting the coffee pot, atop the brick barbecue which Laurel's valet, Jimmy Murphy, designed and built for him.

He said he's been irrigating all morning. Such work, he said, took the place of dieting.

Laurel, then went on to explain the problems he and Hardy had had when making films at the Roach Studios, and concluded with words to the effect that, now they were back together again, they were ready to make some good pictures – which is all they asked to be allowed to do in the first place.

But Fox had no intention of doing what Stan Laurel wanted to do.

The Boys reported to the 20th Century-Fox studios during the second week in July. First thing to do was costume fittings, and then publicity shots. A few days in and, once the scenes had been shot with Laurel & Hardy receiving their brand-new army uniforms, it would seem as though they were asked to "distress" them, i.e. make the uniforms look as though they had been worn. To do this, Stan and Babe chose a rather novel way – over at Hardy's home.

For two people who never saw each other in their private lives – Stan and Babe sure saw a lot of each other in their private lives!

-----0-----

1941 July 01 (*circa*)
        CANOGA VALLEY, California to **VAN NUYS**, California 14 miles
        VAN NUYS, California to **CANOGA PARK**, California 14 miles

-----0-----

Like Laurel, Hardy had entered into the scheme of the "Dig For Victory" campaign, and grew crops on his land – the mainstay being fruit trees. He also kept chickens, ducks, and turkeys; which gave him the added enjoyment of going on a daily egg-collecting run.

From his livestock, Hardy received less of a contribution. In fact, their contribution was negative. His cow ate more in fruit than it gave back in the value of milk, and so eventually had to go. As for the two pigs, they became pets, and so, though they were often served food, they were never served *as* food.

On the day of Laurel's visit, Stan and Babe put on their actual "*Great Guns*" uniforms and set to, working the land to effect the necessary worn appearance of their costumes. They even soaked their feet in Babe's swimming pool, whilst still wearing their boots, so as to give the boots the look of having being used for wading in streams.

Accompanying them on this photo-shoot was their glamorous co-star Sheila Ryan, who wore just a pair of shorts over a swimsuit – which effectively took all the distress out of this "distressing" day.

'Siren' (aka: S. Ryan) – lures the passing G.I.s into her garden.

She enslaves them, and puts them to work. Here they plough the fields ...

.... and scatter the good seed on the land.

Then they're fed and watered, by Sheila's wagging hand!

Fun time over, it was time to return to filming – at which moment it became all too evident to both Stan and Babe that they had no control whatsoever over the scripts, editing, lighting, make-up, or even the conservation of the screen characters of Laurel & Hardy.

To be fair, the Fox negotiators had made it quite clear that, when it came to the actual filmmaking, it was to be strictly under the directions laid down by Fox. However, it had never entered Stan and Babe's thoughts that the restrictions would be so severe. What made it harder to bear for the two comedy stars was that the production team weren't actually capable of producing good comedy. This didn't seem to worry the studio heads, as Fox had five hundred theatres at which their films were shown – regardless of the quality. Consequently *"Great Guns"* fired only blanks.

The man responsible for the misfire was Fox producer Sol Wurtzel, whom Laurel and Hardy had met in September 1933 at the Teatro California, during the premiere of *"La Llorona."* Wurtzel may possibly have understood Spanish, but he definitely didn't understand the Laurel & Hardy brand of comedy.

During the second week in August, the outdoor scenes for the 11th Cavalry Division at 'Fort Merrill' were shot at Inglewood, seventeen miles south of Hollywood. This was no army base, but an old railway station. Shooting of *"Great Guns"* ended a few days later, after which Laurel and Hardy would not be making another film until the next storyline and script had been written – which would turn out to be months away.

A couple of weeks earlier Erskine Johnson had written that, *"Laurel and Hardy have a radio deal in the fire."* Then on the 21 August he aired the claim that:

> Laurel and Hardy, who've just completed "Great Guns" at Fox, are up for two more films – "The Red Mill" at MGM, and "Hit the Deck" at RKO.

All three deals ended up "in the fire."

In mid-September, with the next Fox film some months away, the Boys accepted an offer to appear at yet another event sprinkled with Hollywood stars. The following news release will explain:

Hollywood Sends Expensive 'Cargo' To Milwaukee

> A 21-passenger plane bearing a Hollywood 'cargo' will land at General Mitchell field here Sunday. The 'cargo,' sent here to represent moviedom at the 23rd Annual American Legion National Convention, will consist of producer Darryl Zanuck, and an array of screen talent.
>
> The stars will include Bob Hope, Jane Withers, Carol Landis, Ann Shirley and Jerry Colonna. Stan Laurel of the comedy team will arrive without his sidekick, Oliver Hardy, who was injured in a recent accident.

(*Wisconsin State Journal* – 14 September 1941)

A thorough search turned up no account of Hardy having had an accident, although just a week earlier he had been badly hurt by a claim for almost $100,000 in back taxes for the years 1934-37. (It's growing by the day.)

Whatever the reason, it looked as though Laurel was going to have to make the three and a half thousand mile return journey without his partner, plus spend four days in Milwaukee on his own. For a simple guest appearance, with a group of other stars, it would seem to be a lot of time and effort for little to no reward.

-----0-----

1941 September 14 (Sunday)

LOS ANGELES, California to MILWAUKEE, Wisconsin 1,741 miles

-----0-----

Monday 15 September to Thursday 18 September 1941

MILWAUKEE, Wisconsin – "American Legion Convention"

On Sunday 14 September the plane chartered to fly the Hollywood stars to Milwaukee, for the four-day "American Legion Convention," landed at General Mitchell field. Aboard were Carole Landis, Evelyn Keyes, Florence Lake, Jane Withers, and Anne Shirley; plus Hedda Hopper and several studio press executives, along with Darryl F. Zanuck, production chief of Twentieth

Century-Fox. Upon landing they were greeted by ten thousand fans, and then welcomed by a group of city and Legion officials, headed by Mayor Zeidler.

Three Legion bands paraded with the luminaries around the airport while a battery of newsreel cameramen and photo-journalists, took pictures. An official Legion automobile was assigned to each guest, which then whisked the Hollywood party downtown, escorted by siren-blowing motorcycles.

Several social functions were arranged for the stars during the day and evening. There were cocktail parties and meetings to attend, and broadcasts to make. Monday night was the Commander's Dinner, at which Bob Hope, Jerry Colonna, Louella O. Parsons, and Joe E. Brown were additional guests. Darryl F. Zanuck made the keynote speech, which included the lines.

> Picture business is picking up. The product is better and the competition is keener than ever. A few months ago business was not so good, but now it is on the upgrade.

On Tuesday there was a parade, with Carole Landis leading the Wisconsin contingent, and Jane Withers heading the delegates from Atlanta. In the evening, the premiere of the film "*Hedda Hopper's Hollywood*" was held at Paramount's Palace Theatre. Wednesday was a mixture of auxiliary sessions and personal appearances, plus lots of food and drink. On Thursday the stars flew home.

For Laurel and Hardy to have been here, in the company of their current boss, Darryl Zanuck, was a great opportunity to show him just how popular they were with the public. But with Hardy confirmed as not attending, and with no mention of Laurel in any of the write-ups, it may well be the case that Laurel too never went – and so the opportunity was lost. Maybe the two of them had felt it better to keep their feet on good old terra-cotta!!

On 27 September came an even stranger report of a purported forthcoming live appearance:

> Laurel and Hardy are considering an offer to play at the Harrow theatre in London [England].

It can be said without fear of contradiction that they never went there, either!!

o-o-0-o-o

CHAPTER 24
PILOTS OF THE CARIBBEAN
(1941 pt3)

Whilst still waiting for the call to return to the Fox studios, Laurel and Hardy were able to get back into character when, in November 1941, they undertook a tour of Army and Navy defence bases in and around the Caribbean. The event was sponsored by "Camp Shows, Inc." – an affiliate of the U.S.O. (United Service Organizations). Over a two-week period Stan and Babe would play "live shows," along with five other acts, touring under the company name of *"The Flying Showboat."*

The latter was a bit of a misnomer, as actual flying boats are able to take off from, and land on, water. What the members of this show were actually about to fly in were converted B-18 bombers – but then I guess calling it *"The Flying Bomber Show"* wouldn't exactly have projected the right image.

A week before leaving, Stan wrote to close friend Betty Healy to inform her of the little he knew about the tour – and it was "little."

```
Dear Betty,                           Oct. 25th. '41
Babe & I are getting ready to leave for Bermuda & Trinidad
(British West Indies) for the Government Shows at the
British & U.S. Naval Bases. We are flying from here to N.Y.
& then a naval Bomber picks us up there - think we open in
Bermuda Saturday next.
```

Of the tens of thousands of miles Stan and Babe had travelled during their lifetime, all of them had been on land or aboard ships; as when it came to flying both had left it to the birds. Now both men were going to show tremendous courage by flying an estimated thirteen thousand miles in just nineteen days.

-----0-----

1941 Oct 30 (Thursday)

LOS ANGELES, California to [**AMARILLO**], Texas 935 miles

-----0-----

With courage like that, Stan and Babe deserved an incident free journey, but were almost immediately denied it. Less than a thousand miles out from Los Angeles the plane encountered fog and had to land in Texas, where the passengers spent the night. Looking at the flight path from L.A. to N.Y. one would surmise it must have been northern Texas; in or near Amarillo. So, when the day was dawning, on that Texas Friday morning, they took off again.

-----0-----

1941 Oct 31 (Friday)

[AMARILLO], Texas to **NEW YORK**, New York 1,556 miles

-----0-----

On Friday 31 October 1941, Stan, Babe, and travelling companion Chico Marx, duly rendezvoused on schedule at the New York City air-strip at Mitchel Field, Queens. There they were welcomed by Eddie Dowling, President of the sponsors – Camp Shows, Inc. – who introduced them to the other members of the company: Ray Bolger, Louis Blanski, Mitzi Mayfair, Jane Pickens, and John Garfield. The latter three had been rehearsing in New York for the last week, along with "Radio Songstress" Benay Venuta. The author surmises she was there as back-up in case Chico Marx didn't show; as, when Marx did show up, Venuta dropped out. Louis Blanski was also in the company, as musical accompanist and acting tour manager.

Chico Marx had been at Hal Roach's 20th Anniversary party in December 1933, as well as appearing on the same show as the Boys at Camp Roberts, in June 1941. Hardy and Marx weren't exactly strangers at the race track either.

Front Left: Eddie Dowling. Right: Louis Blanski. Benay Venuta is in front of Hardy. Mitchel Field NY

When interviewed, Stan and Babe were quick to complain about the pain in their legs, brought on by the anti-typhoid shots they had been forced to have. Good job *they* hadn't had five days of dance rehearsals to do.

But then an incident happened which could have put the whole trip in jeopardy. Just as the plane was about to depart, someone put it into Laurel's head that, as he was not an American citizen, he was classed as an alien, and might not be allowed back into the U.S.A. Luckily, among the army brass travelling with the entertainers was Col. William Draper, Asst. Morale Officer at the War Department in Washington. It was he who had obtained the relevant clearance to break the Army regulations prohibiting the transportation of civilians in Army bombers; so he was easily able to assure Laurel that his entry back into the U.S.A. would not be compromised. It was only after getting absolute assurance of this, that Stan was coaxed onto the plane.

-----0-----

1941 Oct 31 (Friday) 9.45pm

NEW YORK, New York to **LANGLEY FIELD**, Virginia 281 miles

-----0-----

With Laurel safely aboard, the party took off on the first leg of their flight south, but they didn't go very far – just two hundred and eighty-one miles in fact, to Langley Field Air Base, Virginia. A photo taken of Laurel, Hardy and Mitzi Mayfair signing autographs for some of the troops at the Langley base shows it to be broad daylight, so one must assume that it was taken after the company had stayed the night there. Whether they did a show there wasn't discovered.

The Boys and Mitzi Mayfair, signing autographs for troops at Langley Field – before leaving for Miami. (31 October 1941)

The troupe were next driven the six miles to Fort Monroe, at Old Point Comfort, Virginia, where a Douglas C-49-A 14-seater Army transport plane, piloted by Maj. J. E. Shuck and co-piloted by Capt. D. E. Williams, was waiting to fly them on the next leg of their journey – to Miami.

Douglas C-49-A 14-seater

-----0-----

1941 Nov 01 (Saturday)

FORT MONROE, Virginia to **MIAMI**, Florida   808 miles

-----0-----

Rain was dripping from Miami's usually blue skies late Saturday when the plane touched down at Municipal airport. First out was Hardy, who sniffed the air, declared "*I smell rain*," complained about his aching legs again, then smiled as he announced: "*It's good to be back in Florida*" (referring to the years he had lived, and done film, work in Jacksonville).

Then, after the fashion of an Army Corporal, Hardy picked up the smallest bag in the pile of luggage, ordered Laurel to bring the rest, and headed for an army transport truck parked nearby. However, after noticing the narrow width of the front seat and the dubious condition of the tyres, Babe switched to the sedan parked next to it, which then took him and the rest of the troupe into town, to the Everglades Hotel.

John Garfield, Ray Bolger, Mitzi Mayfair, Hardy, Jane Pickens (in doorway), Laurel, Chico Marx.
(Miami Airport – 1 October 1941)

Saturday would have gone pretty quickly, with a mixture of rehearsing and relaxation – mainly the former. Let us hope they got a good night's sleep in a comfortable bed, as from now on in they would be roughing it. Sunday saw everyone up at the crack of dawn, and at 7am they took off for Puerto Rico – and not Bermuda, as Laurel had stated in his letter to Betty Healy.

-----0-----

1941 Nov 02 (Sunday)

MIAMI, Florida to **PUERTO RICO**, Greater Antilles   1,014 miles

-----0-----

The scant information available in previous references to the Puerto Rico visit states only that the company did their shows at the Borinquen Field airbase, in San Juan – the capital. But Borinquen is actually on the west coast, eighty-five miles from San Juan, near Aguadilla.

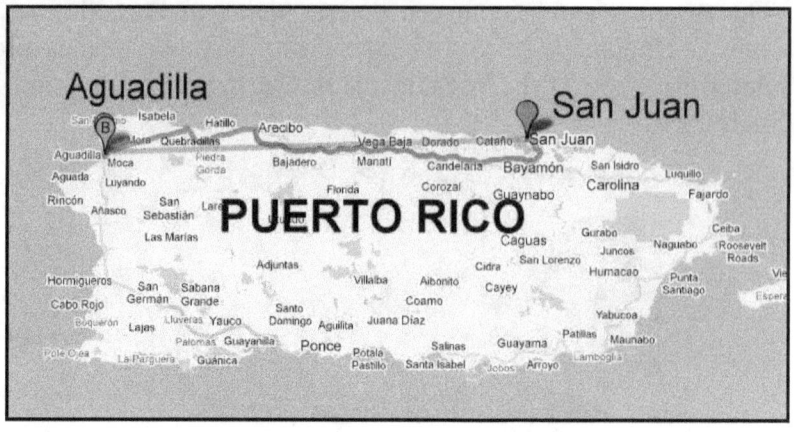

The airfield there had come under the jurisdiction of the U.S. Air Force as late as 1 May 1941, when the immediate tasks had been to build, maintain, and secure the runway – after which, the priority was to ensure that planes could be scrambled at a moment's notice. Identical operations were being carried out on other Caribbean islands, including U.S. bases on Cuba, Haiti, and the Dominican Republic; and on British bases on Bermuda, Jamaica, Antigua, St Lucia, and Trinidad. Other bases were built in Panama, and British Guiana.

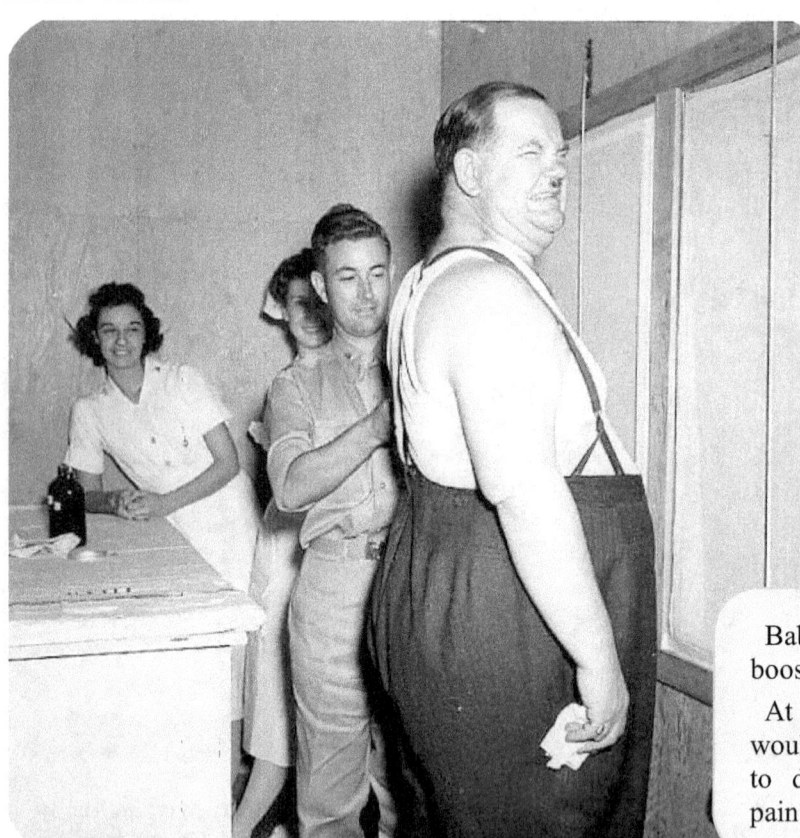

On most of those islands everything was being built from scratch, which actually included levelling jungle to make way for the airstrip. Because of the enormity of the task, and how it had to be expedited, things like "comfortable accommodation" and "facilities" were not covered – which was soon about to become all too evident to the goodwill visitors.

Babe receiving a painful booster typhus injection.

At least both he and Stan would now have something to distract them from the pain in their legs.

As Borinquen was a military base, little information has come out regarding the theatrical company's itinerary, or the troops based there. As best can be determined, the U.S. Air Force companies in residence during November 1941 included the 10th, 12th, 29th, 35th, 40th, 44th, and 45th Bombardment Squadrons; plus the 5th and 27th Reconnaissance – plus medical, weather, and communications units, etc. – totalling around fourteen hundred troops.

(Sunday 2 November 1941)

Borinquen Air Base, Aguadilla, **PUERTO RICO**

On the Sunday evening the troupe gave a show for a fourteen-hundred-strong audience composed of both Army and Navy personnel. The venue was one of the newly built aircraft hangars – so new in fact, it had not yet been completed.

On the left – the hangars under construction. On the right – a finished hangar.

Stan and Ollie on stage in the aircraft hangar at Borinquen Air Base. At least four additional cameras can be spotted in use by the audience.

The makeshift stage was almost as bare as could be, excepting for a microphone, and a piano – the latter placed there for the use of Chico Marx. There was also a piano placed front of stage, for the show's musical accompanist, Louis Blanski.

Here is a typical review of how the show was to run:

> John Garfield, screen tough-guy, this time acted as the genial master of ceremonies. His arrival on stage was greeted by thunderous applause. "*Hello Yankees,*" he addressed them. More thunderous applause. He then laughingly told them how he had learnt to clean his teeth on the plane, and even wash his socks (not on the plane). Only ten days ago he had sat in the same room with Lana Turner having tea (obvious sighs). "*It felt like a troopship.*" (laughter). "*I could tell a million stories about Hollywood but (with a sly wink) I can't tell them now.*
>
> Ray Bolger [best known as the wobbly-kneed scarecrow in the classic film "*The Wizard of Oz*"] came on stage dressed in brown trousers and sports coat with a brown hat perched on the side of his head. The trip was, he said, the most wonderful of

his entire career, and he had travelled some. Ray then did a burlesque dance of the "lovely" trip in the bomber, which "rocked more than a ship," provoking roars of laughter.

Next he did an interpretive dance to the music of Jerome Kern's "*Make Believe*." First movement was almost ballet, then equine, ending up with the humorous split of "*Sunny*" [a film in which Ray stars with Anna Neagle]. Ray had previously warned his laughing audience, "*Doesn't matter what happens to this dance, fellows, I'm only kidding.*"

It was only upon seeing Mitzi Mayfair dancing, that the troops realised what they were fighting for!

BRITISH GUIANA

John Garfield returned, did a bit of cross-patter with Bolger, and then introduced musical-comedy star Mitzi Mayfair. She danced on stage wearing a sensational costume—red skirt and tights, black velvet bodice (sans midriff) with jewelled appliqués. Nicknamed "The Soldiers' Dream Girl," she pirouetted, and high-kicked to the full satisfaction of the audience, and responded to an encore. [With the amount of flesh on display, it is a wonder they ever let her go.]

-----0-----

-----0-----

Chico Marx – the "Italian" member of the infamous Marx Brothers – entered next and, as a phoney excuse for not speaking into the mic', said: "*No speaka gooda English*," which provoked more roars of laughter. He then reproduced the piano playing he was known for from the Marx Bros. films, including one short piece where he played the keys with an orange. There was an encore, and another, and another.

Next came Stan Laurel and Oliver Hardy, performing the

two-man version of "*The Driver's License*" sketch, in which Hardy dominated the stage, the audience and, of course, "Stanley." Wearing their inevitable Derby hats, they soon became involved in a furious argument over Laurel's ability as a chauffeur.

Addressing the audience at the end of the sketch, Hardy, spokesman of the team, said, "*Rising from the ridiculous to the sublime, we should like to thank you, ladies and gentlemen, for your reception of us.*"

Two different camera shots of Stan and Ollie on stage, in the aircraft hangar. Borinquen Air Base, Aguadilla, Puerto Rico. (2 October 1941)

"*Hi soldiers!*" was Jane Pickens' greeting to the audience. Wearing an evening gown of gold lace, she sang, "*When a Gipsy Makes His Violin Cry*," "*I Don't Want to Set the World on Fire*," and "*You and I*." For an encore she chose "*Somewhere, Over the Rainbow*."

Jane, who by then had completely captured the audience with her rich voice and personal charm, did a burlesque of the well-known aria from "*Carmen*," with the aid of a tiara, a string of pearls, an artificial rose, a bandana, and imaginary mosquitoes. The boys simply refused to let Miss Pickens go.

Garfield came back on, this time accompanied by Bolger, to do a vaudeville-type sketch, which ran along the lines:

Bolger: "*John, in your pictures you seem to possess something ordinary fellows like myself do not. I don't know what it is—I look alright.*" (Laughter).

Garfield agreed to give a demonstration of his feminine technique, "to show the Boys a few tricks." He summoned Jane Pickens from backstage, and ordered her to stand before the mic'. "*Now Boys, you now put your arms around her, like this* (suiting actions to words). *Then manoeuvre from behind* (pressing her close to him)."

Garfield (to Jane): "When I look into your eyes, I see the Mediterranean." Then, in an aside to the audience: "Boys, have I traveled!" (Laughter).

Bolger thought he could do even better. He summoned Miss Pickens, and ordered her to put her arms around him. Then he said to her: "Now manoeuvre from behind." (More roars). [I guess you had to be there!]

Then Garfield changed the mood from comedy to tragedy. For five minutes he held the stage, when he read Jane Fowler's epic poem of the historic battle involving the "Jervis Bay." His powerful voice boomed over the microphone, then sinking to almost a whisper, and then rising to a crescendo, with a climax which shattered one silence and created another. Then cheering, and more cheering. But John was spent. No encore.

[Author: The "Jervis Bay" was an Armed Merchant Cruiser with a crew of 254 men. On the 5 November 1940 she was the sole escort for a convoy of 37 freighters on their way from Halifax to Britain, when the convoy was attacked by the German battleship "Admiral Scheer." In the battle which ensued the Captain and 187 officers and crew of the Jervis were lost, and the ship eventually sank.]

Next, "The Soldiers' Dream Girl" Mitzi Mayfair came back and partnered Bolger in a burlesque rumba, which ended with her carrying Ray off the stage over her shoulder, as if he were a sack of feathers. "*Give us a jitterbug*," someone shouted. They obliged with all the well-known routines and some more of their own.

At the end, the sweating Bolger told the soldiers he and his partner had not known what they were doing, but they certainly enjoyed doing it (Laughter). Ray followed with another burlesque—this time of the Louis vs Galento fight.

[On 28 June 1939 Joe Louis fought Tony Galento in a heavyweight title match at the Yankee Stadium. Galento put Louis down in the third, but then Louis stopped Galento in the fourth.]

The last item on the programme was Jane Pickens. She sang, by special request, the current hit "*Intermezzo*" from the Leslie Howard film "*Intermezzo, a Love Story.*" This was followed by "*Let Me Call You Sweetheart*," and "*Shine on Harvest Moon*," which the soldiers readily joined in the singing of.

At the Finale, all the acts came back on stage to take a bow; and then, when Jane Pickens called for the National Anthem, the whole cast and audience joined in the singing of "*The Stars and Stripes*."

["*The Stars and Stripes*" is often misquoted as being the National Anthem. It is, though, known as the "National MARCH" of America.]

One strange inclusion was Jane Pickens singing "*Shine on Harvest Moon*" — a number Laurel and Hardy had popularised in their film; "*The Flying Deuces*," and which there were to finish their stage act with on the 1947 British Tour, with Hardy singing and Laurel doing a soft-shoe shuffle, as per the film. Whether they performed the number in their stage act prior to 1947 I am not able to confirm.

When you are in a Spanish-speaking country, it's the law that you have to look as silly as possible. A sombrero will always do the trick. Ray Bolger looks upset that he didn't get one.
L-R: Chico Marx, Ray Bolger, John Garfield.

Upon leaving Puerto Rico the troupe was split into three parties, each aboard a converted U.S. bomber aircraft. The runway at Borinquen Field air base was enormous (even bigger than the one at the present-day commercial airport in San Juan), so was easily able to facilitate the Douglas C-49-A transport plane they had arrived in. But some of the other airfields they were about to visit were not so big, hence the switch to the smaller B-18 planes.

-----0-----

1941 Nov 03 (Monday)
    PUERTO RICO, Greater Antilles to **ST. CROIX**, Virgin Islands　90 miles

The airfield on St. Croix is located six miles southwest of Christiansted. Stationed there were the United States Army Air Forces 6th Air Force – the 12th Bombardment Squadron (25th Bombardment Group), whose job it was to fly anti-submarine patrols in their B-18 Bolo aircraft.

(Monday 3 November 1941)
ST CROIX, Virgin Islands

Sat in amongst the soldiers, like a couple of regular guys, are Stan and Babe. Seated at their feet can be seen John Garfield and Ray Bolger. It must have been felt that having the ladies there as well would be a little too distracting.

The show was held in daylight, which would seem to indicate that there was no suitable indoor venue which could be blacked out after dark. Illuminating an outdoor stage at night time would have provided too great a risk, because of the possible threat of enemy spotter planes.

The stage is at the foot of a slope, which, for the troops sitting on the slope, gave the impression of being in an amphitheatre.

Having the show in the daytime meant that the troupe did not need to stay overnight at St. Croix, but were able to fly back to Puerto Rico and spend a second night in the superior accommodation there.

LAUREL and HARDY – The U.S. Tours

Show Finale — St. Croix. Between the men in uniform are:
Hardy, Laurel, Jane Pickens, John Garfield (Louis Blanski) Chico Marx, and Mitzi Mayfair.
[Photo courtesy of Paul E. Guerucki]

1941 Nov 03 (Monday)
ST. CROIX, Virgin Islands to **PUERTO RICO**, Greater Antilles 90 miles

-----0-----

1941 Nov 04 (Tuesday)
PUERTO RICO, Greater Antilles to **ANTIGUA**, Leeward Islands 205 miles

-----0-----

MAP of the CARIBBEAN ISLANDS

(Tuesday 4 November 1941)
Coolidge Field, ANTIGUA, Leeward Islands

The next stop-over was Antigua, a relatively short island hop of just over two hundred miles from Puerto Rico. Here they stayed just one day, and did just one show for the 35th Bombardment Squadron, at Coolidge Field Air Base.

-----0-----

Very little information, and no known photos have come out of the visit to the Coolidge Field base, but a recently discovered letter, written by a resident, reveals that Stan and Babe must have had enough of army accommodation, and sought a little luxury away from the base.

This is an extract from a letter written by Laurel, to a Ms. Anne Breton, proprietor of the Antigua Beach Hotel:

[Dated November 19, 1941]

```
Dear Anne,
Thanks so much for your sweet letter and the snaps - so
pleased to hear from you - think the pictures were cute,
especially you - Too bad not clearer, but happy to have
them anyway. I too was sorry we didn't return to Antigua &
your lovely Hotel as I really enjoyed our short visit there
- your Dad - Mother & self were so perfectly charming & did
so much to make us all comfy.
```

Following the one night of luxury, they were off again, bound for the island of Saint Lucia.

-----0-----

(Wednesday 5 November 1941)
Beane Field, **ST. LUCIA,** Windward Islands

1941 Nov 05 (Wednesday)

ANTIGUA, Caribbean to **ST. LUCIA**, Windward Islands 226 miles

----0-----

Here at Beane Field, our intrepid travellers braved the intense heat and mosquitoes, to entertain the 5th and 59th Bombardment Squadrons. This airstrip, too, had only been operational since around May of that year, for which the job of the bombers was to fly the obligatory anti-submarine patrols.

A crowd of St. Lucia natives came out of the hills to join American soldiers in welcoming the troupe at the airport, and then stayed on to watch the show, which was held in daylight under a tropic sky.

Although Ray Bolger, Babe, and Stan are on stage, here at Beane Field, they don't appear to be doing any kind of performance. They're not even engaged in conversation with the troops. Maybe they're waiting for a streetcar.

On Puerto Rico, Oliver Hardy had been made an honorary member of the Bomber Squadron, while Laurel had to content himself with being made a mere member of the ground crew. Stan had later been given the grade of "Third Lieutenant," awarded by the flying officers who were piloting them around the Caribbean. Although Stan thoroughly deserved his "flying wings," it is to be hoped he didn't take this award too seriously, as the grade of "Third Lieutenant" does not exist. This time around Laurel was finally created an "honorary pilot," which prompted a display of false cockiness directed at Babe.

One would expect this family of St. Lucians to be taking snaps of the Hollywood film stars, but it is actually Stan Laurel and John Garfield taking pictures of the family, while Chico Marx and Jane Pickens pick up some local knowledge.

With no show in the evening, the entertainers would have been able to turn in early. But whether or not they were able to sleep would have depended on how well they coped with the heat, the mosquitoes, and the intrusive nocturnal noises issuing from the surrounding jungle.

o-o-0-o-o

CHAPTER 25
HEAT AND DRINK
(1941 pt4)

Next on the itinerary was Trinidad. The first garrison of troops had arrived on the island in April 1941, just a few weeks after the advance party of construction people. A large section of the El Malmo forest had been cleared, and the Aripo river had been diverted to make room for the runway. As the first priority was to construct the airfield, there had been no time or manpower to build barracks, so the troops had had to live in tents. In July work started on building barracks, both there and on the outskirts of Port of Spain; but, at the time of arrival of *The Flying Showboat,*" only half of the troops were accommodated in barracks.

-----0-----

1941 Nov 06 (Thursday)

ST. LUCIA, Windward Islands to **TRINIDAD**, West Indies 229 miles

-----0-----

(Thursday 6 November 1941)
Fort Read, **TRINIDAD, West Indies**

When the planes touched down at 11.30am at Fort Read, opening the aircraft door was tantamount to opening the door to a furnace, as an intense wave of heat hit them.

Hardy was known to be particularly affected by the heat. Even when the atmosphere was little above room temperature he would sweat profusely, and drink huge mugs of tea to compensate for the fluid loss. Here on Trinidad the tropical temperatures had him puffing, blowing, and mopping his brow to try to regulate his body temperature.

The Boys being greeted by local workers on the base in Trinidad, who were there to maintain the runway and build the accommodation.

Because of the heat, most of the company wisely retired to the shelter of their quarters, where they spent the afternoon resting. John Garfield, however, went for a walk around town, and was soon made to regret his decision. In Marine Square he was recognised, and then mobbed by an enormous crowd which started to grow by the second. He later confessed it was the first time in his life he had ever been truly scared.

After Hardy had rested he went to the theatre early and, to pass the time away, actually swept the floor. A reporter caught him there, and described the scene upon his arrival.

> If you saw a little fellow [sic] dressed in what was large enough to be a tent, rolling a cigarette with a one-hand-twist, on pink paper, and pushing a broom at the Fort Read Theatre – that was Ollie.
>
> He was quite proud of the fact that he had lost over fifteen pounds while on the trip.
>
> (*Trinidad Guardian* – 11 November 1941)

They say old habits die hard. Hardy must have been transporting himself back to the years he had worked at the Electric Theater in Milledgeville, Georgia.

In the evening *The Flying Showboat* members gave two performances, on a spotlessly clean stage, to packed houses in the new Fort Read Theatre. The audiences were made up of troops from the Trinidad base command; the 99th Bombardment Squadron, and the 99th Bomb; plus the employees of the construction companies who had built the base and airfield. Locals who worked on the base made up the rest of the audience.

The Hollywood entertainers' next show for U.S. troops involved flying out of the Caribbean, to a British colony near the northern coast of South America.

-----0-----

1941 Nov 07 (Friday)

TRINIDAD, West Indies to BRITISH GUIANA, South America   351 miles

-----0-----

In June 1941 the United States had obtained rights to set up military facilities in British Guiana, as part of an agreement with Britain. In just six days they had cleared a forest and levelled hills, and laid a concrete runway. Atkinson Field – located twenty-eight miles from Georgetown, in Hyde Park – opened on 20 June, and was to become a major staging point for American aircraft crossing the Atlantic, en route to Europe.

Just three days before the entertainers arrived, the 430th Bombardment Squadron (9th Bombardment Group) had been assigned to Atkinson Field, to fly anti-Nazi U-boat sorties in their Douglas B-18 bombers. Another force already stationed there was the 44th Reconnaissance.

-----0-----

(Friday 7 November 1941)

Atkinson Field, Georgetown, **BRITISH GUIANA**, South America

After checking in their bags, and checking out their accommodation, the flying stars were driven into Georgetown itself, to have lunch at the Queen's Park Hotel. This was the first time the entertainers had been introduced into a public place, as at all the other bases they had been confined to camp.

Add to the equation that they were the first troupe of American stage and screen personalities to visit the colony, and you had a formula for mass hysteria. One local newspaper put it:

> Not since Col. Charles Lindbergh paid a flying visit to British Guiana more than a decade ago, has any visitor got as rousing a welcome as the American film stars— John Garfield, Stan Laurel, Chico Marx, Ray Bolger; Mitzi Mayfair, and Jane Pickens.
>
> Iron gates, bolted doors, mounted- and foot-police at the Park Hotel, where the stars lunched, gave way as a fresh wave of enthusiasm swept over the seething crowd on the road, on stationary vehicles, and perched on iron palings, as time and time again the stars left their Creole lunch, went to the balcony overlooking the road, and waved and shouted unintelligible words to the boisterous crowd.
>
> (*Guyana Daily Chronicle* – 8 November 1941)

The crowds had been assembling in front of the Queen's Park Hotel since early morning, in order to see the stars when they arrived at mid-day. But it was actually 1.30pm when they did arrive, by which time the crowds had increased immensely, filling the streets around the hotel.

As soon as the cars were spotted, the crowd gave a deafening cheer. But it was when the stars exited from their cars that things got a little scary. The crowd surged forward, still cheering

Heat and Drink

lustily, and pandemonium broke out. The party responded by waving whilst, with difficulty, edging their way into the Park Hotel. Inside, the numerous autograph hunters who were besieging the VIPs had to be removed by the police, so that the guests could get on with their luncheon.

A second local paper takes up the story.

> John Garfield, Stan Laurel, and Chico Marx bore out the reputation which they have established for popularity in the hearts of the local public. Garfield, undoubtedly, was the favourite with the crowd, and his striking personality attracted the attention of everyone. As for the famous Chico Marx and the inimitable Stan Laurel, no sooner were they in the Hotel than they commenced to perform a number of their characteristic mirth-provoking antics to the intense delight of the crowds. The other members of the party, though familiar to the public, still enjoyed much popularity.
>
> Stan Laurel was comically attired in a white pullover [T-shirt] on the front of which was boldly painted in large black letters "25th Bomb," and a drawing of a bomber finished the design.
>
> At a rakish angle he wore an aviator's cap, and a pair of blue slacks completed his outfit. He did not speak much and, when asked how he liked the City, replied, "Very well."
>
> Incidentally, Hardy, who arrived with the others, was not feeling well enough to join them at the Hotel, and remained behind at Atkinson Field.
>
> When Chico Marx did find time to say a word or two to the Press, he disclosed that he found the city very lovely and tidy. Chico displayed some of his talent by rendering "Roll Out the Barrel" on the piano.
>
> Ray Bolger proved to be a charming conversationalist. He is stately in stature and possesses an imposing personality.
>
> The party had lunch on the cool and spacious veranda of the Hotel, which they interrupted at various intervals and went to the Hotel balcony, waving to the crowd and signalling the "V for Victory" sign.

I wonder if the guy on the left later had a T-shirt printed with "25th photobomb" on it.

(*Guyana Daily Argosy* – 8 November 1941) [Abridged]

The VIPs had been invited to the luncheon as guests of officers of the American Army and Navy, and Local Forces. Present were two captains; a colonel; two lieutenants; two lieutenant colonels; one commander; and three majors. The other local paper gave us more detail about the table arrangements:

> Originally laid for twenty, the table had to have an arm to accommodate extra guests. John Garfield sat near the head, between the two ladies. Ray Bolger and Chico Marx got together at the bend in the table. Laurel ate at another table with some army cronies, and autographed slips for admiring policemen and school-girls in between. He looks rather older than on the screen, and not at all slim. In fact, he is quite half Hardy's size.
>
> Despite a cordon of policemen, barmen and waiters, autograph hunters broke through and reached their objectives. The stars are experts at using a fork and signing their names at the same time.

(*Guyana Daily Chronicle* – 8 November 1941)

Between courses, Stan Laurel, Mitzi Mayfair, Jane Pickens, and John Garfield acknowledge the crowds below, from the balcony of the Queen's Park Hotel, GUIANA. (7 November 1941)

(Newspaper scan)

As the luncheon ended and the party attempted to leave, they were again surrounded by the eager crowd of autograph hunters, so it was with difficulty that they reached their cars. Some of the party slipped away and went sight-seeing. Laurel and Marx dropped in at Lord's the Tailors, where Stan bought a pair of trousers, a couple of sports shirts, and a sun helmet. With shopping over, the celebrities returned to Atkinson Field, where the first thing Laurel did was to see how Hardy was feeling. The rest must have done Babe some good, as he was able to make the evening show. A local reporter reviewed it as follows:

> For two hours Friday night, American soldiers and airmen stationed at Atkinson Field, Hyde Park, forgot the coming war, the petty irritations of army life, the mosquitoes, the heat, the endless sand, and their sickness for home, which some of them had not seen for months. They were indeed at home. Where else but in America could they sit and see, just across the footlights, such a galaxy of stars of stage, screen, and radio, as John Garfield, Chico Marx, Laurel and Hardy, Ray Bolger, Jane Pickens, and Mitzi Mayfair all together.
>
> The illusion was so perfect that, at the end of the evening when Jane Pickens called for the National Anthem, it underlined the most natural thing in the world, to join in the singing of "The Stars and Stripes." [*ibid.*]
>
> For two hours, John Garfield, besides acting as master of ceremonies, recited a poem; Chico Marx played the piano—the same pieces he played in "*A Day at the Races*"; Laurel and Hardy (recovered from the illness which kept him from coming to Georgetown) clowned as only they can clown; Ray Bolger, assistant M.C., burlesqued the Louis-Galento fight in taps, tap-danced solo and rumbaed and jitterbugged with Mitzi Mayfair, who also danced solo, while Jane Pickens sang many songs, some with choral background supplied by the military audience.
>
> Just across the footlights ranged a sea of khaki—eight hundred Yankee faces packed close together, eyes glued on the stage. It was also the official opening of the new theatre, with its polished stage, microphone, loudspeakers, and perfect acoustics. And what an opening! Applause was sometimes almost as long as the items, with rousing cheers the like of which Georgetown has never heard. Encore after encore was demanded, and willingly given, until the performers were, I am sure, ready to drop with exhaustion.
>
> During the prolonged applause at the end of the show, the entire cast came out, and Colonel Draper and Major Boyle, the crew of the bomber that flew them down, were introduced to the audience. Bidding farewell to the stars, Col. Mathews said he hoped they would come back, "the sooner the better." And that was that!

(*Guyana Sunday Chronicle* – 9 November 1941)

-----0-----

1941 Nov 08 (Saturday)

BRITISH GUIANA, South America to **TRINIDAD**, West Indies ✈ 351 miles

-----0-----

Heat and Drink

As at St. Lucia, the local workers turned out to welcome *The Flying Showboat* entertainers at the airport.
TRINIDAD

Ollie orating, while Stan sits secluded.
"The Driver's License"
BRITISH GUIANA

A view of the Boys from backstage at the Atkinson Field theatre.
BRITISH GUIANA

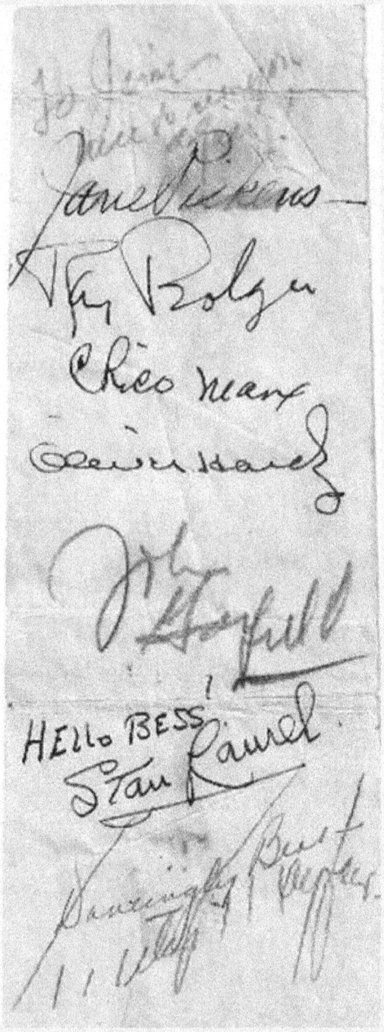

*To Jim
Nice to see you
again*

Jane Pickens

Ray Bolger

Chico Marx

Oliver Hardy

*John
Garfield*

HELLO BESS!
Stan Laurel

*Dancingly Best
Mitzi Mayfair*

The members of 'The Flying Showboat' company may have signed hundreds of autographs, but extant ones are exceedingly rare.

After an overnight stay in British Guiana, our flight-fatigued funsters were flown back to Trinidad. They were now about to spend the whole of Saturday and Sunday on the Docksite Camp, with shows in the evening only. A local reporter observed them during their leisure time:

> Ollie Hardy was interested in conditions among the soldiers, asking questions about their lives, the food down here, and what could be done to improve things for them.
>
> Chico Marx was the most studious of the performers—spending his time reading books and magazines backstage.
>
> Ray Bolger was the clown, always good for a laugh.
>
> As for Jane Pickens and Mitzi Mayfair, all they did was sit and look beautiful. That was more than enough.

(Trinidad Guardian – 11 November 1941)

-----0-----

(Saturday 8 November 1941)

Port of Spain, **TRINIDAD**, West Indies

On the Saturday evening, at 8pm., the troupe performed a two-hour show in the Docksite Camp Theatre, for the United States Officers and men.

(Sunday 9 November 1941)

Port of Spain, **TRINIDAD**, West Indies

On the Sunday, the show was repeated at the Docksite Camp Theatre for the United States Navy (in uniform), the United States Marine Corps. (in uniform), and the United States Army.

Port of Spain, **TRINIDAD** – 8 November 1941.
The entertainers nervously awaiting the start of the show, in a wooden hut, which is serving as a dressing-room at the Docksite Camp.

The gruelling tour was now over, and the troupe of entertainers would soon be back in their own homes, with all the luxury, mod cons and comforts they provided. And how they deserved to be. At the airbases they had visited, the runways had literally been torn from the earth only months earlier, with the result that the surrounding area was a mud bowl when it rained, and a dust bowl when it was sunny. No special accommodation had been built for them. They had had to make the best of what was offered, which in some cases was a wooden shed with a tin roof. These would have been like an oven – by day, and a fridge – by night.

Another discomfort was that, when the jungle had been cleared, no one had told the mosquitoes to leave the area; and so they had stayed on to gorge themselves on the thousands of sweaty human bodies which had replaced their usual animal targets. And mosquitoes weren't the only creatures to cause medical problems. Laurel had a chigger bore into his foot, which caused an abscess which, some months later, needed a minor operation to remove it.

And all this discomfort endured by the performers, just to sing a song, do a dance, play a tune, tell a joke, or act out a sketch. But then it never really was about what happened solely on stage. It was also the very presence of these entertainers on the base, which lifted the spirits of the troops. The stars ate in the enlisted men's mess halls, signed autographs, and posed for pictures by the score.

By making their own sacrifices to be there, even if it were only for two weeks, the Hollywood visitors were saying: "*Look lads and lasses, we know you are here; we know what conditions you are enduring; we know what sacrifices you are making for our country; and we fully appreciate it.*"

Add all this together, and you can see why the troops' morale was lifted sufficiently for them to continue enduring the conditions, in the cause of protecting the U.S. from enemy invasion.

PLANE TALK

Douglas C-49-A 14-seater

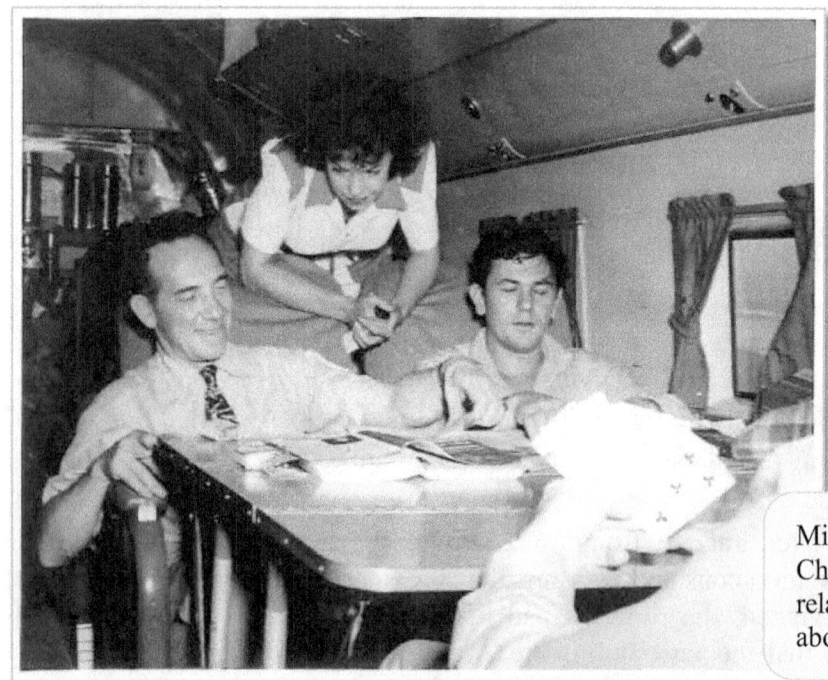

Mitzi Mayfair looks on, while Chico Marx and John Garfield relax over a game of cards – aboard *"The Flying Showboat."*

Laurel, himself, wrote on the back of this photo:
PLAYING SOLITAIRE ON A "C".49 ON THE WAY FROM MITCHEL FIELD TO PUERTO RICO (& SCARED TO DEATH) S.L
Nov 4th 1941

-----0-----

If the other passengers had known that the Chief Navigator was Oliver Hardy, and the pilot was Stan Laurel, they would not have been so relaxed. The real pilot, Lt. Paul Schwartz looks unconcerned.

o-o-0-o-o

Pilot Lt. Paul Schwartz is reunited with his VIP passengers on the set of "*Air Raid Wardens*." If he had turned up on the set of "*The Flying Deuces*," they'd probably have run the other way.

It would have been all so very so easy for *The Flying Showboat* members to have visited troops much nearer to home; but, instead, they had chosen to fly a reported thirteen thousand miles – even though at least two members had an abject fear of flying. Now they could return home feeling justifiably proud of themselves – but not before an exhausting five-thousand-two hundred-mile return trip to Los Angeles.

We will let Laurel have the last word, with these comments in wrote in a letter

> No, I'm not in the least a bit interested in Flying - have made quite a few trips, but it scares me to death, my imaginations run amuck & I'm a nervous wreck. Most of my flying was during the War, Hardy & I were with a show, called the 'Flying Showboat' we were sent by the Government on army bombers to entertain the troops in all the Caribbean Bases, including Georgetown, British Guiana. The whole trip was a nightmare for me, we flew 8 hours or more every day for about three weeks & those old bombers were'nt built for comfort (B.18's) sitting on narrow wooden benches with parachutes on our backs, can you imagine if we'd ever had to 'bail out', we would'nt have known what to do, it really was a frightening experience. On that trip were the late John Garfield, Chico Marx, (Marx Bros.) Ray Bolger, Jane Pickens, Mitzi Mayfair & one or two others you probably do'nt know of. Anyway everybody was very happy when we got back to Miami - needless to tell you that was my last trip in the air, I took the slow train back to Hollywood.

-----0-----

1941 Nov 10 (Monday)
    TRINIDAD, West Indies to **PUERTO RICO**, Greater Antilles   1,076 miles

-----0-----

1941 Nov 11 (Tuesday)
    PUERTO RICO, Greater Antilles to **MIAMI**, Florida   1,095 miles

-----0-----

And a "slow" train it was, taking over 4 days. Here is the possible schedule:

-----0-----

1941 Nov 12 (Wednesday)
    MIAMI, Florida to **WASHINGTON DC** – to **CHICAGO**, Illinois   1,192 miles

-----0-----

1941 Nov 14–16 (Thu-Sat)
    CHICAGO to **LOS ANGELES**, to **VAN NUYS**, California   1,750 miles

-----0-----

The original plan for *The Flying Showboat* was for a different company to fly to the Caribbean on a fortnightly rota. But then, the unthinkable happened. On 7 December 1941, the Japanese bombed Pearl Harbor, Hawaii – thus provoking the Americans into joining the war. It wasn't just U.S. defences in the Atlantic which went on high alert – all the airbases in and around the Caribbean did too; and between 7-13 December all dependent women and children were evacuated to the U.S. mainland.

The entertainment company of Stan Laurel, Oliver Hardy, Ray Bolger, John Garfield, Jane Pickens, Louis Blanski, and Mitzi Mayfair had been the first to tour the Caribbean, and would be the last. *The Flying Showboat* had flown away just in time.

o-o-0-o-o

CHAPTER 26

LAUGH FOR MORALE
(1941 pt5 – 1942 pt1)

As "*The Flying Showboat*" company were making their way back to Los Angeles, the *New York Times* announced:

> Stan Laurel and Oliver Hardy will arrive in Miami tonight after completing an entertainment tour of defense bases in the Caribbean. The comedians will leave for the Coast tomorrow to begin work on "Pitfalls of a Big City," which Sol Wurtzel will produce for Twentieth Century-Fox.
>
> (13 November 1941)

The announcement regarding filming was a little premature. It would be March 1942 before shooting commenced on "*Pitfalls of a Big City*" (released as "*A-Haunting We Will Go*"). Laurel had revealed a revised schedule, in a letter to a friend, some two weeks later:

```
                                              Nov' 26th 1941
We expect to go East next month for about 8 weeks personals
& back for a picture in March.
```

The tour had been hastily put together to fill the gap while the film was being scripted. Here, one might question why Laurel and Hardy were still about to tour, even though the U.S.A. was on war alert. It may be that America had taken a lead from Britain whereby, at the outset of the war some two years earlier, all forms of sporting events and theatrical entertainment had been phased out. It was soon realised, however, that both were necessary to raise morale, enlighten the gloom of war, and ultimately to maintain the war effort. Thus sport and entertainment was quickly reinstated, and encouraged throughout Britain.

In his closing speech at the "Variety Club Seventh Annual Convention" in Atlantic City, back in May 1941, Mayor Taggart had stated on the same subject: "*The morale of the American people must remain on its present high level. No such undermining of government and people must prevail here as did in the fall of France.*" [*ibid.*] Having learned from the past, America continued all forms of entertainment without so much as a one-day break.

It was just as well that Laurel and Hardy's tour was allowed to go ahead, as there was still the matter of the $127,000-plus debt they had to work off.

Paradoxically, just three days after Stan had written the letter re- starting a tour, as opposed to starting a film, Laurel and Hardy were called upon to make a film. However, it was not the usual kind of Laurel & Hardy comedy.

"*The Tree In A Test Tube*" was filmed at the Fox Hills Movietone Studio, West Los Angeles, California, on Saturday 29 November 1941. It was a short, sponsored by the U.S. Department of Agriculture, the aim of which was to inform the public as to the use and value of wood in making numerous products. The film's greatest value to Laurel & Hardy aficionados is not just that they occupy the screen during the full running-time, exhibiting various wood products, but that it was shot in COLOUR.

"The Tree in a Test Tube" reveals Stan to have ginger hair – a characteristic not evident in black & white films — or photos!

LAUREL and HARDY – The U.S. Tours

Two days before heading east, our comedy heroes may also have managed to squeeze in an additional personal appearance, a little closer to home, although confirmation was not found before this book went to print.

-----0-----

1941 December 03 (Wednesday)

LOS ANGELES, California to **SAN DIEGO**, California 121 miles

-----0-----

(Wednesday 3 December 1941 – 1 day only)

SAN DIEGO, California - U.S. Marine Corps barracks

[UNCONFIRMED]

-----0-----

1941 December 03 (Wednesday)

SAN DIEGO, California to **LOS ANGELES**, California 121 miles

-----0-----

Here is the point in this account where we start to untie the Gordian Knot. Past accounts of the coming tour have given a scrambled list of venues, along with inaccurate dates. Author Randy Skretvedt has the tour starting in January 1942, and cites only the following six cities:

Chicago, Detroit, Fort Wayne, Cleveland, Pittsburgh, and Boston.

Whereas author Fred Lawrence Guiles cites twelve cities:

Omaha, St. Louis, Chicago, Milwaukee, Minneapolis, Cleveland, Columbus, Cincinnati, Newark, Buffalo, Boston, Hartford.

It seems as though Guiles has actually given the cities played on the 1940 "*Laurel & Hardy Revue*" tour. Further confusion is added by an entry in the 3 January 1942 issue of *Boxoffice*, which states that: "*L&H have added Memphis – Tennessee, and Columbus – Ohio, to their tour dates.*"

My own attempt to untie the Gordian Knot wasn't as successful as that of Alexander the Great, but it is the best effort made in the last seventy-plus years, and runs as follows.

Chicago, Brooklyn, [somewhere], Fort Wayne, [somewhere], Milwaukee, Chicago, Dayton, Cincinnati, Cleveland, Youngstown, Akron, Boston.

The first stop-over wasn't part of the actual Laurel and Hardy touring show, but just a one-off event in Chicago, at which numerous stars of stage and screen were to appear.

A few days before Stan and Babe set off, the *Oakland Tribune* had informed its readers: "*Jack Oakie, Stan Laurel and Oliver Hardy all have an invitation to go to England and make comedies.*" However, the train driver wasn't convinced, and duly dropped off the comedy couple at the pre-designated city of Chicago. Jack Oakie would not be going to England, either. He was far too busy at Fox even to contemplate the trip.

-----0-----

1941 December 15 (*circa*) Monday

LOS ANGELES to **CHICAGO**, Illinois 2,066 miles

-----0-----

(Wednesday 17 December 1941)

CHICAGO – Chicago Stadium

CHICAGO 9th ANNUAL NIGHT OF STARS

Gala Christmas Benefit Show

Jimmy Durante, Joe E. Brown, Laurel and Hardy, Humphrey Bogart and his wife Mayo Methot, and Jackie Cooper.

Plus every well-known actor currently appearing in Chicago theaters, from Victor Moore to Martha Raye and Vera Zorina, will be appearing.

Laugh For Morale

The twenty-four-thousand-seater Chicago Stadium was sold out, and gate receipts topped $265,000. The extravaganza was to raise money for a civic charity, headed by the Mayor of Chicago, to provide shoes and clothes for eight thousand of Chicago's poor children. Another report quoted the number of children who would benefit as sixty-five thousand – which is some mark-up in numbers, and some mark-down in the amount each child would receive. The show commenced at 8pm and went on until dawn. Six hundred stars of stage, screen, and radio, from all parts of the country, attended this fifty-act show.

Again, one would have to ask what Laurel and Hardy were doing, over two thousand miles from home; as just one of fifty acts; doing a sketch which lasted minutes; on a show that lasted for hours. The motivation certainly wasn't prestige. Plus, they were due to return to Chicago in just five weeks, for a week-long appearance at the Chicago Oriental theatre. Maybe it was good PR for the forthcoming show.

In a special ceremony during their stay in Chicago, Mayor Kelly presented the two Hollywood comedians with "The Key to the City," and then, just like his counterpart in Omaha in 1940, apologetically asked them to return it – explaining: "*I am scheduled to make another presentation tomorrow, but, through oversight, the one I gave you was the last in stock.*"

So Stan and Babe reluctantly gave back the key, but only after Mayor Kelly had promised to have a duplicate made, and sent on to them. After which, I can imagine them checking a local paper to see if Wendell Wilkie was due in town.

-----0-----

[1941 December 21 (circa)   BROOKLYN, New York]

Next on the itinerary was a trip to New York. However, a post-dated article revealed:

> Stan Laurel and Oliver Hardy were forced to cancel out Brooklyn in their forthcoming p.a. tour, and received an irate wire from the Brooklyn 'bums': "Okay! So you're not coming to Brooklyn? Well, you can't dodge the Dodgers – we'll see you in Fort Wayne."

-----0-----

The umbrella title of this tour has somehow become accepted as being "*Hell-a-Belloo,*" but this does not seem to hold up to scrutiny. In Chicago the billing would be simply: "*Laurel & Hardy on the stage IN PERSON.*" Dayton would have only a minor variation of "IN PERSON." Cincinnati too went for "*Laurel and Hardy IN PERSON*" but then put in a subtitle of: "*In a riot of revelry 'HELL-A-BELLOO'.*" Cleveland went for "*SOCKO – Another Smash Show,*" whilst Boston chose: "*Hollywood on Parade.*" And when the Boys themselves were interviewed in Cincinnati, even more confusion to the tour title was added:

> Out of their trip [Laurel and Hardy's Caribbean tour with "*The Flying Showboat*"] grew the idea which they are passing on to the country for their "Laugh for Morale" campaign. They have adopted the symbol of a dash and four dots, which is the Morse code for 'L' and 'H,' which are not only the first and last letters of 'laugh' but also the first initials of L-aurel and H-ardy.

> They report that tap-dancers are working out the dash and four dot routines, and that in some places radio news reporters have picked it up as telegraphic signal background for their broadcasts. The Laurel and Hardy slogan is "Keep 'Em Rolling in the Aisles – Laugh for Morale."

So! the "*Laugh for Morale*" tour went on its way, but there are still some dates and venues which are unknown. First mystery is Laurel and Hardy's whereabouts between the show in Chicago on 17 December, and the next one on 30 December. It is possible they returned to L.A., but that would have taken up at least five days in travel, and involved a journey of over four thousand miles.

-----0-----

1941 December 30 (Wednesday)
        [somewhere] to **FORT WAYNE**, Indiana ??? miles

LAUREL and HARDY – The U.S. Tours

-----0-----

(Wednesday 30 December 1941 to Saturday 3 January 1942)
FORT WAYNE – Palace Theatre

ON STAGE - IN PERSON
Hollywood's Greatest Comedy Team! Make Their First Fort Wayne Stage Appearance
STAN LAUREL
OLIVER HARDY
WITH A LAUGH SHOW THAT'S THE FUNNIEST IN THE HISTORY OF LAUGHTER!
The Bell Troupe
Breath Taking Acrobatics
Rollet & Dorothea
Hollywood Dance Team
Three Harmoniacs
Musical Novelty
JUDY STARR
That Little Mite of Dynamite

AND MANY OTHER PERSONALITIES OF STAGE & RADIO
ON SCREEN: ANN SHIRLEY IN "UNEXPECTED UNCLE"

In Fort Wayne, a local reviewer confirmed that the "*Laugh For Morale*" tour was certainly generating laughter.

> Stan Laurel and Oliver Hardy, Hollywood's funniest comedy team, now appearing on the Palace stage in person, really set records straight when it comes to getting laughs. The Palace audiences this week have enjoyed a laugh-a-second, as a matter of fact, a great many titters come up from the house before Stan and Ollie even walk on the stage.
>
> Once the boys are on the stage, anything can happen … and usually does. They present a skit entitled: "How to Get a Driver's License" which tickles the funny bone of every resident of this state, who has at one time or another taken a driver's test, or stood in line to fill out an application.
>
> In addition, the stage fare also boasts a revue that has been carefully planned to give a variety of entertainment.

(*Fort Wayne Journal-Gazette* – 4 January 1942)

During their week in Fort Wayne, Babe and Stan were autographing photographs for some John Doughboys, when one of the soldiers asked for two.

"Who's the second one for?" asked Hardy.

"It's for the sergeant, if I'm AWOL," explained the draftee, "otherwise it's for my girlfriend."

For this tour, Laurel and Hardy's stage act was back to its basic form of the two-man version of "*The Driver's License*" sketch. As such, it wasn't so much a sketch as a cross-patter act; with the two comedians standing static at the mic', and no need for set or scenery. Being such, it lasted just a few minutes, and so their time on stage was extended by Laurel's rendition of "*I'm a Lonely Little Petunia in an Onion Patch*," and Hardy crooning "*Shine on Harvest Moon*," to which Laurel did a soft-shoe shuffle.

-----0-----

1942 January 04 (Sunday)
    FORT WAYNE, Indiana to [**somewhere**] 🚂 ??? miles

-----0-----

It is possible that Laurel and Hardy played a show between Monday and Thursday 5-8 January, but no record could be found. The next stop-over is, however, confirmed.

Laugh For Morale

-----0-----

1942 January 09 (Friday)

[somewhere] to **MILWAUKEE**, Wisconsin 🚂 ??? miles

-----0-----

(Friday 9 January to Thursday 15 January 1942)

MILWAUKEE – Riverside Theater

RIVERSIDE
The Greatest
STAGE AND SCREEN
combination of them all.
Tomorrow
ON THE STAGE
…. Your
Favorite
Nit Wits
of the screen
In Person
LAUREL
And
HARDY
with
The 7 Freddysons
Alice Dawn
Chriss Cross;
Rollett & Dorothea

The local papers failed to give the show any coverage, but one story did manage to sneak out, via an out-of-town paper: One afternoon, Laurel and Hardy spent some time in the centre of the Plankington Arcade, helping to raise money towards purchasing what was described as "a bombing plane."

This impromptu fund-raising activity would most likely have been on the Saturday – that being the busiest time of the week in a shopping arcade. The Boys manned a section where passers-by had to toss coins into a blanket. A bombing plane is not an item on the usual list of charity causes, so let us hope the people who were throwing the coins had an accurate aim, as "blanket-bombing" is notorious for injuring civilians!!

Not content with giving their services free, Stan and Babe actually doubled the amount raised by matching the ante with a contribution from their own pockets. That's my Boys! Just how they found time to get away from the theatre, whilst playing five shows a day there from 1pm onwards, remains a logistical puzzle.

-----0-----

1942 January 16 (Friday)

MILWAUKEE, Wisconsin to **CHICAGO**, Illinois 🚂 94 miles

-----0-----

Up till now, the dates Laurel and Hardy had played seemed to have been scratch bookings, to break in the show. In fact, previous accounts of this tour have failed to mention any shows prior to this Chicago one. But now the tour proper, planned by the 'Music Corporation of America,' was about to kick in. Let us hope it was the signal for better press coverage.

-----0-----

(Friday 16 January to Thursday 22 January 1942)

CHICAGO – Oriental Theatre

ORIENTAL
RANDOLPH NEAR STATE
Loop's Greatest Amusement Bargain!
Tomorrow
The Lafftime of a Lifetime!
The SCREEN'S FUNNIEST COMEDIANS

LAUREL & HARDY
ON THE STAGE
IN PERSON
With Their Own
HILARIOUS REVUE!
ALICE DAWN
CHRISS CROSS
7 FREDYSONS
Rollett & Dorothea
Ray Lang & Orch.
SCREEN – FIRST LOOP SHOWING
"BOMBAY CLIPPER"

The review in *Variety* (21 January 1942) ran:

> Laurel and Hardy are a smash at the Oriental. It looks like one of the big weeks since this house returned to vaudeville. Comics played town once before, at the Chicago [w/c 18 October 1940], and also did well, but nothing like here.
>
> Hokum skit about trying to get a driver's license had house in an uproar. It is material commonly associated with Laurel and Hardy and effective at all times.

At the hotel, on the Sunday of the stay in Chicago, Babe was presented with a cake, to mark his 50th Birthday.

I wonder if "The Key to the City" had been smuggled in, inside it! (18 January 1942)

Laugh For Morale

On the Thursday night came another of the Boys' charitable acts, when they made a live broadcast over the Mutual network, from the radio station WGN, performing an extract of their stage act. The show was "*Americans at the Ramparts*," which was dedicated to raising funds for infantile paralysis.

This really was a charitable act by the two comedy stars, as they had nothing whatsoever to gain from it, personally. The broadcast came on the last night of their stay in Chicago – too late to attract one single paying customer to the theatre to watch the show.

Broadcasting on WGN
(Note the giveaway on the mic'.)
Chicago – 22 January 1942)

-----0-----

1942 January 23 (Friday)

CHICAGO, Illinois to **DAYTON**, Ohio 298 miles

-----0-----

(Friday 23 January to Thursday 29 January 1942)

DAYTON – Colonial

STARTING TOMORROW ON STAGE
GET SET TO HOWL
... HERE COME YOUR FAVORITE NIT-WITS OF THE SCREEN
IN PERSON
STAN LAUREL
AND
OLIVER HARDY
Plus
ON STAGE
The Singing Star of
Rudy Vallee Radio Program
JUDY
STARR
THE HERZOGS
DeVAL, MERLE AND LEE
FREDERICKS AND LANE
Screen!
"GO WEST, YOUNG LADY"

Stan and Babe arrived in Dayton, Ohio, on the morning of Friday 23 January 1942. In ideal circumstances they would have arrived the evening before the opening night, and held a press dinner or banquet. On this tour, though, the schedule allowed for no such luxuries. In fact, finding time to eat would be a luxury, as the Boys had to do four shows per day – 2.05; 4.35, 7.05, and 9.30pm. So, with time at a premium, the press had to gather what they could from our subjects over breakfast at the Biltmore Hotel, where they were staying the week.

A welcome addition to the melange was former Roach Studios' actress Virginia Karns Patterson. Back in 1934 Virginia had played the part of 'Mother Goose' in the Laurel & Hardy film "*Babes in Toyland*," and so the three of them had a happy reunion. Meeting over, it was time to get to the Colonial Theatre for the first show. The *Dayton Daily News* opined:

> Laurel and Hardy are seemingly more funny on stage than they are on screen. This is not to condemn their pictures, but rather to compliment their personal appearance, for they do more than we have learned to expect from Hollywoodians at the Colonial.

Much as it is pleasing that the reviewer enjoyed Laurel and Hardy live, it is beyond belief that their stage act was funnier than their films – unless the only Laurel & Hardy film he had ever seen was their most recent, "*Great Guns*."

If Friday in Dayton had seemed one heck of a full itinerary, then Saturday was about to make it seem positively relaxing. The Saturday and Sunday shows had been increased to FIVE, with the first performance starting at 1.14pm, and the last one at 9.42pm.

If this weren't gruelling enough, come early morning, the Boys elected to make an appearance at the local U.S. Air Force base. Having given so many "Laughs" on the "*Laugh For Morale*" tour, it was time to add the "Morale" part.

Here at Patterson Field they mixed with members of the 11th Bombardment Group, who had been drafted in to fly patrol-and-search missions off Hawaii. Stan and Babe would have had something in common with the flight crews, as the latter had trained in B-18s, the same type of aircraft they themselves had flown in throughout their U.S.O. tour of the Caribbean (although the pilots here had since received B-17s for operations).

As they couldn't even fix a TV aerial on a roof, what chance do they have an aircraft engine?

The Non-Flying Deuces
Composite image – showing what the full view of the B-17 bomber would have looked like.

The *Dayton Daily News* reported that the two comedians were made "Honorary First Sergeants," in recognition of their work in the comedy "*Great Guns.*" (The only other award this film was to receive was a "Golden Turkey.")

After Stan and Babe's poor efforts to repair the engine on the army bomber, the award was rescinded, and they were demoted to "Goodwill Representatives of the Fairfield Air Depot" – the latter being adjacent to the base.

Stan receiving his award as "Honorary First Sergeant."
He gave the original of this photo to Virginia Karns, on which he had written:
"WE'RE IN THE ARMY NOW, VIRGINIA!
Stan & "Ollie"

From Patterson Field, the two comedians had to make a dash to the Colonial Theatre to fulfil their quota of appearances. Five shows later, the Boys' day still wasn't over. Their hosts at Patterson Field had requested that they show their faces at a dance for enlisted men, at the Temple Israel, in Dayton. The event drew a capacity crowd, swelled by those wishing to see Laurel and Hardy, plus Judy Starr – no doubt.

Sunday also featured an extra-curricular event but, mercifully, it wasn't in the morning, so the Boys may have had time to recuperate from the previous day's schedule. After the last of their five Sunday performances, Stan and Babe went to a party at Bill and Virginia Patterson's house, along with a further fifty-plus invitees.

The Boys are so close to Virginia in the Dayton photo (top) and on the set of "*Babes in Toyland*" (right) that you'd think she really was their mother.
Left: Virginia in costume as 'Mother Goose.'

While at Virginia's house party, Stan was fascinated by the Pattersons' twin babies, and insisted on taking each guest in turn up to their bedroom to observe them sleeping.

Hardy, however, plumped himself into a comfortable easy-chair, and there he stayed. Maybe his hosts didn't realise it, but this was Hardy's way of saying that he didn't want to be there. It was also a sign that he wasn't too well.

o-o-0-o-o

CHAPTER 27

TOUR DE FOX
(1942 pt2)

The local newspapers in Dayton gave Laurel and Hardy little to no coverage for the rest of the week, and so they left without fanfare and moved on.

-----0-----

1942 January 30 (Friday)

DAYTON, Ohio to **CINCINNATI**, Ohio 🚂 50 miles

-----0-----

With only a fifty-mile train journey to Cincinnati, the Boys managed to make it for breakfast at the Netherland Plaza Hotel, where they held a press conference:

> A pair of soberly-dressed—dark blue suits, quiet ties, white shirts—business men walked into the hotel dining room. The head-waiter said, "Over here, Mr. Hardy. Over here Mr. Laurel."
>
> And the gentlemen of the press gandered at Hollywood's most celebrated clowns: Oliver Hardy and Stan Laurel, veterans of more than 150 films [*sic*] devoted to the thesis that a good fall is one of the funniest things ever invented by man.

> Mr. Hardy promptly dispelled the enveloping solemnity by admitting that he was once a boy soprano, and by refusing to have anybody test the reality of the infinitesimal moustache which is part of his stock-in-trade.
>
> It was once tested, he said, by a doubting fan who pulled his 306 pounds along by a single hair.
>
> Mr. Hardy is in the enviable position of not having to worry about his weight: So his breakfast was a good hearty one of ham and eggs, interrupted briefly to allow the photographers to catch him and Mr. Laurel in a series of funny poses.
>
> "Photographers," observed Mr. Hardy, "are all gag-men at heart."
>
> This is Mr. Hardy's first visit to Cincinnati, but Mr. Laurel was here once on what may now be described as an historic occasion. He and a young fellow named Charlie Chaplin played the Empress in 1913 in a production called Fred Karno's "Night in an English Music Hall."

[Stan had actually played in Cincinnati THREE TIMES with the Karno Company: February 1911, January 1912, and October 1912. He is mistaken about their having played there in 1913.]

> It is an astonishing thing to watch them change at command from solid citizens having breakfast with friends, into the comics known to millions: A rearrangement of the facial muscles, a twist of the wrist and body, and there they are.

(*Cincinnati Post* – 30 January 1942)

-----0-----

(Friday 30 January to Thursday 5 February 1942)

CINCINNATI – Shubert Theatre

> The Stage Goes Daffy
> In An Explosion of Mad Mirth!
> It's the funniest, goofiest,
> laugh show on earth ….
> IN PERSON
> ## LAUREL & HARDY
> First Cincinnati appearance of the famous screen comedians in the topsy-turvy riot of revelry.
> ## "HELL-A-BELLOO"
> Featuring the Clown Prince of Hilarious Hokum
> **MILT BRITTON**
> AND HIS MAD MUSICAL MANIACS
> WORLD'S CRAZIEST ORCHESTRA
> **TOMMY RAFFERTY**
> **TITO, JOE BRITTON**
> Dave Van Horn
> 4 Skating Marvels
> **JUDY STARR**

A local paper said of the show:

> 'Frightened bewilderment' and 'angry exasperation,' as expressed to a "T" by Stanley Laurel and Oliver Hardy, trundled onto the Shubert stage Friday night and set to work with the familiar mannerisms and expressions which have popularised them with a vast movie following.
>
> They argued and they sang. Ollie smoothed his Derby hat with his cuff innumerable times, waved his tie at the crowd, and suffered untold mental pain from the crude manners of his pal.
>
> Master Stanley, to the intense delight of the audience, screwed his face into the familiar grimace and scratched his head. Occasionally he broke into tears and cried in a high squeak, which brought responsive cheers.
>
> Laurel and Hardy have identified themselves on the screen countless times with their famous mannerisms.
>
> They bring the whole caboodle to the Shubert stage this week, and the antics were popular enough Friday night to call for four encores—something you don't see very often in these days of streamlined stage shows.
>
> The two buffoons are assisted by an excellent stage show, a considerable part of which is devoted to the antics of Milt Britton's Band.
>
> (*Cincinnati Post* – 31 January 1942)

A second local paper went with:

Laurel and Hardy in Shubert Revue

> Stan Laurel with his goony and bewildered smile, and his ponderous, patient and long-suffering comedy partner, Oliver Hardy, lead the parade of clowns, musicians, singers, dancers, skaters, and stage hands who appear in the spotlight of the new stage show which opened yesterday at the Shubert.
>
> Presented with the well-timed but apparently careless informality and abandon of "Hellzapoppin'," this vaudeville clambake clicks in all departments and gives especial emphasis to slapstick features.
>
> Laurel and his partner, unlike some of the screen actors who put in a personal appearance from time to time, can do more than bow and reminisce about the pictures they have played in.

Their act, which closes with a silly song by Laurel ["*I'm a Lonely Little Petunia in an Onion Patch*"] involves them in a series of misunderstandings about an application for an auto license.

These misunderstandings roll up a good score of laughs as Hardy tries to enlighten his addled partner, with his exasperation mounting as confusion increases to a point where his familiar black bangs nearly stand up on end.

(*Cincinnati Enquirer* – 31 January 1942)

Although the tour was not a fund-raising event, Stan and Babe did a promotional photo-shoot for buying United States Savings Bonds and Stamps, at the Headquarters of the Hamilton Defense Savings Committee. The photographs were then used for an illustrated feature in one of the local newspapers, and a magazine.

The address of the Defense Savings Committee was 408 Walnut Street.
I hope the Boys didn't get confused and go to 1127 Walnut Avenue!

-----0-----

1942 February 6 (Friday)
        CINCINNATI, Ohio to **CLEVELAND**, Ohio 247 miles

-----0-----

(Friday 6 February to Thursday 12 February 1942)
        CLEVELAND – Palace

This local newspaper gave us a better-than-average review:

> Laurel and Hardy, those comics who have been entertaining you from the screen for the last 17 years, assailed yesterday what seemed to me to be the "coldest" Cleveland audience any entertainers have encountered here for a long time.
>
> Before they came to the footlights, Clyde McCoy and his orchestra, together with some entertainers varying from good to weak, had been slowly congealing the crowd.

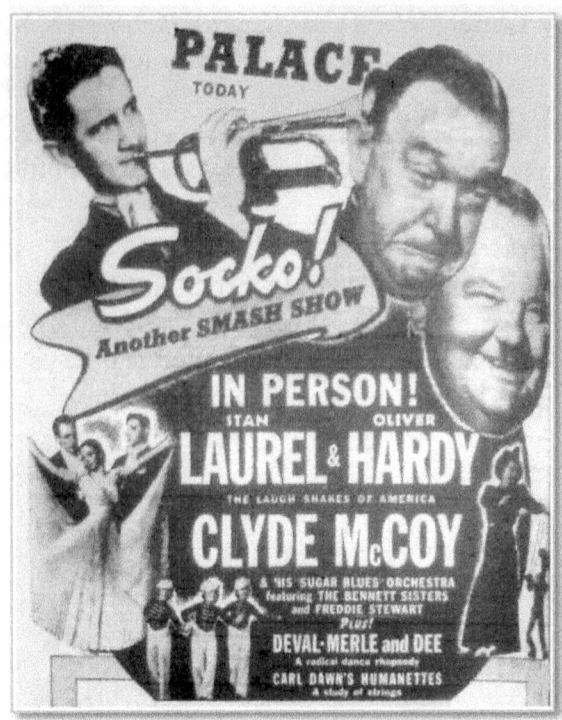

**CLEVELAND
PALACE**
TODAY
Sock!
Another SMASH SHOW
IN PERSON
STAN   OLIVER
LAUREL & HARDY
THE LAUGH SHAKES OF AMERICA
CLYDE McCOY
& HIS SUGAR BLUES ORCHESTRA
featuring **THE BENNETT SISTERS**
and **FREDDIE STUART**
Plus!
DEVAL - MERLE and DEE
A Radical Dance Rhapsody
CARL DAWN'S HUMANETTES
A Study of Strings

Perhaps I am stressing my own opinion when I report that the audience seemed to me to be downright weary of another orchestra with its boy and girl singers, offering the same songs we have been hearing for weeks on end.

That gets us back to Laurel and Hardy. They give one of their best acts, doing exactly what they (and no-one else) have been doing on the screen for a long time, with one whimpering and playing stupid and the other beaming and smiling, raging and brow-beating by turns.

After they have entertained with material which seems to be ad-libbed, but is not, they turn to the business of getting Mr. Laurel a driver's license – with the usual funny results.

By the time they had ended their skit yesterday afternoon, they had the audience sufficiently thawed to demand several encores, during which each sang a solo … and stole the show.

(*Cleveland Plain Dealer* – 07 February 1942)

Hurrah! Hurrah! At last an affectionate review, written by a local journalist, instead of one of those cynical, sneering, scathing statements which the trade papers seem to prefer.

-----0-----

1942 February 13 (Friday)
CLEVELAND, Ohio **YOUNGSTOWN**, Ohio 🚂 74 miles
-----0-----
(Friday 13 February to Monday 16 February 1942)
YOUNGSTOWN – Palace Theatre

The show in Youngstown had been scaled right down. Clyde McCoy & His Sugar Blues Orchestra had split, and were appearing as bill-toppers in their own right at the Palace Theatre in Akron, Ohio, fifty miles away. Back in were Milt Britton and his Mad Musical Maniacs, who had recently supported the Laurel & Hardy Show in Cincinnati. However, missing from the featured acts on the Cincinnati bill were Dave Van Horn, Joe Britton, and Judy Starr. The number of stage shows had been cut to just three – at 3, 7 and 10pm; and the whole package was booked in for just four nights – Friday to Monday.

The review in the Youngstown Vindicator was short, but, er …. short:

Stan Laurel and Oliver Hardy, whose faces are familiar on screens all over the world, are on the Palace stage as the headliner, with Milt Britton's acrobatic band.

YOUNGSTOWN PALACE
IN PERSON
The Laugh Shakes of America
STAN
LAUREL
OLIVER
HARDY
in
"HELLA-BALLOO"
EXTRA! LAUGH ATTRACTION!
MILT BRITTON
AMERICA'S CRAZIEST ORCHESTRA
Featuring
TOMMY RAFFERTY – TITO
4 SKATING MARVELS
ON THE SCREEN
"CADETS ON PARADE"
Freddie Bartholomew

The comedians have a little skit about getting a driver's license, which they have put on in many army camps. They sing a song or two from their pictures, and stay in character the whole time on the stage.

Britton's orchestra generally kick the welkin around. Members smash fiddles over each other's heads, they wear make-up in one scene, they tear their clothes, and generally disport themselves like something strayed from "Hellzapoppin."

On the Friday, anxious as always to do a bit of extra publicity, Stan and Babe secured themselves a live radio spot on the programme "*Old Family Almanac*" – broadcast on WFMJ. Stan spoke of his hobby of fishing, while Hardy cited gardening as his. On that same day, 14 February 1942, the trade paper *Boxoffice* published the following snippet.

Two Theatres Return to Vaude-Film Policy

AKRON—The Palace here and the Palace at Youngstown, after several weeks of a straight film policy, switched again to vaude-films. Friday when Clyde McCoy's band and revue opened at the local house for four days and Laurel & Hardy, screen comics, topped a stage bill at the Youngstown house for the same period. The units switch houses to complete the week.

On the Tuesday, Clyde McCoy & His Sugar Blues Orchestra duly left Akron to take over the stage at the Youngstown Palace, while the Laurel and Hardy Company moved out. However, the people of Akron were left disappointed, as it was only a re-release of the Laurel & Hardy film "*The Flying Deuces*" which made it to the Palace Theatre there. The question now is, in the three days Stan and Babe were to have spent in Akron, "Where did they went?"

The next engagement, after what should have been Akron, was Boston. Had Laurel and Hardy been booked into a venue much nearer to Boston so that, come the Friday, they wouldn't have anything like the six-hundred-mile journey Akron to Boston would have entailed? The answer lay in the following week's newspapers, in Boston. It wasn't good news!

-----0-----

1942 Feb 18 (Wednesday)
YOUNGSTOWN, Ohio to **BOSTON**, Massachusetts 601 miles

-----0-----

(Friday 20 February to Thursday 26 February 1942)
BOSTON – RKO-Boston Theatre (aka: Keith's)

The Thursday evening edition of the *Boston Globe* contained a large ad-block proclaiming:

RKO BOSTON
Starts TOMORROW On Stage
HOLLYWOOD comes to BOSTON!
ALL IN PERSON
LAUREL & HARDY
IN A NEW REVUE
**HOLLYWOOD
ON PARADE**
SUSAN MILLER
singing star of "Swing It Soldier"
AL SIEGEL
"The Starmaker"
LORRAINE & ROGNAN
Comedy Stars of "The Fleet's In"
ON SCREEN
**The ANDREWS SISTERS
"WHAT'S COOKIN'"**

However, come Friday's edition, the bad news was broken to theatregoers that:

> Oliver Hardy, of the Laurel and Hardy team, left here last night [19 February] by plane for California, forced to cancel a Boston engagement that was to have begun today, because of illness. Dave Apollon rushed from New York to fill his place at the RKO Boston Theatre.
>
> With his smaller partner Stan Laurel, the movie funny man Hardy arrived Wednesday from Youngstown. He was suffering from a throat ailment, which made it almost impossible for him to speak. His managers [*sic*] had wired ahead, requesting that physicians be called on his arrival.
>
> He was placed under the care of doctors, and all visitors were barred, in an effort to ensure his being able to go on stage at the RKO-Boston. Yesterday morning, what voice he had left had completely disappeared, and doctors ordered that he be bundled off to California for the sunshine.

(*Boston Post* – 20 February 1942)

-----0-----

1942 Feb 19 (Thursday)
    BOSTON, Massachusetts to **LOS ANGELES**, California   3,017 miles

-----0-----

Luckily there were no further cities on the tour, as it had always been scheduled to end in Boston; so only theatregoers from Akron and Boston were left disappointed at not seeing the comedy duo. The reason the tour dates hadn't been extended beyond Boston was that Stan and Babe had to be back in Hollywood, and ready to start filming on 15 March.

But even when Hardy recovered, and the Boys reported to the Fox set on schedule, not much film would have ended up in the can as, just six days in, the two comedians went off to Mexico for another live appearance.

The number in the touring party was one hundred and thirty-two, of whom fifty were Hollywood stars, and the rest their entourages. The junket was organised by the 'Motion-Picture Society for the Americas,' which was a section of the 'Rockerfeller Latin-American Relations Committee' combined with the 'Hollywood Victory Committee.' The delegation left Hollywood on 21 March 1942, on a special train, and spent the night at San Diego.

The stars boarding the Hollywood Special for San Diego check out their route, using the Atchison Topeka and Sante Fe Coastal Route brochure. (Getty Images)
L-R: Mark Sandrich, Lucille Ball, James Cagney, Joan Blondell, Stan Laurel, Dick Powell, Jinx Falkenburg, Kenneth Thomson, Ann Miller, Oliver Hardy.

The following morning came the hard bit, when the remaining seventy-five miles was done by coaches, some of it over the mountains, to the Mexican Military Headquarters at Ensenada.

-----0-----

1942 March 21 (Saturday)
        LOS ANGELES, California to **SAN DIEGO**, California 121 miles
1942 March 22 (Sunday)
        SAN DIEGO, California to **ENSENADA**, Mexico 75 miles

-----0-----

Ensenada is located on Mexico's Baja Peninsula coast, just sixty-eight miles south of the border crossing-point at Tijuana. Special diplomatic arrangements had been made for transferring the party across the Mexican border and, from thereon in, they had been shadowed by a motor-cycle escort of both American and Mexican law officers. On the April 1941 "Goodwill Visit" to Mexico City, President Avila Camacho himself had welcomed the Hollywood stars, but here the honour was given to Lieut. Asner Zertina to officiate on his behalf.

(Sunday 22 March 1942 – 1 night only)
ENSENADA – Teatro Mayan

Stan Laurel and Oliver Hardy, James Cagney, Lupe Velez, Joan Bennett, Ann Miller, Lucille Ball and Desi Arnaz, Jinx Falkenburg, Rosita Moreno, The Nicholas Brothers, Adele Mars, Francis Dee, the Merry Macs, Mary Martin, Marlene Dietrich, Dick Powell, Joan Blondell, Joel McCrea, Linda Grey, Katherine Booth, Martha O'Driscoll, Barbara Britton, Arturo de Cordoba, Mr. & Mrs. Kenneth Thomson, Irving Berlin, and Nat Young's 14-piece orchestra. Producer – Mark Sandrich.

On the evening of Sunday 22 March 1942, the visitors gave a four-hour show at the Teatro Mayan (Mayan Theatre), on Ensenada's main street, in front of a packed house of two thousand five hundred Mexican soldiers and sailors. The reviews proclaimed the show to have been: "*The biggest show in the United States international goodwill program to date.*" "The goodwill" was directed towards the Mexican soldiers and sailors stationed in that area.

The Commander in Chief of their garrison was General Lázaro Cardenas, who had actually been the President of Mexico from 1934-1940. The reason for the presence of such a large number of troops was that the United States, and its ally Mexico, feared that the Japanese would invade the Pacific coast through Baja California.

Intriguingly, the show was recorded – copies of which were sent to all the Latin-American nations. [Can someone send me a copy, please!]

-----0-----

ENSENDA
22 March 1942

While waiting backstage at the Teatro Mayan, Stan and Ollie try to figure out a way of splitting up Hollywood starlets Linda Grey, Katherine Booth, Martha O'Driscoll, and Barbara Britton.

When Stan gets a hold of Linda Grey, he gives her a good old "Spanky McFarland."

When Ollie tries the same with Martha O'Driscoll and Katherine Booth, he finds himself on the receiving end.

Travelling with the Ensenada show party was official "Life" photographer JOHN FLOREA. Here, Hardy is showing him how it's done.
[off stage – Teatro Mayan]

1942 March 23 (Monday)
        ENSENADA, Mexico to **SAN DIEGO**, California   75 miles
1942 March 24 (Tuesday)
        SAN DIEGO, California to **LOS ANGELES**, California   121 miles

-----0-----

One would have thought that, after the events in Mexico City eleven months earlier, Laurel and Hardy would have considered a second visit to Mexico unwise. Although they hadn't returned to the capital, there had still been more than enough fans around to cause them severe discomfort, if not injury. So just why had the two Hollywood comedians twice made long and arduous trips to Mexico? The answer would seem to lie in two newspaper reports, which came out just six weeks after the junket to Ensenada:

> I hear that a deal is now cooking for Oliver Hardy and Stan Laurel to make a picture for the Azteca Film Company in Mexico City. Their attorney, Ben Shipman, flew to Mexico today to make final arrangements.
>
> I happened to be in Mexico City with Babe and Stan and you've never seen such popularity. Everywhere they went the Mexicans would shout affectionately, "Mr. Fat and Mr. Thin!" – and that's going to be the title of their Mexican picture; or, in Spanish, "*El Gordo y El Flaco*."

                                                                    (Louella O. Parsons – 8 May 1942)

A second article, a few days later, claimed the deal was not just for one picture, but for a series:

> Laurel & Hardy, through their attorney, Ben Shipman, are ready to close a deal to make a series of Spanish language comedies for Azteca Studios in Mexico City this summer. Shipman left here last week to sign the papers. Contract will not interfere with 20th-Fox, which calls for two pictures a year for five years. Mexican productions will be for Latin-American distribution.

                                                                         (*Variety* – 13 May 1942)

Upon their immediate return from Mexico, before these reports were released, the Boys had gone straight back to the Fox studios to complete "*A-Haunting We Will Go*." Laurel firmly believed that, this time around, things on set would be different; but it wasn't to be, and again they were forced to play uncharacteristic roles, and speak humourless lines. Filmmaking wasn't fun anymore!

o-o-0-o-o

o-o-0-o-o

CHAPTER 28

ON THE RIGHT TRACK

(1942 pt3)

The Boys followed up their appearance in Ensenada by joining "*The Hollywood Victory Caravan.*" This was another revue-style company of Hollywood stars, who were about to embark on a thirteen-city tour, by train, playing at the largest venues the cities had to offer. All the monies raised would be going to the joint 'Army-Navy Relief Fund' – with the target figure being set at seven hundred and fifty thousand dollars. Three-quarters of a million pounds seems like a phenomenal amount of money until, that is, you compare it to the total amount of money needed to be raised by the sale of War Bonds, which was, wait for it! – one BILLION dollars per MONTH.

Being Hollywood stars, the members of the company were allowed to rehearse at both the 20th Century-Fox and the Paramount studios in the days prior to the departure date.

The full company boarding the 10-car Santa Fe special train at Los Angeles Union Station, on Sunday 26 April 1942, consisted of fourteen musicians; three press agents; three hairdressers; two wardrobe women; three assistants; fourteen stars: Pat O'Brien, Rise Stevens, Joan Blondell, Joan Bennett; Desi Arnaz, Eleanor Powell, Charlotte Greenwood, Frank McHugh, Charles Boyer, Bert Lahr, Cary Grant, Ray Middleton, Oliver Hardy, and Stan Laurel; and eight starlets: Katherine Booth, Alma Carroll, Frances Gifford, Elyse Knox, Fay McKenzie, Marie McDonald, Juanita Stark, and Arleen Whelan. Musical Director Alfred Newman accompanied the stars, in both meanings of the word.

Other acts were to make their way by plane to the first stop-over in Washington D.C. These were: Bob Hope, Frances Langford, Jerry Colonna, James Cagney, Groucho Marx, Joan Bennett, Olivia de Havilland, Merle Oberon, and Claudette Colbert.

[N.B. Frances Langford and Jerry Colonna posed for pictures at Union Station, but are believed to have stayed behind in L.A. to make a radio broadcast with Bob Hope on the Tuesday evening, after which all three of them flew to Washington.]

Many big names in film production had also contributed their considerable talents and expertise to the show. The skits and sequences had been written by such renowned writers as George S. Kaufman, Moss Hart, Russell Crouse, and Howard Lindsay; while the music and lyrics had come from such luminaries as Jerome Kern, John Mercer, Frank Loesser, and Arthur Schwartz. Sets were by Milt Gross; and dance-direction under Danny Dare. The show's producer was Mark Sandrich – best known as producer of most of the Fred Astaire-Ginger Rogers film musicals.

-----0-----

1942 April 26

LOS ANGELES, California to **WASHINGTON**, D.C. 🚂 2,762 miles

The passengers shrunk down in size, to allow a view of the HVC train. (*Corbis*)

-----0-----

The easy bit was when Hardy squatted for this photo. The hard bit came when he had to stand up again. Also lining up in front of the train engine are:
Cary Grant, Rise Stevens, Charles Boyer, Desi Arnaz, Joan Blondell, Hardy, Laurel. (*Corbis*)

At 9am on the morning of Wednesday 29 April, close on three days after leaving Los Angeles, the Sante Fe Special pulled in at Union Station, Washington, DC. Upon detraining, the passengers were met by a salvo of camera flashes, a thrust of microphones, a whole bank of movie cameras, and more flatteringly, a guard-of-honour by army and navy of soldiers. **[FILM]**

From exiting the station, the Hollywood entourage were shepherded into a cordoned-off zone, to the accompaniment of the United States Army Band. With everyone ringed around a rig of microphones, the visitors were given a welcoming speech by Rear Admiral Charles Hepburn. In reply, producer Mark Sandrich (in white raincoat) expressed what a privilege and an honour it was for the company to serve the military, and how thrilled they were to be doing their little bit. The stars then filed past Rear Admiral Hepburn and Lieut. Col. Curtiss Mitchell (representing the Army), both of whom shook hands with each star in turn.

WHERE'S STAN?
If you think that's Laurel next to Hardy – you've been fooled! It's Pat O'Brien.
Stan is just behind Rear Admiral Hepburn – between the second and third mic's.
(Washington Union Station – 26 April 1942)

With formalities over, the celebrities climbed into a motorcade of jeeps. Sharing with Stan and Babe were Rise Stevens, Eleanor Powell, and Desi Arnaz. All the jeeps then pulled out and took the stars, parade-style, on a circuitous route past the Capitol Building.

First stop was at the Army & Navy Club, where the VIPs were treated to a hearty army breakfast. They were going to need all the nourishment the meal provided, as what was to follow would be the longest day of their lives.

Breakfast over, the performers were taken to the Willard Hotel where, after a quick freshen-up and a change of clothes, they commenced an arduous stint of rehearsals.

WASHING LINE
During rehearsals at the Willard Hotel, some of the stars line up for a publicity-shot. L-R: Desi Arnaz, Cary Grant, Pat O'Brien, Rise Stevens, Joan Bennett, Charlotte Greenwood, Claudette Colbert, Eleanor Powell, Stan Laurel, Oliver Hardy, Bert Lahr.

Following evening meal, there was more rehearsing until late. But then "late" became "very late" when the whole cast had a full dress rehearsal over at Loew's Capitol Theatre – which lasted from midnight till 8am.

Rehearsals started again after breakfast on Thursday morning, and continued throughout the day in both ballrooms of the Willard Hotel.

But then between 5 and 6pm the performers had to abandon all thoughts of their stage acts, as no less than the first lady had invited them all to tea. **[FILM]**

In a letter written some years later, Stan Laurel recalled:

```
                                        APRIL 25th. 1960
Dear Mrs Marie Hatfield:
When we played in Washington, we were all invited to the
White House & graciously entertained by Mrs Roosevelt on
the front lawns, refreshments were served in a large tent
while the White House Band played for us, it was a
wonderful experience, Mrs. R. was a charming Hostess, very
cordial. We were shown through the House, but the President
was in some conference, so we did'nt have the opportunity
to see him, but he did wave to us all from his window &
threw us a kiss.

                        Stan
                       -----0-----
```

Groucho Marx was engaging Eleanor Roosevelt in a discussion about Jerry Colonna's moustache, when the U.S. Marine Band, composed of ancient veterans (described by Bert Lahr as "God-awful") struck up a patriotic fanfare. With split-second timing, Groucho looked at Mrs. Roosevelt and quipped: *"No wonder the Old Man didn't come."*

Mrs. Roosevelt obviously took the joke well, and even went to the show that evening, at the risk of receiving more insults from the joker supreme.

Apr 30 (Thu)   **WASHINGTON** – Loew's Capitol Theatre (3,450)

> Thursday 30 April 1942
> Loew's Capitol Theatre, WASHINGTON DC
> 70 HOLLYWOOD STARS
> IN PERSON!
> GIGANTIC HOLLYWOOD THREE-HOUR SHOW
> All proceeds to Army-Navy Relief
> The greatest idea – and show of the century!
> 8.30pm – 11.30pm

The show, emceed by Bob Hope, started at 8:30pm in the Capitol Theatre, and went on till gone midnight. Now comes the bit that is hard to write. The trade paper *Variety* singled out two performances as being disappointing:

> Groucho Marx was restrained by the limitations of his old "Who's Olive?" sketch, in which he worked with Olivia de Havilland. Like most of the sketches, it was much too long for the amount of humor given off.
>
> Also sufferers from lack of material were Laurel and Hardy, with their 'Simple-Simon' cross-talk.

Ouch! It would have been nice for all Laurel & Hardy fans to hear that "Laurel & Hardy got the biggest laughs of the night, and the longest ovation," but one can only state the truth – even though it is not what one wishes to hear.

Taking hundreds of photographs throughout the tour was noted photographer Gene Lester, to whom we all owe a great debt for capturing so many wonderful images of this historic event.

(Standing L-R) Merle Oberon, Eleanor Powell, Arlene Whelan, Marie McDonald, Fay McKenzie, Katharine Booth, Mrs. Eleanor Roosevelt, Frances Gifford, Frances Langford, Elyse Knox, Cary Grant, Claudette Colbert, Bob Hope, Ray Middleton, Joan Bennett, Bert Lahr, Mark Sandrich (director), Jack Rose (writer), Stan Laurel, Jerry Colonna, and Groucho Marx,
(Seated L-R) Oliver Hardy, Joan Blondell, Charlotte Greenwood, Charles Boyer, Rise Stevens, Desi Arnaz, Frank McHugh, Matt Brooks (writer), James Cagney, Pat O'Brien, Juanita Stark, Alma Carroll.

[Library of Congress]

RUNNING ORDER
Hollywood Victory Caravan

OPENING: chorus of starlets singing two specially written numbers. **BOB HOPE** joins the girls in the last refrain, then into a monologue about the Hollywood-to-Washington cross-country trip.

Hope introduces **DESI ARNAZ** who sings and plays his signature tune, the conga drum number "*Babalu*."

Hope introduces **GROUCHO MARX** and **OLIVIA DE HAVILLAND**, for the sketch "**WHO'S OLIVE?**" **CARY GRANT** joins Hope and together they do the "**FIRST WASHINGTON QUICKIE**." Grant introduces **JOAN BLONDELL** who enacts a cod-striptease act; with some unwanted attention from Cary Grant, Desi Arnaz, and Groucho Marx.

Hope and Grant do the "**UMBRELLA QUICKIE**," then Grant introduces **LAUREL & HARDY** with "**THE DRIVER'S LICENSE**" sketch. Next, Hope does a bit of patter with **CHARLES BOYER**. Cary Grant and Bob Hope follow with the "**SECOND WASHINGTON QUICKIE**."

Grant introduces **CHARLOTTE GREENWOOD**, who sings "*Shall I be an Old Man's Darling, or a Young Man's Slave*," followed by one of her famed eccentric dance numbers. Hope introduces **CLAUDETTE COLBERT**, and assists her in a skit. Next comes **GROUCHO MARX** in a sketch entitled "**THE BARKER**" featuring "*Lydia*" – assisted by **PAT O'BRIEN**. Hope and Grant do "**THE PRESIDENT'S QUICKIE**." Grant introduces **FRANCES LANGFORD**, who sings "*Windmill Under the Sky*" and one other number.

CHARLES BOYER does a serious scene about German repression titled "**THE LAST CLASS**" – assisted by Olivia deHavilland, Pat O'Brien, Desi Arnaz, and the Starlets. Grant introduces **RAY MIDDLETON**, who sings "*Spread Your Wings*."

FRANK McHUGH and **FAY McKENZIE** act out a bedroom farce, and **PAT O'BRIEN** does a piece from his role in the film "Knute Rockne."

BOB HOPE returns, for a bit of kidding with **JOAN BENNETT**.

BERT LAHR follows with the "*Income Tax*" sketch, assisted by Grant and Middleton. **CARY GRANT** makes an appeal, for the buying of War Bonds.

RAY MIDDLETON closes the first half with a patriotic song, backed by the chorus of eight starlets.

INTERVAL

Part 2

Alfred Newman's "**OVERTURE**" signals the start of the second half. **BOB HOPE** opens with a monologue, and then introduces **JERRY COLONNA** for some cross-patter. **COLONNA** sings and plays trombone in solo spot.

Cary Grant introduces **CLAUDETTE COLBERT** and **FRANK McHUGH** in the "**AIR RAID WARDEN**" sketch. **MERLE OBERON** recites a piece of verse. Then it's **GROUCHO MARX** and a chorus of nurses in the skit "**DR. HACKENBUSH**."

"**THE LADIES**" features **JOAN BENNETT, OLIVIA DE HAVILLAND** and **JOAN BLONDELL** doing a nostalgic "*Shuffle Off to Buffalo*" number about ladies in uniform. Pat O'Brien introduces Metropolitan Opera singer **RISE STEVENS** – who sings "*My Hero*" and "*The Moon is Down*."

Cary Grant introduces **ELEANOR POWELL**, who dishes out rhythm in a special tap-dance routine.

PAT O'BRIEN and **FRANK McHUGH** do a war sketch, entitled "*BATAAN.*"

O'Brien sets up the theme of "**AMERICA**" with his version of the lyrics, then **JAMES CAGNEY** enters singing "*I'm a Yankee Doodle Dandy.*" Next, several of the cast return in a sketch titled "*So Long Sam.*"

BERT LAHR does his "**SONG OF THE WOODSMAN**" speciality.

BOB HOPE and **BING CROSBY** [when available] exchange some friendly banter. **CROSBY** croons a couple of his best-known numbers.

Bob Hope introduces **JAMES CAGNEY IN A SPECIALITY** which includes a hoofing routine to "*Grand Old Flag.*"

The whole male cast performs "*Sweater Boy,*" and **HOPE** and **COLONNA** encore with more cross-patter. Bob Hope then says all the "Farewells" and brings out the entire company for the **FINALE**, with **RAY MIDDLETON** leading a rendition of "*Keep the Light Burning Bright.*"

In the second chorus **ELEANOR POWELL** enters, decked out in red, white, and blue, symbolising 'Uncle Sam.'

The **ENTIRE CAST** sing "*The Star Spangled Banner.*"

THE END

[Twenty-eight acts. Running time = 180 minutes]

It was now, upon leaving Washington, that the Sante Fe Special, on which the entertainers had travelled from Los Angeles, was about to come into its own. Between cities the VIPs would eat and sleep on board, whenever need be. With the schedule they had, there was going to be a lot of "need be."

To make sure they did get some rest, the 10-car special would be shunted into rail sidings, regardless of the time of arrival in any particular city, and the passengers left there undisturbed. Then, at 1pm on the day of the show, the posse of policemen who had been guarding the train would escort the stars from the train to their cars, and lead them in convoy to their hotel. This was to be billed as a "parade," and would allow the locals to get a look at the screen icons.

At the hotel, once the stars were booked in, the floors would be blocked off to all visitors. At 7:30pm the cast members would be escorted to the venue, ready for the show at 8:30. No one other than those involved with the show would be allowed backstage, and there was to be no autograph signing at the stage door.

-----0-----

1942 May 01 (Friday)
        WASHINGTON, D.C. to BOSTON, Massachusetts 🚂 440 miles

-----0-----

May 1 (Fri)   **BOSTON** – Boston Garden (24,000)

In Boston, the next stop-off, an estimated one million people turned out to watch the evening "Parade of Stars" from the Statler Hotel to the Boston Garden stadium. One report claimed:

> The Hollywood Victory Caravan Show was such a sensation that there's talk around here it will live in history along with another great Hub event, the Boston Tea Party.

The show had now been cut by some forty minutes, from the three hours and twenty-six minutes it had run in Washington, which must have been a blessing for audience and acts alike.

Of our comedy heroes, we were told only:

> Laurel and Hardy, Groucho Marx, and Bert Lahr gave to the show a music-comedy producer's idea of a lavish Broadway comedy.

On the Right Track

CLOSING THE SHOW WITH "The Star Spangled Banner" IN BOSTON.
L-R: Bob Hope, Charles Boyer, Joan Blondell, Bert Lahr, Cary Grant, Eleanor Powell, Oliver Hardy, Stan Laurel, Charlotte Greenwood, Desi Arnaz, Frances Langford, James Cagney.
(Newspaper scan)

-----0-----

1942 May 02 (Saturday)
      BOSTON, Massachusetts to **PHILADELPHIA**, Pennsylvania 312 miles
-----0-----

May 2 (Sat)   **PHILADELPHIA** – Convention Hall (16,000)

Upon the Victory Caravan's arrival at 9am at Broad Street Station, Philadelphia, there was an immediate lock-down of the surrounding area, to stop any unauthorised persons from entering. However, an army of pressmen and photographers were there to witness the stars disembarking. The Sante Fe Special had been backed into the station, so that the rear coach acted as a kind of stage, upon which the Hollywood stars made their entry in small groups, and then exited – stage left.

The first to step out were Claudette Colbert and Oliver Hardy. Babe, grinning broadly, remarked that it was a case of "beauty and the beast." When Laurel next scampered down the train steps he was advised to go back, as the police had not yet cleared a way through to the exit. He got the hint, and made a quick turnabout – but not before treating the assembly to his grimace and cry.

Plans had been made for the Hollywood visitors to be paraded to the City Hall to meet the Mayor, and then on to Independence Hall, but these were cancelled at the eleventh hour. It would seem that the one million turnout in Boston had been too overwhelming for the stars, and too big for the organisers to control, so no one wanted to risk such numbers congregating again. Instead, at 1pm, the visitors were driven directly to the Ritz-Carlton Hotel, with an escort of honour from the women of the Navy League (Nells).

Despite the change in plans, twenty-five thousand Philadelphians jammed the streets between the station and the hotel, hoping to get a pre-show glimpse of the stars; but it was the photographers who caused most trouble for the police cordon.

The show itself was staged at the Convention Hall, in front of a sixteen-thousand-strong audience, and was scheduled to run from 8.15 till 11-15pm. The *Philadelphia Inquirer* reported:

The comedians were out in force – Laurel and Hardy, Bert Lahr, Charlotte Greenwood and Groucho Marx, not to forget Bob Hope—but the "Ooh's and ah's" of an enthusiastic crowd was reserved for the glamor-boys and glamor girls, with honors about evenly-divided. Charles Boyer, Claudette Colbert, Olivia De Havilland, and Joan Bennett were among those who scored heavily.

Within the brief summary of each act, the *Philadelphia Inquirer* further gave us:

Laurel and Hardy held their usual choice spot in the hearts of last night's fun-loving audience. They didn't have to say much. But the laughs were theirs for the looking.

When the cast members came to leave the stadium, they had to be escorted through the thousands of fans who, unable to gain admission, had waited outside to see them leave. This kept the guard of ninety-five police patrolmen, twelve mounted policemen, and an eighty-five-strong cavalry detachment busy till well past midnight.

-----0-----

1942 May 03 (Sunday)

    PHILADELPHIA, Pennsylvania to **CLEVELAND**, Ohio 🚂 431 miles

-----0-----

May 3 (Sun)   **CLEVELAND** – Public Hall (10,721)

Thousands of enthusiastic fans greeted the Hollywood party as they detrained at Pennsylvania East 55th St. Station, Cleveland, at 1.30pm. In the afternoon, the stars rested up at the Statler Hotel, in preparation for the 8.30 show.

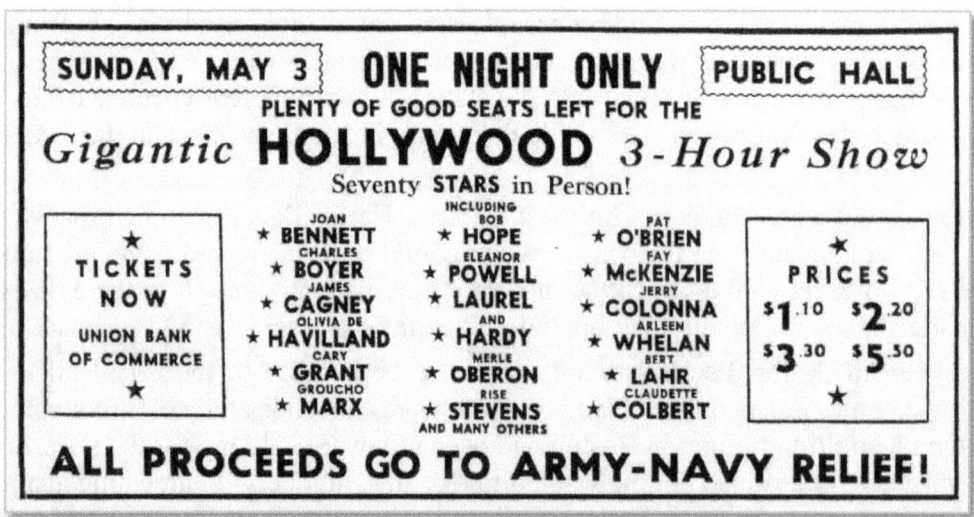

The near-eleven-thousand audience greeted each star with applause and loud cheers, but Bob Hope was singled out for the loudest and longest applause, as he was considered to be a "hometown boy made good." Hope was actually born in Eltham, South London, England, but maybe the residents of Cleveland were working on the principle, "Possession is nine-tenths of the law."

Of the show, the local paper included only a lukewarm comment regarding our comedy subjects:

> Laurel and Hardy repeated their "license skit," which they did a few weeks ago in the Palace, and it was still good.
>
> (*Cleveland Plain Dealer* – 4 May 1942)

The *Hollywood Reporter* was a little warmer in its report:

> It [the show] has Laurel and Hardy in their ever-popular comedy routine.

And *Boxoffice* said:

> Laurel and Hardy presented their regular vaudeville act.

Anyone would think from these comments that Laurel & Hardy were a vaudeville act, who had been touring the same act for years.

-----0-----

1942 May 04 (Monday)

CLEVELAND, Ohio to **DETROIT**, Michigan 168 miles

-----0-----

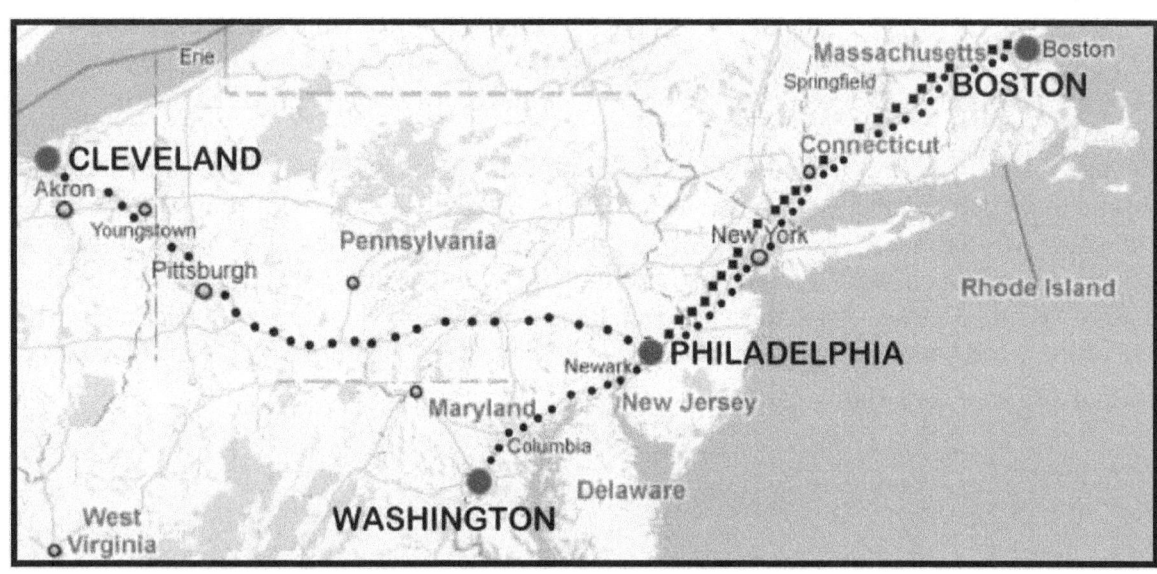

WASHINGTON–BOSTON–PHILADLEPHIA–CLEVELAND

May 4 (Mon)   **DETROIT** – Coliseum (State Fair Grounds) (14,000)

In Detroit, the now-familiar arrival scenes this time took place at Michigan Central station, after which the Hollywood entourage was whisked away to the Hotel Statler. During a press conference there, many of the stars expressed interest and amazement at the scope and intensity of the war production drive in the city whose main industry, until a few months ago, had been the manufacture of automobiles.

Bob Hope assured the reporters that there was no artistic temperament being shown by any of the show's members. He added that the stars drew lots for the best dressing rooms, and the losers willingly accepted humble and barren accommodation. At one stop there were only two dressing rooms, so all the men had to crowd into one, and all the ladies into the other. Things got even worse at another venue where, Bob Hope purported, the dressing room was an elephant stall. Let us hope the elephant had taken the night off.

While in Detroit, some of the company decided to visit a group of orphaned children. This meant breaking the "No Outside Appearances" rule, as the orphanage they had selected, which was – in CANADA. An outsider being told this could immediately imagine the risks involved in travelling all that way, and getting back in time for the show. But then an outsider would not know that a tunnel runs under the Detroit River and brings one into Windsor, Ontario, just TWO MILES away, which is where the orphanage was situated.

The escapees were Pat O'Brien, James Cagney, Cary Grant, Joan Blondell, Bert Lahr and, of course, Stan and Babe –who entertained the children for an hour, before returning to their hotel. There they received a good dressing down from Mark Sandrich, who outlined the repercussions of such actions, which could be missed rehearsals or even missed trains. Feeling thoroughly chastised, our well-doers chorused: "Sorry sir! We won't do it again, sir! Sandrich, though, was quietly proud of them.

The show itself, held in the Coliseum at the State Fair Grounds, Detroit, was seen by fourteen thousand audience members, who paid $55,000 for the privilege. Tucked in among the reviews of the show was the line: "*Laurel and Hardy did a familiar comedy turn.*" Whether it was funny – it doesn't say. Why it was "familiar" is questionable, seeing as this was Laurel and Hardy's one and only visit to Detroit. Stan, the screen character, would not have been displeased with the usage of the word "familiar" as his logic might well have been: "Familiarity breeds content."

You can add your own Hardy correction to that!

o-o-0-o-o

CHAPTER 29

TRAIN KEEPS A ROLLIN'
(1942 pt4)

1942 May 05 (Tuesday)
          DETROIT, Michigan to **CHICAGO**, Illinois 🚂 342 miles
-----0-----

May 5 (Tue)   arrived at Union Station, Chicago.

On Tuesday 5 May our caravanners arrived in Chicago but, as the show wasn't until the following evening, they had a rest day – in which the word "rest" can probably be expanded to mean: "a few drinks, then a sing-along, followed by general unruly behaviour."

May 6 (Wed)   **CHICAGO** – Stadium (19,823-seater – attendance 23,884)

Although having been told off for their visit to the orphanage in Detroit, Stan, Babe, and Pat O'Brien managed to get out of Mark Sandrich's bad books and, accompanied by Desi Arnaz and Ray Middleton, were allowed to go and watch the Chicago Cubs in action, after which the four of them autographed a baseball bat for player, Stanley Hack. **[FILM]**

> Oliver Hardy, Desi Arnaz, Pat O'Brien, Ray Middleton – signing a bat for Stanley Hack of the Chicago Cubs.
> (Newspaper scan)

Of the evening's show at the Chicago Stadium, the part of the review mentioning our Boys was a little more affectionate than the ones to date: (*Daily Tribune* – 7 May 1942)

> Stan Laurel and Oliver Hardy brought joy to the hearts of their fans in the Laurel and Hardy manner.

-----0-----

1942 May 07 (Thursday)
CHICAGO to **ST. LOUIS**, Missouri 🚂 299 miles
-----0-----

May 7 (Thu)   **ST. LOUIS** – Municipal Auditorium
                                      (12,369)

In St. Louis, the company was joined by Bing Crosby, who had cancelled a couple of radio broadcasts to be there. His presence, plus a fund-raising golf match early in the day with legendary rival Bob Hope, captured the headlines and kind of diverted attention away from the main show.

The only word on Laurel and Hardy was: "Laurel and Hardy clowned in the way they have in numerous film collaborations."

(L-R standing) Eleanor Powell, Bert Lahr, Frank McHugh, Ray Middleton (obscured), Groucho Marx, Rise Stevens, Desi Arnaz, Stan Laurel, Oliver Hardy.
(Seated:) Charlotte Greenwood, Joan Bennett, Joan Blondell, Claudette Colbert, Charles Boyer, Cary Grant, Pat O'Brien.

It was always gone midnight by the time the show company were able to get to the train, where most of them immediately retired to their sleeping quarters. However, with there being no show on the Friday, a gang of them decided to stay up late, and entertain themselves for a change.

Collecting chairs from the lounge coach, they all sat around the piano in the bar, and launched into a free-and-easy of sing-along songs, and solo performances.

It was a chance for some of the lesser-known stars to showcase their talents in front of the established acts, and a chance for the established acts to show off talents they weren't known for.

Faye McKenzie, Stan, Francis Langford, Pat O'Brien, Rise Stevens, Frank McHugh (seated on piano), Charlotte Greenwood.

The surprise here is Groucho playing the piano – a skill normally associated with Chico. But more so, Jimmy Cagney, who was normally one of the first to retire, but who stayed on to join in the fun. He later selected it as one of the highlights of the tour.

Because there was no show on Friday 8 May, one may think it could be classed as a rest day, but there were still daytime public appearances to make, and press conferences to attend. Following their near six-hundred-mile journey from St. Louis, the Very Important Passengers did get a few hours extra to themselves as, instead of the usual 1pm slot, their arrival time was switched to 5pm. Good job, too, especially for those who had stayed up till the wee small hours.

-----0-----

1942 May 08 (Friday)

      ST. LOUIS, Missouri to **ST. PAUL**, Minnesota 560 miles
      ST. PAUL, Minnesota to **MINNEAPOLIS**, Minnesota 9 miles

CHICAGO – ST. LOUIS – MINNEAPOLIS – ST. PAUL – DES MOINES

First reception of the day was at the Union Depot in St. Paul, Minnesota; where, as the stars exited the train, they were welcomed on the lower platform by the sounds of the 'Great Northern Drum and Bugle Corps.' At the rear of the platform the color bearers of a second drum and bugle corps, the 'East Side American Legion,' formed a guard of honour for them to walk through.

A six-foot-high platform had been erected at the south end of the concourse, which the stars made their way towards. However, between the platform and the improvised stage were three thousand star-struck fans, all anxious to get within touching distance of their screen favourites. The organisers, though, had cleverly placed a double line of colour, sound, and bodies between the fans and the movie stars, in the form of a troupe of two hundred brightly costumed drum majorettes, which effectively held the crowd in check.

The hosting of the Victory Caravan show in Minnesota had been organised by the Winter Carnival committee. The figureheads of which were King Boreas VIII and Queen Martha – not to be confused with "real" royalty. They were seated at the foot of the stage, and welcomed the Hollywood peasants to their kingdom, before bestowing on them a citation naming them as "Subjects of the Rollicking Realm of Boreas." Each guest then received a royal scroll enrolling them in "The Court of King Boreas VIII" – which would no doubt have appealed to the Boys' sense of humour.

Cary Grant being given a royal welcome by Queen Martha and King Boreas VIII. The other peasants will have to wait their turn.

[Stan and Babe not pictured]

After speeches from members of the city's welcoming committee, Mark Sandrich thanked the assembled crowd on behalf of the travelling troupers, for what he described as, "*the most heart-warming reception we have had in any city.*" The praise seems to have been well-deserved. Sandrich then introduced the members of his troupe, at which cue each actor and actress ascended the steps to the stage, waved to the crowd, took a bow, and exited.

When it was Laurel and Hardy's turn, they said not a single word, but just stood there and looked dumb – which was enough to get a huge laugh. The whole entourage was then played off by a fourth band as they left the concourse. Retracing their steps, the party boarded the train to go just nine miles up the line, to Minneapolis, to receive yet another welcome.

The "Hollywood Special" got into Minneapolis thirty minutes late, owing to the Mayors of both St. Paul and Minneapolis extending the welcoming ceremony in St. Paul. Several hundred fans were on the platform, while across the road, in Washington Avenue, a few thousand more lay in wait. They were kept entertained by the sounds of the drum corps of the St. Paul American Legion, plus the sights of their baton twirlers doing some fast and fancy moves.

The stars at first came out individually, maybe so as to receive more attention. One reporter said of Babe:

Oliver Hardy – stalking in melancholy mood like Hamlet – trod the boards alone, carrying a sprig of lilacs, and humming softly to himself. His alter-ego, the dour Stan Laurel, wasn't in sight just then.

Detraining at Minneapolis. In line, nearest the track are: Mark Sandrich, Frank McHugh, Charlotte Greenwood, Stan Laurel (with Hardy on his right) Bing Crosby, and starlet Katharine Booth.

But then the stars began to emerge in quick succession, and moved toward the exit gates in a group. Just before emerging into Washington Avenue, they passed through a guard of honour made up of sailors from the naval reserve at Wold-Chamberlain field, on the one side, and soldiers from Fort Snelling, on the other. Members of the Minnesota Defense Force, and the local police force then escorted the stars to four waiting buses, to the accompaniment of the drum corps and deafening cheers from the thousands of spectators.

Getting off the bus outside the Nicollet Hotel in Minneapolis are L-R:
Babe Hardy, Katharine Booth, Stan Laurel, Frances Gifford, and Mark Sandrich.

The cheers emitted by the star spotters lining the route, continued all the way to the Nicollet Hotel. Upon the stars' arrival, a posse of sixty-five Military Police escorted them in the elevators to the eighth floor, which had been reserved in its entirety for them. The military presence was to remain on guard for the duration of the Hollywood party's stay, with orders to protect them from autograph hunters and curiosity seekers – and thieves, I would imagine.

> Having no show on the Friday night, some of the stars went to the State cinema to watch the latest film release, "*My Favorite Blonde.*" Those who did not attend would later have got the cold shoulder from Bob Hope and Bing Crosby – the first being the star of the picture, and the second having a cameo role.

It is hoped that all the troupe members woke up well refreshed on the Saturday as, that day, they had TWO shows to perform. Bob Hope and Bing Crosby must have certainly felt good. First thing Saturday morning they were off for another round of golf, at which they raised a further $1,000 towards the Army-Navy Relief Fund. Hope, by the way, and his best pal Jerry Colonna had flown in from Chicago.

May 9 (Sat)   **ST. PAUL** – Auditorium (12,500) (2.30pm)
May 9 (Sat)   **MINNEAPOLIS** – Auditorium (9,700) (8.30pm)

The planning and organisation at each and every city was like a military operation, but, on this day, the workload would be doubled. It was just as well that the military was actually on hand to assist, as the hundreds of soldiers, state guardsmen, and police officers there to protect the film stars were kept busy throughout the day.

To do the first show involved a return train journey to St. Paul for the 2.30pm matinee at the twelve-and-a-half-thousand-seater Auditorium. [Why do cinemas and theatres always use "matinee" to describe an afternoon performance, when the word means "morning"?] Then it was back to Minneapolis, for the evening show in the Auditorium, to an audience of just under ten thousand.

The monies raised in St. Paul, by box-office receipts and other fund-raising activities, turned out to be one of the best of the whole tour. This was a pretty commendable achievement, especially when one considers that St. Paul was one of the smaller cities, and had direct competition from its near neighbour Minneapolis – on the SAME DAY. In weighing up everything – organisation, security, reception, and the warmth of its populace – the Hollywoodians must have rated St. Paul as one of their favourite visits. However, one newsman was about to put a blot on his landscape paper.

In every town and city Hardy visited, throughout his celebrity life, there was always someone ready to challenge him over who had the biggest waistline. Here in St. Paul it was Frank Mondike – Head of the Morals Squad.

Local journalist James Gray of the *Saint Paul Pioneer Press* wrote an affectionate review of the show, in which he briefly described each act, before tagging his article with the words: "I hope I haven't forgotten anyone." But he had – LAUREL & HARDY!

-----0-----

MINNEAPOLIS AUDITORIUM
When you are a little dot, on a stage, miles away from the audience …

… you need a BIG pencil.

The reviewer from the *Minneapolis Journal* did little to make amends. All he wrote was: "*Laurel and Hardy went through a skit having to do with Laurel's driving license.*" Not much to go off there, but he did redeem himself when he highlighted a bit of business that no one else mentioned in any other reviews, including future ones:

Frank McHugh and Fay McKenzie acted in a bedroom farce, with Stan Laurel coming in for the blackout."

Meanwhile, Bert Lahr (best remembered as the cowardly lion in "*The Wizard of Oz*") got two reviews:

> Bert Lahr and Cary Grant appeared in a hilarious income tax sketch, which had Grant laughing so hard he missed lines.

And for his second act:

> Lahr convulsed the audience with a song about a woodsman.
>
> (*Minneapolis Journal* – 10 May 1942)

Lahr must have kept those two reviews at the top of his lifetime collection of memorabilia, and yet he might well have burned the one from the previous show in St. Louis, which ran:

> Bert Lahr didn't come off so well with his complaints about the size of his income tax, in a skit in which Cary Grant assisted.

And yet, the night before that, we were told:

> Bert Lahr almost stopped the show with an income tax skit.

It just goes to show that, on a different day, with a different audience, in a different city, in a different arena, with different acoustics, and different sight lines, you are bound to get different reactions. So we shouldn't feel too bad if Laurel and Hardy's sketch did not always get the reaction we would have liked.

[I wonder if Bert Lahr ever realised his surname is an acronym of "Laurel and Hardy Revue"!!]

-----0-----

1942 May 10 (Sunday)

MINNEAPOLIS, Minnesota to **DES MOINES**, Iowa 243 miles

-----0-----

May 10 (Sun)   **DES MOINES** – Shrine Auditorium (4,500)

The cities most recently visited had, under orders, scaled down or even cancelled the circus-style parade of the Hollywood stars from their train to the hotel, and/or hotel to the show venue. But Des Moines wasn't going to let the occasion pass without some pageantry. Days in advance the *Des Moines Register* had declared:

> Des Moines streets will be decorated with flags, bunting and streamers for the parade at 1pm Sunday featuring the 23 top Hollywood film celebrities who will visit the city.
>
> Stars will parade west on Locust Street from the Statehouse to Fourteenth Street [later extended to Eighteenth] in open cars, and then will go straight to Shrine Auditorium for the Hollywood Victory Caravan show at 2.30pm. The actors and actresses will ride one star to a car, so that everyone will have a great opportunity to see them.
>
> A holiday spirit will prevail during the mile-and-a-half-long parade. Airplanes will fly over the line of march, there will be aerial bombs and daylight fireworks, and confetti will be tossed down from loop buildings.
>
> More than 250,000 Iowans are expected to be in Des Moines to see the parade, which will include several bands, the West Des Moines drum and bugle corps, 300 state guardsmen, 500 Boy Scouts and an escort from the army, navy, and marine corps.

On the day itself, the Sante Fe Special arrived at Des Moines Rock Island Station at 8am, whence it was promptly surrounded by a contingent of the Iowa State Guard, who patrolled the area with billy-clubs in hand, just to make everyone aware that the train was off-limits.

Most of the stars didn't leave their berths till around 11am, and it was 12.50pm before they started to emerge from the train. The first three were Groucho Marx, Stan Laurel, and Oliver Hardy. Stan and Ollie made familiar gestures and mannerisms to acknowledge the crowds, as did Groucho – but his familiar gestures didn't receive the same response, as few recognised him without his prop moustache and black-rimmed glasses.

As if the general conditions of the tour weren't strenuous enough, during the parade the three aforesaid comedians actually put themselves in physical danger – in the name of entertainment. Groucho Marx ascended a fire truck, on which he improvised clowning around on the upraised ladder, while Laurel and Hardy consented to being driven in a midget car.

For Groucho, whose normal exertions as physical clown were confined to moving his jaw, the choice of swinging from rung to rung on a ladder, mounted high up on a fire truck, was very ill-advised. Buster Keaton – yes! but Groucho Marx – NO!

As for Stan and Babe, they had to sit on the *back* of the midget car, as it wasn't big enough to sit inside – not for Hardy anyway! The precariousness of their position revealed itself when the car hit a bump, and they had to struggle to prevent themselves being pitched backwards off the car.

In the review of the matinee show, acts were varyingly reported as "scoring heavily," being "the people's choice," "stopping the show," or being "hilarious" – whereas Stan and Ollie were accredited with only "Laurel and Hardy presented an amusing skit."

THE BIG BOYS
Stan and Babe in their midget car, during the Des Moines street parade.

Maybe if they had fallen off the back of the car, they would have been "hilarious."

REAR VIEW
From this shot, you can see just how precariously they were perched.

Hope they didn't have to travel all the way to the next city in that car.

o-o-0-o-o

CHAPTER 30

LAST TRAIN TO SAN FERN ... CISCO

(1942 pt5)

1942 May 11 (Monday)

DES MOINES, Iowa to **DALLAS**, Texas 🚂 696 miles

-----0-----

May 11 (Mon)   **DALLAS** – Fair Park Auditorium (4,500)

The eleventh city stop of "The Star-Spangled Special" was Dallas, Texas. It was scheduled to arrive at Union Terminal at 2.00pm, but pulled in forty-five minutes late. This didn't dampen the enthusiasm of the mass of people in and around the station, nor those lining both sides of Houston Street, as all stayed on for the big arrival.

On the platform to welcome the stars was a deputation of organisers from the Army-Navy Relief Fund, plus a handful of local dignitaries. The Hollywood visitors next had to pass through a guard of honour, made up of fifty sailors and fifty soldiers, who then broke ranks and not only escorted the stars to the fifty open-top cars parked outside, but drove them parade-style to their hotel. The route was lined with a solid bank of fans on either side and, once at the destination, the police had trouble getting the celebrities through the mass of fans crowding the entrances to both the Baker and Adolphus Hotels.

It is not known which hotel Stan and Babe were allocated to; but, at the Adolphus, a party of the stars made for the Variety Club function room – which makes one believe this is the one the Boys would have selected. At least eight of the stars left the comfort and security of the hotel, to spend part of the afternoon selling War Bonds at the nearby Neiman-Marcus store, but not Stan and Babe. Good job too! The presence of Laurel and Hardy in a store would have made a bull in a china shop the lesser of two disasters. Stan and Babe were otherwise employed, attending the 3pm press conference in the hotel. Al Fisher, Assistant Producer of the show, told the pressmen:

There hasn't been a beef or a squawk from nearly two-dozen celebrities who [would normally] make complaints and tantrums a technique of doing business. They have suffered all kinds of inconveniences and have been pushed around as you don't push around Hollywood extras. In one place they all had to dress in a common dressing room, which had recently served as a horse stable [or was it an elephant?]. They took it laughing.

They turn out at all hours for pictures or for anything else the press department asks. There hasn't been a fuss or a feud on the trip. If these actors were performing for pay it would be a different story. Since they are giving their service, they are perfect darlings. I love actors like I've never loved 'em before.

In the evening, following the "Parade of Stars" from the hotel to the show venue, the full-house of nearly five thousand paying customers at the Fair Park Auditorium saw the biggest assembly of Hollywood stars they had ever witnessed. In a show of twenty-eight acts, Laurel & Hardy went on in tenth place, sandwiched between actress-singer-comedienne-dancer Charlotte Greenwood, and glamorous star Joan Blondell. Some sandwich!!

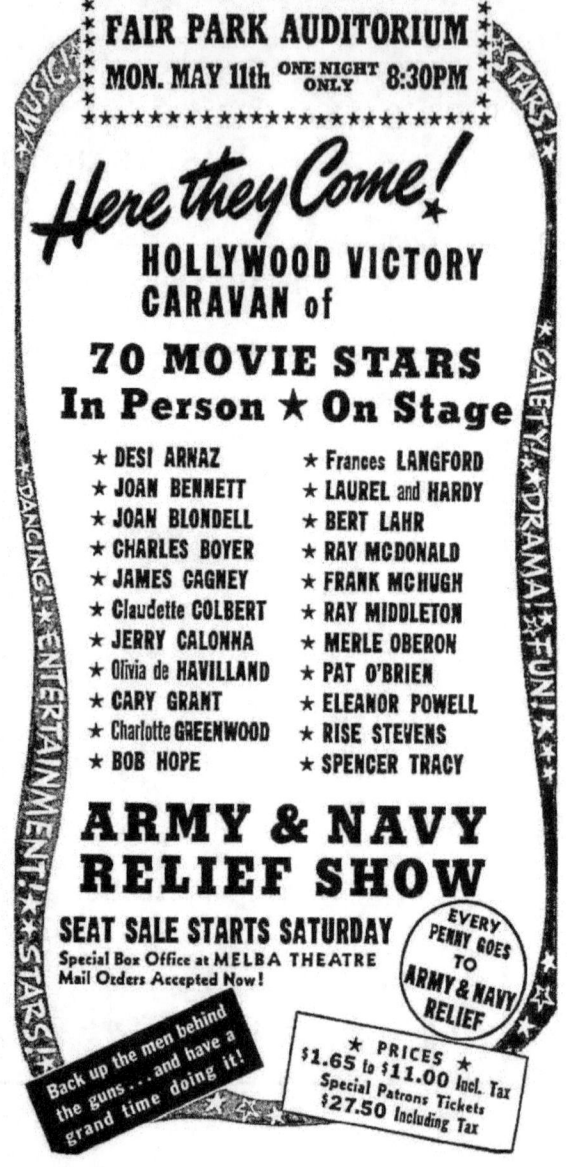

> Laurel and Hardy, timid Stan, and disgusted Oliver, with the gestures so familiar in the films, arguing out the question of Stan's new driver's license. Hardy claims the 1913 one he's been using is somewhat outdated.

So! No sign of just how they were received. Shame!

It was as late as 3am, after a long, long day, when the company finally left Houston and, it is hoped, managed to get some sleep on "The Star-Spangled Special" as it cut its way through the Texas night.

-----0-----

1942 May 12 (Tuesday)

                DALLAS, Texas to **HOUSTON**, Texas 242 miles

-----0-----

May 12 (Tue)   **HOUSTON** – Coliseum (12,500)

The Union Station was packed with would-be star spotters when the Victory Caravan arrived, and hundreds of them stayed on for several hours when it was learned that the majority of stars would not leave the train until it was time to go to the show. Those stars who did leave were chauffeured in jeeps driven by the Ellington Boys Cadets to the Rice Hotel, where a crowd had been gathering since early morning waiting for a glimpse of their favourite actors.

Other locals were shocked and surprised to spot Joan Blondell shopping in Levy Brothers, and Jerry Colona and Groucho Marx going walkabout through the streets. It was 7pm before the stars came out in formation, when they paraded down Texas Avenue to Main, and on to the Coliseum – cheered by solid lines of Houstonians along the whole route.

Some of the acts practically gave two performances – the scheduled one at the Coliseum, and an improvised one in the Music Hall. At the latter, Bob Hope was making a broadcast in front of an invited audience made up of the Ellington Field Cadets. Consequently, Hope was a half an hour late for the show at the Coliseum, where Bing Crosby stood in until he arrived.

After three columns of reviews on the majority of the acts, the *Houston Chronicle* focussed in on the comedy performers. "Oh good!" I hear you cry. "Now we can read how Laurel & Hardy stole the show." Well, maybe not!

At Houston station, the Boys are caught trying to steal the spare wheel off this jeep, having heard of the precious wartime value of rubber.

The greater part of the three-hour show was devoted to fun and frivolity, with Bob Hope, Bing Crosby, Pat O'Brien, and Cary Grant occupying the spotlight the greater part of the time. Most of the comedy was fresh and new, with quips being taken at Houston weather, crowded conditions at Washington, and Mrs. Roosevelt's extensive travels.

> Charlotte Greenwood is another grand old trouper who received an ovation from the audience. Another comedy highlight was an income tax skit staged with great skill by Bert Lahr and Cary Grant. Other comedy skits were staged by Olivia de Havilland and Groucho Marx; by Frank McHugh and Fay McKenzie; Laurel and Hardy in a comedy routine; Jerry Colonna, who convulsed the audience with his rendition of "Ah! Sweet Mystery of Life," and Groucho Marx and the chorus in "Dr. Hackenbush."
>
> Claudette Colbert received an ovation when she appeared with Grant in a comedy skit. Cute little Joan Bennett won favor with the audience, too, as she appeared in a skit with Grant and Hope, and later with Joan Blondell and Olivia de Havilland.

Olivia DeHavilland seems to be saying: "I don't know how I ended up in the same dressing-room as this clown." While Laurel seems to be saying: "Suits me."
[N.B. The snipe states that this photo was taken in San Francisco but, as Olivia DeHavilland didn't play San Francisco, backstage at the Houston Coliseum would be the best call. AJM]

So from this last review we can see that two acts got "an ovation," one was a "comedy highlight," one "won favour," and one "convulsed the audience." Laurel and Hardy, meanwhile, were "in a comedy routine." Hmmm! Praise conspicuous by its absence here! And that, sadly, is all the coverage Houston chose to give on the two comic legends. But that isn't to say the audience didn't love them.

Houston was the penultimate show, but first would come a return to Los Angeles, and a brief respite. From leaving L.A. to getting back had been nineteen exhausting days, in which the Victory Caravan troupe had played shows in twelve cities, and clocked up over eight thousand miles in train travel.

-----0-----

Looks like a deleted scene from "*Berth Marks*," but it is actually starlet Alma Carroll trying to pass the Boys in the corridor of the "Sante Fe Special."

Last Train To San Fern … Cisco

On the subject of trains, here is another photo taken by Gene Lester aboard the Sante Fe Special.

MAKING a RACKET in the on-board recreation room are: Laurel, Hardy, Bert Lahr (obscured); Katherine Booth, Groucho, and (front) Marie MacDonald.

Bert Lahr following his own advice to: "Put 'em up!" Hardy reacting by testing how hard his biceps are; Bing Crosby giving a look of "Can you believe this guy;" and Cagney looking on with shock horror.

265

1942 May 13 (Wednesday)
HOUSTON, Texas to LOS ANGELES, California 🚂 1,549 miles

-----0-----

The original plan had been for the stars to return to Hollywood in triumph, and for the local populace to make their own contribution to the war effort, by giving generously to the show in their city. After all, what would a "Hollywood Victory Caravan" full of Hollywood stars be, if it didn't play in Hollywood, for the people of Hollywood?

Jack Benny had been contacted to emcee the show, as Bob Hope wouldn't be available. However, by now, the Hollywoodians had had enough of fundraising, as other parties had been milking them since the U.S.O. concert the previous year.

The lack of a decent venue, too, was another problem cited for the cancellation. The Hollywood Bowl would seem to be the perfect choice, but it was deemed to be too cold at that time of year. "Too cold" in the spring, in California, seems very questionable to an outsider, but locals ought to know their own weather.

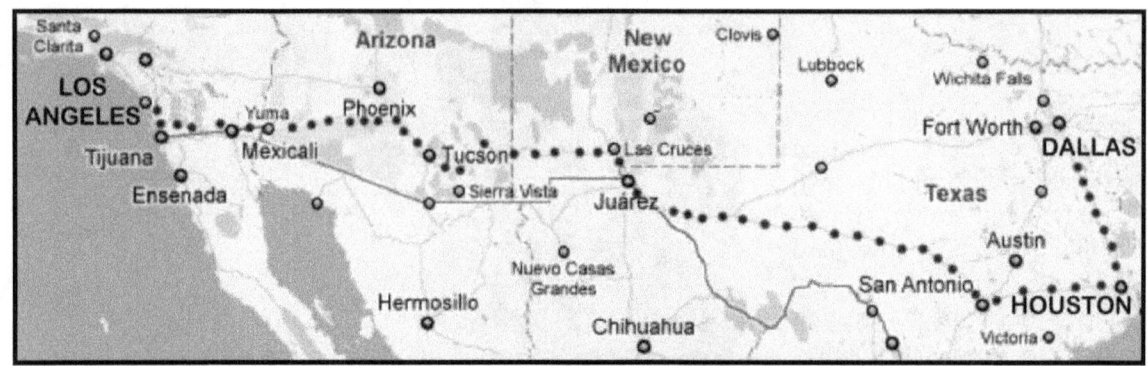

DALLAS – HOUSTON – LOS ANGELES

And so, on 14 May, after a near two-day train ride from Houston to Los Angeles, the travel-weary stars returned home for some well-earned rest. Because the travelling party were known to be so darn exhausted, no formal welcoming committee had been arranged, and so the stars had just their loved ones waiting to welcome them home.

Four days later, the engine of the "Sante Fe Special" was once again fired up – for the last trip on the Victory Caravan tour.

-----0-----

1942 May 18 (Monday)
LOS ANGELES, California to **SAN FRANCISCO**, California 🚂 382 miles

> Tuesday 19 May 1942
> Civic Auditorium, SAN FRANCISCO
> HOLLYWOOD VICTORY CARAVAN
> Army and Navy Relief Benefit Show
> 8.30 – 11.30

-----0-----

San Francisco was going to be no anti-climax. The members of the Hollywood Victory Caravan were about to team up with the members of "Walter Winchell's Navy Relief Fund." With the addition of other Hollywood stars to this one-off show, the entourage had almost doubled in number – from seventy to one hundred and twenty-five. Consequently it took four hotels – the Mark Hopkins, the Saint Francis, the Fairmont, and the Empire – to accommodate them all. For those who simply need to know – Laurel and Hardy stayed at the Fairmont Hotel.

Most of the original members of the troupe were returning, but others had had to pull out due to work commitments. Gone were Bing Crosby, Olivia DeHavilland, Claudette Colbert, Bob Hope, Francis Langford, and Jerry Colona. The latter three were off for adventures of their own, which would recur for many years to come.

To replace Hope as M.C. it took four new members: Walter Winchell, Al Jolson, Eddie Cantor, and Milton Berle – which must be an indication of just how big a contribution Hope had made to the show. In came the Andrews Sisters, Ben Bernie, the De Marcos, Dinah Shore, and Abbott & Costello.

-----0-----

May 19 (Tue)   **SAN FRANCISCO** – Civic Auditorium (11,000)

The show at the Civic Auditorium raised a further $45,000 towards supporting the families of servicemen and women on the warfront. Little was reported of the content of the show, except that it over-ran (8.50-12.30). This wasn't too difficult to predict. Previous shows had overrun, and this one had additional acts.

An interesting question is naturally raised by the presence of the two comedy double-acts on the bill: "Whose humour would fare best – Abbott & Costello's, or Laurel & Hardy's?" Well, the *San Francisco Chronicle* said of the former:

Bud Abbott and Lou Costello got entangled in a verbal mix-up about baseball, with confusion about a first-baseman named "Who."

SAN FRANCISCO programme, showing some of the new faces who came into the show – although Bob Hope was an old face, who went out.

And of Laurel & Hardy's act the *Chronicle* said: ... er ... NOTHING! So we will never know if the young pretenders were ever thought to have dethroned the "Kings of Comedy."

-----0-----

1942 May 20 (Wednesday)

SAN FRANCISCO, California to **LOS ANGELES**, California 🚂 382 miles

-----0-----

Having now completed their thirteen-city tour, the stars of the Hollywood Victory Caravan were returning to their normal employment, having raised the combined total of $650,000 towards the Relief Fund, with more money yet to filter through. They would now be able to face the movie cameras again, without a look of guilt in their eyes.

With notes made from his father's accounts of the Victory Caravan tour, John Lahr, son of Bert Lahr, wrote in the biography "*Notes on a Cowardly Lion*":

No matter how early Bert arrived at a venue, Stan and Babe were always there first. They would be sat at the corner of the long dressing-table, their make-up neatly set out with a clean towel neatly folded over it, and a full bottle of whisky placed between them. After Laurel and Hardy had got themselves ready, they would wait quietly as all the other actors came in one-by-one, and slowly but surely most would make their way over to the corner to share a chat and a shot.

A second account came from Groucho Marx, which backs up the claim about the drink:

I shared a dressing room with Laurel and Hardy. I've never drunk so much alcohol, but these two were pleasantly sloshed all the time I was with them. This, I thought, would be the leg-up I needed to outshine them. No way!

John Lahr goes on to reveal that Frank McHugh told him that, "When the orchestra played Laurel & Hardy's sign music, you've never heard such an ovation."

The last words on the Hollywood Victory Caravan itself come from the version of events given by Bert Lahr, to his son John. He describes the poignant moment when the end of the tour came, a tour that had seen many new friendships forged. Some flew back to Los Angeles from San Francisco, but most returned by train. As they were disembarking at Glendale Station, California, and saying their final "Goodbyes" Bert, who was himself fighting back the tears, spotted ...

... the massive Babe Hardy, so outgoing and confident a funny-man, trying to look away from his friends to hide his tears. He looked large and rumpled from the journey. 'Don't let's lose this. Keep in touch.' He looked, I don't know how to say it – he looked so isolated, so alone.

(Notes on a Cowardly Lion – John Lahr)

Soon, the feeling of abandonment and isolation would increase many-fold for both members of the comedy couple.

o-o-0-o-o

CHAPTER 31

FORT AND LOST

(1942 pt6 – 1945 pt1)

Just over a week after making the trip to and from San Francisco, the nomadic Laurel and his constant companion Hardy were off on the same trail, but only half-way along this time, to San Luis Obispo.

-----0-----

1942 May 29 (Friday)

LOS ANGELES, California to **SAN LUIS**, Obispo 🚂 199 miles

The occasion was the opening of the Fremont Theatre, 29 May 1942. Other stars who attended were: Carole Landis, Carole Bruce, Constance Bennett, John Carroll, Charlie Ruggles, Max Baer, Nat Pendleton, and actor Jackie Cooper.

Upon alighting from the bus which had brought them from the station, the Hollywood icons firstly went to an area across the road from the theatre, which had been laid out for the purpose of selling War Bonds to the public.

Selling bonds to Mayor Kimble.   Shaking on the deal.

Stan and Ollie skipped the public and sold their quota to the top man, Mayor Kimble, before making their way back across the street through the crowds of on-lookers. From the theatre foyer they, and the other VIPs, were escorted inside by the uniformed usherettes.

Once the lights had gone up, and the sixteen-hundred-strong audience had gasped at the revealing of the magnificent interior, the visiting stars took to the stage and began their fund-raising appeal. It was then on with the entertainment proper, which was a screening of the newly released wartime film "*This Above All*." No reports were found of any of the guest stars doing a live performance.

Babe and Stan as members of the audience, for once, at the opening of the Fremont Theatre – proving they enjoyed having a laugh as well as giving one. The lovely lady is actress Carole Bruce.

Fox Newsreel filmed parts of the event, to show at Fox cinema outlets. Whether it was intentional or not, the news-clip would have nicely complemented the trailer for the most recent Fox-Laurel & Hardy film, "*A-Haunting We Will Go*". **[FILM]**

-----0-----

1942 May 30 (Saturday)

SAN LUIS, Obispo to **LOS ANGELES**, California 199 miles

-----0-----

Saturday 30 May 1942 was 'Memorial Day' – the equivalent to 'Remembrance Day' in the U.K. To mark the occasion, a special tribute show was broadcast:

c11.05p.m. – Variety Hour (WIBA) for United Service Organisations

Mary Martin, Fanny Brice, Red Skelton, Meredith Wilson's Orchestra, Max Terr's Chorus, Joe E. Brown, Charles Butterworth, Linda Darnell, Deanna Durbin, John Garfield, Judy Garland, Laurel and Hardy, Hugh Herbert, Chico and Harpo Marx, Aldolpe Menjou, Chester Morris, Ritz Brothers, Mickey Rooney, Rosalind Russell, Ann Rutherford, Ann Sheridan, Spike Jones' City Slickers.

The format of the show – whether live, pre-recorded, or audio clips from recent U.S.O. tours – is not known.

Whatever happened in Laurel and Hardy's lives, throughout June, July, and August, happened in private. The only news to come out was that they had exercised the freedom given them in their contract with Fox, and signed a concurrent contract with MGM. It would be December, when filming began on their first MGM film, before they found out if the choice had been a good one. Oh! one more thing: Stan and Babe had invested in a turtle farm, based in Mexico. This wasn't a breeding programme to boost turtle numbers, but quite the opposite. The turtles were being farm-reared for their meat. (Surely it is far easier raising chickens for meat – plus, the shells are much easier to open!)

Meanwhile, during the second and third week in September, a nationwide drive was being launched, to promote sales of $100,000,000 in War Bonds and stamps. Fronting the drive would be thirty film stars who, between them, would be visiting three hundred U.S. cities. The event, sponsored by the United States Treasury Department, was labelled "Salute to Our Heroes Month," with the adopted slogan: "Buy a Bond to Honor Every Mother's Son in Service."

The thirty recruits were mostly drawn from those who had just finished making a film, which gave them the added bonus of being able to shamelessly plug their film's current or imminent release. The stars were split into seven travelling groups. In the Boys' group was the lovely actress Jean Parker, who had been Hardy's love interest in the Laurel & Hardy feature, "*The Flying Deuces*." The fourth member was Richard Arlen, who had just completed making "Alaska Highway" with Ms. Parker.

The following schedule has been compiled to be as close as possible to the original one:

STARS OVER AMERICA
"Salute To Our Heroes"

1942 Sep 10	MONTANA, Helena
1942 Sep 10	MONTANA, Butte
1942 Sep 11	MONTANA, Billings
1942 Sep 12	NORTH DAKOTA, Bismarck
1942 Sep 12	NORTH DAKOTA, Fargo
1942 Sep 14	WISCONSIN, Superior
1942 Sep 15	MINNESOTA, Duluth
1942 Sep 15	MINNESOTA, Eveleth
1942 Sep 16	MINNESOTA, Hibbing
1942 Sep 16	MINNESOTA, St. Cloud
1942 Sep 17	MINNESOTA, Minneapolis
1942 Sep 18	SOUTH DAKOTA, Sioux Falls

1942 Sep 19	IOWA, Sioux City
1942 Sep 20	SOUTH DAKOTA, Mitchell

I could go on to describe how Laurel and Hardy were met by a reception committee at each town they visited; the crowd reactions; their hotels; and the functions they performed; if it weren't for one thing – Laurel and Hardy NEVER MADE IT!

On 9 September the *Daily Variety* gave out the disappointing news:

> Because Oliver Hardy has been ordered by his doctor to rest a few days on account of laryngitis, he and Stan Laurel will delay joining 'Stars Over America' bond selling tour for a week to hook up with troupe in Duluth end of this week.

But five days later the same newspaper had to retract the statement.

> Ralph Bellamy replaced Laurel & Hardy, whose participation in the campaign had to be postponed because of Hardy's illness. Bellamy will join Richard Arlen and Peggy Diggins today in Duluth.

(*Daily Variety* – 14 September 1942)

Babe was never well enough to make any part of the tour, and so Bellamy covered throughout its run. Fans of Montana-based actress Jean Parker were also disappointed. She had pulled out before the Boys had.

Reports that Hardy had eloped with Ms. Parker, to get married in secret, were found to be untrue.

A later press release claimed:

> New volunteers for the film industry's September Bond Drive are Fred Astaire, Bette Davis, Hugh Herbert, Gene Tierney, Chester Morris, Laurel and Hardy, Richard Arlen, Susan Hayward, and Jinx Falkenburg, who are now touring major cities throughout the country.

(*Associated Press* – 23 September 1942)

Considerable research turned up no evidence that Laurel and Hardy, nor any of the other named stars, were still touring at this later date.

-----0-----

Fox film starlet Elena Verdugo, valet Jimmy Murphy, Stan, and Babe doing their bit for the "Dig For Victory" scheme – (*circa* 28 October 1942).

Stan explaining that this South American breed of Muscovy ducks are "quackless."

-----0-----

After picking off the best fruit the trees in Laurel's garden had to offer, what could be better than eating it?

Having had October and November in which to recuperate, Hardy was well enough to join his comedy partner in December, when work began on their first feature for MGM – "*Air Raid Wardens.*" Stan and Babe were obviously hoping the whole set-up at MGM would be a vast improvement on the one at Fox. It wasn't! Here, too, the film suffered from bad scripting and the suppression of the Laurel & Hardy characters.

So 1942 came and went, with disappointment at the projects and events Laurel and Hardy had *failed* to make, and disappointment with the film they *had* made!

1943 started off with promise, but then broke the promise:

> Riding high on a wartime comedy wave, Stan Laurel and Oliver Hardy are busier between films these days than when before the camera. They're working out a radio show, planning a Broadway play, and managing the affairs of a turtle business in Mexico.
>
> (30 January 1943)

The business in Mexico wasn't the only thing there to turn turtle on them. On 27 February 1943 *Boxoffice* announced:

> As soon as their commitments at *Metro* and *Fox* permit, Laurel and Hardy will co-star in a film version of the lives of Don Quixote and Sancho Panza. Titled "*Don and Sancho,*" the screenplay will be written by the comedy team and produced by the Azteca Studios, Mexico City, in Spanish and Portuguese. Later the picture will be produced in Hollywood for worldwide release.

Talk of Laurel and Hardy making films in Mexico had been going on since May the previous year, and that is all it turned out to be – TALK! However, two films did make it to print: the Fox-produced feature "*Jitterbugs*" (filmed mid-February to late March 1943); followed by a second Fox film "*The Dancing Masters*" (completed around the end of June).

Then in early July came news that:

> Oliver Hardy and Stan Laurel are writing a book, very appropriately titled "*Thru Thick and Thin.*" They'll mention all of their leading ladies, and they have quite a bevy, what with the late Jean Harlow, Paulette Goddard, Janet Gaynor, Lupe Velez, and their latest, Trudy Marshall.

This too never materialised, and nor did the next Laurel and Hardy film project at Fox – "*The Servant Problem.*" Maybe they couldn't get the staff!

Fast forward to November 1943, and we find one of the Boys' sketches being aired via, what was for them, a new working medium – RADIO. The sketch was titled "*The Wedding Party*" (although it is also known by two other titles).

Meant as the pilot for a series of Laurel & Hardy radio sketches, it was broadcast on the show "*Mail Call,*" which went out on the Armed Forces Radio Service on 24 November.

The premise of "*The Wedding Party*" – with Stan (the groom); Ollie (best-man); and Patsy Moran (the bride-to-be) – was knocking a judge out of bed to marry Stan and Patsy. Stan needs a bit of Dutch courage, and begins to take shots from a bottle of prune punch. This further impairs his already impaired faculties. A series of unhelpful responses to the wedding vows, by the bride and groom, results in the judge refusing to marry them. After reconsideration he continues with the ceremony, but his frustration soon rises to a point where he can take no more, and tells them to clear out. As they are about to leave, Stan asks Ollie for another shot (meaning: "of the prune punch"). Ollie responds with a shot from a gun.

THE END

-----0-----

One would surmise that "*The Wedding Party*" was well-received by the radio listeners of the Armed Forces it had been aired to as, less than four months later, a second Laurel & Hardy sketch was broadcast LIVE – on NBC

Fort and Lost

MR. SLATER'S POULTRY MARKET

Recorded to disc on 6 March 1944 [May or may not have been broadcast on NBC]

In this sketch, Laurel and Hardy are working for a supplier of chickens and chicken meat. Through a mix-up, they arrive at the hideout of a bunch of gangsters, who mistake them for a pair of hit-men they are about to hire to execute a rival gangster.

During questioning of how they conduct their 'business,' Stan and Ollie describe how they kill chickens, which the gangsters take for how they despatch the people they are hired to kill. This convinces the gangsters that the two are cold-hearted killers. The police turn up in time to arrest the gangsters before their mistake is discovered, thus saving the Boys from retribution.

The second scene finds the Boys in prison, where they then have to convince the police they aren't killers.

-----0-----

Before there were any further thoughts of a series of Laurel & Hardy radio sketches, the Boys were called back to the Fox studios to sell their souls again. "*The Big Noise*" (filmed April 1944), is about an eccentric inventor who invents a bomb. The biggest bomb wasn't *in* the film, but *was* the film. This was followed in June 1944 by a switch to the MGM studios for filming of "*The Home Front*," which came to be released as "*Nothing But Trouble.*"

Knowing that, with Fox and MGM, they were never going to be allowed to make films how they wanted to, Stan and Babe still kept up the search for a way to produce their own films:

> Mexico City is beckoning comics Stan Laurel and Oliver Hardy. In a few weeks, after completing "The Home Front" for MGM, they'll fly south to establish their own company which will have the high-sounding title: "Produciones Cinematograficas. S. de R. L." The boys will make both Spanish and English versions. The first two will be musicals: "Don Quixote" and "Fra Diavolo."
>
> (7 July 1944)

To be fair, the Boys did fly south to Mexico, but it wasn't on private business, but on another junket – this one to Monterrey, Nuevo Leon.

-----0-----

1944 October 01 (*circa*)

LOS ANGELES, California to **MONTERREY**, Mexico ✈ 1,228 miles

Rare photo at a barbecue, during the 'Goodwill' trip to Monterrey, Nuevo Leon, Mexico.

These visits of Hollywood stars to Mexico were designed to cement diplomatic relations between the two countries, but this one seems to have gone a little awry – owing to one Oliver Hardy!

> Most hectic incident of the Hollywood junket to Monterey, Mexico, was NOT carried in the wire stories. As Stan Laurel and Oliver "Babe" Hardy approached one of Monterey's breweries, a hefty local seized Hardy's arm and almost jerked it out by the roots. As the party came out, the same gent, using his paunch as a weapon, tried to butt Babe head over heels. Instead, Babe, who sports a mean paunch himself, butted back and floored the bully. Five hundred witnesses cheered hysterically.
>
> (Harrison Carroll's 'Hollywood" column – 6 October 1943)

So much for "Goodwill!' "

1943 October 04 (*circa*)

MONTERREY, Mexico to **LOS ANGELES**, California 1,228 miles

-----0-----

The next Laurel & Hardy picture, "*The Bullfighters*" (MGM), filmed November-December 1944, made a feeble attempt to pay homage to Mexico and its national "sport" of bullfighting; but by now Stan and Babe had had enough of fighting. With both the Fox and the MGM contracts now completed, and realising that to negotiate any form of extension would be assigning themselves to further purgatory, Laurel and Hardy gave a sour goodbye-kiss to the world of films.

Before the two comedians could sink into a life of depression and despair, the world suddenly became a brighter place: 5 May 1945 witnessed the unconditional surrender of the Germans, and signalled the end of the war in Europe. The Japanese capitulated on 14 August after receiving the *very loud* and *very clear* messages which the Americans delivered to Hiroshima and Nagasaki.

Less than three weeks after the declaration of peace in Europe, Ruth Laurel too ceased hostilities. On 24 May her attorney filed to dismiss a separate maintenance suit against Stan, following Ruth's doctor's advice that the worry of the court case was retarding her recovery from a recent illness.

The case coincided with Stan putting Fort Laurel up for sale. Maybe he thought there was no further need to be surrounded by a seven-foot-high wall, although it is still uncertain whether the wall was to keep out the Japanese, the Germans, reporters, or the ex-wives. The sale almost certainly conveyed to Ruth that there was no money left in the coffers.

Babe visiting Stan to reminisce over old times at Fort Laurel, before the bell is rung to call "Last Orders" for the last ever time.

Just before Stan vacated Fort Laurel, Hollywood columnist Bob Thomas went along to meet him there:

> "Yep, I sold it," he said. "I'm moving into the city. Don't know where yet, but I've got a couple of possibilities."
>
> "I had to sell the place because I just couldn't get the help to keep it up," Laurel explained. "I had a man here for three days last week, but unfortunately I paid him in advance. I haven't seen him since."
>
> Stan was seated in the playroom of Fort Laurel. It is a large room with a bar, and many pictures of show business people on the walls.

If one assumes this issue of *Spy Smasher* is current, then Hardy's visit can be dated as on, or shortly after, 28 October 1942. The same date can also be allocated to the series of "Dig For Victory" photos included in this chapter, in which Fox starlet Elena Verdugo was sent along to provide the glamour.

Unfortunately, the lovely Miss Verdugo was not rewarded with a part in any of the subsequent films the two comedians were to make at Fox. Shame!

N.B. This picture is not related to the current article, nor date of sale.

> "I'll show you something," he said, and turned a switch.
>
> Outside the window, water began to drip from the roof. Stan assured me the rain effect was very helpful in keeping the place cool in the summertime. It has also been good for a few laughs.
>
> "When we had parties, I would turn it on and people would think it was raining. They would run all the way out to the street to roll up their car windows, before they realized they weren't getting wet." Stan emitted that high, horse-like laugh of his.

(28 May 1945)

The "For Sale" advert described Fort Laurel as:

> 3 houses on a 105ft x 415ft [1 acre] plot – beautiful grounds, completely enclosed with 6ft [*sic*] brick wall. One house has bar room with beautiful 15ft bar and unique back bar. 6,000 sq.ft. of concrete in driveways and walks – huge patio and barbecue.

Since 1941, Laurel had conscientiously partaken in the "Dig for Victory" campaign, whereby he had grown his own fruit and vegetables, and raised chickens, ducks, and rabbits. But now, everything was in a state of neglect. Weeds had taken over the gardens; the greenhouse was empty; and the chickens, ducks, and rabbits had found their way into cold-storage, with no feathers or fur to keep them warm.

Laurel's own life reflected the fate of his garden: forlorn, abandoned, and all the fruitful years behind him. When he looked back at the friends who had visited; the parties they had enjoyed; and the laughs they had shared; it must have made him very sad to know he was leaving.

Laurel would be leaving behind the wishing well at Fort Laurel, but the loss wouldn't be that great, as he had long-since realised that it didn't work.

When Stan first married Ruth he had a trailer, a boat, and a big house. Now they were all gone – including his wife – and he was sentencing himself to the life of a single man – in an apartment (believed to be in The Garden Court Apartments, 7021 Hollywood Blvd., Hollywood). But with Laurel's in-built burning desire always to have a partner by his side, he would not remain a single man for long.

o-o-0-o-o

CHAPTER 32

THE BOYS IN FOREIGN
(1945 pt2 – 1948)

Laurel's hopes of a financial upswing were kept alive during the next few months, by talk of him and Babe Hardy doing a Broadway show in the fall. This was followed on 17 December 1945 by an announcement that: *"Laurel and Hardy are due to go to London in the spring to do a picture."* Bah humbug!

On 30 April 1946 Ruth's divorce from Stan was granted on the grounds of three years' separation. Her parting shot at Laurel was: *"When he has something, he doesn't want it – but when he hasn't got it, he wants it."* Ruth then announced she was immediately about to marry another man. If Ruth thought she was cocking a snook at Stan, because *she* had found another partner, her gesture would have been ineffective. Laurel already had is next wife waiting in the wings; and on 5 May 1946, just five days after his divorce from Ruth, he was a married man again.

His **new** wife – not a recycled one, although many were to draw comparisons with one of the former ones – was Ida Kitaeva Raphael. Ida (pronounced "Eeda") was Laurel's second *Russian* wife, another blonde, and a singer who had worked both the east and west coasts. Also, the way Stan and Ida met was near-identical to Stan's first meeting with Illiana, which was in a Russian restaurant. But there, any comparisons with Illiana ended. As Hardy had found peace and happiness with Lucille, so too had Stan with Ida, and they were to live together till death did them part! Fred Lawrence Guiles reveals details of that first meeting:

In 1945, Stan took a party of ten for dinner at the Moskwa, in the San Fernando Valley. Seated across the room was a compelling-looking blonde, imperious, blue eyes flashing, a diva, he learned. "Please send her over," he asked, and Ida Kitaeva (Keaton) Raphael entered Stan's life.

Ida's Russian accent intrigued Stan at once. She was recently a widow; he was in the process of getting a divorce. It seemed a repetition of his meeting with Virginia Ruth Rogers, except for one small detail. Ida Kitaeva Raphael was in show business herself. She had a small career going, with a few impressive movie credits, mostly from her work with director Preston Sturges.

In 1944 Sturges had used Ida in *"Hail the Conquering Hero,"* as a prima-donna who bursts forth into song to hail home the "marine war hero." At the time she met Laurel she was working on Harold Lloyd's last film *"The Sin of Harold Diddlebock."* Within days Stan was chauffeuring her to the studio. She said it was heartbreaking to see him each morning since he was the one who should have been going before the cameras.

When they first met, Ida had no idea who Stan Laurel was, and so was shocked to learn he had been a major star. She was later to say to author John McCabe: *"He seemed quite lonely, and that won my heart more than anything."*

LAUREL and HARDY – The U.S. Tours

-----0-----

1946 May 06

HOLLYWOOD, California to **YUMA**, Arizona 302 miles

-----0-----

To get married, Stan and Ida eloped to Yuma, Arizona. It was Laurel's third time there, so you would think he would have known the way. But no! He got lost. It was five in the morning when they finally got there; whereupon, in a scenario straight from the script of the Laurel & Hardy radio sketch "*The Wedding Party*" (*ibid.*) the couple knocked the Peace Justice [*sic*] out of bed. The place was called "Cupid's Corner." Laurel thought it said "Stupid's Corner" and went right on in!

Mercifully, the ceremony went off without incident, and the PJ was able to get back into his PJs and go back to bed. The Laurels, meanwhile, stopped off at San Diego on the way back, for a short honeymoon at the Grand Hotel. Nothing to report there, except that no past wives came banging on the door of their room shouting verbal abuse.

-----0-----

1946 May 06

YUMA, Arizona to **SAN DIEGO**, California 169 miles

1946 May 09 (*circa*)

SAN DIEGO to **HOLLYWOOD**, California 133 miles

-----0-----

Stan was fifty-six, Ida was thirty-nine. Some years into their marriage, Stan wrote a letter to a friend, in which he gave her résumé as follows:

```
Mrs. Laurel was a singer, she was trained in China for
opera, she had a very fine voice, but being a stranger here
& unknown also unable to speak the language, it was
difficult to get an opportunity to work in opera, so her
only chance was to work in Russian night clubs in New York,
Chicago, & Hollywood, then when she married me, she decided
to give it up and quit the business. I still think she was
very foolish, am sure if she had continued she would have
made a great career for herself.
```

Immediately after the marriage, Stan and Ida moved into a two-storey house at 4238 Matilija Avenue, Sherman Oaks. Meanwhile he and his working partner were at a loose end. Even though WWII was ended, filming was obviously a closed door, and visiting Army bases was too uncomfortable, too exhausting, and not exactly what one could term "a future." Nor did it pay the bills. They had enjoyed their entry into stage work, but to do this on a permanent basis, in America, was not an easy prospect. Vaudeville boasted only about a dozen remaining theatres, so artistes had to be prepared to work night clubs, cabaret venues, and in cinemas, to keep in full-time employment. After working the cinemas, with their massive auditoriums, seating up to six thousand people, and having to perform up to six shows per day, on a bill shared with a feature film, Laurel and Hardy realised that even this, the best option, was not the right medium for their soft-approach humour.

With the Boys floundering, a life-line appeared from an unexpected source, when, over in England a young entrepreneur, Bernard Delfont, took advantage of the sailing de-restrictions across the Atlantic and invited Laurel and Hardy to come to London. Delfont's first idea had been for Stan and Ollie to play in pantomime; but, when Laurel informed him about "*The Driver's Licence*" sketch, he changed his *modus operandi* and booked them on a provisional twelve-week engagement of British Variety theatres.

For Stan Laurel it was the beginning of a whole new life. With the sailing of the *Queen Elizabeth* from New York, it is ironic to reflect that, thirty-five years after deserting the British stage to go and seek a new life in America, Stan Laurel was returning in the hope of mending the pieces of his broken fortunes.

-----0-----

The Boys in Foreign

1947 January 31 (*circa*) Friday
      LOS ANGELES, California to **NEW YORK**, New York 🚂 2,814 miles
1947 February 05
      Queen Elizabeth sails for **SOUTHAMPTON**, England.

-----0-----

In a sense, the war years had preserved Laurel and Hardy. The British had been more concerned about their battles with the Germans, than about Laurel and Hardy's battles with Roach, Fox, and MGM, and were unaware of the comedians' decline. After the declaration of peace, it was as if a pause button had been released; and to find that, out of the recent darkness, this glowing light was about to appear in their midst, gave cause for tremendous excitement. And so on 10 February 1947, as the *Queen Elizabeth* sailed in to Southampton Docks, Laurel and Hardy were stunned to see thousands of fans waving, cheering, and whistling *The Cuckoo Song*.

Look who I've brought with me.
Arrival at Southampton on the *Queen Elizabeth* — 10 March 1947

There were to be similar gatherings every time the comedy couple turned up at a railway station, a hotel, a theatre, or any public event. In Glasgow, Edinburgh, and Liverpool, the crowds were so huge and so pushy that police on horseback had to be used to control them.

Following extended runs at the world-famous London Palladium, and the London Coliseum, the Hollywood screen comedians played a week at two other London theatres, after which provincial theatres began to book them.

Between May and September, Laurel and Hardy played the No.1 circuit of Variety theatres: the Moss Empire theatres in Glasgow, Edinburgh, Newcastle, Liverpool, and Swindon; plus the Hippodrome theatres in Birmingham, Dudley, Bristol, and Coventry; along with provincial theatres in Manchester, and Hull; and also theatres in the seaside resorts of Morecambe, Blackpool, Butlins Skegness, Southsea, Margate, and Boscombe. The tour then concluded back in London, with shows at Finsbury Park Empire, and Chiswick Empire.

[For a complete account of the 1947 tour, see my book "LAUREL & HARDY – The British Tours."]

LAUREL and HARDY – The U.S. Tours

Word of Laurel and Hardy's popularity and box-office appeal had spread to Europe and so, commencing 1 October, dates were played in Denmark, Sweden, France, and Belgium – where the mob scenes and packed audiences repeated at each and every public appearance and show.

In Copenhagen, Laurel and Hardy were treated like Royalty, and driven in style, in a liveried Landau, from the railway station to the Palace. [Not THE Palace.]

----0----

In Odense, DENMARK, they were appointed honourable members of the bowling club, and received medals, plus a diploma on which were their caricatures. [23 October 1947]

----0----

282

Laurel and Hardy being greeted by Stan & Oliver in the foyer of the Lido de Paris, FRANCE [28 October 1947]

Just before the scheduled six-week run at the Lido, in Paris, Stan and Babe were recalled to England to appear in the *Royal Variety Performance*," at the London Palladium, in the presence of King George VI, the Queen Mother, Princess Elizabeth (later Queen Elizabeth II) and her fiancé Philip Mountbatten.

The entire company singing "*The National Anthem*" at the Finale of the 1947 'Royal Variety Show,'
London Palladium – 3 November 1947.
Stan and Babe – front row, 7th and 8th from the right.

The two comedians then resumed the European tour which, after Paris, ended in Belgium on 9 January 1948, and the Boys were finally able to return home. Their provisional **twelve-week** engagement had lasted almost exactly **twelve months**.

-----0-----

1948 January 15   Hardys sail from Antwerp on board MV *Bastogne*, bound for New York.
1948 January 28   Laurels sail from Southampton, on board *Queen Mary*, bound for New York.

-----0-----

After their one-year absence, Laurel and Hardy had to face being treated with indifference by most of the American public, and also come to terms with a younger generation who didn't even know them. But then, in May, an offer of work did come in – but it wasn't for a film:

> If Stan Laurel and Oliver Hardy are able to unshackle themselves from Hollywood, Broadway will see them cavorting in "So Merrily We Sail," a musical comedy to be produced by Sherman Krellberg. Without them, Mr. Krellberg said yesterday, he will be forced to drop the venture.
>
> For several weeks the comics have been studying the script. They are sufficiently interested to have volunteered suggestions and final word from the pair is expected within ten days.

(24 May 1948)

Ten days passed, and then another four months of nothing, before the next offer came in. This time it *was* for a film. Fingers crossed!

> Glenn McCarthy, independent producer, has announced that his next film, "You Can't Do That," will be a comedy, written by Monty Collins and Frank Gill, about life in a motion-picture cartoon studio. He will seek the services of Stan Laurel and Oliver Hardy for the leading roles.
>
> Laurel and Hardy will play themselves, but won't have to carry the picture, as they will be only two of six stars.

(8 November 1948)

Exactly twelve months earlier, in November 1947, while Stan and Babe were still doing stage shows in Paris, Hollywood columnist Erskine Johnson had announced: *"Stan Laurel and Oliver Hardy will return to the screen in a series of comedy shorts, when they return from Europe."* But, come the end of 1948, neither this nor the other two aforementioned projects had come to fruition. 1949 was bound to bring something — wasn't it?

o-o-0-o-o

CHAPTER 33

AT WHAT PRICE?
(1949 – 1951 pt1)

Come March 1949, fourteen months after their return from Europe, Laurel and Hardy had made no films, no radio shows, and no known personal appearances, although Stan is known to have attended a Testimonial Dinner, at the Masquers Club on 28 January.

Stan Laurel (indicated by the arrow) at the Masquers Testimonial Dinner to honour Jean Hersholt. 28 January 1949. [He is not sitting near anyone instantly recognisable.]

-----0------

Three weeks later, it was Hardy's turn to get involved with a Masquers Club event. Over forty members had formed a drama company, and were about to go on a short tour with the production: "*What Price Glory.*" On 21 February 1949 they staged the final dress-rehearsal at the Masquers Club, in front of an audience of 450 invited guests and brass.

The stars among the 40-plus company were: John Wayne, Gregory Peck, Ward Bond, Maureen O'Hara, Pat O'Brien, Alan Hale, Sr., Ed Begley, Henry O'Neill, Herbert Rawlinson, Harry Carey, Jr., Luis Alberni, and one Oliver 'Babe' Hardy.

The following night, "*What Price Glory?*" opened in Long Beach, beginning a six-city tour of one-night stands in California, as follows:

Feb 22	LONG BEACH,	
Feb 25	OAKLAND, Auditorium Theatre	
Feb 27	SAN FRANCISCO, Opera House	
Mar 1	PASADENA, Civic Auditorium	
Mar ??	LOS ANGELES, Philharmonic Auditorium. [Thought to have been cancelled]	
Mar 11	HOLLYWOOD, Grauman's Chinese Theater	

None of the cast took a salary, so that the entire proceeds of the production could go to the "Military Order of the Purple Heart" – to aid wounded veterans in hospitals, or those unable to follow their trades or professions.

Audiences were awestruck when some of Hollywood's biggest stars actually walked out on stage, and were still in total disbelief when the whole cast re-appeared for the end-of-play walk-down.

And so what of our comedy hero, Hardy? Well, *Variety* printed a review of the Masquers dress-rehearsal, in which they revealed:

> Oliver Hardy, in for the bit as the town's mayor in the would-be marriage ceremony, turns in an hilarious bit of timing.

But then another review, in a later show, cited a different role:

> Not forgetting, of course, Oliver Hardy – who had only a walk-on part as a French Major.

It may well be a typing error, and "Major" was typed instead of "Mayor." It is also quite possible that minor roles were switched around during the run of the play, when certain actors weren't available, and another one had to stand in. Either way, at least we know Hardy was in it and that, as we also well know, he was extremely capable of stealing the laughs for even the most-minor of roles.

> Laurel & Hardy biographer John McCabe, was told by James Cagney (when compiling Cagney's biography) that Hardys performance: "… was the funniest thing I think I have ever seen. Roland Winters and I had to hang onto each other, we were laughing so much."

[Additional material from an article by Michael F. Blake, whose father, Larry Blake, was one of the cast.]

Then, in March, both Laurel AND Hardy were on the invitation list to go on a junket, by train, to and from Houston, in the company of a whole host of other Hollywood stars. They must have believed that this might go some way to re-establishing their status as Hollywood stars themselves.

The original passenger list reads like pages from "*Who's Who in the Movies*" – as, along with Messrs. Stan Laurel and Oliver Hardy, it included: Dorothy Lamour, Clark Gable, Andy Devine, Hugh Herbert, Joan Davis, Edgar Bergen, Van Heflin, J. Carrol Naish, Walter Brennan, Errol Flynn, Constance Moore, Sonja Henie, John Wayne, Maureen OHara, Ward Bond, Dennis O'Keefe, Robert Ryan, Dennis OShea, Ellen Drew, Leo Carrillo, Kirk Douglas, Buddy Rogers, Monty Collins, Gale Storm, MacDonald Carey James Cagney, Pat O'Brien, Bud Abbott and Lou Costello, Alan Hale, and Chester Morris.

The last six would have been well known to Stan and Babe: O'Brien, Cagney, Abbott, and Costello had been fellow passengers on the "Victory Caravan," while Hale, Morris, and again Costello had appeared in Laurel & Hardy films.

On Monday 14 March, when the 16-coach Santa Fe Railroad streamliner train "The Shamrock Special" left Pasadena station, at least four invitees were missing from the original guest list: Clark Gable, Bud Abbott, John Wayne and, most disappointingly of all, Oliver Hardy. Maybe Hardy was burned-out from the tour of "*What Price Glory?*" – which had ended just three days

At What Price?

earlier; giving him only two days to recover and prepare. Or maybe there is some other reason. Read on!

On board were sixty movie personalities, on a junket said to be "just about the costliest and most spectacular ever staged, anywhere." In addition, some one hundred newspapermen and women from national magazines, news syndicates and newsreel companies were to travel with them to record the activities over the whole five-day excursion.

-----0-----

1949 March 14 (Monday)
>LOS ANGELES, California to **CLOVIS**, New Mexico 🚂 1,007 miles

-----0-----

First stopover was Tuesday afternoon in Clovis, New Mexico, where two thousand residents were congregated on the railway platform, ready to greet the Hollywood entourage.

-----0-----

1949 March 15 (Tuesday)
>CLOVIS, New Mexico to **LUBBOCK**, Texas 🚂 100 miles

-----0-----

Two hours and fifteen minutes after leaving Clovis, similar scenes were enacted at the Santa Fe station, in Lubbock, Texas.

-----0-----

1949 March 15 (Tuesday)
>LUBBOCK, Texas to **HOUSTON**, Texas 🚂 518 miles

-----0-----

It was Wednesday morning when the train finally arrived at its destination – Houston Union Station, where a crowd estimated at five thousand was waiting to welcome the visitors to their city. In the afternoon, a smaller crowd was at the airport for the arrival of another forty-five Hollywood stars.

The now one-hundred-plus actors and actresses had come to Houston at the invite of Glenn McCarthy, a multi-millionaire who had made his fortune by working his way up from rancher and oilfield worker, to oilman, banker, and then newspaper and radio station owner. His latest incarnation was that of film producer, and all those now assembling in Houston were there to promote the premiere of his first picture, "*The Green Promise*," to be shown on Friday.

Just four months earlier, McCarthy, it may be remembered, had been planning to star Laurel and Hardy in "*You Can't Do That*," but the film, about life in an animation studio, seems not to have made it to the drawing-board.

If going from rancher to film producer weren't a big enough financial risk, consider that McCarthy's concurrent venture was that of hotelier, with the stars also being in Houston for the opening of "The Shamrock" – his brand new 1,100-room, 18-storey hotel, four miles outside downtown Houston, which had set him back $20 million.

On the Wednesday afternoon the Hollywood actors attended a press reception, in two of the hotel's sumptuous lounges. On the Thursday afternoon, Dorothy Lamour, Pat O'Brien, and McCarthy himself officiated at the cutting of the green ribbon to mark the hotel officially open. It was St. Patrick's Day, which gave even more cause for celebration.

At the 7pm champagne reception, the guest list had been swelled by a further nineteen hundred invitees. These were made up of additional Hollywood stars, plus writers, state officials, dignitaries, and three hundred millionaires – including the normally publicity-shy Howard Hughes. **[FILM]**

Friday saw the premiere of "*The Green Promise*" – paradoxically, the Hollywood entourage DIDN'T. The premier was held at two cinemas in downtown Houston, for which a five-mile torchlight parade from the Shamrock Hotel to the cinemas had been organised. Although the stars did partake, by waving from their fifty open-air limousines to the eighty-thousand-strong crowd lining the route, once they arrived at the cinemas they were excused duties.

When asked why he had spent $600,000 bringing more than one hundred Hollywood stars on a three-thousand-mile return journey, then sent them home without seeing his movie, McCarthy replied: "I just didn't think they'd want to be bothered sitting through it." Maybe he felt that everyone could not help but praise the merits of the hotel, but might be less kind about the film.

-----0-----

1949 March 18 (Friday)
        HOUSTON, Texas to **LOS ANGELES**, California   1,675 miles

-----0-----

With hundreds of column inches being written about the Houston celebrations, and with so many stars in attendance, it is little wonder that Stan Laurel's inclusion in the write-ups was in name only – which must come as a disappointment to those readers wanting to know of his involvement. Our glasses must be raised, therefore, to the one journalist who short-listed our comedy hero for due praise in a postscript.

Under the banner headline: "Big Name Movie Stars Take a Back Seat to Homely Comics in Public," Wood Soanes wrote:

> The three most popular players in pictures are, in the order named, Andy Devine, Hugh Herbert and Stan Laurel. This may sound a little silly but the fact remains that, on the tour of the special train chartered by McCarthy for the transportation of the stars from Hollywood to Houston, it was Devine that the populace wanted to see most of all; Herbert with whom they whoo-whooed most enthusiastically; and Laurel around whom they swarmed, demanding to know where his partner, Oliver "Babe" Hardy, was.
>
> Devine appears occasionally as a subordinate player; Herbert has done very little in recent years; and Laurel is practically an unknown quantity. Yet young and old knew the three men at once and passed up all the glamor girls and the pretty boys in their favour.
>
>   (*Oakland Tribune* – 27 March 1949) [Abridged]

One can safely say that, if Laurel had been accompanied by his iconic partner Hardy, the demonstration of fan adoration would have increased manyfold. Which begs the question: "Where was Hardy?" and prompts the second question: "Why did Laurel give up a week of his time to go on this train ride?" Well, both answers can be found in a newspaper article, based on an interview Hardy gave on the very day the "Shamrock Special" steamed out of Santa Fe:

> I found round, firm and fully-packed Hardy in a buckskin outfit, on the set of John Wayne's "A Strange Caravan." He admitted that a couple of cows gave their lives to supply the costume. I asked if his present role meant a permanent split with the wistful Laurel.
>
> "No, no," Babe assured. "This is just temporary until we get active again. In fact, my salary goes to our joint corporation. We've been incorporated since 1935." [*sic*]
>
> Babe said he had discussed the single role with Stan, who said to go ahead. "He called me up at seven this morning to wish me luck on my first day," Hardy said.
>
> Hardy is going ahead with his separate career and will do a role in "Riding High" with Bing Crosby. But the boys may get back together in a picture for Glenn McCarthy Productions.
>
>   (*Oakland Tribune* – 14 March 1949) [Abridged]

Hardy had probably secured his role of 'Willie Paine,' Wayne's sidekick, following a friendship the two had built up while appearing in "*What Price Glory*." Thankfully, Hardy's part in the film was far bigger than the one he had had in the play, for which Babe gave a very creditable performance in a straight acting role.

At What Price?

THE FIGHTING KENTUCKIAN – Willie Paine and Johnny Wayne
The film started its life as "*Eagles in Exile*," was released in the US in 1949 as
"*A Strange Caravan*," but then as "*The Fighting Kentuckian*" in the UK in 1950

Good to report, too, that the Bing Crosby film "*Riding High*" also made it onto the screen (released 1950). Hardy's part was only a cameo, but allowing Oliver Hardy on screen for even just a few seconds is long enough for the man to steal the plaudits, as the following review of "*Riding High*" will confirm:

> When the final counts are in, there are only three performances of any real merit: William Demarest as a race-track character; Oliver Hardy as an unhappy bettor; and a Japanese bantam chicken, which didn't get credit.

RIDING HIGH

Given an insider tip … Hardy runs to the Tote window …

 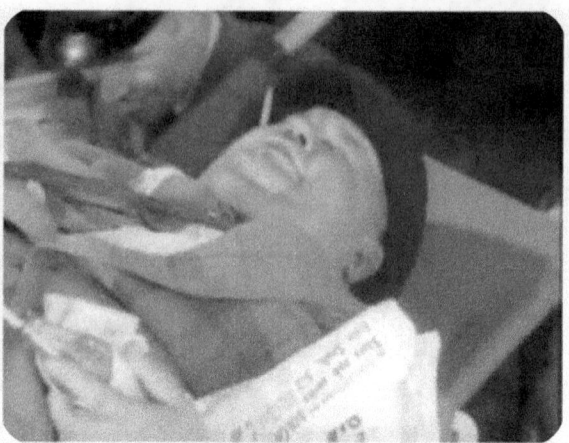

| … and places his own money, plus his wife's life savings on 'Doughboy.' | He exits on a stretcher, after fainting at the shock of losing it all. |

So what of the revelation that Laurel and Hardy "may get back together in a picture for Glenn McCarthy Productions"? Well, it would seem that thoughts of making "*You Can't Do That*" were certainly on the cards back in January:

> Although no names are on dotted lines yet, it looks as though the comedy team of Stan Laurel and Oliver Hardy is headed for featured roles in "You Can't Do That," a comedy, naturally, about life in a movie cartoon studio, which Glenn McCarthy Productions will make independently for RKO release. The production, written by Monty F. Collins, a former film comic himself, is tentatively set to go in April, and the company also plans to use other "names" in the cast.
>
> (*New York Times* – 16 January 1949)

Three weeks later it was still a goer, but with a different title:

> Glenn McCarthy, independent producer, today announced that his next picture for RKO will be "My Darling Is a Kangaroo," a screen comedy about life in an animated cartoon studio, which Monty F. Collins and Frank Gill have written.
>
> (*New York Times* – 5 February 1949)

Strange though that, within weeks of reports that Laurel and Hardy were about to get back together, another was claiming they had separated:

Oliver Hardy May Get New Comedy Partner

> Oliver Hardy, associated almost inseparably with Stan Laurel on the screen for twenty-two years, may have a new comedy partner soon. Hardy is reported to be discussing a deal with a producer who wants to star him with Charles Coburn as a comedy team—again without Laurel.
>
> (*Associated Press* – 9 April 1949)

With hindsight, the rumour that Laurel and Hardy were about to separate seems absolutely ludicrous. Right up to his last days, Laurel always claimed that he and Hardy had never had a falling out – not even a cross word. But a contemporary letter, written by Laurel to Chicago attorney Lauritz P. Hwass, is proof that the rumour was actually true, and that Laurel had done a cover-up.

```
                                                         14th Feb. '49
My Dear Larry:-
Am sorry that Benny Benefico disclosed a near fact before
it was definite. However, I am trying my utmost to avoid a
seperation of the team regardless of our personal
grievences. Anyway, it is entirely up to Mr. Hardy. I expect
to get a showdown this week. Will advise you of the result.
```

Stan

At What Price?

With phrases like: "*I am trying my utmost to avoid a seperation [sic]*," and: "*I expect to get a showdown,*" this was obviously a real rift, and one that had the potential to become a permanent split between the comedy couple.

The idea for teaming Hardy with Coburn quickly evaporated, but McCarthy's plans for a film had more substantiation. So how come it was never made? It was the spring of 1950 before the answer was provided: (*Oakland Tribune* – 17 April 1950)

> Glenn McCarthy's plan to do a film with Laurel and Hardy, based on a story by Monty Collins, has apparently failed to materialize.
>
> At the time "The Green Promise" was previewed in Houston, just about a year ago, everything seemed to be in the bag. Nothing happened in the intervening 12 months, and now an announcement has come from Oliver 'Babe' Hardy that the two zanies are preparing to get together again for the first time in five years.
>
> They go to Paris this summer to make a picture, temporarily called "Atoll K," by John Klorer and Frederick Kohner. It will be produced by Tim Whelan, with French and American backing, and the cast will include Fernandel – the French comedian; and Toto – the Italian clown.
>
> Laurel and Hardy expect to follow "Atoll K" with another picture to be made abroad, probably in Italy.

Still in 1949, Hal Roach too seemed to believe Laurel and Hardy might still have some mileage, and offered them a new film deal:

> If you are wondering about those Laurel and Hardy comedies you've been seeing on television, here's the inside: Hal Roach sold the TV rights for $750,000. The buyer expects to make about $250,000 on the deal.
>
> Roach tried to talk Stan and Babe into making a series of 14 shorts, running 12 minutes each, expressly for television, but they turned him down, saying the price wasn't right.

Wow!! Three quarters of a million dollars in 1949. That was a LOT of money. There were only two reasons the TV company paid that much for the Laurel & Hardy films – one was the name "Laurel," the other was the name "Hardy" – and yet neither of those two gentlemen got a single cent.

The only other change during 1949, apart from the four seasons, was that on 26 August 1949 Stan and Ida bought a new house, at 1111 Franklin Avenue – Santa Monica. I say "bought," but Stan couldn't afford to buy it outright, and put down just a $1,000 deposit on the purchase price of $16,500.

The property was described as a "frame-and-stucco, single dwelling, 7-room, 2-bathroom, 2-car garage, and garden." The Laurels were to live there for the next seven years, until it became too big for them to manage.

So, on the work-front, 1949 ended almost as disappointingly as had 1948. Hardy had done okay with creditable roles in a play and in two films, but all Laurel was known to have done was go on the junket to Houston; attend another meeting of the Masquers Club on 28 September; and then appear at a children's Christmas Party, organised by the Sherman Oaks Chamber of Commerce, on 8 December. And, of those, only Hardy's two film roles had put any money into the coffers of "Laurel & Hardy Feature Productions."

So, with 1950 showing no further promise of work in the U.S., it was the offer to go and make a film in France, which the Boys grasped with both hands.

> 'The deal sounds like the best we've had in years,' Hardy said today. 'We have a good story, and that's important.'
>
> 'We've had many Hollywood offers, but none have included good stories. Producers feel that all we need to do is some slapstick and that's enough.'
>
> (17 March 1950)

To be fair it was a lucrative offer, but there would be a price to pay, and that price was twelve months of squabbling, frustration, anger, embarrassment, despair, and life-threatening illnesses. For starters, Laurel had recently been diagnosed as diabetic.

Had the two ageing comedians not had so much debt to pay off, by way of back-taxes and alimony, they might well have opted to remain in the U.S.; which, hindsight reveals, would have kept them out of another unfunny mess.

On 3 April 1950 the Laurels rented out 1111 Franklin Avenue to a family, on a month-to-month basis, while they went to France to make "*Atoll K*." It would turn out to be a very wise rental investment, as the months were about to add up.

-----0-----

1950 April 03 (circa)

LOS ANGELES, California to NEW YORK, New York 2,814

-----0-----

Stan and wife Ida set off first, sailing on the *RMS Caronia*, and arriving in Paris on 13 April 1950. Using the Prince de Galles Hotel as a base, Stan spent weeks with two other scriptwriters, trying to knock out a working script for "*Atoll K*." The task was almost impossible, as all three writers had different ideas, and had to try to communicate in three different languages – English, Italian, and French. A later change to English-speaking writers did little to improve the situation.

Babe and Lucille Hardy joined Laurel in Paris in mid-June, nearly ten weeks after work had

> When the Hardys arrived at St. Lazare Station, Paris, Babe's first action was to pick out Stan from a line-up of fans, all wearing masks of Laurel's likeness.
> 17th June 1950

first started on the script – but still it wasn't ready.

So, while the other writers stayed in Paris to continue work on the script, the two star comedians went on a publicity tour of Italy, to promote a film that hadn't even been written. But the fans didn't know or care about that, and at every stopover – Marseilles, San Remo, Genoa, Milan, and Rome – the Boys were mobbed.

Of the Milan visit, Laurel later wrote in a letter:

At What Price?

```
The L&H film version of 'Fra Diavolo' is still shown every
year in Italy, it was showing in Milan when Hardy and I
were there in 1950, the English was 'dubbed' in Italian
language, I got a big kick out of L&H speaking Italian just
like the natives!
```

The Boys were back in Paris before June was out, where Laurel had to make major alterations to the rubbish the writers had written in his absence. It was 5 August before the script was deemed workable, at which point everyone set off for Marseilles to start filming. The next seven or eight days were spent shooting outdoor scenes in Marseilles harbour.

Cast and crew then moved to St. Raphael, on the Côte d'Azur. Shooting commenced on 16 August on a peninsula called Cap Roux which, in the film, is the actual atoll – with its specially built bamboo and palm-leaf huts, in and around which most of the action takes place.

The hardships of the daytime shooting began to cause the Boys severe health problems. Hardy was now around 330lbs, and the excess weight he was carrying, combined with the intense heat he was exposed to daily, caused him to develop heart fibrillation.

As for Laurel, he was losing weight faster than Hardy was gaining it. His diabetes, coupled with another illness, rendered him so weak he was able to film for only minutes at a time. He struggled gainfully on and, God bless him, managed to shoot all the location scenes, plus those done at the studios, in Nice, over the weeks which followed.

No filming was done between the end of October and the first two weeks in January, owing to Laurel's continuing illness and eventual hospitalisation. It was 17 January 1951 before filming recommenced, in Paris. The following day, shooting on-set was interrupted for the presentation of a huge cake, and a magnum of champagne. It was Hardy's 59th Birthday.

Unsure whether Ollie is about to blow or sneeze, Stan keeps the potted plant at a safe distance. — Paris Studios Cinéma. [18 January 1951]

Both stars struggled on with filming till the end of March, before finally hearing, what was for them at the time, the most glorious four-letter word in the English language – it's a "WRAP."

The film was eventually released under three different titles, in three dubbed language versions, and in varying lengths, by various releasing companies.

Anyone watching the finished film, no matter which version, cannot help but notice Laurel metamorphosing from 165lb (11st 11lb) to 114lb (8st 2lb) – anyone, that is, who can bear to watch it through.

Before they went to France, Laurel and Hardy had had an offer to star in the RKO picture "*Two Tickets To Broadway.*" However, because of the interminable length of time "*Atoll K*" had taken to complete, their parts had been given to another comedy double-act. And so "*Two Tickets To Broadway*" became, instead, the final film of the vaudeville act 'Smith and Dale.'

In February 1951, while Stan and Babe were still shooting "*Atoll K,*" there had been a deal pending for them to go to Australia to make another film, as soon as they were free. But, by now, all they wanted to make was THEIR BED, and to lie in it for several months.

The Boys had come to France expecting to spend just twelve weeks there. This had turned into twelve MONTHS – twelve months of sheer torture. Laurel wasn't going to extend it by one more day than was absolutely necessary. He and Ida left France on 17 April, aboard the *RMS Queen Elizabeth*, and sailed for home. The Hardys, meanwhile, were happy to stay on for a short holiday, finally departing from Belgium on 23 April 1951, aboard the *MS Washington*.

From now on the stage would be the only medium in which Laurel and Hardy were to work. On the film-making front, they had made the final cut.

o-o-0-o-o

CHAPTER 34

PROMISES, PROMISES
(1951 pt2 – 1953 pt1)

If Laurel hadn't yet come to terms with his film career having ended, then the first event he attended, less than two weeks after getting home, would almost certainly have driven it home to him:

OLD TIMERS OF SCREEN PAID TRIBUTE

Film greats of the day-before-yesterday gathered last night [8 May 1951] at a movie paying them tribute. In a ceremony under the auspices of the Hollywood Chamber of Commerce, cinema stars who reigned years ago received homage at the Academy Award Theater.

Jack Benny was master of ceremonies for the salute to the former stars. Among those honoured were Betty Blythe, Francis X. Bushman, Chester Conklin, Heine Conklin, Pauline Garon, Julia Faye, William Farnum, Helen Gibson, Stan Laurel, Elmo Lincoln, Hank Mann, Mae Murray, Eddie Polo, Herbert Rawlinson, and Mack Sennett. John B. Kingsley, president of the Hollywood Chamber, and Ronald Reagan, president of the Screen Actors Guild, also took part in the ceremony.

The movie immortals, who played important parts in the birth and growth of a giant industry, were issued citations "For your help in making Hollywood the film capital of the world."

A greeting committee of today's young stars and starlets, including Julia Adams, Tony Curtis and Piper Laurie, escorted the old timers to the special premiere of the film "Hollywood Story," at the Academy Theater.

(Associated Press – 9 May 1951)

["*Hollywood Story*" was a 'Universal-International' fictional feature film, which a bunch of silent stars had been suckered into appearing in. Laurel was not one of them.]

But retirement wasn't on Laurel's mind just yet. Only three weeks later came a report that Laurel and Hardy would be touring again soon.

Come September, Laurel and Hardy return to Europe to star in a revue that will tour the principal cities of Italy. These zanies are so popular in Italy that their old hit "Fra Diavolo," is in its third month at a movie house in Rome.

(2 June 1951)

On 2 June 1951 *Boxoffice* announced:

It is rumoured that Laurel and Hardy may come to Australia soon to make a film. A representative of the comedy team has been in contact with principals here, and the only matter to be finalized is that of finances.

It is hard to believe that Stan and Babe would even want to consider going to make a film in Australia, so soon after the traumatic experience of their year in France. In a letter to Betty Healy, Laurel speaks only of projects a little closer to home:

```
                                                 June 20th. '51
Expect to leave for Italy - France & Spain for a years run
in a Revue about Sept - if the War business does'nt upset
our plans.

                                   Stan
```

[Laurel may be referring to the 1951 strikes in Spain, which started in Barcelona then spread throughout other cities, including Madrid, causing civil unrest.]

295

When Stan next wrote to Betty, he had just returned home following a couple of days in hospital. One newspaper reported he had gone in for major surgery; but he was quick to put in a retraction that he had gone in only for a check-up, and everything was OK. This was great news, as offers for work were coming in from different media.

Firstly, Stan and Babe went into talks with Hal Roach, Jr. about a profit-sharing TV deal; then, according to the *New York Times:*

> Offers are piling up for this unique and beloved team—offers for TV series, for an Italian stage revue, a Japanese cinema; for their life story in a Billy Wilder movie. Hollywood or no Hollywood, the world is not likely to let this Silver anniversary pass unnoticed.
>
> (8 July 1951)

Come September there was still no word on the Roach TV deal, when in came yet another idea for a film:

> Jerry Wald and Norman Krasna are concluding a deal that will bring Stan Laurel and Oliver Hardy back to the screen after an absence of six years.
>
> The picture will be the forthcoming RKO Radio, Technicolor musical, "The Girls Have Landed," which stars Tony Martin.
>
> Veterans of many USO tours, Laurel and Hardy will fit aptly into the cast of "The Girls Have Landed," the story of the USO in World War II.
>
> (7 October 1951)

This was yet one more film which seems never to have got past the planning stage. However, the possibility of doing TV shows was still simmering. Because some of the fifty-two films Hal Roach had sold to the TV network were now regularly being screened on television, the audiences who had missed them first time around on cinema release were clamouring for more. The Boys' old friend, Hollywood columnist Erskine Johnson, interviewed them on the subject:

> For the first time in five years Stan Laurel and Oliver Hardy will be on your neighbourhood theatre screens this winter in a feature comedy, "Atoll K." And they're being deluged with TV offers.
>
> "A whole new generation of kids have discovered us," Hardy beamed.
>
> There are no big casts and no big flossy production numbers in the blueprints for new Laurel and Hardy comedies, whether they are for TV or movie theatres.
>
> "It will be the same situation comedy," Hardy made it clear, "with one set and no more than three other actors in the cast. We have to be together. Split us up and put us with other people and we're gone. Everything that happens to us happens in a little corner.
>
> "Laurel, as usual, will be supervising and helping us write the scripts.
>
> "We've been accused of being temperamental because we want to supervise our own stuff," Hardy let it fly. "Well, that's not true. We know just what's right for us.
>
> "We refused to do a picture for a certain producer at Fox. He called us to his office and said:
>
> "'Sit down, boys, and tell me what you don't like in the script.'
>
> "We asked him, 'Have you read it?'
>
> "He replied:
>
> "'Well, no, I've been a busy man lately.'
>
> "That's when we quit. How can you do a movie when the producer hasn't even read the script?"
>
> (16 November 1951) [Abridged]

But it wasn't only TV in the U.S. which wanted Laurel and Hardy. According to a letter written by Stan, interest was coming in from the U.K.

Promises, Promises

```
My Dear Betty:-                          December 6th. '51
Glad to tell you, I never felt better, I now weigh 149 and
look like my old self again & expect to leave for England
in February for personal appearances also Television shorts
over there. Needless to tell you I can't wait to get back
in harness again. To be very frank I never thought I would,
last year at this time I weighed only 110 lbs. I shall know
definitely next week re the trip so of course will let you
know. Well Betty, will close now. Am busy digging up a new
act to take over, know you understand.
```

Eleven days later, the details were confirmed:

```
Dear Betty:                              December 17th. '51
We are leaving for England end of January, due in London
Feb. 3rd. so as you can imagine I am up to my neck in
preparation, a million & one things to do.
Yes, Babe is going too. Our name L&H is magic over there,
it's amazing after all these years, they don't even want to
remember you over here.
```

It is quite understandable, therefore, why Laurel and Hardy were off to England, to begin a six-month tour of variety theatres. The other one-hundred-and-one offers they had been made over the last seven years would have to wait until they got back.

Accompanying Stan and Babe on the 1952 British Tour were their wives – Ida and Lucille. Here they are at Los Angeles Union Station (23 January 1952) about to catch the train for New York, where they will board the *Queen Mary*.

1952 January 20 (circa)
        LOS ANGELES, California to NEW YORK, New York 🚂 2,814 miles
1952 January 23   Queen Mary sails for England

LAUREL and HARDY – The U.S. Tours

When Laurel and Hardy disembarked at Southampton, on 28 January 1952, they were entering a different Britain from the one they had experienced in 1947. The biggest change for them would be the decline in popularity of variety shows, with theatres around the U.K. struggling to fill seats. Laurel and Hardy were still idolised as screen comics but, as it was twelve years since they had made anything resembling a decent film, they had lost a whole generation of prospective new fans. Having their films shown on television would have popularised them with the youngster who had missed the cinema releases; but, in Britain, the purchase of TVs was limited to the very rich. At £110 a set, one can see why.

However, every faith remained with Laurel & Hardy's box-office appeal, and Bernard Delfont had booked them back on the No.1 circuit – namely, the Moss Empire theatres at Glasgow, Newcastle, Edinburgh, and Liverpool, with the addition of those at Sunderland, Nottingham, Leeds, Sheffield, and Swansea; plus the Hippodromes at Birmingham, Dudley, Bristol, and Coventry. Out were the seaside resorts of Morecambe, Blackpool, Skegness, and Margate; but in came Brighton, Southend, and Southport.

In the provinces would be a return to the city of Manchester, but the rest of the venues would involve first-time visits to Peterborough, Hanley, Shrewsbury, Bradford, Sutton, Southampton, and Portsmouth. Wales was represented with dates in Rhyl, Cardiff, and Swansea; and so too were Northern and Southern Ireland, with weeks in Belfast and Dublin.

There were however no bookings in London theatres, even though Laurel and Hardy had done exceptionally good business in London in 1947. Babe explained this away, to one reporter, as though it had been a matter of personal choice:

> "We both like the provincial theatres. It is here where our act is best appreciated – especially by the children."

The shows were the same format as those in 1947, with six to eight support acts which would include a mix of dancers, a juggler, a cartoonist, a ventriloquist, acrobats, a magician, musicians, and even a comedy impressionist. The *"Driver's Licence"* sketch had been replaced with a new one penned by Stan, *"A Spot of Trouble,"* the premise of which was taken from their 1929 film *"Night Owls."*

Reviews of the sketch were mixed. The *Birmingham Evening Despatch* opined:

The sketch in which Laurel and Hardy appear is woefully thin, but what of it? The old, odd antics are still there, although perhaps less exuberant than in the old days.

Whereas the *Coventry Standard* could not have given more praise:

I salute these masters for reducing their audience to the point of near-hysteria simply by exploiting absurdities; and for leaving us limp with laughter, but refreshed.

But the *Dublin Times* summed it up best in the first two lines of their review:

What Laurel & Hardy have to say to each other doesn't really matter. They merely have to appear on stage, and the house rocks, shrieks and hoots with laughter.

Breaking into the Chief of Police's house lands them in:
"A SPOT OF TROUBLE" — (1952 British Tour)

Promises, Promises

It was hinted that the tour might be extended into December, so that Stan and Babe could do a Christmas pantomime, but the reason this fell through was explained in a later interview.

Double Tax Sends Stan & Ollie

Stan & Ollie were asked to stay to do a pantomime, but if they had done so they would have had to pay tax here as well as in America. As Stan put it, 'We would have owed ourselves money.' But they are coming back next year for a longer visit and hope to do a pantomime then.

(Portsmouth *Evening News – 1952)*

Stan treated it all philosophically. In a letter to fellow English comedian Stan Anniston, he wrote:

```
                                              Aug. 19th. '52
We sail back to the States again Oct 8th "Queen Elizebeth"
so only have six more weeks to play. Really hate to leave,
but have to on account of Tax situation - Understand if we
don't return here till Oct 1953 - we can stay a whole year.
So all being well, we intend to do that - except if we
don't get tied up in TV. Anyway a good rest won't do me any
harm & will give me plenty of time to prepare another act.
```

-----0-----

1952 October 08   Queen Elizabeth sails for New York.
1952 October 15

NEW YORK, New York to LOS ANGELES, California 2,814 miles

-----0-----

It had been a totally exhausting tour, and neither Stan nor Babe was getting any younger. All doors now seemed to have closed and, as they sailed home, they must have felt that spending the rest of their days "behind closed doors" was a real possibility.

The tour hadn't served any purpose in securing work, but it had achieved its number-one aim of earning the former screen comedians some urgently needed cash to pay off at least some of their American creditors.

Hopefully, when Stan and Babe got home there would be viable offers of work which would help them to continuing doing just that.

In September 1952, while the Boys were still playing theatres in Britain, word had come through that, as soon as they returned home, they would resume talks with the Hal Roach Studios about a TV show. But, in the first four months after doing so, only three offers came in. None were from Roach.

The first, revealed in a newspaper column, was for a film:

George Pal tells us that he still has the film version of "Tom Thumb" on his schedule. He's already tested a boy for the title role and made him pint-size by trick photography. Stan Laurel and Oliver Hardy, just back from a long tour of Europe, will likely play the two thieves who kidnap Tom and endeavour to enlist him in their life of crime. The story will stick very closely to the original fairy tale.

(23 October 1952)

This is one of the rare instances when a film offered to Laurel and Hardy was actually made. Sorry to say, when it was finally made, in 1958, it came too late for our comedy heroes; but two other comedy heroes did justice to the parts – namely Terry-Thomas and Peter Sellers.

The next offer was to play in a nightclub, as told to us by Mr. Laurel:

```
                                              Nov. 17th. '52
Dear Betty:-
We have been contacted again to play the SAHARA in Las
Vegas, but don't think we could manage with our scenery
```

etc. Stage isn't big enough - but may take a trip there &
look it over. Anyway I don't intend to do anything till
after New Year.

-----0-----

1952 November 18 (Tuesday)
      SANTA MONICA, California to **LAS VEGAS**, Nevada   275 miles

1952 November 19 (Wednesday)
      LAS VEGAS, Nevada to **SANTA MONICA**, California to   275 miles

-----0-----

Here is what Laurel had to say after his reconnaissance trip: (Nov. 29th. 52)

Dear Betty:-

I went to las Vegas a week ago last Tuesday & came back
next day. A quick trip to see the place & find out re size
of stage etc. Too small & no facilities to hang scenery -
so impossible for us to play there with this act. They want
us to put on a new act - more suitable for night clubs
where we wouldn't require a lot of scenery & props. Am not
too enthusiastic about it - especially that type of
audiences. Anyway, I can't be bothered right now.

   Just had an offer to go to the Malay States - Singapore -
Hong Kong etc. & Japan & Bankok (Siam) which sounds
interesting - but will have to do a pantomime act to avoid
language difficulties. We have a terrific following in
these places & they are anxious for us to open next March -
we are checking now re getting Dollars out. Will let you
know if anything develops.

                                                 Stan

The third offer, again revealed in a gossip column, was for the Boys to appear in a play:

"Omnibus" got a turn down last week from a pair of famous comics, Stan Laurel and Oliver Hardy. They were offered roles in an upcoming play by Bill Saroyan, but they figured it was too highbrow for their brand of foolery.

It's too bad that Stan and Ollie felt this way, because, in the opinion of many viewers, "Omnibus" could stand a dash of what some critics label as lowbrow comedy.

Both of these veteran funnymen say they won't do a regular video show until the medium can afford them. They want a budget which will allow them to come up with the quality they attained in those old two-reelers which are being seen on TV now, and which don't bring them a penny.

[William Saroyan was a prolific playwright. So much so that he was featured on two stamps – one in the U.S.A. and one in Russia. One of his plays, "*The Oyster and the Pearl*," was televised in 1953, so <u>may have been</u> the one offered to Laurel and Hardy.]

So, after turning down work in the last three media, Stan began to focus his attention on a fourth – that of returning to the variety stage:

                                             February 4th. '53

Dear Ed [Patterson]-

No, we are not making any film at present - just busy
taking it easy. We have offers to play in Tokio for eight
weeks also a tour of Australia & Panto at the Opera House
in Belfast this next Xmas for a 10 week run "Babes In The
Wood" & of course a tour in Variety to follow in England
again, but nothing definite to date.

                                                 Stan

Ida Laurel – pleased to have her man at home with her.
[1111 Franklin Avenue]

Three weeks earlier, columnist Hal Humphrey had interviewed Stan and Babe regarding their views and hopes for TV work. After the two of them had expressed a philosophical resignation to not getting a cent for their films being shown on TV, Hardy added: *"There's one blessing. It certainly keeps us alive with the public."*

Reservations about making new films for TV were then expressed:

> Stan has always written most of the material for everything they did. This is one of the reasons they've turned down offers from NBC to do those "Comedy Hour" and "All Star Revue" shows.
>
> "This may sound immodest, but we can't learn anything from those TV guys today," Ollie explained. "Most of them are writing stuff we did 20 years ago. Stan knows our characters, and what we can do, but we know those TV guys wouldn't let us do it our way."
>
> Stan and Ollie have another problem. When they do go into TV today they've got to compete with themselves. If their "live" appearances aren't as good as the old films the viewers are watching, they're finished!

(13 January 1953)

So how would Stan and Babe react when, at the end of February, an offer to make TV shows with Roach was re-submitted to them?

> Stan Laurel and Oliver Hardy in a new series of comedies filmed especially for television may be the next big video announcement from Hollywood. Hal Roach Sr., who produced the original series in the 30s, has made the offer, and the comics are thinking it over.

(28 February 1953)

They obviously didn't think it over for very long as, over the next six weeks, all their plans were for playing theatre dates overseas, as Stan confirms in this letter:

> April 25th. '53
>
> My Dear Betty:-
> I am feeling lots better, & getting the urge to get moving again. We are either going to England or Australia this year or maybe both, arrangements not completed as yet, but will be, pretty soon now, so am busy preparing a new act.

> The picture bus. is in uproar with the 3rd. dimension medium., studios are closed down for a few months as they are not sure which way to go, so of course there are a million & One actors idle. TV seems to be slowing down too, a lot of Sponsors are cutting out the big expensive shows as they will soon be able to get a backlog of old but good pictures from the studios, so they won't have to pay for actors or bother with productions & will be much cheaper, so things do'nt look too bright in Hollywood for a lot of Thespians. It's lucky we are able to go abroad & not be affected.

In the same letter, Stan revealed a recent social event he had attended:

> April 25th. '53
>
> My Dear Betty:-
>
> The Masquers Club gave a dinner for Louella Parsons last Thursday night [23 April], it was quite an affair. I met Shemp Howard, but did'nt get a chance to talk to him very much, I think he re-joined the Stooges again, do'nt know what they are doing right now.

[Betty Healy was the former wife of Ted Healy, who formed an act called 'Ted Healy and his Stooges,' from which 'Curly, Larry, and Moe' defected, and went on to became the film trio 'The Three Stooges."]

Come June, the only talk of TV was regarding the televising of the Coronation of Queen Elizabeth II. Meanwhile, Laurel was still preparing for an overseas tour:

> June 4th. '53
>
> My Dear Betty:-
>
> The Australian trip has been postponed, we will have to wait till the Tax situation is cleared up or no use of us going. So now its back to England for a year & maybe by that time things will get straightened out for Australia. We open in London for eight weeks in Oct. then tour the provinces again.
>
> I am busy trying to work out a new act, have a rough idea. If it does'nt pan out, I'll have to shake my head again.

A letter sent five weeks later to a friend in Liverpool, covered the same topic:

> July 10th. '53
>
> My Dear Jock [Weaver]:-
>
> We are returning to England again sometime in September, so will probably sail on one of the "QUEENS"
>
> Glad to tell you I am feeling much better in the health dept. gained back a lot of weight & all ready to GO again. The nice long rest did wonders for me.
>
> *Stan*

Just seven weeks later, Stan did "go again." Disappointed and disillusioned by the failure of the networks to offer them TV work, he and Hardy packed their trunks and went to join the circus ... sorry! ... went to play British variety theatres.

o-o-0-o-o

CHAPTER 35
THE LAST STAGE
(1953 pt2 – 1954)

1953 August 30 (*circa*)
        LOS ANGELES, California to NEW YORK, New York 2,814 miles

1953 Sept 02   *SS America* sets sail. -----0-----

The Hardys and the Laurels posing on the deck of SS *America*.
(The strange-looking ship's wheel is just the photographer's artwork.)

Oliver Hardy's work permit prohibited him from setting foot on British soil until a year after he had left, which meant not before 9 October 1953. To get around this the Hardys and the Laurels landed at Cobh, in Southern Ireland.

The party spent the next five weeks at the Royal Marine Hotel, in Dun Laoghaire, near Dublin. There, Stan dedicated most of his time to writing and rewriting the new sketch "*Birds of a Feather*" – before bringing over the other three cast members to rehearse it.

Why Laurel didn't write the sketch before leaving California, then all the party simply sail directly to England in October, is puzzling to say the least. One presumes there was a good reason.

The basic plot for "*Birds of a Feather*" is as follows:

> The two friends meet outside a public house. Stan informs Ollie of a vacancy which might suit them. The job entails tasting whisky, with the incentive seeming to be: "the more you drink, the more you earn." They take the job, but strive a little too keenly to fulfil demands, with the result that Ollie ends up in hospital after launching himself through an open window, in an effort to fly.
>
> With the introduction of a doctor, a nurse, and an undertaker, mix-ups occur over just who is the patient, and who is the visitor. Confusion is increased by the presence of some eggs in Ollie's bedside cabinet which Stanley brought for Ollie, but which the nursing-staff think were laid *by* Ollie. The sketch ends with Laurel and Hardy walking around clucking like hens, after being fed bird seed. The pandemonium is added to when the doctor opens the bedside cabinet doors and two pigeons fly out.
>
> The two comedians then come front-of-tabs and sing "*Trail of the Lonesome Pine*" (from their film *Way Out West*), before saying their customary "Goodnight."

Ollie and Stan in the hospital scene in "*Birds of a Feather*."

["*Birds of a Feather*" is quoted by many as having been based on the Laurel & Hardy film "*County Hospital.*" In both, Stan goes to visit Ollie in hospital, but there any similarity ends.]

From Ireland it was a short sail to England, and then a rail journey to London where they would begin to publicise the tour. This would normally have been done solely by newspaper articles, and public appearances, but now they had the advantage of technology which would project them right into the living room of hundreds of thousands of people around Britain. And so, on Saturday 17 October 1953 Stan Laurel and Oliver Hardy made their first ever (known) live appearance on television.

When Stan and Babe had been in England the previous year, few working-class homes had a TV set; but the live broadcast of the Coronation of Queen Elizabeth II had acted as the catalyst in TV sets being manufactured at a more affordable price. In the U.S., television broadcasting had been established for a few years; which, as we know, led to Laurel & Hardy being discovered by a whole new generation. But in America, even their newly found popularity had not resulted in any work.

Here in England, the two comedians had always remained popular, even without TV exposure, but now the very medium used to promote live theatre was the one that was also killing it, as people were staying at home to watch television. The use of TV exposure was truly a case of, "You're damned if you do, and you're damned if you don't."

But the two Hollywood stars still had the full backing of the theatres, and were re-engaged at the Empire theatres in Glasgow, Edinburgh, Newcastle, Liverpool, Sunderland, Nottingham, Leeds, and Sheffield; the Hippodromes in Birmingham and Brighton; plus Portsmouth Royal, and Bradford Alhambra. They were even about to make a return to London, with dates at Finsbury Park Empire, Chiswick Empire, and Brixton Empress.

However, because Laurel and Hardy had missed the 1953 summer season, and would be leaving before the 1954 one, Bernard Delfont, their British agent, had had to put them into theatres he would not otherwise have considered. These were the Hippodromes at Manchester, Wolverhampton, Norwich, and Aston; the Palace theatres at Hull, Grimsby, and Plymouth; plus Carlisle Her Majesty's and Northampton New –theatres which were run-down and/or never did good business.

The Last Stage

Stan and Babe were going to need all their mental and physical health, combined with popularity and box-office draw, to make this tour a success – but the odds were stacked against them. Not only was Variety on its last legs, but so too were the two comedians.

The tour started off well in the town of Northampton. Of the opening night, one review read:

> Laurel & Hardy had a warm reception from an audience that was strangely mixed. There were adults who had rocked at Stan and Ollie when the films were literally the 'flicks'. Secondly, there were the children – before the curtain it was almost like a panto matinee – whose acquaintance probably dated from the time the family TV set was installed.
>
> Nostalgia, and a love for a comedy couple re-born – ironically by a medium the experts say will one day kill the stage – these were two main ingredients in the Laurel & Hardy success. But that was certainly not all. There was for the discerning the pleasure of watching two masters of their craft at work.
>
> <div align="right">(<i>Northampton Chronicle & Echo</i>)</div>

Some weeks later, after a visit to his beloved North East, Laurel wrote:

> The bus. [business] was shocking in Sunderland - Worst week of our tour - The audiences were blasé, - so a miserable week was had by all.

The Manager's Report Form echoed Stan's claims:

> Well received. They are working well indeed, and their material is much stronger than on their previous visit here, but, even so, they are not going more than well in any part of the house, and their ability to attract has greatly diminished.

One bright moment on the tour was Babe's 62nd birthday party, attended by the whole company (18 January 1954, Portsmouth). But the advancing years weren't being kind.

The Boys struggled on though bad houses and bad illness, until it all came to a dead-stop. On the second night of their week in Plymouth, Hardy was unable to appear, having suffered a mild heart attack, complicated with pneumonia. It was hoped he would recover to complete the tour, but the devastating truth was – Laurel and Hardy had played their last ever performance.

Stan and Babe had worked so hard, and gone through so much misery in trying not to disappoint their fans, but in the end it was their bodies and not their spirit which let them down, and forced them to curtail the tour. And so, on 3 June 1954, the former stage and screen legends boarded the merchant vessel the *Manchuria,* bound for Los Angeles – and retirement.

Lifeboat drill on board the *Manchuria*.
(With kind permission of John Peterson
Courtesy of the DPI)

-----0-----

1954 June 03

MV Manchuria sets sail from Hull, bound for Vancouver – via Los Angeles.

-----0-----

With no films or public appearances being made, and with both their wives not breaking the law, or taking them to court, Stan Laurel and Oliver Hardy's lives were now no longer covered by newspaper articles. Luckily for Laurel and Hardy scholars, one man who knew them better than any other stepped forward and documented all their later years in detail. His name – STAN LAUREL.

Stan had always religiously replied to fan mail but, now that he had more time on his hands, and there was peace in his home, his rate of letter-writing increased dramatically – and not just to fans, but to friends and former work colleagues. So, where applicable, we will let the man himself inform us what was going on during those quiet times – starting with:

```
We arrived back home June 26th. Am glad to be back to take
a rest for a while.

We sailed from Hull Eng. June 3rd. on a Danish Cargo ship,
the voyage took 23 days, stopped in at St. Thomas (Virgin
Islands) Curaco Christobal & through the Panama Canal it
was very interesting, especially the Canal.

The accommodations were very nice - good food & calm sea
all the way, I really prefer traveling this way as you
do'nt have to dress up for meals etc. as you do on the big
passenger ships.
```

```
There was only 10 passengers (12 is the limit they carry)
so its practically like being on a private yacht.
```

Back in March, a press announcement had come out claiming that the comedy duo were about to make films for U.S. television, upon their return to California:

> Stan Laurel and Oliver Hardy are planning to make their screen comeback in a television series for Hal Roach. He plans to re-team the comics because of the popularity of the revival of their old films on television. They weren't interested a year ago.

The Last Stage

Stan then substantiated the plans, in a letter to a friend in England:

```
                                              March 12th. '54
Dear Leslie Link:-
Doubt if we will make any more Cinema Pictures as the TV in
the States is the most important now - especially for
comedians, so we shall be making short subjects for that
medium, which of course - in time will be seen over here.
                      Stan
```

During the first four weeks back in California, it would seem that L&H were getting ever closer to finally brokering a deal with Roach, following the public's renewed interest in them.

> About three years ago Hal Roach, Jr., one of Hollywood's leading on-film TV producers, released 52 old two-reelers featuring the near-ancient comedy team of Laurel and Hardy. The response was tremendous. A new generation went wild over the old comedy team, and the oldsters accepted them once more.
>
> So enthusiastic has the welcome become that Roach is going to sign his "new finds" to long-term contracts. All of which is not too bad considering Stan Laurel is now a youngster of 64 and his robust partner is 62.
>
> Roach has several plans in mind for the duo. Foremost is a weekly show tentatively titled "Cavalcade of Fun." It would be a 60-minute affair in which a dozen name comedians would be featured. The leading members of the cast would be Laurel and Hardy.
>
> According to Roach, the entire project will get going as soon as Hardy feels well enough to begin work. The plump comic is reported to have had a bad attack of pneumonia during a European tour. "He may need a few weeks to build back his strength," Roach declared.
>
> Incidentally, the "rookies" will be making something in the neighbourhood of $2,500 a week when they return to work.
>
> (Robert L. Sokolsky – 23 July 1954) [Abridged]

From a letter written by Laurel in March 1956, it would appear that, around two years earlier, a private approach had been made to him for Laurel and Hardy to make a TV series with the team responsible for the Buster Keaton TV shows:

```
                                              March 20th. '56
Dear Jack:-
Clyde Bruckman (who directed "Battle of the Century")
committed suicide a couple of years ago, poor guy. He came
to see me a few months before this, he was directing Buster
Keaton in some TV shorts at the time & was trying to get us
to make a series to alternate with Buster.
```

Bruckman committed suicide on 4 January 1955. He shot himself with a gun he had borrowed from Buster Keaton, after telling Keaton he wanted it to go hunting. There seems to be no evidence to back up Stan's belief that Bruckman was directing the Buster Keaton TV shows. Bruckman had indeed been a director, and among his credits were three Laurel & Hardy silent films: "*The Battle of the Century*" (1927), "*Leave 'Em Laughing*" (1928), and "*The Finishing Touch*" (1928). His last picture as director was 1935, after which he had turned to writing. However, during the last six years of his life his only credited work was as writer on eight Jules White films.

It may be that Bruckman had wanted to ingratiate himself with the Keaton production team, by bringing them the heads of Stan Laurel and Oliver Hardy, in the hope of getting a writing job, or even directing. Either way, his plan didn't work and he died penniless – unable even to leave money for his funeral arrangements.

In September 1954 Laurel wrote:

```
Hardy is feeling better, & we have several offers on hand
to make TV films also a deal to make a picture in London,
which would be in February next. I doubt if we shall come
over for anymore Variety tours as Hardy prefers film work,
doesn't like the traveling every week.
```

Laurel and Hardy's next appearance was not on the big screen, nor even on the small screen, but at the opening of a new shop:

Nov. 9th '54

```
My Dear Betty:-
My son-in-law Rand Brooks has just opened a Western Store.
It is quite attractive & think he will do very well.
Enclosed is our invitation card to the opening. They had
quite a celebration.
```

HOWDY PARTNER
Rand Brooks meets his father-in-law and partner.

HOWDY PARTNERS
In costume for the opening of
Rand Brook's western store

Rand Brooks was a TV cowboy, known for his role of 'Lucky Jenkins' in the 1952-54 "*Hopalong Cassidy*" series, and later as 'Randy Boone' in the third season of "*The Adventures of Rin Tin Tin*" (1956-57).

This was to be Stan and Babe's last-ever public engagement

Laurel's next letter to Betty Healy was regarding Laurel and Hardy being the recent subjects on Ralph Edwards' "This Is Your Life," (1 December 1954):

Dec. 7th. 54

My Dear Betty:-

Thanks for the compliments on our TV appearance - frankly I was shocked & embarrassed, being put on the spot totally unprepared - I still havent gotten over it.

I appreciated the honor bestowed, but sincerely wished it had never happened - I felt like 5 million viewers were saying "So what"!! seemed like a nightmare.

I enjoyed seeing some of the old gang again after the show, had a lovely party at the Roosevelt Hotel.

The way Stan and Babe were tricked into appearing on "*This Is Your Life*" is as follows: First part was to fly Bernard Delfont – the man who had booked them for their three post-war British Tours – from London to Los Angeles. Delfont was then primed to telephone the two comedians, tell them he was in Los Angeles for just one night, and ask would they like to come and meet him at the Knickerbocker Hotel. The ruse worked and, as the three old friends were reminiscing about the British Tours, the camera crew came out of a side-room and surprised them; accompanied by a voice-over from Ralph Edwards informing them: "Stan Laurel, Oliver Hardy – these are your lives." **[FILM]**

The Last Stage

The two ageing comedians then had to make their way over to the TV studio, to have their history revealed to the viewing millions. In the seemingly interminable time it took Stan and Babe to arrive, TV host Ralph Edwards did some cringe-worthy ad-libbing. Things didn't improve when the Boys did arrive, as Edwards struggled to call them by their correct names, and then at times spoke to them as if they were senile.

There were quite a few embarrassing blank pauses, when Stan and Babe failed to recognise some of the guests from the customary backstage voice-overs. In fact, a few weren't even recognised when they showed their faces. Also, the accuracy of at least three of the stories told by guests was very questionable, as they seemed to contain gross exaggeration – to say the least. One guest claimed that, during filming on "*Liberty*," Hardy fell twenty feet, then a further twenty feet, on to and through a safety platform (built on the framework of girders where they filmed the main scenes). A second claimed Laurel was almost killed by a bull; and a third claimed they were BOTH nearly killed by a lion. Other stories went the opposite way, in that they had no punchline at all.

Both Stan and Babe forced polite smiles in the right places, but were obviously ill at ease and embarrassed throughout the whole proceedings – hence Stan's unappreciative comments.

Host Ralph Edwards (left) handing out presents to Ida and Lucille, at the end of "*This Is Your Life*." Far right is Bernard Delfont.

Ralph Edwards' Company redeemed themselves to some extent, with one of their post-show presents. They had had an impressive plaque made up, with a fine dedication on it, which was then put on display on the Roach Lot.

It was more than fourteen years since the Boys had worked at the Hal Roach Studios, but the man himself, although conspicuous by his absence on the TV show, turned up there for the dedication ceremony.

Stan had been filled with utter disappointment that, after all these years of struggling and fighting to get onto American TV, the only appearance they had made was the "*This Is Your Life*" debacle – and FOR FREE! But at least it had resulted in the Boys reuniting with Hal Roach.

LAKE LAUREL AND HARDY
SO NAMED
BECAUSE THESE TWO
WORLD-FAMOUS COMEDIANS
WERE FIRST TEAMED HERE AT
THE HAL ROACH STUDIOS
AND BECAUSE THEY,
MORE THAN OTHERS,
WERE IN AND OUT OF
THESE WATERS.
"THIS IS YOUR LIFE"
DECEMBER 1, 1954

Left: Hal Roach Jun., and right: Hal Roach – who, all those years on, honoured the two stars who had put the studios on the world map.

Two other people who deserved to be honoured are: MRS. Laurel and MRS. Hardy – pictured here.

Ida Laurel and Lucille Hardy were always by their husbands' side; and it can be said with confidence that, had they not accompanied the Boys on their three post-war British Tours, the two comedians would not have lasted as long as they did.

Although further tours were unlikely to ever happen, there was still an outside chance that Laurel and Hardy would get to make their own TV shows as, four weeks earlier, it had been announced that:

> Stan Laurel and Oliver Hardy have agreed to NEW half-hour films for TV—if their agent can find a sponsor.

(5 November 1954)

Now all we have to do is hope that a sponsor is found before all the sand runs out of the two old-timers!

o-o-0-o-o

CHAPTER 36

A MAN OF LETTERS

(1955 onwards)

A picture may paint a thousand words, but Stan's typewriter wrote a thousand letters in one year alone. [That's an average of three a day – EVERY day.]

Three weeks into the new year, negotiations were still on for Laurel and Hardy to make films for TV, with Roach:

My Dear Betty: Jan. 21st. 55

We are negotiating with Hal Roach Jr to make four one-hour films for TV & with added footage to be released abroad in the theatres. We have a meeting tomorrow at the Studio & it looks like we may close the deal. However will let you know if anything happens.

Next to get some insider information was Ernie Murphy, who had continued his role as Laurel's secretary since his Roach years.

My Dear Ernie   Jan. 27th. 55 :

Dont faint - we are negotiating with Hal Roach Jr. for a picture deal - four one hour shows for TV which will also be released abroad in the cinema. They are to be costume period in color á la "Bohemian Girl" etc. (musical) Think it will work out this time as we dont have Roach Sr. to contend with & his "you know what I mean" stories - however will let you know if & when the deal is closed.

Meanwhile Erskine Johnson, Hollywood columnist, had obtained information from the other party: – (*NEA* – 28 January 1955)

Stan Laurel and Oliver Hardy are close to a big TV announcement—a return to the Hal Roach studio for a still hush-hush tele-film project. Hal Roach Jr. confirmed the news to me, admitting negotiations are in progress. But he would reveal only one clue—"It's an idea I have, but will not be a weekly series. That's all I can say until the papers are signed."

Five weeks on, after being so excited when he had first told Betty Healy of the possible deal with Roach, Laurel was definitely downbeat:

LAUREL and HARDY – The U.S. Tours

Feb. 28th. '55

My Dear Betty:-

Sorry delay in reply to your previous letter, which was due to my waiting to be able to give you some news on the Roach deal. However, nothing has developed as yet, have'nt heard a word further since I last wrote you about it, seems strange, especially as young Hal was so very enthusiastic. Anyway, if nothing comes of it, it wo'nt break my heart by any means.

-----0-----

It would seem, therefore that, in Erskine Johnson's next article, he was peddling old news:

> It looks like the first hour-long filmed features for TV will be made by Stan Laurel and Oliver Hardy, under the production banner of Hal Roach Jr. As tipped here, talks have been going on between Roach and the comedians for weeks. The blueprint calls for six features to be made over a one-year period. Then, the footage will be re-edited into two feature-length pictures for European theatre showings.
>
> (*NEA* – 2 March 1955)

In mid-April, Stan was well enough to attend a social evening, with some of his peers:

> The Masquers, Monday night [18 April] presented its George Spelvin Award to George Gobel "for his great contribution to entertainment."
>
> In a rare tribute, many of show business' old-timers honoured and ribbed Gobel in four hours of speechmaking.
>
> Art Linkletter was roastmaster at the dinner, and among those who roasted Gobel were Leon Ames, Gene Autry, Preston Foster, Joe Frisco, Jack Haley, Don Hartman, Alan Mowbray, Pat O'Brien, Edgar Bergen, Walter Brennan, Wally Ford, and Rhys Williams.
>
> In the audience were many more great old-time names, including Stan Laurel and silent screen star Jack Mulhall.
>
> (James Bacon (*AP*) – 19 April 1955)

A few weeks later, it would seem that the premise of the first Laurel & Hardy TV film had actually been decided upon:

> The first hour-long film for TV, starring Stan Laurel and Oliver Hardy, goes before Hal Roach Jr.'s camera as soon as Stan puts finishing touches on his own script. The plot has them playing pilgrims.
>
> (Erskine Johnson (*NEA*) – 16 May 1955)

Again Erskine Johnson was peddling old news, as what he didn't know, and nor did Hal Roach for that matter, was that, at the time the article went out, Stan was in the middle of a lengthy stay in hospital.

June 6th. '55

My Dear Betty:-

Sorry so long in reply to yours of May 10th., when I got your letter, I was in the Glendale Sanitarium - was in there for three weeks - had a bad attack of high blood pressure with slight stroke on my left side. Have been home for a couple of weeks now & pleased to tell you I am up & able to get around again. I was certainly lucky, could have been very serious for me, anyway, the Dr. says I should be back to normal in a couple of months. This of course has delayed the Roach deal, altho' they know nothing of my illness, I do'nt want to make any commitment until I am in condition to go ahead with it. I am feeling OK, but still very weak & have to get my strength back.

A Man of Letters

But Laurel came out of the sanitarium still determined to make the Roach TV films, as told to an English cousin:

July 1st. '55

Dear Nellie [Bushby]:-
I had a stroke, my left leg & left arm was paralyzed for quite a while. As soon as I am ready & able, I have four feature films to make with Hardy, we are going back to our old Studio (Hal Roach) needless to tell you how happy I am - never thought I would ever work again.

Stan

It turns out the previous letter was written while Laurel was taking some rest and relaxation away from home – as was this next one:

July 2nd. '55

My Dear Betty:-
Am spending a week of two in La Jolla - lovely spot - but weather not so good - hope it will soon break & get some sunshine - its warm but very dull. Will write you on return home.

-----0-----

1955 June 24 (*circa*)
        SANTA MONICA, California to **LA JOLLA**, California 125 miles

1955 July 8 (*circa*)
        LA JOLLA, California to **SANTA MONICA**, California 125 miles

-----0-----

Having had a jolly holiday in La Jolla, Laurel wrote from his Santa Monica home:

July 14th. '55

My Dear Betty:-
I came back from La Jolla a week ago, apart from dull weather I enjoyed the change & I think it did me a bit of good - am walking better anyway - I ate out in restaurants so the exertion of getting in & out of the car etc. helped me a great deal - it was exercise for me.

Stan

-----0-----

In August, Erskine Johnson was still determined to print an exclusive on the Laurel & Hardy TV films:

> News item: "Stan Laurel and Oliver Hardy To Star in Two 90-Minute Color Films for NBC-TV." Remember?—you read it here months ago.
>
> (*NEA* – 15 August 1955)

But Johnson was again way behind time, as the following letters, written by Laurel to a fan, show:

Sep. 6th. '55

Dear Earl Shank Jr.:-
So sorry the long delay in reply to your very nice letter of last April 26th. Reason is, I took ill & went into hospital for several weeks & some of my mail got mislaid, & in clearing my desk this AM I just came across it.

Pleased to tell you my health has greatly improved & hope to be in good shape soon now to make some more films.

Stan

Laurel reiterated comments about the improvement in his health to Trixie Wyatt, a friend in England. Stan had first got to know her when the two of them were touring England in a juvenile pantomime company, in 1907, when she was still Trixie Knight.

```
                                           Sep. ??. '55
My Dear Trixie:-
Sorry dear so long in reply to you letters - fact is I have
been ill & spent several weeks in hospital taking
treatments for High blood pressure which had caused a
slight stroke of my left arm & leg & was not allowed to
attend to any correspondence however am back home again &
feeling better & able to get around a bit with a crutch.
Dr. says I shall be back to normal again in a few weeks.
I am of course very weak & taking exercises every day to
get my strength back. Not much more to tell you dear - Eda
sends love - she has had a trying time taking care of
everything & is working hard. I will write you again soon.
                      -----0-----
                                           Sep. ??. '55
Dear Trixie:-
Thank you Dear for your nice letter Aug. 29th. was pleased
to hear from you - I should have written you before this, &
intended to - but I have such a lot of unanswered mail that
it seems I will never get started on it & every day more
piles up on me. I think I shall finally have to get a
secretary in for a few days to help me clear up this
correspondence. Pleased to tell you I have improved a great
deal & feeling pretty good, but am still very weak from the
shock - I will be OK again as soon as I regain my strength.
```

When word of Stan and Babe making a film for TV did finally come in, it was not exactly the one they had been hoping for:

```
                                           Sep. ??. '55
Dear Trixie:-
On TV. (BBC) Oct 9th. the "Water Rats" are putting on a
show & we have been asked to make some film which will
appear on the show (about 3 or 4 minutes) so you might
possibly be seeing us again. We are going to try and Make
it & ship it over - I think we can manage to do it on time.
```

The "Grand Order of Water Rats," to give it its full title, is a British charitable organization made up of members drawn exclusively from show business, with many "Companion Members" from the U.S. Stan and Babe were made members of the Order, way back in March 1947, when they were in London.

```
Dear Trixie:-                              Sep. 30th. '55
No we are not coming to England. We made a bit of film here
yesterday which will be put into the Water Rats show on Oct
9th. B.B.C. TV. - hope you get a chance to see it, so you
can let us know how it turned out. We haven't seen it of
course so don't know how it looks.
```

Stan and Babe made their "bit of film" at Stan's home – 1111, Franklin Street, Santa Monica, California. Babe would have driven the twenty miles from his home in Van Nuys, in the heart of the San Fernando Valley, for the recording session.

[Puzzlingly, the Laurels' address changed from Franklin Avenue to Franklin Street, circa 1954.]

-----0-----

A Man of Letters

1955 September 29
        VAN NUYS, California to **SANTA MONICA**, California   20 miles

1955 September 29
        SANTA MONICA, California to **VAN NUYS**, California   20 miles

-----0-----

Filmed on 29 September, the clip was flown to London, and broadcast on 19 October [and NOT the 9th – as first scheduled], on a BBC live variety show, titled: "*This Is Music Hall.*" **[FILM]**

                                                                         Nov. 4th. '55

```
Dear Trixie:-
Glad you saw the "Water Rats" show on TV. & got a Kick out
of seeing us, even tho we didn't do anything — was pleased
to be in it. Hope we photographed alright without make-up —
wish I could have seen it, but it was made in a hurry — had
to be sent to London the same day.
                         Stan
```

-----0-----

Two more letters to friends in England followed. The first to North East comedian Vic Silver.

                                                                         Nov.12th. '55

```
My Dear Vic:-
Due to my recent illness I have'nt been doing much of late
- just resting & taking things easy till I'm fit & able
again - have four Feature films to make as soon as I get in
shape to work.
                         Stan
```

The second was to the variety artiste 'Lorraine' – whose act was as a cartoonist, assisted by his wife:

                                                                        Dec. 24th. '55

```
My Dear Jeanette & Lawrie:-
Both Babe and I have been on the sick list for several
months. On account of heart trouble Babe had to go on a
strict diet to reduce weight - lost about eight stone. Then
to make matters worse, I had a slight stroke (left arm &
leg paralyzed) & was in hospital several weeks for
treatment. However pleased to tell you I made a wonderful
recovery & am nearly back to normal again thank God.
I was very lucky indeed. We were preparing to make some new
pictures at our old studio (Hal Roach) when this thing
happened, so the deal had to be postponed till I am in
shape again - the Dr. figures I will be OK by April & will
be fully able to continue.
```

-----0-----

A week later Laurel informed a fan in Maryland of his continuing recovery:

                                                                         Jan. 3rd. '56

```
My Dear Earl Shank:-
Pleased to tell you I have improved a great deal, Dr.
thinks I shall be in shape to work again about next April.
Needless to tell you I am looking forward to getting back
in harness once more - it sure has been a long road back,
but am out of the Woods now & things look brighter Thank
God.
                         Stan
```

Dear Betty:-   Jan. 9th. '56

We had dinner with Eda's Brother & Wife on Xmas – we took them to dinner New Year's Eve to "The Fox & Hound" (a restaurant near here) the food was wonderful – then we all came home and opened a bottle of champagne to celebrate the New Year's Eve, we tuned in (TV) on big crowd at the Ambassador Hotel – they were all singing "lang Syne" so we felt we were in the party too & helped us to get in the spirit of things – so a good time was had!

Stan and Ida – living out their later years as just an ordinary man and wife.

Come the turn of the New Year it would seem, according to one newspaper item, that things had definitely improved on the health front:

> I'm glad to report that comedian Stan Laurel, who had a stroke several months ago, is coming along so well that his doctor assures him he will be able to work within two months.
>
> The other half of the Laurel and Hardy team, Oliver Hardy, also has been doing something about his health. The rotund Hardy went from 312 to 260 pounds, a total loss of 52 pounds.
>
>   (15 January 1956)

In the letter written Christmas Eve, Stan stated that Babe had lost about eight stone [112 pounds] so the figure of 52 pounds is way off.

Stan next reiterates his own improvement in health to another English girlfriend from his mid-teens.

Dear Ellina Turner [nee Irwin]:-   Jan. 26th. '56

I have been on the sick list since last April, had a slight stroke which paralyzed my left arm and leg, but happy to tell you I made a wonderful recovery, & soon be in good shape to return to work.

We have a new series of films to make at our old studio (Hal Roach) so am looking forward to being back in harness once more. I have certainly been very fortunate Thank God – thought for a while I'd never be able to walk again, it really was an awful experience to go through.

The only news to emerge during the next twelve weeks was that, in mid-February, the super-slimmed-down Hardy spent some time in Palm Springs recuperating.

A Man of Letters

-----0-----

1956 mid-February (*circa*)
      VAN NUYS, California to **PALM SPRINGS**, California 125 miles

1956 late-February (*circa*)
      PALM SPRINGS, California to **VAN NUYS**, California 125 miles

-----0-----

On 19 April, Laurel wrote of the current work situation to Ernie Murphy:

```
Young Roach called me last week re going back to work, but
of course it's out of the question right now - with the
health situation of us both - altho' I am feeling good and
greatly improved. I doubt I could take on anything
strenuous for a while yet. We certainly have been
unfortunate in the health dept. this year or so. Anyway we
are lucky our old films have kept the name alive on TV
otherwise we would have disappeared entirely.

We just had a deal offered to Tour Australia & New Zealand
for a year - only eight shows a week - think I could manage
that, but Babe does'nt like personal appearances or the
Traveling, so I guess that's out.
```

Stan

-----0-----

One reporter obtained information on Laurel's eating-out habits: (3 July 1956)

> Former comic great Stan Laurel, and actor Raymond Burr, have been dropping in at different times recently for dinner at Jack's Corsican Room, 5430 E. 2nd St. Naples. Laurel, looking a little older than he does in those still-hilarious old comedies on TV, absolutely raves about the quality of Jack's $2.95 'prime rib au jus' dinner.

On 29 July 1956 a huge newspaper article came out, detailing a visit Stan Laurel had recently made to Oliver Hardy at his home. The Hardys were now living at 5429 Woodman Avenue, Van Nuys, where they had moved the previous year, as the property at Magnolia Boulevard had become all too big for them to manage.

-----0-----

LAUREL
1956 July 20 (*circa*)
      SANTA MONICA, California to **VAN NUYS**, California 20 miles

-----0-----

No doubt Stan went there to talk over whether he and Babe were going to be up to the demands of making the proposed TV films. Journalist Bob Thomas (*Associated Press* – 29 July 1956) was on hand to record some of the conversation. First topic up was Hardy's weight loss – which was almost three stone more than the last weigh-in:

```
"Yes, I've lost 150 pounds [10st 10lb]," he remarked, as he
seated himself in his study. "I got pneumonia when we were
touring England two years ago. My heart was jumping around
a bit, and I got asthma too. When we got back here I went
to the hospital for a check up, and the doctors told me I
should lose weight.

"My wife, who is a good taskmaster, kept me on a strict
salt-free diet, with a limit of calories. No, I don't miss
eating. I never really was a tremendous eater. It was the
drinking. I drank a lot of beer."

Hardy said they had been unable to resume work because his
partner suffered a stroke about a year ago.
```

LAST PHOTO-SHOOT
Stan visiting Babe at the Hardy home — Van Nuys, California.
(circa 20 July 1956)

"But he's better now," he added, "and as soon as Stan is feeling up to it, we want to start a new series. It will be on film, not live. All the comedians on live shows have heart-attacks or get sick; that's not for us."

He remarked that they get more fan mail and public recognition now than at the peak of their movie fame. "Kids are always coming to the door and saying, 'Are you Hardy?' he said. "I give 'em a picture and they go away happy."

Although Stan has been seriously ill, he was able to laugh about his condition. "I'm coming along fine now, but I can't do any skiing right away."

He explained that paralysis of his left side started a year ago and affected the use of his arm and leg. But recently he has been more active, hence this visit.

"These things take time," Laurel remarked, "but I'm really improving. I'm able to walk up and down stairs now. I might be able to start a series now, but I want to wait until I'm sure I would be able to get through it. I wouldn't want to get started and then let people down.

"I'm anxious to get some new films on TV so we can get those darned old ones off. It makes me so mad to see them because they are cut so poorly. The TV people just measure off so much film and make a cut."

There is a well-known extant piece of colour footage of Stan and Babe meeting up, which is described as the last film of them together. I firmly believe that the only date this could have been taken is the same day as this photo-shoot. I surmise that Laurel was driven to Hardy's house, where they then did the interview and photo-shoot — after which, Babe changed into more casual clothes, and went with Stan to his daughter's house in Tarzana.   **[FILM]**

-----0-----

1956 July 20 (*circa*) – HARDY
        VAN NUYS, California to **TARZANA**, California 🚗 10 miles
        and return journey.

1956 July 20 (*circa*) –LAUREL
        TARZANA to VAN NUYS to SANTA MONICA 🚗 30 miles

-----0-----

Of his reaction to seeing Hardy, at the beginning of this visit, Laurel wrote:

```
Dear Earl Jr.:-                             Sept. 14th. '56
I saw Mr Hardy a few weeks ago, didn't look too good - lost
so much weight, don't think you would recognize him on the
street, he dropped from 360lbs. to 210, I was really
shocked to see such a change.
```

What Stan didn't know whilst writing this letter was that, just the day before, Babe Hardy had suffered a massive, debilitating stroke.

It was over!

o-o-0-o-o

THE LAST WORD

During the six-year duration of World War II, Stan and Babe were pretty well in continuous employment. But then, in the eleven years 1946-1956 inclusive, they had had NOT ONE DAY of paid employment on American soil. Nor had they been paid for any radio or TV appearances, nor any live guest appearances at public and show business events.

American media companies had made fortunes out of the Laurel & Hardy films during this period, with their continual showing in cinemas and then, later, on TV; plus the use of their characters for advertising purposes – but Stan Laurel and Oliver Hardy got NOT ONE CENT out of it.

It was a sad indictment of the world's favourite funny men. As Oliver Hardy might rightly have said: "It's enough to make a man burst out crying."

Let us just hope that the Boys rated all the enjoyment they have given the world as payment enough. Their legacy of comedy films is unsurpassed, and the world is all the better for the laughter that Laurel and Hardy have generated on-screen, on stage, and – IN PERSON.

o-o-0-o-o

AKNOWLEDGEMENTS

U.K. LIBRARIES
To the British Newspaper Library, whose newspapers extend far beyond the U.K.

U.S. LIBRARIES
The following U.S. Libraries were also helpful in the extreme:

Akron Summit County – Jane Gramlich; Antigua – anon; Atlantic City – Pat Rothenberg; Boston Public Library – Henry F. Scannell (Curator); Chicago – anon; Cincinnati – Marianne Reynolds; Columbus – anon; Dallas – Rachel Howell; Fort Wayne Allen County – Linda; Hartford – anon; Houston – anon; Indianapolis – M. Perkins; Miami-Dade – Helen Muir; Milwaukee – Kathy; Minneapolis – Ian Stade; New York – Steve Massa; Philadelphia – James Quinn; Pittsburgh Carnegie Library – Marilyn Holt and Suzanne M. Johnston; Puerto Rico University, Alma Torres; St. Louis – Trent Sindelar; St. Lucia – anon; St. Paul – Ron Paulson; San Diego – Debra Dixon; Washington – anon; Youngstown – Sally Freaney

WEBSITES
Boystown: www.boystown.org/discover/history/yesterday
US Army Center Of Military History: www.history.army.mil
Ida May: www.idamay.org

To the Ellis Island Foundation I extend my utmost gratitude for access to the New York Immigration Records, which were invaluable in tracking Laurel, and Hardy, and associates, across the great pond.

PHOTOGRAPHS and ILLUSTRATIONS
Bernie Hogya; Michael Ehret; Bob Salk; Marian Daniels; Gil Williams; Rob Stone; John Petersen and the DFI; Paul E. Gierucki; Paul Hasse; David Tomlinson; Trevor Dorman; Tyler St. Mark Collection; John Ullah; and Ray Andrew – Charlie Hall archives.

And to 'Google Map,' which made tracking the tour routes so very easy.

[It isn't that long ago when the only way to receive photographs was by negatives or prints being sent by post. Nowadays, with email, and especially with thousands of images available to download from the Internet, keeping tabs on the source of photographs is nigh on impossible. My apologies, therefore, to anyone whose name I have omitted.]

Photo Agencies and Archives:
Getty Images. Corbis

[Every effort was made to trace the present copyright holders of the photographs and illustrations contained within these pages. Anyone who has claim to the copyright of any of those featured, please make representation to the publishers, who will be only too pleased to give appropriate acknowledgement in any subsequent edition(s).]

Film Clips
To YouTube and the people who share footage, from which some of the frame-grabs were obtained.

Sincere thanks also to:
The following U.S. Laurel and Hardy scholars who, for neither fee nor favour, volunteered to spend many hours searching for information to share with other L&H scholars: Hooman Mehran – New York; Bernie Hogya – New Jersey; Flip Lauer – Cleveland; Trever Rook – Omaha; Bruce R. Weaver – Chicago; and Ken Runyan – Dayton. You have my heartfelt appreciation.

Stan Laurel Letters:

A massive thank you to Ali and Dave Stevenson for the Stan Laurel-Betty Healy letters. Additional snippets came from www.lettersfromstan.com. The rest are from the author's own collection.

AKNOWLEDGEMENTS

Author Simon Louvish – who gave me access to his research material; Kate Guyonvarch – Chaplin Archives; and David Wyatt – for providing catalogue details of some of the U.S. Tours footage.

To Miguel Johnson, and Reverend Gonzalez – two locals on Puerto Rico, who gave such wonderful hospitality to an eccentric Englishman, which made for one of the most memorable days of his life, looking around Borinquen Air Field, on Puerto Rico.

The author is deeply indebted to: Rob Lewis, whose support and assistance kept the project going. TT Litho – Allen, Paul, and Correen – without whom, the book would not have got into print. Ali Stevenson – by whose brilliant perceptions, and much appreciated suggestions, the text was greatly enhanced; and to Chris Seguin who corrected a number of mistakes I made in the First Edition, and added useful information which was not known at that time.

And lastly, a massive "Thank You" to Bob Dickson and his team of associates, without whose dedicated and diligent research the details of many of these events would never have been found.

o-o-0-o-o

BIBLIOGRAPHY

"LAUREL and HARDY – The Magic Behind the Movies," Randy Skretvedt

"STAN – the Life of STAN LAUREL" Fred Lawrence Guiles (Stein & Day)

"LAUREL or HARDY - The Solo Films," Rob Stone and David Wyatt (Split Reel)

"The LAUREL & HARDY Scrapbook," Jack Scagnetti (Jonathan David)

"Mr. Laurel & Mr Hardy," John McCabe (Signet USA)

"BABE – The Life of Oliver Hardy," John McCabe (Robson)

"The Comedy World of STAN LAUREL" John McCabe (Doubleday)

"Notes on a Cowardly Lion – the biography of BERT LAHR," John Lahr

"On the Trail of CHARLIE HALL," Ray Andrew (self-published)

"STAN and OLLIE – The Roots of Comedy," Simon Louvish (Faber & Faber)

"LAUREL and HARDY – From the Forties Forward," Scott MacGillivray (iUniverse)

"ATOLL K – The Final Film of Laurel and Hardy," Norbert Aping (McFarland)

o-o-0-o-o

U.S. FILM FOOTAGE

1932 August 31 (*circa*) [or July 15 or 16] – NEW YORK, Broadway

Laurel and Hardy are seen being driven down New York Broadway in an open-top horse-drawn taxi carriage (curiously named a "sea-going hack"). Rather than being a mute clip of them waving to the crowds, the film takes a surprising diversion: A New York cop stops the carriage, and we are treated to a full-blown sketch, wherein the cop goes through the procedure of issuing them with a ticket for going through a red light.

Considering this was done on location, in ONE-TAKE, after what can have been only a hurried talk through, it emerges as a delightful piece of footage. Hardy is engrossing throughout, staying within character and delivering what appears to be some brilliant ad-libbing. At one point, when the cop says he wants to speak to the driver, Hardy utters the killer line: "I don't think the driver can talk. In fact, I don't think the driver can see."

Hearst Metrotone News [page 48]

-----0-----

1937 July 03 – DEL MAR, Race Track

Clip opens with Bing Crosby manning the turnstile, at the inaugural opening of the Del Mar race track. A panning shot of the stands reveals film stars Robert Taylor and "his inseparable companion Barbara Stanwyck;" plus Una Merkel. As the race finishes, we see Babe Hardy tearing up his losing ticket in frustration.

Hearst Metrotone News [page 102]

-----0-----

1937 July 31 – DEL MAR, Race Track

A specially shot gag sequence sees Crosby closing the payout booth, after counting up the day's takings. Babe Hardy arrives late and presents Crosby with four winning tickets "right on the nose." After paying Hardy out, Crosby issues the line: "They told me there was a profit in these places," to which Hardy retorts: "You're dealing with 'Longshot' Hardy, my friend."
Crosby takes real delight in watching Hardy act and ad-lib.

[page 112]

-----0-----

1937 December 25 – SANTA ANITA, Race Track

This coverage of the "Christmas Day Stakes" catches Hardy outside the stand, secretively checking the racing form. In the stands we see actress Virginia Bruce on her honeymoon; plus Al Jolson, and Bing Crosby. [page 107]

-----0-----

1938 December 31 – SANTA ANITA, Race Track

Virginia Bruce, Bing Crosby, Guy Kibbee, Adolphe Menjou, Spencer Tracy, and other stars carry on as if the camera wasn't present. But then Babe Hardy brightens up the screen with yet another ad-libbed piece of business: After watching the race through binoculars, he gives some wonderful looks to camera, then throws up his hands in despair as the race finishes. [page 128]

-----0-----

1940 October 11-16 – MILWAUKEE, Riverside Theater

After the briefest of clips of the preceding dance numbers on the bill of the "Laurel & Hardy Revue," Stan and Ollie appear front of tabs. We see (but don't hear) some brief introductory patter, before the curtains open to reveal the interior of a police station, with a cop sat at a desk. After the shortest of short clips of them performing *The Driver's License,* the Boys appear front of curtain again, take a bow then exit.

An amazing rare piece of footage – one of only two known clips of L&H on stage in the U.S.A. Both are extra notable in that they are in colour.

Privately owned home-movie [page 153]

-----0-----

1941 May 17 – ATLANTIC CITY, Traymore Hotel

"Variety Club Seventh Annual Convention"

The main footage is of the Sunday night "Humanitarian Awards Ceremony," but there are some out-takes in which Stan and Babe can be spotted leading Saturday's 'Grand Parade' through Atlantic City.

Pathé Newsreel [page 187]

-----0-----

1942 April 26 – LOS ANGELES, Union Station – 'Hollywood Victory Caravan'

First scene is Laurel and Hardy walking between a guard of honour of soldiers on one side, and sailors on the other. All the Hollywood stars line up beside the train for a photo shoot. Next is another group shot, with half of the number on the observation car at the rear of the train, and the rest on the track below. Just before the train pulls away, a group of soldiers and sailors surround the back of the train to shake hands with the stars. Some of the bolder ones climb up, and get a goodbye kiss from the girls.

[page 242]

-----0-----

1942 April 29 – WASHINGTON, Union Station – Hollywood Victory Caravan

The stars are seen getting off the train and walking along the platform. Upon exiting the station they crowd around a bank of microphones. A 'Welcome' speech is given by Rear Admiral Charles Hepburn. Mark Sandrich replies on behalf of the visitors; and then R.A. Hepburn shakes hands with all the stars, whilst seemingly not recognising any of them. The stars get into jeeps, and the convoy parades through Washington.

Pathé Newsreel [page 243]

Laurel and Powell look at the view, while the others look at the view-finder.

The Boys in their jeep, passing the Capitol building.

U.S. Film Footage

1942 April 30 – WASHINGTON, White House
> The whole of the Hollywood entourage are seen assembled on the lawn of the White House for a photo-shoot. Tucked in amongst them is Eleanor Roosevelt. They break, and make for a nearby refreshment tent. [page 246]

-----0-----

1942 May 06 – CHICAGO, Chicago Stadium
> A 28-second clip of a documentary about the "Hollywood Stars" being the most popular and successful team in the PCL in the thirties and forties. In the dying seconds, Babe Hardy, Desi Arnaz, and Pat O'Brien can be glimpsed on a baseball pitch, signing a bat. Though this is great to see, it is a bit of a con as it has NOTHING to do with the subject of the documentary. The bat signing sequence is actually of Hardy, Arnaz, and O'Brien's visit to Chicago with the Hollywood Victory Caravan. [page 253]

-----0-----

1942 May 29 – FREMONT, San Luis Obispo – Fremont Theater
> After a shot of the façade of the newly-built, Fox-owned Fremont Theatre, and the crowds outside, the camera alights upon Laurel and Hardy, selling a block of bonds to Mayor Kimble. The rest of the stars file past a commentator from KVEC, who temporarily stops each one to say a quick word at the microphone. Featured are: Carole Landis, Carole Bruce, Constance Bennett, John Carroll, Charlie Ruggles, Max Baer, Nat Pendleton, and actor Jackie Cooper.
>
> Fox Newsreel [page 269]

-----0-----

1949 August 18 – HOUSTON, Texas – Opening of the Shamrock Hotel
> From the brief description available, it would seem that the footage is not of the actual opening ceremony, but a short clip of the evening's champagne reception.
> Of the one-hundred-plus actors; and the two-thousand two-hundred-plus other invitees, the only known faces spotted in this short clip are actors Stan Laurel, Hugh Herbert, Pat O'Brien, Ward Bond, Andy Devine and Joan Davis.
>
> Paramount News [page 287]

-----0-----

TELEVISION

1951 February 21 – Hollywood Reel – TV Newsreel – Presenter: Erskine Johnson.
> TV Guide reads: "Quite a group on "Hollywood Reel" over KTLA, including Don DeFore, Belita, Joel McGuiness, Stan Laurel, Johnny Sheffield, and Lita Baron.
> The timing of this broadcast throws up a conundrum, as Laurel was still in France, filming "Atoll K," so could not have shot any "Hollywood" footage.

  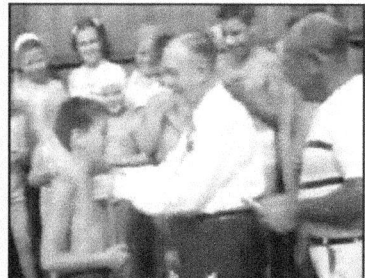

On your marks … … get shot ..er .. set! Where to pin the medal?

> If this is the swimming gala clip broadcast on 21 February 1951, then it must have been taken at least 10 months earlier, before Laurel went to Paris (April 1950).
>
> [Chapter 33]

-----0-----

1954 December 01 – LOS ANGELES – *"This Is Your Life"*

Among the "surprise guests" were Leo McCarey – who had directed some of the early L&H-Roach films; Frank Fouce, who had worked on the solo comedies Laurel made with G.M. Anderson; and Roland Park, a boyhood pal of Stan's.

Park had been flown over from North Shields, England, to reminisce about his and Stan's upbringing there, but goes into a long apocryphal story about Stan's first appearance as a comedian on a stage in Glasgow.

Caught by Delfont ...   ... imprisoned by Edwards   ... chewed by Blaine.

Vivian Blaine, too, went off-subject. Instead of talking about being Laurel and Hardy's, the female lead in *Jitterbugs*, she chose to tell of Stan and Babe's arrival in Southern Ireland, just prior to their 1953 UK stage tour. Disappointing, too, is that Delfont, the man who kept Laurel & Hardy "alive" from 1947 onwards, was not given any speaking time.   NBC TV, USA (30 min. TV slot) [page 308]

-----0-----

1955 October 19 – "This Is Music Hall" — BBC TV transmission in Britain   [page 314]

During this 90-second piece-to-camera, Hardy reads out a list of American members of the British-based charity organisation 'The Grand Order of Water Rats,' to which Stan adds a description of the type of act they performed.

Both sign off with a heartfelt "Goodbye" to their "Brother Water Rats, and many friends and fans."

-----0-----

STAN VISITS OLLIE (aka: LAUREL & HARDY AT HOME) – 1956

The title is a mis-nomer. Hardy is doing the visiting, and not at Laurel's home – but his daughter's. Firstly, Stan, Ida Laurel, Stan's daughter, husband (Rand Brooks), and their two children are shown sitting around a picnic table in the garden. In the next scene, Stan is with Babe, and they mug for the camera. Laurel is still recovering from the effects of a mild stroke, but the startling difference is in Hardy's appearance, as he has lost 150lb, and looks almost emaciated.

Evidence suggests this occurred on the same day as the photo-shoot at the Hardy home – circa 20 July 1956.   [See page 318]

It is not the way we would like to remember them, but, sadly, it remains the last-ever time they were filmed together.   [Shot in colour by a fan – Andy Wade.]

-----0-----

N.B. This is not an attempt to catalogue every known piece of footage of Laurel and Hardy, but merely to expand on information supplied in the text.

My grateful thanks to film archivist David Wyatt, for sharing his catalogued lists of footage, originally printed in the *"Laurel & Hardy Magazine,"* which were an invaluable source for this section.

The catalogue notes have, however, been replaced by the author's own comments in most of the entries.

o-o-0-o-o

LAUREL & HARDY – The British Tours
Part 1 – Screen to Stage [1926 to 1951]

Second Edition – Extensively revised, reformatted and expanded

The story starts where our comedy heros meet up at the Hal Roach Studios, and become an inseparable partnership. We then fast forward to the promotional tour of major cities in England and Scotland, which they undertook in the summer of 1932.

Fast forward again to their 1947 British stage tour, for which readers are given a full account of every theatre engagement and every act they worked with; their travel arrangements; the hotels they stayed in; the people they met; previously undocumented public appearances. and descriptions of the crowds of thousands who mobbed them and left them reeling from the onslaught.

Second Edition. 210 pages. Lavishly illustrated — Softback — A4 [297mm x 210mm]
(ISBN 978-0-9521308-8-8) — Available via lulu.com

-----0-----

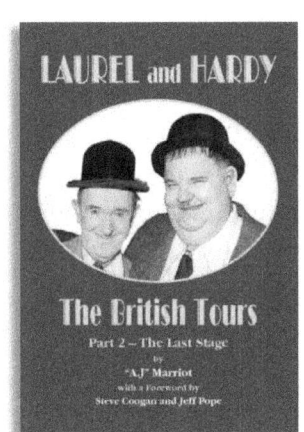

LAUREL & HARDY – The British Tours
Part 2 – 'The Last Stage.' [The 1952 and 1953-4 Tours]

Second Edition – Extensively revised, reformatted and expanded
This engaging book is the story of the love which the British and Irish retained for these two comedy legends after the USA had turned its back on them, and how they adapted from film- to stage-work, and survived through the changing *modes* of comedy, and the changing *moods* of theatre audiences. Readers are given a full account of the theatres they played, the acts they worked with, their travel arrangements; the hotels at which they stayed; the people they met; and their many public appearances – all complemented by scores of rare photographs from these tours.

Second Edition. 208 pages. Lavishly illustrated — Softback — A4 [297mm x 210mm]
(ISBN 978-0-9521308-8-8) — Available via lulu.com

-----0-----

LAUREL and HARDY – The European Tours

"The European Tours" details not only the 1947-48 stage tours Laurel and Hardy played around Denmark, Sweden, France, and Belgium, but the year the two Hollywood comedians spent in France, during the making of their 1950-51 film *Atoll K*. Included in this is a promotional visit to Italy; plus details of two earlier visits to France — one by Laurel in 1927, and one by both comedians in 1932.

Readers will get to see the real men behind the screen characters of "Stan and Ollie" — how they coped with being mobbed everywhere they went; the exhaustion of a life of touring; and how they both worked on through serious illness to complete their last film.

From it all, Stan Laurel and Oliver Hardy emerge as lovable, but vulnerable, men – and readers will experience their every emotion throughout these previously undocumented tours.

Second Print. 128 pages – 200 illustrations. Softback – A4 [297mm x 210mm]
(ISBN 978-0-9521308-4-0) — Available via lulu.com

A Lot of Fun

LAUREL – Stage by Stage

"LAUREL - Stage by Stage" is the prequel to Marriots previous Laurel and Hardy's "Tours" books; and is a companion to "CHAPLIN – Stage by Stage."

It narrates for the first-time-ever all of Stan Laurel's stage shows, from his earliest appearances in British pantomime (as the teenage Stanley Jefferson), right up to his last-ever stage show before entering films.

Along the way he spends over three years touring with Charlie Chaplin, in the most-famous of all comedy troupes – the Fred Karno Company.

The next eight years are spent touring in U.S. vaudeville, playing in song-dance-and-comedy sketch acts with various partners.

Readers will experience every low and high as this comic genius tries to unshackle himself from the hardship and tedium of vaudeville, during a number of attempts to get into the world of film comedy. The amount of detail revealed about these "lost" tours is astounding.

272 pages – 200 illustrations. Softback – A4 [297mm x 210mm]

Second print (ISBN 978-1-78972-555-1) — Available via lulu.com

-----0-----

CHAPLIN – Stage by Stage

Contains every known stage appearance Chaplin made in the UK and, for the first time ever, the ones he made in Vaudeville, touring America with the Fred Karno Company of Comedians.

Along the way, many myths and mistakes from other works on Chaplin will be corrected, and many lies and legends exposed. But, in destroying the negative, a positive picture is built up of the very medium which created the man and the screen character "Chaplin."

Includes extracts from the scripts of the plays and sketches in which Chaplin appeared, complemented by reviews and plot descriptions, all of which help to complete the picture of the influences which affected Chaplin's later film work. Read and be Amazed!

[Although it is a companion to "LAUREL – Stage by Stage" it contains far more text relating to Chaplin, plus numerous different and previously unpublished photos of him.]

Chaplin Stage by Stage *provides a unique and indispensable record of Chaplin's career on the British stage and music hall and in American vaudeville in the formative fifteen years before he entered films. Marriot's phenomenal research gives us an exhaustive chronicle of Charlie's stage appearances – in addition to those of his father and his brother Sydney.* — [DAVID ROBINSON – Chaplin biographer.]

258 pages – 130 illustrations. Paperback – A4 [297mm x 210mm]

Second print (ISBN 978-1-78972-556-8) — Available via lulu.com

-----0-----

Have you bought your copies yet?

A sincere "Thank You" to those who have.

"A.J" Marriot

For information on the First Editions, and how to purchase, go to the author's website:

www.laurelandhardybooks.com

OR e-mail: ajmarriot@aol.com for any enquiries.

o-o-0-o-o